# Conservation in a changing world

As evidence for the rapid loss of biological diversity strengthens, there is widespread recognition of the need to identify priorities and techniques for conservation action. Much progress has been made in the development of quantitative methods for identifying priority areas based on what we know about species distributions, but we must now build an understanding of biological processes into conservation planning. Here, using studies at global to local scales, researchers consider how conservation planners can deal with the dynamic interactions of species in a changing world, where human impacts will continue to affect the environment in unprecedented ways. This book will be a source of information for postgraduates, researchers and professionals in conservation biology, wildlife management and ecology.

GEORGINA M. MACE is a Senior Research Fellow at the Institute of Zoology, Zoological Society of London. She has been awarded the Marsh Award for Conservation Biology (1993) by the Zoological Society of London, the President's Medal of the Chicago Zoological Society (1995) and the OBE for services to conservation (1998). She is also co-editor of *Creative Conservation* (1994) with P. J. Olney and A. T. C. Feistner, and co-editor of the journal *Animal Conservation*.

ANDREW BALMFORD is a lecturer in conservation biology, until recently at the University of Sheffield, and now at the University of Cambridge. He is on the editorial boards of *Animal Conservation, Biological Reviews,* and *Oryx.*

JOSHUA R. GINSBERG is the Director of the Asia Program at the Wildlife Conservation Society in New York, where he administers 75 projects in 14 countries. He is associate editor for *Issues in International Conservation*, for the journal *Conservation Biology*, and is on the editorial board for *Oryx.* He is also deputy Chairman for the IUCN Canid Specialist Group, and a member of four other IUCN Specialist Groups.

**Conservation Biology**

Conservation biology is a flourishing field, but there is still enormous potential for making further use of the science that underpins it. This new series aims to present internationally significant biology. It will focus on topics where basic theory is strong and where there are pressing problems for practical conservation. The series will include both single authored and edited volumes and will adopt a direct and accessible style targeted at interested undergraduates, postgraduates, researchers and university teachers. Books and chapters will be rounded, authoritative accounts of particular areas, with the emphasis on review rather than on original data papers. The series is the result of a collaboration between the Zoological Society of London and Cambridge University Press. The series editors are Professor William Sutherland of the University of East Anglia and Professor Morris Gosling, Director of the Institute of Zoology in London. They hold the common belief that there are unexploited areas of basic science that can help define conservation biology and bring a radical new agenda to the solution of pressing conservation problems.

# Conservation in a changing world

Edited by
GEORGINA M. MACE
ANDREW BALMFORD
AND JOSHUA R. GINSBERG

CAMBRIDGE
UNIVERSITY PRESS

THE ZOOLOGICAL    CONSERVATION
SOCIETY OF LONDON  INTERNATIONAL

PUBLISHED BY THE PRESS SYNDICATE OF THE UNIVERSITY OF CAMBRIDGE
The Pitt Building, Trumpington Street, Cambridge CB2 1RP, United Kingdom

CAMBRIDGE UNIVERSITY PRESS
The Edinburgh Building, Cambridge CB2 2RU     UK http://www.cup.cam.ac.uk
40 West 20th Street, New York, NY 10011-4211     USA http://www.cup.org
10 Stamford Road, Oakleigh, Melbourne 3166, Australia

© Cambridge University Press 1998

First published 1998

Printed in the United Kingdom at the University Press, Cambridge

Typeset in FF Scala 9.75/13 pt [VN]

*A catalogue record for this book is available from the British Library*

*Library of Congress Cataloguing in Publication data*

Conservation in a changing world / edited by Georgina M. Mace, Andrew Balmford,
and Joshua R. Ginsberg
    p.   cm.
    This book derives from papers presented at a joint Zoological Society of
London and Conservation International Symposium held in London in September 1996 – Pref.
    Includes bibliographical references (p.     ) and index.
    ISBN 0 521 63270 6 (hardback). – ISBN 0 521 63445 8 (pbk.)
    1. Biological divesity conservation—Congresses.   2. Conservation biology—Congresses.
    I. Mace, G. M. (Georgina M.)   II. Balmford, Andrew, 1963–   .   III. Ginsberg, Joshua Ross.
    QH75.A1C6658   1999 /1998
    333.95'16–dc21   98–24393 CIP

ISBN 0 521 63270 6 hardback
ISBN 0 521 63445 8 paperback

# Contents

List of contributors   [vii]

Preface   [ix]

1   The challenges to conservation in a changing world: putting processes on the map   [1]
ANDREW BALMFORD, GEORGINA M. MACE AND
JOSHUA R. GINSBERG

2   Anthropogenic, ecological and genetic factors in extinction   [29]
RUSSELL LANDE

3   Integrating endangered species protection and ecosystem management: the Cape Sable seaside-sparrow as a case study   [53]
AUDREY L. MAYER AND STUART L. PIMM

4   The dynamic response of plants to environmental change and the resulting risks of extinction   [69]
BRIAN HUNTLEY

5   Ecological and evolutionary importance of disturbance and catastrophes in plant conservation   [87]
WILLIAM J. BOND

6   Butterfly distributional patterns, processes and conservation   [107]
CHRIS D. THOMAS, DIEGO JORDANO, OWEN T. LEWIS,
JANE K. HILL, ODETTE L. SUTCLIFFE AND JEREMY A. THOMAS

7   Continent-wide conservation priorities and diversification processes   [139]
JON FJELDSÅ AND CARSTEN RAHBEK

8   Endemism and species turnover with elevation in montane avifaunas in the neotropics: implications for conservation   [161]
DOUGLAS F. STOTZ

9   Indicator taxa for biodiversity assessment in the vanishing tropics   [181]
SACHA SPECTOR AND ADRIAN B. FORSYTH

10  Key sites for conservation: area-selection methods for
    biodiversity   [211]
    PAUL H. WILLIAMS

11  Integrating population abundance, dynamics and distribution into
    broad-scale priority setting   [251]
    A. O. NICHOLLS

12  Global biodiversity priorities and expanded conservation
    policies   [273]
    NORMAN MYERS

13  Global conservation and UK government policy   [287]
    ROBERT M. MAY AND KERRY TREGONNING

    *Index*   [302]
    *Colour plates*   [facing 180]

# Contributors

ANDREW BALMFORD
Department of Animal and Plant Sciences,
University of Sheffield, Sheffield S10 2TN,
UK
Present address: Department of Zoology,
University of Cambridge, Downing Street,
Cambridge CB2 3EJ, UK

WILLIAM J. BOND
Department of Botany, University of Cape
Town, Private Bag, Rondebosch 7700,
South Africa

JON FJELDSÅ
Centre for Tropical Biodiversity, Zoological
Museum, University of Copenhagen,
Universitetsparken 15, DK-2100
Copenhagen Ø, Denmark

ADRIAN B. FORSYTH
National Museum of Natural History,
Smithsonian Institution, Mail Stop 105,
10th Street and Constitution Avenue,
Washington DC 20560, USA

JOSHUA R. GINSBERG
Asia Program, Wildlife Conservation
Society, 2300 Southern Boulevard, Bronx,
NY 10460–1099, USA

JANE K. HILL
Department of Biology, University of
Leeds, Leeds, LS2 9JT, UK

BRIAN HUNTLEY
Department of Biological Sciences,
University of Durham, South Road,
Durham DHI 3LE, UK

DIEGO JORDANO
Departamento de Biología Vegetal y
Ecología, Facultad de Ciencias,
Universidad de Córdoba, Avenida San
Alberto Magno, s/n, 14701 Córdoba, Spain

RUSSELL LANDE
Department of Biology, University of
Oregon, Eugene, OR 97403-1210, USA

OWEN T. LEWIS
Department of Biology, University of
Leeds, Leeds LS2 9JT, UK

GEORGINA M. MACE
Zoological Society of London, Regent's
Park, London NW1 4RY, UK

ROBERT M. MAY
Department of Zoology, University of
Oxford, South Parks Road, Oxford OX1 3PS,
UK

AUDREY L. MAYER
Department of Ecology and Evolutionary
Biology, University of Tennessee,
Knoxville, TN 37996-0910, USA

NORMAN MYERS
Green College, University of Oxford,
Oxford OX2 6HG, UK

A. O. NICHOLLS
CSIRO Division of Wildlife and Ecology,
PO Box 84, Lyneham, ACT 2602, Australia

STUART L. PIMM
Department of Ecology and Evolutionary
Biology, University of Tennessee,
Knoxville, TN 37996-0910, USA

CARSTEN RAHBEK
Centre for Tropical Biodiversity, Zoological
Museum, University of Copenhagen,
Universitetsparken 15, DK-2100
Copenhagen Ø, Denmark

SACHA SPECTOR
Department of Ecology and Evolutionary
Biology, University of Connecticut, 75
N. Eagleville Road, U-43, Storrs, CT
06269, USA

DOUGLAS F. STOTZ
Environmental and Conservation
Programs, Field Museum of Natural
History, Roosevelt Road at Lake Shore
Drive, Chicago, IL 60605, USA

ODETTE L. SUTCLIFFE
Environmental Information Centre, NERC
Institute of Terrestrial Ecology, Monks
Wood, Abbots Ripton, Huntingdon,
Cambridgeshire, PE17 2LS and Department
of Biology, University of Leeds, Leeds LS2
9JT, UK

CHRIS D. THOMAS
Department of Biology, University of
Leeds, Leeds LS2 9JT, UK

JEREMY A. THOMAS
NERC Institute of Terrestrial Ecology,
Furzebrook Research Station, Wareham,
Dorset BH20 5AS, UK

KERRY TREGONNING
Office of Science and Technology,
Department of Trade & Industry, 94–98
Petty France, London SW1H 9ST

PAUL H. WILLIAMS
Biogeography and Conservation
Laboratory, The Natural History Museum,
Cromwell Road, London SW7 5BD, UK

# Preface

Conservation biology has grown enormously in size, scope and stature over the past decade. Nevertheless, there is a growing worry that the diverse array of approaches taken in tackling conservation problems focus in large part on current patterns of biological diversity, while generally neglecting detailed consideration of the biological and anthropogenic processes which variously underpin and threaten those patterns. The natural world we are attempting to conserve is not a static place: populations persist by interacting with one another and with other organisms; they respond to external challenges in dynamic ways; and the nature of these challenges is itself changing as the scale of the human enterprise continues to expand. If today's conservation strategies are to yield long-term benefits, process-related concerns must be integrated into conservation planning at an early stage.

This book is about identifying the sorts of natural and anthropogenic processes that conservation practitioners need to be concerned about, yet which conservation biologists are at present largely ignoring. We have deliberately avoided dividing the book into sections, as many of the chapters tackle cross-cutting themes. Nevertheless, there is a broad shift in emphasis through the book, from the empirical through to the practical.

The book begins with an introduction in which we highlight what we see as some of the key emergent themes from later chapters, and we set out the case for focusing on processes when thinking about conservation in a changing world. After this, Lande provides essential background for the rest of the book by summarizing the main deterministic threats to biological diversity, and reviewing recent ideas about the sizes at which small (and indeed not so small) populations begin to be threatened by stochastic genetic and ecological processes. Mayer and Pimm then demonstrate the large scale over which even existing anthropogenic threats operate by exploring the causes of the continued decline of the Cape Sable seaside-sparrow, a bird entirely restricted to the 9000 km$^2$ reserve system designed to conserve the Florida Everglades. Two further, growing challenges to biological diversity are considered in detail in Chapters 4 and 5. Huntley explores the likely biological implications of human-induced changes to the global climate, in the light of how species have coped with climate change in the geological past, and of how those dynamic responses may now be compromised by habitat and population fragmentation. In Chapter 5, Bond continues this theme of biological responses to external challenges, pointing out that many plant species have adapted to and are nowadays dependent on the kinds of large-scale disturbances (such as fire and grazing pressure) which have accompanied human modification of many habitats since the advent of agriculture. If we are to maintain those species and the communities to which they belong, we will often need to manage disturbance regimes accordingly.

Next, Chapters 6–8 use detailed case studies to illustrate some of the dynamic demographic, genetic and evolutionary processes which enable free-ranging populations to persist, yet which are not readily captured by a simple pattern-based approach to priority-setting. Thomas and colleagues provide empirical evidence to support the role of both niche theory and metapopulation theory in accounting for the population biology of butterflies, and draw several important (but not necessarily intuitive) messages for conservation practitioners: that we should conserve vacant but suitable habitat as well as occupied patches; that we might in some instances need to discourage dispersal from small patches; and that we should focus efforts most on relatively healthy populations at the core of species' ranges, rather than those in decline near range margins. Fjeldså and Rahbek use a large-scale analysis of the distribution patterns of neotropical birds to identify centres of endemism and, in particular, areas of likely importance for the generation and maintenance of evolutionary novelty. And Stotz focuses in on patterns of elevational turnover in the same group of species, and concludes that important demographic processes may increasingly be disrupted by mid-elevation deforestation, which interrupts both altitudinal migration and postulated source-sink population dynamics.

The last five chapters consider the practical scope for taking account of process-related concerns. Spector and Forsyth assess the performance of one readily assessed group as an indicator for wider conservation priorities, and provide rarely reported data on the high costs of even short-cut methods of biodiversity inventory. Williams describes how these, and other sorts of data, can be used by increasingly sophisticated computer-based algorithms to identify efficient networks of priority areas. Nicholls then tackles the enormous challenge of thinking about how these procedures could be further refined so as to incorporate into reserve networks concerns about the conservation of ecological and genetic processes. He concludes that several process-linked concerns are, in principle, analytically tractable, but that our capacity to tackle them in any realistic timeframe will be limited by data availability. Myers takes a broad and imaginative view of the way forward, adding new data to substantiate his earlier work on the critical importance of a relatively small number of biodiversity hotspots, and explaining why one of the major challenges to conservationists is not biological at all, but rather lies in eliminating existing incentives by governments which subsidize non-sustainable development. In the closing chapter, May and Treggoning further explore the importance of policy instruments, showing how many of the issues raised in the book can be tackled by government, in sometimes surprisingly simple ways.

This book derives from papers presented at a joint Zoological Society of London and Conservation International Symposium held in London in September 1996. We are grateful to both of these organisations for the financial and logistic support which made the meeting possible. We owe a debt to ideas that arose at an earlier Royal Society Discussion Meeting (Lawton & May, 1995), and to a key paper on the importance of processes in conservation biology (Smith *et al.*, 1993). We thank all the authors and a host of anonymous reviewers for their work on the chapters presented here, our spouses for coping with our stochastic schedules, the editorial staff at Cambridge University Press for producing the book so efficiently, and Unity McDonnell at ZSL for shepherding the process despite the fragmented distribution of the authors and the male-biased emigration of the editors. GMM thanks NERC for support; AB and GMM were assisted by a NERC grant; JRG's contribution was facilitated by the Wildlife Conservation Society.

### References
Lawton, J. H. & May, R. M. (eds) (1995). *Extinction rates*: Oxford University Press, Oxford.
Smith, T. B., Bruford, M. W. & Wayne, R. K. (1993). The preservation of process: the missing element of conservation programs. *Biodiv. Lett.*, 1, 164–7.

# The challenges to conservation in a changing world: putting processes on the map

ANDREW BALMFORD, GEORGINA M. MACE AND JOSHUA R. GINSBERG

## INTRODUCTION

By common consensus, a single species, somewhat inappropriately named *Homo sapiens*, is now on the verge of precipitating an extinction event which may rival the Big Five mass extinctions of the geological past (Pimm *et al.*, 1995; May & Tregonning, this volume). Recent estimates are that impending rates of species loss are between three and five orders of magnitude higher than background extinction levels (May *et al.*, 1995; Pimm *et al.*, 1995). In tropical forests alone, human activities are probably committing between 0.1 and 0.3% of species to extinction every year. From the perspective of providing goods and services, populations are more important than species, yet new work suggests that extinction rates of populations are far higher, with annual losses running at around 0.8% (equivalent to about 1800 populations every hour: Hughes *et al.*, 1997).

The causes underlying these losses are well established, and are succinctly reviewed by Russ Lande in Chapter 2. The chief anthropogenic threats responsible for the current extinction crisis are habitat clearance and degradation (including pollution and habitat fragmentation), overexploitation (itself exacerbated by unregulated access to common-property resources and by economic discounting), and the myriad impacts of introduced species (Vitousek *et al.*, 1997). Once populations are substantially reduced by these deterministic challenges, they may in turn become vulnerable to both intrinsic threats such as the stochastic demographic and genetic perils of small population size, and extrinsic threats such as chance environmental fluctuations, and random catastrophes (Lande, this volume).

Conservation biologists have responded to this stark situation in three main ways. Most fundamentally, a great deal of effort has been devoted to identifying and attempting to reverse the likely causes of species decline – an empirical approach which, in his lucid review of the state of the field, Graeme Caughley labelled the declining population paradigm (Caughley, 1994; Caughley & Gunn, 1996). In addition, since the founding of modern conservation biology in the late 1970s, theoretically based work in both genetics and demography has examined the effects of small population size itself (an approach dubbed the small population paradigm by Caughley). The third, most recent wave (reviewed in depth by Paul Williams in Chapter 10) links empiricism with computer-based algorithms in an effort to identify priority areas where nature reserves and other *in situ* conservation initiatives could be most efficiently concentrated.

In our view, these approaches, while extremely valuable, suffer from an important limitation: they are very largely based on contemporary patterns of the distribution of biodiversity and the threats which it faces. Concerns about processes are generally limited to the internal dynamics of small and isolated populations. Yet the world is dynamic at broader scales as well. Conserving biodiversity requires more than just representing its more tangible elements (such as species or intraspecific genetic variation) in static protected areas. Rather, it requires maintaining the dynamic genetic and ecological processes which characterize and sustain free-ranging communities (see T. B. Smith *et al.*, 1993). Beyond this, humans are also changing the world in novel ways. Future threatening processes will not simply be current threats writ larger. Conservation strategies must, wherever possible, anticipate future threats as well as address contemporary ones if they are to prove effective over the long term.

This book is about starting to identify the sorts of natural and anthropogenic processes which we as biologists should think about when designing strategies to meet the challenge of conservation in a changing world. This opening chapter provides a brief overview of what we consider to be some of the book's emergent themes, and tries to embed them in the context of the recent literature. We begin by presenting evidence indicating that process-related concerns are inadequately reflected in current work. The bulk of the paper then highlights what we see as the key process-related issues that we need to address, and examines the likely consequences of failing to do so, before closing with a series of critical recommendations for planners and practitioners.

## THE PROBLEM

Clear evidence that a conservation agenda based solely on contemporary patterns often fails to tackle process-related concerns comes from thinking about how we identify priority sites for conservation. This work is critical to ensuring limited conservation resources are focused efficiently, and as Paul Williams shows in Chapter 10, area-selection methods have become extremely sophisticated in recent years. They are now capable of identifying near-optimum networks of sites which contain as much biodiversity (measured in different ways) as is practically possible within limits set by the availability of land or resources (see also Csuti et al., 1997). However, the input to these algorithms consists, in the main, of simple snapshots of where different organisms are found at a particular time (Flather et al., 1997). The analyses take little or no account of any dynamic features of the systems under study, such as movements of individuals, the temporal viability of different populations, the population processes that contribute to longer-term viability, or ecological interactions within communities.

This, in turn, is reflected in the output of these sorts of procedures (Nicholls, this volume). Selected sites commonly fail to include the core of species' ranges, where populations may be most abundant and most resilient to anthropogenic activities (see also below). Moreover, patterns of occupancy may be sufficiently fluid that key sites picked in one year turn out, with the benefit of hindsight, to be alarmingly poor at representing the same species or populations even in subsequent years (Margules et al., 1994; Nicholls, this volume). This problem is likely to be greatly amplified over the much greater timescales that characterize most ecological and evolutionary processes. Further quantitative studies of the consequences of neglecting process-related issues during priority-setting are clearly needed, but the message from work to date is that by themselves, pattern-based algorithms may generate only rather limited solutions to long-term (and necessarily process-dependent) conservation goals.

A second way in which we can examine the mismatch between contemporary conservation biology and perceived conservation need is to compare the sorts of questions conservation practitioners ask with the types of questions conservation biologists are presently answering. Here, data on questions asked come from a survey conducted by Hilary Swain and colleagues of 50 conservation managers in Florida (Swain et al., 1996); data on the sorts of questions that are answered come from an analysis of the abstracts of 214 contributed papers appearing in the journal *Conservation Biology* be-

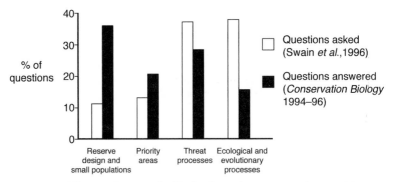

Fig. 1.1 Differences between the kinds of questions conservation practitioners are asking and those which conservation biologists are answering. Data on questions asked come from a survey of 50 conservation managers in Florida (Swain *et al.*, 1996). Information on questions answered comes from an assessment of 214 papers contributed to *Conservation Biology*. Results are qualitatively similar if data are taken from *Biological Conservation* instead.

tween 1994 and 1996. Sorting questions into four broad categories (three of which correspond to the main approaches discussed above) reveals a clear disparity between the problems managers feel they want answered, and the research activities of professional biologists (Fig. 1.1).

Questions relating to the detailed design of reserves and the fate of small populations are evidently more interesting to scientists than to conservation practitioners. The same appears true, although to a lesser extent, of questions linked to the identification of overall spatial priorities for conservation. In contrast, two sorts of questions are answered less often than they are raised. Both are explicitly process related: questions dealing with the dynamics of the threats to different species; and questions involving the ecological and evolutionary dynamics of the systems of conservation concern. Managers are clearly very worried about how interactions will be maintained in small reserves, and how both natural and anthropogenic processes in the wider landscape will impinge on the contents of protected areas. As yet, conservation biologists are not providing the answers.

## WHAT SORTS OF PROCESSES?

In broad terms we suggest that the key process-linked issues which conservation biologists should think more about fall into three groups (see Table 1.1): threatening processes; dynamic responses of organisms to external

**Table 1.1**

*Some process-related concerns of importance for the conservation of biological diversity in a changing world*

*Threatening processes*
Established threats are changing over time in different ways
Threatening processes operate over wider temporal and spatial scales than we commonly think
Cumulative effects can be unpredictable
Novel threats are emerging

*Dynamic responses to external challenges*
Species have coped with past environmental change by shifting ranges, but this is now hampered by the rate of change and by habitat fragmentation
Adaptive evolution to new challenges requires large population sizes
To persist, some species may now depend on continued exposure to natural or anthropogenic challenges to which they are adapted

*Intrinsic ecological and genetic processes*
Maintenance of metapopulation dynamics requires multiple, clustered habitat patches separated by a relatively benign matrix
Migratory populations depend on the conservation of all their habitats
Some communities rely on dispersal over very large distances
Long-term genetic viability of small populations can be threatened by stochastic problems of inbreeding depression, excessive loss of genetic variation, and mutational meltdown
Genetic integrity of sympatric species requires the maintenance of mechanisms of reproductive isolation
Certain kinds of areas ('species factories') may be disproportionately responsible for the generation of evolutionary novelty

challenges (either natural or anthropogenic); and intrinsic ecological and genetic processes by which free-ranging populations and communities persist. We will now look at examples of each of these sorts of processes, and think in particular about why they may be inadequately dealt with in a conservation agenda driven largely by consideration of present-day patterns.

## Threatening processes

As the conservation status of more and more species is assessed by IUCN and other agencies using new, quantitative criteria (IUCN SSC, 1994), we are acquiring an increasingly detailed picture of current levels and causes of threat (see IUCN, 1996; G. M. Mace & A. Balmford, unpublished data). To the extent that the new categories of threat can nominally be equated

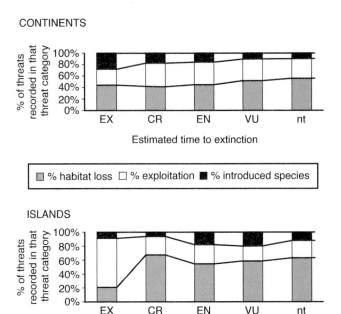

CONTINENTS

Estimated time to extinction

□ % habitat loss  □ % exploitation  ■ % introduced species

ISLANDS

Estimated time to extinction

Fig. 1.2 Likely changes in the time course of different threatening processes to continental and island mammals. Species are classified according to their IUCN threat category, with the estimated time to extinction increasing from left to right. EX = extinct; CR = critical; EN = endangered; VU = vulnerable; nt = near-threatened. The analysis deals only with those species for which threats have been published. Island species are those entirely restricted to islands; continental species are all others.

with fixed probabilities of extinction within a given time frame (Mace, 1994), it is tempting to try to use these assessments to predict the future course of anthropogenic extinctions. However, our ability to infer future losses (and their causes) from existing patterns of threat is limited by several important considerations.

First, there are major temporal (as well as spatial and taxonomic) differences in the relative impacts of different threats. Figure 1.2 illustrates this point with data derived from an analysis of threatened mammals. Using the IUCN categories of threat as rough measures of the relative time before different species are likely to go extinct, we see that, among mammal species on continents, the relative importance of losses due to introduced species is likely to decline in future, while the proportion of extinctions due to habitat loss is likely to increase. The picture is further complicated by consideration of mammals restricted to islands. Here, habitat loss is again set to increase in relative importance, but the threat classification data indicate that introduced species are likely to present a continuing (rather than declining) threat. Any meaningful extrapolation of the future impact of existing threats must take these sorts of detailed variations in the dynamics of particular threatening processes into account.

There is also growing evidence that, so far, we have underestimated the wide-ranging, long-term and sometimes unpredictable impacts of certain sorts of contemporary threats. For instance, detailed dissection by Audrey Mayer and Stuart Pimm in Chapter 3 of the possible causes of the decline of the Cape Sable seaside-sparrow (*Ammodramus maritimus mirabilis*) reveals that the most likely reasons involve recent and profound changes to the hydrology (and associated fire phenology) of the Everglades National Park. The whole of the seaside-sparrow's range is contained within a reserve network totalling over 9000 km$^2$. Yet, despite this formal protection, extensive flooding in the western part of the park, and desiccation (and hence increased incidence of fires) in the eastern part – both brought about by activities in agricultural zones beyond the park's boundaries – have between them greatly decreased the availability of breeding habitat. Threatening processes can evidently operate over much wider spatial scales than we sometimes think.

Shifting to a temporal scale, even well-known threats can also have cumulative and unpredictable effects. Long-term consequences of sustained anthropogenic pressures on natural ecosystems may often be characterized by discontinuous, threshold (rather than linear) responses (Ehrlich & Holdren, 1971; Myers, 1995). A good example of this comes from a recent reassessment by Jeremy Jackson of the most likely cause of the collapse of coral reefs in the Caribbean (Jackson, 1995, 1997; see Fig. 1.3). Newly synthesized historical evidence clearly demonstrates that, prior to the arrival of Europeans, the region supported extraordinary densities of large vertebrates, including green and hawksbill turtles (*Chelonia mydas* and *Eretmochelys imbricata*), sharks, rays, groupers, manatees and monk seals (Jackson, 1997). Their combined biomass probably exceeded that recorded for all ungulates in the Serengeti by at least one or two orders of magnitude, yet by the time modern reef ecology began in the late 1950s, intense overexploitation meant that all these species were already reduced to a fraction of their previous abundance. Nevertheless, this dramatic faunal collapse apparently had little if any immediate impact on the struc-

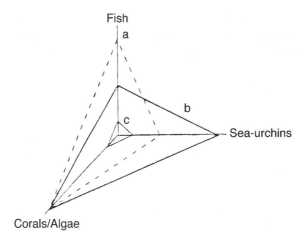

Fish

a

b

Sea-urchins

c

Corals/Algae

Fig. 1.3 Schematic representation of the apparent response of Caribbean reef communities to overexploitation of fish (leading to an increase in sea-urchins and a shift from plane a to plane b) and subsequent sea-urchin disease (leading to overgrowth of corals by macroalgae, and collapse of the system from plane b to plane c). (From Jackson 1995, by permission of Oxford University Press.)

ture of Caribbean reef communities (Jackson 1995). Smaller fish continued to consume both macroalgae and *Diadema* sea-urchins (plane a in Fig. 1.3), and only after these smaller species themselves became the target of overexploitation (during the course of the twentieth century) did pronounced changes in community composition take place. Overfishing and the ensuing decline in fish predation on sea-urchins allowed *Diadema* to increase in abundance. Even then, because this urchin is a heavy grazer on macroalgae, the ratio of corals to algae remained high (plane b in Fig. 1.3). It was not until disease decimated *Diadema* populations in 1983 that the underlying fragility of this now simplified system was fully revealed. The ensuing precipitate reduction in grazing pressure released macroalgae, which have since been overgrowing corals throughout the Caribbean. The region's reefs now appear locked into a low diversity, algal-dominated state (plane c in Fig. 1.3), but the sudden nature of the switch to this condition belies the chronic and cumulative nature of its underlying cause.

One final reason why basing conservation strategies solely on present-day human impacts is inadequate is that entirely new threatening processes are emerging, and will continue to do so. Probably the most important of these to have been documented to date is climate change (Huntley, this volume). Despite continued lack of clarity in the details of how global warming is expected to proceed, there is growing consensus surrounding the overall picture (IPCC Working Group I, 1996; Mahlman, 1997). Human activities have already warmed the earth by an average of around $0.5\,°C$ this century, and by 2100 continued emissions of $CO_2$ and other greenhouse gases are likely to have led to a further increase in mean surface temperatures of between 1.5 and $5\,°C$, with a consequent mean rise in sea levels of $50 \pm 25\,cm$. More precise estimates will hinge on resolving the many uncertainties in existing climate models, and will be strongly affected by exactly when and by how much we decide to curb greenhouse emissions. But, given the evidence (for review see Huntley in Chapter 4) that macroclimatic conditions play a primary role in determining the distribution of many species, the impacts of global warming on biological diversity are very likely to be substantial.

### Dynamic responses to external challenges

The overall effect of any external challenge on a population will be determined not just by the magnitude of the challenge itself but also by the population's own capacity to respond in an adaptive manner. Natural populations have always been subject to external challenges of one sort or another, yet some have evidently persisted despite them. We therefore need to think in more detail about the kinds of dynamic responses which have conferred resilience to environmental challenges in the past. Climate change again provides a useful arena in which to examine these process-related concerns.

As Brian Huntley describes in Chapter 4, the global climate has oscillated dramatically over the course of the Quaternary, and new palaeoecological analyses yield valuable insights into how species have coped. One very common response to changed environmental conditions has been a shift in the geographical ranges of species. As climate zones have moved latitudinally and/or altitudinally, species have persisted by tracking these shifts, in effect occupying the same envelope of climatic conditions through time, in spite of global climatic instability. A striking illustration of this sort of response is provided by G. R. Coope's work on fossil beetles (Coope, 1995). Of more than 2000 species recovered from Quaternary deposits in Britain, well over 99% are still extant, but the great majority are nowadays restricted to other parts of Palearctic, which are either colder or warmer than contemporary Britain (depending on whether

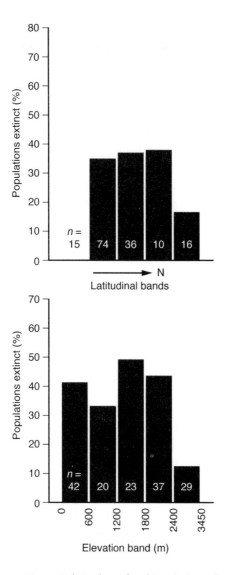

Fig. 1.4 Relative loss of 151 historical populations of Edith's checkerspot butterfly in western North America, as a function of latitude and elevation. Populations at the warmer margins of the species' historical range (i.e. those at low latitudes and altitudes) exhibited higher extinction than others. (Reprinted with permission from Parmesan, 1996, © Macmillan Magazines Ltd, 1996.)

the species occurred here during glacials or interglacials, respectively).

As predicted by these observations, evidence is now accumulating that ongoing anthropogenic climate change is already leading to the differential loss of populations at the warmer margins of species' ranges (see Fig. 1.4 for the example of population losses in Edith's checkerspot butterfly, *Euphydryas editha*). However, it is less clear whether we can expect that, as in the past, species will be able to compensate for this by expanding their ranges into regions that were previously too cold. Present forecasts suggest that impending rates of climate change will be at least an order of magnitude greater than those experienced in the recent past (IPCC Working Group I, 1996). In Chapter 4, Huntley uses spatial and dynamic modelling, coupled with data on known dispersal distances of plants, to show that many species may be simply incapable of spreading fast enough to track the rapidly shifting areas within which their climatic requirements are satisfied.

This problem is compounded by the effects of habitat fragmentation. Whereas in the past, individuals dispersing from a marginal habitat in a warming (or cooling) world may have found more suitable conditions close by, nowadays the likelihood is that they will be separated from the nearest patch of more appropriate habitat by a considerable expanse of agricultural or other unsuitable habitat. Fragmentation thus greatly reduces the probability of successful dispersal and establishment. Artificial and natural corridors between remaining habitat patches may become increasingly important in facilitating range shifts through today's highly fragmented landscape, although we suspect that large protected areas, with sufficient topography to embrace a series of climatically discrete habitat types, may be of even greater value (see Hunter *et al.*, 1988; Coope, 1995; Huntley 1995, this volume).

A second sort of response enabling species to persist despite marked environmental change is to stay put and adapt to that change directly. Although it was previously thought that the speed and frequent reversal of climate change over the Quaternary probably precluded any major evolutionary responses, in Chapter 4 Huntley reviews newly published work showing that small-scale, apparently adaptive changes in morphology (and presumably related aspects of physiology and ecology) have occurred over the course of recent climatic cycles (see Fig. 1.5). These shifts in mean morphology still lie within the span of present-day phenotypes, suggesting they have arisen through changes in the frequencies of existing genotypes, rather than via selection of entirely new alleles. We can expect to see similar

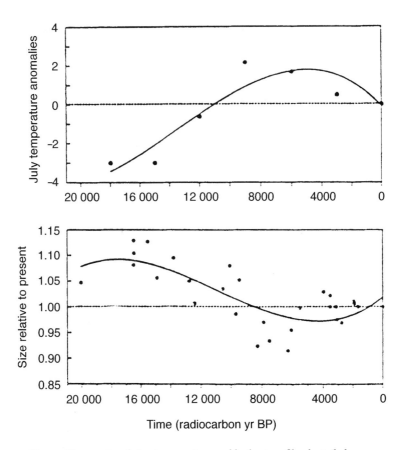

Fig. 1.5 Changes in relative temperature and body size of bushy-tailed
woodrats (*Neotoma cinerea*) as estimated from the size of faecal pellets
recovered from fossil middens, over the past 20 000 years. As temperatures
increased, woodrats showed an adaptive decrease in size, as predicted by
Bergmann's rule. (Reprinted with permission from F. A. Smith *et al.*,
1995, © American Association for the Advancement of Science, 1995.)

adaptive changes in phenotype as global warming proceeds. However, as
Lande shows in Chapter 2, calculations from theoretical models and laboratory populations indicate that sufficient genetic variation for such adaptive
evolution may require the long-term maintenance of effective population
sizes of 5000 or more. This number is far greater than that needed to
ensure short-term persistence (on either genetic or demographic grounds).
By reducing populations of many species well below this level, we may be
further compromising their ability to cope with a rapidly changing world.

Palaeoecology has one other rather obvious message here: faced with major environmental change, species that fail either to relocate their ranges or else adapt accordingly simply go extinct (Coope, 1995; Jackson, 1995; Huntley, this volume). How far we can maintain the potential for dynamic responses such as adaptive evolution and range shifts, despite population reductions and habitat fragmentation, may be a key determinant of the impact of the sorts of new and rapidly developing anthropogenic challenges we can expect over the next century.

One further, vital consideration related to the response of organisms to external challenges is the idea that many species have already evolved strategies to cope with particular natural or anthropogenic processes which they have encountered in the past. This may mean that the persistence of these species depends on continued exposure to such processes now. William Bond provides very clear examples of this in Chapter 5. Many plants of open formations are evidently well adapted to fire and to vertebrate herbivory. Although these disturbances have been widespread since the late Miocene, humans have accelerated their spread, particularly since the advent of agriculture. However, in the developed world, the tendency of both conservationists and other sectors of society has been to curb these disturbances, with the result that the open vegetation types that depend upon them are now threatened by succession to more closed communities. The same is less true for pre-industrial countries, where disturbance is still intense and closed formations are consequently under greater threat than open ones.

Additional illustrations of the importance of maintaining disturbance are provided by work on the impacts of damming (and consequent restriction of floods) on the community structure of North American rivers (see Fig. 1.6), and by new data on the fate of native plant species in the few remaining fragments of Wisconsin prairie (Leach & Givnish, 1996). In this latter case, resurveying sites visited 30 to 50 years earlier revealed that, despite remaining structurally intact (and being adequately conserved from a pattern-based perspective), each patch had lost an average of 0.5 to 1.0% of its species every year. Moreover, the pattern of loss was consistent with it being due to the suppression, through land-use changes and habitat fragmentation, of anthropogenic fires to which many prairie species are adapted. As in Bond's examples, retaining fire-adapted species in remnants of prairie will require active maintenance of historical fire regimes. More generally, the need for such interventive management of landscape-scale processes seems set to rise, as the world becomes increasingly

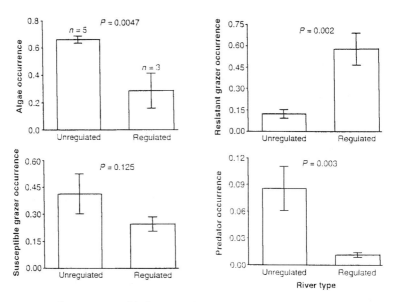

Fig. 1.6 Occurrence of different trophic groups in unregulated rivers (which flood regularly) and regulated rivers (where damming prevents flooding) in northern California. Grazers whose large caddises make them predator-resistant are susceptible to rolling rocks during flooding of unregulated rivers. However, their occurrence is substantially increased (leading to corresponding decreases in algae, predator-susceptible grazers and hence predators) when rivers are dammed and flooding eliminated. Damming thus has major indirect effects on foodweb structure, which could perhaps be offset by pulsed water releases to maintain occasional riverbed scouring. (Reprinted with permission from Wootton *et al.*, 1996, © American Association for the Advancement of Science, 1997.)

urbanized and developed, and the frequency of some natural and long-standing human-caused disturbances declines.

### Intrinsic ecological and genetic processes

The last group of process-related concerns raised repeatedly in this book derive from a suite of ecological and genetic processes which are part of business as usual for free-ranging populations. We must ensure that these continue if we are to have any hope of retaining functional biological communities over the long term.

One very important set of such processes relate to population dynamics (see Thomas *et al.*, and Stotz, this volume). Pattern-based priority-setting often treats populations as discrete and static entities, whose survival is independent of events in other populations (see the chapters by Williams and by Nicholls). In reality, this assumption is rarely met: at at least some temporal and spatial scales, nearly all populations are interconnected, and their long-term persistence depends on the continued movement of individuals between areas.

In metapopulations, for example, single populations are connected by low levels of dispersal across a network of occupied and unoccupied habitat patches (Gilpin & Hanski, 1991). Individual populations are prone to extinction, but metapopulations persist provided that extinction rates are exceeded by rates of recolonization from populations nearby. As Chris Thomas and colleagues discuss in Chapter 6, thinking about populations in this way highlights the importance of retaining suitable patches of vacant as well as occupied habitat, and underlines the need to consider the size and degree of isolation of habitat patches when generating guidelines for the management of species which exist as metapopulations. The condition of the matrix between habitat patches may also be critical. For instance, in Chapter 8, Doug Stotz suggests that, in neotropical forests, lowland habitats may hold source populations of wide-ranging species, and export individuals to sink populations at higher altitudes. The significance of this is that, even if the habitat of both source and sink populations remains intact, we can expect that sink populations may be lost as a result of the intensive deforestation now taking place in intervening, medium altitude habitats through which dispersing birds must pass.

Most importantly, metapopulation theory indicates that, when resources are limiting, conservation efforts should be concentrated on the best patches of habitat within the core of species' ranges (Thomas *et al.*, this volume). Marginal habitat quality and greater isolation mean that conserving populations at the edges of species' ranges can be extremely difficult and may make only a limited contribution to the persistence of metapopulations as a whole. Yet this emphasis on the cores of species' ranges (derived from thinking about population processes) may often be directly at odds with current conservation policy. A fire-fighting tradition in conservation means that efforts are sometimes more readily marshalled around very small or rapidly declining (rather than relatively healthy) populations (see Fig. 1.7 for the example of the marsh fritillary butterfly (*Eurodryas aurinia*) in Britain). Moreover, site-selection algorithms are frequently geared to identify those areas with highest species richness. But these are often rich simply because they straddle several habitats, and the populations they contain may each be less viable than those found in areas of lower overall

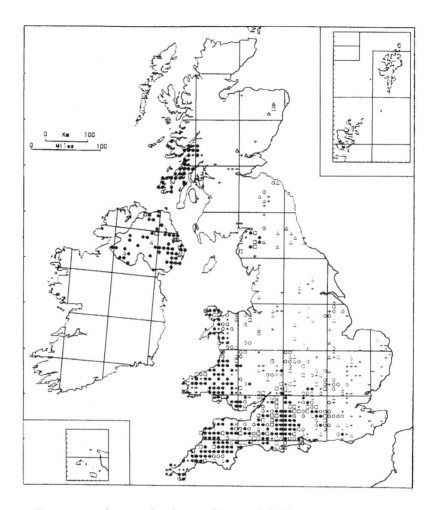

Fig. 1.7 Past and present distribution of the marsh fritillary in the UK and Ireland in 1990, plotted on a 10 km grid. Large filled circles definitely retained colonies in 1990, and small dots possibly did; all other symbols refer to now extinct colonies. Historically, disproportionate effort has gone into conserving habitats and populations in eastern and central England (where the species is scarce and declining), whilst little serious attention has been given to conserving more robust populations (with greater long-term viability) in north-west Scotland and south-west England. (Reprinted from Warren, 1994, with permission from Elsevier Science Ltd.)

species richness in the core of each habitat type (Branch *et al.*, 1995; Nicholls, this volume). This conflict between conserving cores and edges of habitats and species' ranges is a topic we will return to in the final part of the chapter.

Movements of individuals between discrete areas of habitat can be critical to population persistence in other situations as well. We have obviously known for a very long time that many organisms exhibit lengthy annual migrations between tropical and temperate regions. Over the past 15 years, evidence has accumulated that large numbers of species of birds and insects that never leave the tropics also undergo extensive annual migrations, commonly across elevational gradients, or between wet- and dry-season habitats (Stiles, 1985; Janzen, 1987; Stotz, this volume). Recent radio-tracking data on the resplendent quetzal (*Pharomachrus mocinno*) in Costa Rica, for instance, reveal that much of the area that individuals use in the course of a year of altitudinal migration lies beyond the reserve network designed to conserve this flagship species (Powell & Bjork, 1995). The persistence of species like this is obviously dependent on the continued unrestricted movement of individuals up and down elevational gradients. When any of the habitat types on which these populations depend are eliminated, such species will of course disappear even from those areas where they are properly protected (Stotz, this volume).

At an even bigger scale, new work on coral reefs suggests that their fate may commonly be determined by events 100–200 km away (Roberts, 1997; see Fig. 1.8). Recruitment at reefs depends not just on local reproduction but also on the extent to which this is supplemented by pelagic larvae transported from 'upstream' reefs by surface currents. By mapping prevailing currents in relation to reef locations across the Caribbean, Callum Roberts has been able to show that, while some reefs have only a relatively small upstream catchment (so that local recruitment is likely to be the overwhelming determinant of their persistence), others receive larval imports from (and are hence dependent on) a vast area of upstream reefs. The other side of this dispersal coin is that management needs to focus on the conservation, in particular, of those reefs responsible for seeding large areas of reef downstream, and on ensuring that marine reserves are sufficiently clustered that these large-scale exchanges of individuals can continue to take place (Ogden, 1997; Roberts, 1997). These key insights gleaned from examining the demographic processes underpinning reef dynamics may be critical to the future management of coral reef ecosystems.

The final set of process-related issues we want to emphasize here is a

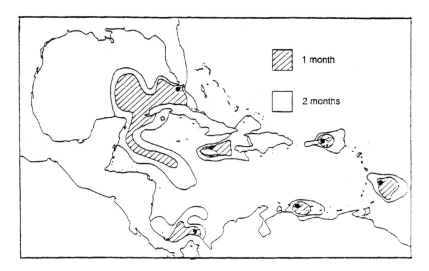

Fig. 1.8 Areas from which six Caribbean reefs (represented by dots) are likely to receive viable larvae, depending on whether larvae survive for one or two months. These upstream catchments vary in extent by an order of magnitude. (Reprinted with permission from Roberts, 1997, © American Association for the Advancement of Science, 1997.)

series of genetic concerns. The small population paradigm has already identified the sorts of stochastic genetic challenges facing small populations (summarized briefly in Table 1.1), and developed a series of recommendations about how big populations need to be for these problems to be minimized (see Lande, 1995 and in this volume). Two other, more deterministic concerns have perhaps received less attention.

Where closely related species occur sympatrically, their genetic integrity is obviously dependent on the maintenance of reproductive isolation. While, in many instances, there are likely to be multiple barriers to interbreeding, in the case of species flocks of cichlids in Great Lakes of Africa (Fig. 1.9), their relatively recent divergence means sympatric species are still capable of producing fertile hybrids. Instead, reproductive isolation of these species is maintained via mate choice based on the bright, species-specific colouration of males. However, dramatic increases in water turbidity (due to eutrophication caused by agriculture and forest clearance) now threaten this process (Seehausen et al., 1997). In Lake Victoria, light quality has apparently declined to the point that female choice is compromised, males are becoming increasingly dull-coloured, and local species diversity in areas of recent eutrophication is more closely related to light availability

Fig. 1.9 *Labrochromis ishmaeli*, a cichlid from Lake Victoria. Until recently, the lake housed at least 500 species of haplochromine cichlids, yet very many have disappeared in the past 20 years (Barel *et al.*, 1985). This is usually attributed to the introduction of the predatory Nile perch, but new evidence suggests it may in part be due to pollution, which has reduced light quality and so disrupted reproductive isolation of species by interfering with female mate choice based on bright male colouration (Seehausen *et al.*, 1997). Photograph courtesy of Zoological Society of London.

than to any other environmental measure. By disrupting the process responsible for maintaining cichlid diversification, this form of habitat deterioration may be having a greater impact on the fate of this extraordinary radiation than more commonly blamed culprits such as the introduced Nile perch (*Lates* spp.).

Lastly, several of the chapters here (by Lande, Myers, Huntley and others) consider the need to maintain the evolutionary potential of populations to generate novel adaptations and indeed new species. We have already discussed these ideas briefly in the context of species' responses to external challenges, where we thought about the effective size that populations need to be if they are to retain a capacity for adaptive evolution.

New work is now beginning to address the related question of where such populations might be most likely to occur. According to Fjeldså and Rahbek (Chapter 7), the generation of new species is focused in particular areas; these sites might therefore merit especially high conservation priority. Using detailed maps of the distribution of South American birds, they identify a series of typically high altitude sites, characterized by a long history of climatic and ecological stability, where both ancient and more recent endemic species are clustered. They suggest that these areas represent species factories, from where new species have spread into lower elevation

Fig. 1.10 Ecotone habitat between rainforest and savanna in Cameroon. Work on the morphology and genetics of forest birds suggests such transition zones may be important areas for the generation of evolutionary novelty via natural selection (T. B. Smith *et al.*, 1997). Photograph courtesy of M. W. Bruford.

forests, and where older species have survived despite climatic fluctuations elsewhere. A somewhat different (but by no means contradictory) view comes from research by Tom Smith and colleagues on the genetics and morphology of little greenbuls (*Andropadus virens*) across the forest–savanna ecotone in Cameroon (T. B. Smith *et al.*, 1997; Fig. 1.10). Their results indicate that natural selection acting on populations in the ecotone may play an important role in generating evolutionary novelties in this predominantly rainforest species.

These studies offer the first detailed insights into the question of where new species arise. It may turn out that novelties appear both in ecotones between rainforests and savannas and in climatically stable cloud forests. From a conservation perspective, there is an additional and important message here. Both these kinds of habitat are associated with intense human population pressures. People too have apparently long thrived near the stable environments of cloud forests (see Fjeldså & Rahbek, this volume. Fig. 7.6), while rainforest margins in Cameroon and elsewhere are now experiencing rapid encroachment by pastoralists, agriculturalists and fuelwood gatherers (Balmford & Long, 1994; Enserink, 1997). A further irony is that, in the case of high altitude forests, their long-term stability may now mean that their biological communities have relatively little resilience to new and increasing anthropogenic pressures (Fjeldså and Rahbek, this volume).

## RECOMMENDATIONS

The principal purpose of this chapter (and indeed the whole book) is to identify process-related issues of conservation concern, rather than necessarily propose ways of resolving them. Nevertheless, a handful of recommendations do emerge repeatedly in the papers which follow. We therefore conclude this chapter by summarizing some of these ideas for future action, in the hope that this list can be used as a framework for future discussions.

### Try to integrate process-related concerns into priority-setting procedures

Identifying priorities for future investments is an essential component of efficient conservation, and the chapters by Williams and by Nicholls both suggest imaginative ways in which process-related information could, in principle, be incorporated into existing, largely pattern-driven algorithms (see also Flather *et al.*, 1997). Some information about processes may be quite readily acquired – for instance, if future work confirms the evolutionary importance of ecotones or ecoclimatically stable areas, these elements could easily be mapped and given disproportionate weighting in site-selection exercises. However, being realistic, obtaining other sorts of process-related data will often be extremely hard. As Spector and Forsyth illustrate in Chapter 9, even acquiring straightforward information about distribution patterns for a reasonably well-known and potentially valuable indicator group such as the dung beetles may be prohibitively expensive except over relatively small scales. Getting reliable data on population abundances, on linkages between populations, or on their genetic substructuring will be even more difficult. And integrating information of this kind into priority-setting algorithms is at present extremely expensive in computational terms, and the results are hard to interpret (Nicholls, Chapter 11). These sorts of problems may in part be offset by the free exchange of information and expertise between countries (see examples by May & Tregonning, and Spector & Forsyth, this volume), and by pragmatic assessments of the performance of potential short-cut survey methods. Nevertheless, the practical difficulties in building process-related issues into conservation planning should not be underestimated.

### Tackle the fundamental problems underlying the erosion of biological diversity

We are used to thinking about man's negative impact on the biosphere as being very largely due to our rapid population growth. However, unsustainable patterns of resource exploitation by humans, and harmful economic and political structures, are equally important underlying causes of the present extinction crisis (Ehrlich and Holdren, 1971; Deacon, 1994; Ehrlich, 1995). Several authors in this book highlight these latter concerns, and suggest possible ways in which they could be tackled. Thus Norman Myers details the extent of so-called 'perverse subsidies' paid by governments in the developed world to support environmentally unsustainable activities, largely concentrated in the agricultural, energy and transport sectors. Myers argues persuasively that, in the long-term interests of society, many of these subsidies should now be eliminated, simultaneously reducing negative human impacts, easing financial pressures on governments, and releasing funds for conservation investments. In Chapter 4, Huntley stresses that any serious attempts to tackle the problems posed by global warming must first and foremost involve stringent and immediate measures to limit emission of greenhouse gases. And, in considering the implications of their avifaunal analyses for future conservation priorities in South America, Fjeldså and Rahbek argue that, while conserving endemics on the slopes of the Andes and in the Atlantic forests of Brazil requires the expansion of the existing network of reserves, conserving the more widespread species typical of the Amazon basin will be much more effectively achieved by implementing sustainable macroeconomic policies at a regional scale.

### Conserve at least some very large areas with relatively limited human access; managing a network of postage stamp-sized reserves is both expensive and difficult

Many of the process-related problems raised in this chapter arise because of increasing habitat and population fragmentation. If conservation areas are extremely large, and especially if they have widely varying topography, then they may be capable by themselves of sustaining many of the ecological, demographic and genetic processes we have discussed (see also Tilman, 1996; Jackson, 1997). Very big reserves may contain whole metapopulations, or the entire ranges of elevational migrants; populations may be large enough retain their evolutionary potential; landscape-wide processes (such as fire and flooding) may be allowed to continue unchecked; and in the face of climate change, species may even be able to shift their ranges altitudinally yet remain within the confines of the protected area.

However, we should not underestimate how large such ideal reserves would need to be. The vast protected-area network surrounding Florida's Everglades is evidently still too small to buffer one of its most important inhabitants against external land-use changes (Mayer & Pimm, this volume). Elsewhere, new work on large carnivores suggests that, for species with enormous home ranges that take them out of protected areas and into direct conflict with humans, even reserves as big as 10 000 km$^2$ may simply not be big enough (Woodroffe & Ginsberg, 1998). Yet, reserves this large are few and far between (Mayer & Pimm, this volume), and the scope for gazetting new reserves this size is extremely limited. Promising new ideas in this area include recognition of the value of linking up reserves that span international boundaries (Kim, 1997; Hanks, in press), and of the potential conservation significance of military land. In the UK, for instance, 1% of the land surface (much of it of considerable conservation interest) is in the hands of the Ministry of Defence (May & Tregonning, this volume) – nearly six times as much as that covered by all fully protected areas under the control of national conservation agencies (Groombridge, 1994).

The other enormous hurdle here is how to protect very large reserves at all effectively. One elegant suggestion from work on Amazonian reserves, where illegal access is nearly always achieved along rivers, is that reserve boundaries should, wherever possible, match those of watersheds (Peres & Terborgh, 1995). Policing efforts can then be concentrated where the river draining the protected area crosses its boundary – which in effect represents the single point of exit and entry for the whole reserve. The most controversial question is how far conservation in these areas can be reconciled with the development needs of local people. We detect a groundswell of opinion from conservationists working in the field, suggesting that the model of conservation through sustainable exploitation may not always be feasible. Given even current population densities and patterns of resource tenure, some biological systems may simply be incapable of satisfying local human demands on a sustainable basis (for examples, see Redford, 1992; Ludwig *et al.*, 1993; Jackson, 1997). In these situations, conservationists and policy-makers are faced with the stark choice of either severely limiting human access to protected areas, or else accepting that resource utilization will lead to the ecological extinction of certain exploited species (Kramer *et al.*, 1997).

### Identify critical habitat patches and significant populations and focus conservation actions judiciously; this is essential where full protection can be afforded only to small, fragmented areas

The problem here is what (if any) rules of thumb can be used to identify which habitat patches are best. Metapopulation theory suggests that isolated populations in small habitat patches at the edges of species ranges may be less valuable than large, core populations (Thomas *et al.*, this volume). Consideration of global warming also leads to the conclusion that focusing on populations towards the centre of species' ranges may be most rewarding (Huntley, 1995). In the context of the UK, for example, the status of species at the northern edge of their distribution will generally be improved by climate change, while species at the very southern margin of their distribution may well be lost irrespective of any management intervention. Conservation efforts may instead have most impact on those species for which the UK represents core habitat. These arguments must be weighed against the fact that places where several habitats come together will often contain more species per unit area than similar sites located entirely within single habitats, and the evidence from Cameroon that ecotones may perhaps be species factories (T. B. Smith *et al.*, 1997). There is clearly a great deal of scope for additional work on this important topic.

### In small and isolated reserves, actively manage those ecological processes to which species are adapted, or else be prepared to accept the loss of such species

This book contains several examples of the sorts of large-scale ecological processes which become altered or eliminated in fragmented, developed landscapes. Conservation practitioners need to be aware of the serious repercussions which changes in these processes can have, and manage isolated habitat patches accordingly (Tilman, 1996). It may be possible (for some well-known groups, at least) to identify the kinds of species that are most vulnerable to changes in disturbance regimes (see Bond in Chapter 5 for an example based on plant life histories). One other important point here is that managing wide-ranging ecological processes within protected areas may have additional benefits which may offset conflicts between conservation and human development. For instance, many important sites for endemic birds in the Andes are close to areas of high human population density (Fjeldså & Rahbek, this volume). Protecting those forests for their biological diversity should simultaneously help stabilize water catchments on which tens of thousands of people depend.

### In fragmented landscapes, think seriously about conservation in the intervening, human-dominated matrix

What happens in human-dominated habitats beyond reserves is the key to the future of biodiversity for two reasons. First, the wider matrix is enormously important in its own right. In Kenya, for example, until recently around 80% of large mammals lived outside the country's famed network of national parks and reserves (Western, 1989). And in most parts of the world, protected areas are unlikely ever to cover much more than 5% of the land surface (Mayer & Pimm, this volume). If this non-reserved landscape is thoroughly hostile (so that very few species persist in it), and if reserves are distributed at random with respect to biological diversity (and there is alarming evidence that this assumption may be quite close to the truth – Pressey 1994), then simple application of the species–area relationship predicts that this 95% loss of available habitat should lead to the extinction of around 50% of all species – even if no species are lost from protected areas (Mayer & Pimm, this volume).

The condition of the matrix will also have a profound effect on the status of biological communities within reserves (Janzen, 1986; Franklin, 1993). As we have seen repeatedly in this chapter, parks are not islands (Janzen, 1983), and their fate is intimately tied-up with processes occurring beyond their boundaries. A relatively benign matrix may reduce negative edge effects around protected areas. In the context of this book, a less hostile human-dominated landscape would also do much to alleviate process-related concerns about the movements of individuals between reserves, over both ecological and evolutionary time.

## ACKNOWLEDGEMENTS

Many of the ideas presented here were developed using a Small Grant from NERC (to AB and GMM) and a research grant from the University of Sheffield. GMM thanks NERC for support. We thank Emile Lefebvre for assistance and Tim Birkhead for comments on an earlier version of this chapter.

### References

Balmford, A. & Long, A. (1994). Avian endemism and forest loss. *Nature*, **372**, 623–4.

Barel, C. D. N., Dorit, R., Greenwood, P. H., Fryer, G., Hughes, N., Jackson, P. B. N., Kawanate, H., Lowe-McConnell, R. H., Nagoshi, M., Ribbink, A. J., Trewavas, E., Witte, F. & Yamaoka, K. (1985). Destruction of fisheries in Africa's lakes. *Nature*, **315**, 19–20.

Branch, W. R., Benn, G. A. & Lombard, A. T. (1995). The tortoises (Testunidae) and terrapins (Pelomedusidae) of southern Africa: their diversity, distribution and conservation. *S. Afr. J. Zool.*, **30**, 91–102.

Caughley, G. (1994). Directions in conservation biology. *J. Anim. Ecol.*, **63**, 215–44.

Caughley, G. & Gunn, A. (1996). *Conservation biology in theory and practice.* Blackwell Science, Oxford.

Coope, G. R. (1995). Insect faunas in ice age environments: why so little extinction? In *Extinction rates*: 5–74. (Eds Lawton, J. H. & May, R. M.). Oxford University Press, Oxford.

Csuti, B., Polasky, S., Williams, P. H., Pressey, R. L., Camm, J. D., Kershaw, M., Kiester, A. R., Downs, B., Hamilton, R., Huso, M. & Sahr, K. (1997). A comparison of reserve selection algorithms using data on terrestrial vertebrates in Oregon. *Biol. Conserv.*, **80**, 83–97.

Deacon, R. T. (1994). Deforestation and the rule of law in a cross-section of countries. *Land Econ.*, **70**, 414–30.

Ehrlich, P. R. (1995). The scale of the human enterprise and biodiversity loss. In *Extinction rates*: 214–16. (Eds Lawton, J. H. & May, R. M.). Oxford University Press, Oxford.

Ehrlich, P. R. & Holdren, J. P. (1971). Impact of population growth. *Science*, **171**, 1212–17.

Enserink, M. (1997). Life on the edge: rainforest margins may spawn species. *Science*, **276**, 1791–2.

Flather, C. H., Wilson, K. R., Dean, D. J. & McComb, W. C. (1997). Identifying gaps in conservation networks: of indicators and uncertainty in geographic-based analyses. *Ecol. Appl.*, **7**, 531–42.

Franklin, J. F. (1993). Preserving biodiversity: species, ecosystems or landscapes ? *Ecol. Appl.*, **3**, 202–205.

Gilpin, M. & Hanski, I. (eds) (1991). *Metapopulation dynamics: empirical and theoretical investigations.* Academic Press, London.

Groombridge, B. (ed.) (1994). *Biodiversity data sourcebook.* World Conservation

Press, Cambridge.

Hanks, J. (1998). The role of transfrontier conservation areas in southern Africa in the conservaion of mammalian biodiversity. In *Future priorities for the conservation of mammalian biodiversity* (Eds Entwistle, A. & Dunstone, N.). Cambridge University Press, Cambridge. (in press)

Hughes, J. B., Daily, G. C. & Ehrlich, P. R. (1997). Population diversity: its extent and extinction. *Science*, **278**, 689–91.

Hunter, M. L., Jacobson, G. L. & Webb III, T. (1988). Paleoecology and the coarse filter approach to maintaining biological diversity. *Conserv. Biol.*, **2**, 375–85.

Huntley, B. (1995). Plant species' response to climate change: implications for the conservation of European birds. *Ibis*, **137**, S127–38.

IPCC Working Group I (1996). *Climate change 1995. The science of climate change*. Cambridge University Press, Cambridge.

IUCN Species Survival Commission (1994). *IUCN Red List categories*. IUCN, Gland.

IUCN (1996). *1996 IUCN Red List of threatened animals*. IUCN, Gland.

Jackson, J. B. C. (1995). Constancy and change of life in the sea. In *Extinction rates*, 45–54. (Eds. Lawton, J. H. & May, R. M.). Oxford University Press, Oxford.

Jackson, J. B. C. (1997). Reefs since Columbus. *Coral Reefs*, **16**, S23–32.

Janzen, D. H. (1983). No park is an island: increase in interference from outside as park size decreases. *Oikos*, **41**, 402–10.

Janzen, D. H. (1986). The eternal external threat. In *Conservation biology. The science of scarcity and diversity*: 286–303. (Ed. Soulé, M. E.). Sinauer Ass., Sunderland.

Janzen, D. H. (1987). When, and when not to leave. *Oikos*, **49**, 241–3.

Kim, K. C. (1997). Preserving biodiversity in Korea's demilitarized zone. *Science*, **278**, 242–3.

Kramer, R., van Schaik, C. & Johnson, J. (eds). (1997). *Last stand. Protected areas and the defense of tropical biodiversity*. Oxford University Press, New York.

Lande, R. (1995). Mutation and conservation. *Conserv. Biol.*, **9**, 782–91.

Leach, M. K. & Givnish, T. J. (1996). Ecological determinants of species loss in remnant prairies. *Science*, **273**, 1555–8.

Ludwig, D., Hilborn, R. & Walters, C. (1993). Uncertainty, resource exploitation and conservation: lessons from history. *Science*, **260**, 17, 36.

Mace, G. M. (1994). Classifying threatened species: means and ends. *Phil. Trans. R. Soc. Lond.* B, **344**, 91–7.

Mahlman, J. D. (1997). Uncertainties in projections of human-caused climate warming. *Science*, **278**, 1416–17.

Margules, C. R., Nicholls, A. O. & Usher, M. B. (1994). Apparent species turnover, probability of extinction and the selection of nature reserves: a case study of the Ingleborough limestone pavements. *Conserv. Biol.*, **8**, 398–409.

May, R. M., Lawton, J. H. & Stork, N. E. (1995). Assessing extinction rates. In *Extinction rates*: 1–24. (Eds Lawton, J. H. & May, R. M.). Oxford University Press, Oxford.

Myers, N. (1995). Environmental unknowns. *Science*, **269**, 358–60.

Ogden, J. C. (1997). Marine managers look upstream for connections. *Science*, **278**, 1414–15.

Parmesan, C. (1996). Climate and species' range. *Nature*, **382**, 765–6.

Peres, C. A. & Terborgh, J. W. (1995). Amazonian nature reserves: an analysis of the defensibility status of existing conservation units and design criteria for the future. *Conserv. Biol.*, **9**, 34–46.

Pimm, S. L., Russell, G. J., Gittleman, J. L. & Brooks, T. M. (1995). The future of biodiversity. *Science*, **269**, 347–50.

Powell, G. V. N. & Bjork, R. (1995). Implications of intratropical migration on reserve design: a case study using *Pharomachrus mocinno*. *Conserv. Biol.*, **9**, 354–62.

Pressey, R. L. (1994). *Ad hoc* reservations: forward or backward steps in developing representative reserve systems? *Conserv. Biol.*, **8**, 662–8.

Redford, K. H. (1992). The empty forest. *BioScience*, **42**, 412–22.

Roberts, C. M. (1997). Connectivity and management of Caribbean coral reefs. *Science*, **278**, 1454–7.

Seehausen, O., van Alphen, J. J. M. & Witte, F. (1997). Cichlid fish diversity threatened by eutrophication that curbs sexual selection. *Science*, **277**, 1808–11.

Smith, F. A., Betancourt, J. L. & Brown, J. H. (1995). Evolution of body size in the woodrat over the past 25,000 years of climate change. *Science*, **270**, 2012–14.

Smith, T. B., Bruford, M. W. & Wayne, R. K. (1993). The preservation of process: the missing element of conservation programs. *Biodiv. Lett.*, **1**, 164–7.

Smith, T. B., Wayne, R. K., Girman, D. J. & Bruford, M. W. (1997). A role for ecotones in generating rainforest biodiversity. *Science*, **276**, 1855–7.

Stiles, F. G. (1985). Conservation of forest birds in Costa Rica: problems and perspectives. In *Conservation of tropical forest birds*: 141–68 (Eds Diamond, A. W. & Lovejoy, T. E.). International Council for Bird Preservation, Cambridge.

Swain, H. M., Gordon, D. R., Brennan, L. A. & Fitzpatrick, J. W. (1996). Ecologists as problem solvers? Well what are the important problems? Developing priorities for conservation biology research in Florida. *Supplement to the Bulletin of the Ecological Society of America*, **77 (3)**, 432.

Tilman, D. (1996). The benefits of natural disasters. *Science*, **273**, 1518.

Vitousek, P. M., D'Antonio, C. M., Loope, L., Rejmanek, M. & Westbrooks, R. (1997). Introduced species: a significant component of human-caused global change. *New Zealand J. Ecol.*, **21**, 1–16.

Warren, M. S. (1994). The UK status and suspected metapopulation structure of a threatened European butterfly, the marsh fritillary *Eurodryas aurinia*. *Biol. Conserv.*, **67**, 239–49.

Western, D. (1989). Conservation without parks: wildlife in the rural landscape. In *Conservation for the twenty-first century*: 158–65 (Eds Western, D. & Pearl, M. C.). Oxford University Press, New York.

Woodroffe, R. & Ginsberg, J. R. (1998). Edge effects and the extinction of populations inside protected areas. *Science*, **280**, 2126–8.

Wootton, J. T., Parker, M. S. & Power, M. E. (1996). Effects of disturbance on river food webs. *Science*, **273**, 1558–61.

# Anthropogenic, ecological and genetic factors in extinction

RUSSELL LANDE

## INTRODUCTION

Conservation biologists focus disproportionately on particular vulnerable, threatened and endangered species. The large number of such species, and their frequent multiplicity even within local planning areas, makes it clear that effective conservation and restoration must be done in the context of comprehensive landscape and ecosystem approaches that consider biodiversity and large-scale ecological processes. Species-based approaches should play an essential part in formulating and monitoring large-scale conservation plans in order to ensure that ecologically important species, or those that are sensitive indicators of ecosystem health, are properly managed. Understanding the factors that contribute to the extinction risk of particular species therefore remains of vital importance even within landscape and ecosystem approaches to conservation and restoration.

Anthropogenic factors constitute the primary causes of endangerment and extinction: land development, over-exploitation, species translocations and introductions, and pollution. These primary factors have ramifying ecological and genetic effects that contribute to extinction risk. For example, land development causes habitat fragmentation, isolation of small populations and intensification of metapopulation dynamics. All factors affecting extinction risk are ultimately expressed, and can be evaluated, through their operation on population dynamics. Following an overview of anthropogenic, ecological and genetic factors contributing to extinction risk, I briefly discuss their relative importance and interactions in the context of conservation planning.

## ANTHROPOGENIC FACTORS

### Land development

Human population growth and expansion and economic activity cause the conversion of vast areas for settlement, agriculture and forestry. This results in the ecological effects of habitat destruction, degradation and fragmentation which are among the most important causes of species declines and extinctions. Habitat destruction contributes to extinction risk of three-quarters of the threatened mammals of Australasia and the Americas and to more than half of the endangered birds of the world (Groombridge, 1992).

### Overexploitation

#### Unregulated economic competition

Open access to common-property renewable resources, such as fisheries and many species of wildlife, creates competition among resource extractors. Unregulated or inadequately regulated competition is one of the major causes of over-exploitation and depletion of such resources (Ludwig, Hilborn & Walters, 1993; Rosenberg et al., 1993). About half of the fisheries in Europe and the United States were recently classified as over-exploited (Rosenberg et al., 1993). Hunting and international trade contribute to the extinction risk of over half of the threatened mammals of Australasia and the Americas and over one-third of the threatened birds of the world (Groombridge, 1992) and have caused local extinctions of many forest-dwelling mammals and birds even in areas where habitat is largely intact (Redford, 1992).

#### Economic discounting

With sole ownership or co-operative management of a renewable resource, other economic factors can cause severe over-exploitation for short-term profit at the expense of long-term sustainability. A nearly universal economic practice is discounting of future profits at a rate at least as large as the difference between the monetary interest rate and the inflation rate. Annual discount rates employed by many governments and resource exploiters are often in the range of 5% to 10% or higher. A standard goal of economic enterprises is maximization of the cumulative discounted profit. Under this goal, discounting causes overexploitation of renewable resources because a unit of harvest now is perceived as more valuable than the same unit harvested in the future.

Clark (1973, 1990) showed that, in many cases, there is a critical discount rate above which the optimal strategy from a narrow economic viewpoint is immediate harvesting of the population to extinction (liquidation of the resource). In simple deterministic models with a constant profit per individual harvested, the critical discount rate equals the maximum per capita rate of population growth, $r_{max}$, because money in the bank grows faster than the population (May, 1976). Organisms with long generation time and/or low fecundity, such as many species of trees, parrots, sea turtles and whales, have $r_{max}$ below the prevailing discount rate and are frequently threatened by over-exploitation.

Stochastic fluctuations in population size reduce the size of sustainable harvests (Beddington & May, 1977, Lande, Engen & Sæther, 1995). Modifications of optimal harvesting strategies to reflect management goals of reducing extinction risk as well as maximizing sustainable harvests have only recently been developed. Such harvesting strategies generally involve thresholds at very substantial population sizes below which no harvesting occurs when the population fluctuates below the threshold, and above which harvesting occurs as fast as possible (Lande, Engen & Sæther, 1994, 1995; Lande, Sæther & Engen, 1997).

## Introduction of exotic species

Artificial translocation of animal and plant species beyond their natural ranges is the third major anthropogenic factor contributing to extinction risk. Massive numbers of species are transported and released in foreign environments accidentally, incidentally and deliberately in private and commercial transportation, live animal trade, ornamental plantings and biological control.

Introduced species, mainly predators and competitors, seriously affect about one-fifth of the endangered mammals of Australasia and the Americas and birds of the world (Groombridge, 1992). Introduced rats are responsible for extinctions of many island-endemic birds (Atkinson, 1989). In some National Parks in Hawaii, up to half of the plant species are non-native (Vitousek, 1988) and constitute a serious risk for the endangered flora. Introduced strains and species of parasites and diseases are also a serious problem for many endangered species (Dobson & May, 1986).

## Pollution

Agricultural and industrial pollution have had both localized and widespread effects. Long-lasting pesticides, such as DDT, become concentrated in terrestrial and aquatic food chains, and have endangered several birds of prey such as the American bald eagle and peregrine falcon. Although bans on most long-lasting pesticides in the USA helped recovery of both these species, they are still used in many countries. About 4% of endangered birds of the world and 2.5% of mammals of Australasia and the Americas are at risk from pollution (Groombridge, 1992). These figures under-estimate the extent of morbidity, mortality and fertility impairment caused by pesticides in many non-endangered species.

Acid rain has had intense regional effects on terrestrial plant communities in western Europe and on freshwater ecosystems in the eastern USA. In Germany, about one-fourth of the native species of ferns and flowering plants are endangered or extinct; the proportion of these endangered or extinct species at risk from various sources of pollution are 5% from air and soil pollution, and 5% from water pollution (ODEC, 1991).

## ECOLOGICAL FACTORS

### Environmental fluctuations and catastrophes

All natural populations fluctuate because of changes in their physical and biotic environments that alter birth and death rates. Unexploited vertebrate populations have coefficients of variation (standard deviation/mean) in annual abundance usually in the range of 20% to 80% or more (Pimm, 1991). Exploited populations also are highly variable (Myers, Bridson & Barrowman, 1995), not only because of environmental stochasticity, but because commonly used exploitation strategies, such as constant-effort or constant-rate harvesting, tend to reduce population stability (Beddington & May, 1977; May et al., 1978). Catastrophes are an extreme form of environmental fluctuation in which the population is suddenly reduced in size by a large proportion, usually caused by extraordinary climatic conditions, such as droughts or severe cold, or by disease outbreaks (Young 1994).

In stochastic population models with density dependence and either normal environmental fluctuations in population growth rate or random catastrophes, for a population initially near carrying capacity the mean time to extinction $T$, scales asymptotically (for sufficiently large populations) as the carrying capacity raised to a power. With normal environmental fluctuations the power depends on the ratio of the mean to environmental variance in annual rate of population growth. With random catastrophes, the power depends on the average frequency and magnitude of catastrophes. In both cases the power may be either greater than or less than one. Thus, comparing populations with different carrying capacities, under low environmental stochasticity, $T$ increases faster than linearly with increasing carrying capacity, whereas under high environmental stochasticity, $T$ increases less than linearly with increasing carrying capacity (Lande, 1993). Logarithmic scaling of $T$ with initial population size is characteristic of a declining population, in which the mean growth rate is negative, regardless of whether the decline is deterministic or stochastic (Lande, 1993). Asymptotic scaling laws for various risk factors are summarized in Fig. 2.1 and Table 2.1.

Previous authors incorrectly suggested that, with normal environmental stochasticity, $T$ increases at most linearly with carrying capacity, and that with random catastrophes, $T$ would only increase as the logarithm of carrying capacity (Goodman, 1987a, Ewens et al., 1987). Goodman (1987b) and Quinn & Hastings (1987) used these erroneous results to argue that population subdivision generally prolongs the mean time to extinction, and is therefore an advisable strategy for nature preserves. While this may be true in some circumstances, it is not correct in general. If subdivision substantially reduces the correlation in environmental stochasticity among the localities, e.g. considering one large contiguous reserve versus several small distant reserves of the same total area, then subdivision can increase $T$. For example, when single populations are subject to major catastrophes, occurring randomly among populations, then population subdivision can clearly be advantageous for persistence (Burkey, 1989). Subdivision can also increase persistence in the presence of catastrophic epidemics, not only by reducing the transmission of epidemics among localities, but in some cases by reducing their frequency because many epidemics require a threshold population size or density to become started (Hess, 1996). On the other hand, if the small reserves are located in the same general area, and subject to nearly the same environmental stochasticity, then subdivision is likely to decrease persistence by making the small reserves more subject to edge effects, Allee effects and demographic stochasticity.

Above the species level, ecosystem function is likely to be enhanced in large reserves without landscape fragmentation; species diversity would tend to be larger, at least initially, in several small reserves spread over a

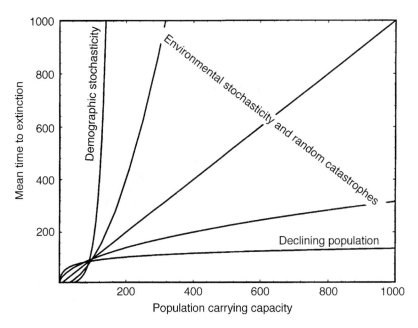

Fig. 2.1 Asymptotic scaling laws for the mean time to extinction as a function of population carrying capacity under different risk factors (see Table 2.1).

larger geographic area, but these would suffer more rapid local extinctions. Designs for nature reserves systems must balance these advantages and disadvantages of subdivision. From a review of data on several natural and artificial archipelagoes, Burkey (1995) concluded that, on a single large island, the rate of species extinctions is initially faster, but ultimately slower, than on several small islands.

**Metapopulation dynamics**

Like population subdivision, dispersal among local populations, patches of suitable habitat or 'islands' can have advantages and disadvantages for persistence. The major advantage is that dispersers can recolonize suitable habitat after local extinctions, allowing a metapopulation to persist in a balance between local extinction and recolonization (Levins, 1970; Hanski & Gilpin, 1997). In the original metapopulation model of Levins (1970) the equilibrium proportion of islands occupied by a species is $p = 1 - e/m$, where $e$ is the rate of local extinction and $m$ is the colonization rate. Metapopulation persistence then requires that $m > e$. This, and other demo-

**Table 2.1**

*Asymptotic scaling laws for mean time to extinction, T, from different ecological and genetic risk factors, as a function of the initial actual size, N, or effective size, $N_e$, of a population at carrying capacity*

| Risk factor | Proportional scaling of T |
|---|---|
| Declining population[a] | $-(\ln N)/\bar{r}$ |
| Environmental stochasticity[b] | $N^{2\bar{r}/V_e - 1}$ |
| Demographic stochasticity[c] | $(1/N)e^{2Nr/V_I}$ |
| Fixation of new mutations[d] | $N_e^{1 + 1/c^2}$ |

[a] In this case only, mean population growth rate, $\bar{r}$, is negative.
[b] Mean and variance of annual growth rate are respectively $\bar{r}$ and $V_e$.
[c] Mean and variance of individual Malthusian fitness are, respectively, $r$ and $V_I$.
[d] Coefficient of variation of selection against new mutations is $c$.

graphic and genetic benefits of dispersal (see below), have spurred interest in various methods of facilitating dispersal, from artificial transport of individuals or germ cells to preservation or creation of habitat corridors connecting islands of suitable habitat. The efficacy of corridors has hardly been tested (Andreassen, Halle & Ims, 1996), but for many species they may be of little value because of edge effects.

The major disadvantage or cost to dispersal is caused by habitat heterogeneity in the form of increased mortality and decreased fecundity during movement through unsuitable habitat. For species in which individuals or mated pairs hold exclusive territories, or home ranges with small overlap, the basic effects of habitat destruction and fragmentation can be taken into account, along with life history, age-structured population dynamics and individual dispersal behaviour (Lande, 1987). Identifying the individual territory as the local unit in a metapopulation, local extinction then corresponds to the death of an individual, and colonization represents successful dispersal into a suitable, unoccupied patch of habitat. Patches of suitable habitat the size of individual territories are assumed to be randomly or evenly distributed across a large region (not clumped on a spatial scale much larger than the mean individual dispersal distance), and the proportion of the region composed of suitable habitat is $h$. The equilibrium proportion of suitable habitat occupied by the species is $p = 1 - (1 - k)/h$. The parameter $k$, termed the 'demographic potential', depends on the life history and dispersal behaviour of the species and generally lies between 0 and 1; it gives the maximum occupancy of suitable habitat in an entirely suitable region ($p = k$ when $h = 1$).

This model reveals two general and robust features important for conservation planning. First, unoccupied suitable habitat may be as important as occupied habitat for long-term persistence of a metapopulation. Continual destruction of unoccupied habitat will doom a metapopulation to early extinction. Secondly, as the amount of suitable habitat in a region decreases by habitat destruction and fragmentation, the equilibrium occupancy of suitable habitat decreases. Because the population size is a product of the amount of suitable habitat and the occupancy of suitable habitat, this implies that, with habitat destruction and fragmentation, the equilibrium population size generally declines faster than the rate of habitat loss. This also entails an 'extinction threshold' or minimum density of suitable habitat in a region necessary for population persistence, $h = 1 - k$ (since $p = 0$ when $h \leq 1 - k$). A population may become extinct in the presence of a large amount of suitable habitat if this is too sparsely distributed.

This model was developed for application to conservation of the northern spotted owl, *Strix occidentalis caurina*, in the Pacific north-west of the USA (Lande, 1988a). Subsequent analyses of this subspecies, accounting for more details of spatial distribution of suitable habitat and degrees of habitat suitability (Doak, 1989; Thomas *et al.*, 1990; McKelvey, Noon & Lamberson, 1993), confirmed the general existence and robustness of an extinction threshold in the population dynamics of territorial species, and eventually led to the consideration of more than 1000 different animal and plant taxa in conservation plans for the old-growth forest ecosystem on which the northern spotted owl depends (FEMAT 1993).

Few attempts have been made to analyse the effects of dispersal and local population dynamics on metapopulation persistence that could be applied more generally, including to non-territorial species. Some steps in this direction (Hanski & Gyllenberg, 1993; Hanski *et al.*, 1995, Lande, Engen &Sæther, 1998) suggest the existence of alternative equilibria: an unstable equilibrium with low occupancy of suitable habitat, and a stable equilibrium with high occupancy of suitable habitat. These alternative stable equilibria arise because of interactions between local and global population dynamics. At low habitat occupancy, emigration from an occupied patch is not compensated by immigration, which can render isolated populations vulnerable to extinction. Increasing habitat occupancy in the metapopulation increases the number of immigrants to any site, decreasing the rate of local extinction (the 'rescue effect' of Brown & Kodric-Brown, 1977) and increasing the probability of successful colonization ('establishment effect' of Lande, Engen & Sæther, 1998). If there is ample suitable habitat for metapopulation persistence, but the chances of successful dispersal and colonization are low owing to costs of dispersal or difficulties in colonization of suitable habitat caused by demographic stochasticity and Allee effect, then there may be an unstable equilibrium at low habitat occupancy, constituting a kind of Allee effect at the metapopulation level.

## Small population size

### Demographic stochasticity

Random individual variation in vital rates of mortality and reproduction, and random segregation of X and Y chromosomes in sex-determination, cause fluctuations in the per capita rate of population growth. The magnitude of these fluctuations is inversely proportional to population size because independent random events among individuals tend to cancel in a large population. In contrast to environmental stochasticity, which may operate with comparable intensity in both large and small populations, demographic stochasticity affects small populations most strongly. In simple models with the population initially at carrying capacity, under demographic stochasticity alone the mean time to extinction scales asymptotically almost exponentially with carrying capacity (Fig. 2.1, Table 1). Demographic stochasticity is generally thought to be of relatively little importance in populations larger than roughly 100 individuals (MacArthur & Wilson, 1967; Richter-Dyn & Goel, 1972; Lande, 1993). In small populations demographic stochasticity may be the dominant stochastic factor in population dynamics, posing a greater risk of extinction than environmental stochasticity. Demographic stochasticity can create a type of Allee effect such that in populations below a certain population trajectories most sample paths tend to decrease (Lande, 1998c).

### Allee effect

Co-operative social interactions occur in many animal species, including group defence against predators, physical or chemical conditioning of the environment (e.g. huddling for warmth), communal nesting and increased per capita efficiency of group foraging for resources. Individuals in populations below a certain size or density may suffer reduced fitness from insufficient co-operative interactions with conspecifics. More generally in small or sparsely distributed populations, individuals may have difficulty encountering potential mates. These effects can make population growth negative in small populations, creating an unstable equilibrium at small population size below which the population tends to decline to extinction (Allee et al., 1949; Andrewartha & Birch, 1954). For example, the Lakeside Daisy is a self-incompatible perennial, and the last individuals in Illinois were found to be incompatible and hence incapable of reproduction (De-Mauro, 1993).

*Edge effects*
Habitat destruction and fragmentation create new edges and may reduce habitat quality for considerable distances inside suitable habitat patches, by causing microclimatic alterations and facilitating incursion or invasion of exotic species. For example, clearing tropical rainforests for pastureland causes desiccation and vegetational changes up to hundreds of metres inside remnant forest patches (Lovejoy et al., 1986). Fragmentation of temperate zone forests by agriculture and settlement facilitates the invasion of cowbirds that parasitize the nests of other birds, some of which are endangered (Robinson et al., 1995).

Another type of edge effect arises from dispersal beyond the boundary of suitable habitat. The rate of dispersal into unsuitable regions determines the minimum size of a geographically isolated patch of suitable habitat that can support a stable population, known as the critical patch size. With random dispersal, lethal surroundings and a low intrinsic rate of increase per generation, the critical patch size is much larger than the average individual dispersal distance (Kierstead & Slobodkin 1953). More hospitable surroundings, high intrinsic rate of increase and habitat selection behaviour decrease the critical patch size (Okubo, 1980; Pease, Lande & Bull, 1989).

## GENETIC FACTORS

### Maladaptive translocation and hybridization

A low rate of interspecific hybridization often occurs between closely related species and may be beneficial in augmenting intraspecific genetic variance and adaptive evolution (Lewontin & Birch, 1966; Grant & Price, 1981). Artificial disturbance of habitats facilitates contact and hybridization between normally non-interbreeding species. Interspecific contact and hybridization also can occur through invasion or introduction of exotic species. Abnormally high rates of interspecific hybridization are likely to be maladaptive because of partial sterility and reduced viability caused by a variety of post-zygotic reproductive isolating mechanisms that usually exist between species (Dobzhansky, 1970), which can impose a heavy cost on a rare species hybridizing with a common species (Levin, Francisco-Ortega & Jansen, 1996). When natural reproductive isolating mechanisms are mainly prezygotic, interspecific hybridization may not threaten the demographic stability of a species but can nevertheless destroy its genetic integrity. To give some examples, fragmentation of old-growth forests in the Pacific north-west of the USA has facilitated range extension of the barred owl which is now hybridizing with the northern spotted owl. Molecular genetic evidence indicates that domestic dogs are hybridizing with the endangered Simien jackal (Wayne, 1996). The diversity of subspecies and species of cichlid fish in Lake Victoria has declined with artificial increases in water turbidity that decreases colour vision, sexual selection and mate choice (Seehausen, van Alphen & Witte, 1997).

Intraspecific hybridization can also produce maladaptive effects by eroding the genetic basis of adaptations to local environmental conditions. This often occurs when non-local genetic strains are used for restocking game fish and forest trees. Until recently, little attention was given to the genetic properties of introduced stocks, which has resulted in widespread decreases in fitness of stocked populations and maladaptive hybridization with remaining wild stocks. This is one of the major factors contributing to massive declines and numerous local extinctions of salmon runs in the Pacific north-west (Nehlsen, Williams & Lichatowich, 1991; Ratner, Lande & Roper, 1997).

### Selective breeding and harvesting

Exploited populations are frequently subject to intense selective harvesting based on size, age and behavioural characteristics. This can induce evolutionary changes in life history and social structure which will usually decrease the fitness of the wild population, as well as diminishing the quantity and quality of future harvests. Selective harvesting is thought to be a factor in body-size declines of many exploited stocks of anadromous fish (Stokes, McGlade & Law, 1993).

Intense selective pressures can also occur during artificial propagation of captive populations, because artificial rearing conditions usually differ substantially from natural environments (Arnold, 1995). The resulting evolutionary changes are again likely to be maladaptive for wild conditions.

Artificial propagation for the purposes of augmentation and reintroduction of endangered or extinct populations should be done in as few generations under as naturalistic conditions as possible. Indefinite restocking programmes, such as fish hatcheries, may be doing more harm than good in the long run, and should not be viewed as an adequate substitute for habitat restoration (Allendorf & Waples, 1996).

## Small population size

### Inbreeding depression

Matings between closely related individuals tend to produce offspring with reduced fitness due to the expression of (partially) recessive deleterious mutations in homozygous form. In historically large, outcrossing populations this inbreeding depression in fitness typically results in a loss of fitness of a few to several percent per 10% increase in the coefficient of inbreeding or consanguinity (Ralls & Ballou, 1983; Falconer & Mackay, 1996). Thus, in species of domesticated animals, experimental propagation by continued brother-sister matings generally results in extinction of a high proportion of lines within five or ten generations (Soulé, 1980; Frankham, 1995a). Species, and populations within a species, differ substantially in the magnitude of inbreeding depression (Soulé, 1980; Lacy, Petric & Warneke, 1993).

The genetic basis of inbreeding depression is best understood in species of *Drosophila*, in which roughly equal parts are contributed by nearly recessive lethal mutations and by partially recessive, mildly deleterious mutations (Simmons & Crow, 1977). Both recessive lethal and mildly deleterious mutations arise at thousands of genetic loci throughout the genome in eukaryotic species (Simmons & Crow, 1977). Theory and experiment indicate that gradual inbreeding allows natural selection to purge recessive lethal mutations from a population as they become expressed in homozygotes, whereas it is difficult or impossible to purge mildly deleterious mutations (Lande & Schemske, 1984; Charlesworth & Charlesworth, 1987). However, for populations with extremely high inbreeding depression, such as some tree species and gynodioecious plants, it may be difficult to purge even the recessive lethals by close inbreeding because if nearly all of the selfed offspring die before reproduction the population is then effectively outcrossed and no purging occurs unless the selfing rate exceeds a threshold value (Lande, Schemske & Schultz, 1994).

Substantial loss of fitness is an almost inevitable consequence of sudden reduction to very small population size, unless the population rapidly recovers to a large size thereby allowing selection to reverse the short-term effects of inbreeding and random genetic drift (e.g. Keller *et al.*, 1994). The more gradual the reduction in population size, the greater the opportunity for purging recessive lethal mutations and avoiding a large part of the inbreeding depression. Thus, inbreeding depression is not simply proportional to the inbreeding coefficient routinely calculated for selectively neutral genes. The rule suggested by Franklin (1980) and Soulé (1980), supported by extensive practical experience in animal and plant breeding, is that inbreeding depression can be largely avoided in populations with effective sizes larger than $N_e = 50$. However, inbreeding depression may be more severe in natural environments than in laboratory populations (Jiménez *et al.*, 1994) and in stressful than in optimal environments (Keller *et al.*, 1994; K. Biljsma, pers. comm.).

Inbreeding depression can be easily reversed (at least temporarily) by introduction of several unrelated individuals into an inbred population, and permanent prevention of inbreeding depression can be accomplished by continued immigration every one or two generations of a single unrelated individual into each local population regardless of their size (Lande & Barrowclough, 1987). Such a plan was recently instituted for the endangered Florida panther, motivated by strong circumstantial evidence of inbreeding depression in the small remnant population, and low genetic divergence from other conspecific populations (Hedrick, 1995). Although this genetic augmentation may be sufficient to reverse inbreeding effects without swamping any important local adaptations that might exist, the Florida panther still faces the ecological threats of small population size due to past habitat destruction and high mortality from automobile impacts.

### Loss of genetic variation

Finite population size causes random changes in gene frequencies, attributable to Mendelian segregation and variation in family size, which result on average in a loss of genetic variance from a population. The expected proportion of selectively neutral genetic variance lost from a population per generation is $1/(2N_e)$, where $N_e$ is the effective population size. For wild populations the effective size is usually substantially less than the actual size because of large variance in family size, unequal sex ratio among breeders and fluctuations in population size through time (Wright, 1969). The ratio of effective to actual size of wild populations is often on the order of 0.1 (Frankham, 1995*b*). Weakly selected genes become effectively neutral with respect to the action of random genetic drift if the magnitude of selection on them is much less than $1/(2N_e)$ (Wright, 1969).

To lose a large fraction of its genetic variance measured by heterozygosity in molecular genetic polymorphisms or heritable variance in quantitative characters, a population reduced to a small effective size, $N_e$, must remain small for at least $2N_e$ generations. Following its loss in such a population 'bottleneck', genetic variance can be regained by immigration or by mutation. An isolated population that passes through a bottleneck must regain large size and remain large for a long time in order for mutation to replenish normal levels of genetic variance. Metapopulation structure, with frequent local extinction and colonization, can reduce $N_e$ of the metapopulation orders of magnitude below its actual size, mimicking the genetic effects of a population bottleneck (Wright, 1940; Maruyama & Kimura, 1980; Hedrick, 1996).

Although all kinds of genetic variance are lost at the same rate by random genetic drift, in an isolated population different kinds of genetic variance are replenished at different rates depending on their mutability. Stable populations of different sizes also maintain unequal proportions of different kinds of genetic variance depending on the balance between random genetic drift, mutation and selection (see Table 2.2). Among small or moderate populations of given size, there may be substantial variance in the amount of inbreeding depression (Lacy *et al.*, 1993), in the heritable variance in a given quantitative character (Bürger & Lande, 1994), or in the heterozygosity at a given set of loci (Wright, 1969). One should therefore not expect a close concordance in different types of genetic variance among populations of different size, contrary to the suggestion of Soulé (1980). In particular, populations with moderate effective size, on the order of $N_e = 10^3$ to $10^4$, may maintain low molecular heterozygosity for point mutations, with substantial heritable variance in quantitative characters, and nearly normal inbreeding depression and heterozygosity for repeated DNA.

A low rate of dispersal, on the order of a few individuals exchanged among populations per generation, is sufficient to prevent much genetic differentiation at quasineutral loci, such as most molecular genetic polymorphisms (Wright, 1969; Crow & Kimura, 1970). In contrast, adaptive differences among populations can be maintained by natural selection with high levels of dispersal and gene flow (Endler, 1977). Lack of differentiation between populations at molecular genetic loci therefore does not imply lack of adaptive differences.

**Table 2.2**
*Mutability, order of magnitude of time scale in generations for replenishment, and minimum effective population size ($N_e$) for maintaining typical levels of different types of genetic variance in a randomly mating population*

| Genetic variance | Mutability | Time scale | Minimum $N_e$ |
|---|---|---|---|
| Inbreeding depression | High | $10^2$ | 50 |
| Quantitative characters | Moderate | $10^4$ | 5000 |
| Molecular heterozygosity | | | |
| Point mutations | Low | $2 \times 10^4$ to $10^5$ | $10^4$ to $10^5$ |
| Repetitive DNA | high | $10^3$ | 500 |

Molecular and quantitative variance are assumed to be quasineutral (excluding strongly selected mutations).

Genetic variability allows adaptive evolution in response to changing environments. Polygenic, quantitative (continuously varying) characters of morphology, behaviour and physiology are particularly important for long-term adaptability and population persistence. Quantitative characters are usually under stabilizing natural selection toward an intermediate optimum phenotype that may fluctuate with time. Like unconditionally deleterious mutations such as those contributing to inbreeding depression, heritable variance in quantitative characters therefore imposes a fitness cost or 'genetic load' on a population, which is the price it must pay for long-term adaptability (Crow & Kimura, 1970; Lande & Shannon, 1996). Thus, under normal environmental conditions, including temporal fluctuations, there is an optimal level of genetic variance for maintaining both current fitness and future adaptability.

There is, however, a maximum rate of directional or random environmental change that a population can tolerate by adaptive evolution without becoming extinct, depending on the amount of genetic variability it can maintain (Lynch & Lande, 1993; Bürger & Lynch, 1995; Lande & Shannon, 1996). Rapid, extreme environmental changes, such as anthropogenic global warming, will place a premium on genetic variability and adaptability of many populations in fragmented environments during the coming centuries (see Discussion).

To maintain typical levels of heritable variance in quantitative characters, based on experimental estimates of their mutability, Franklin (1980) and Soulé (1980) recommended a minimum effective population size of $N_e = 500$. Recent experimental evidence indicates that a large fraction of the mutational variance in quantitative characters is associated with recessive lethal and semi-lethal effects (Lopez & Lopez-Fanjul, 1993a,b; Mackay,

Lyman & Jackson, 1992), such that the quasineutral, potentially adaptive mutational variance is roughly one-tenth as large as previous estimates. Lande (1995) therefore suggested that the Franklin–Soulé number should be increased by a factor of 10 to $N_e = 5000$. Maintenance of rare alleles with major effects on disease resistance may require much larger populations (Roush & McKenzie, 1987).

### Fixation of new mutations

In contrast to recessive lethal mutations which generally are kept at low frequencies by natural selection, random genetic drift can fix mildly deleterious mutations in a small population and gradually erode its fitness. Mildly deleterious mutations arise at many loci, with a total genomic rate on the order of one per generation in a variety of organisms; individually they produce an average fitness loss of a few to several percent and are only partially dominant (nearly additive). When enough deleterious mutations become fixed, the population is genetically inviable ($r_{max} \leq 0$) and rapid extinction ensues. For a population in a constant environment, at carrying capacity with no demographic stochasticity, the mean time until genetic inviability from fixation of new deleterious mutations scales asymptotically as a power of the effective population size at carrying capacity; the power depends on the coefficient of variation of selection against new mutations (Lande, 1994, 1995). For realistic distributions of selection on mildly deleterious mutations, the coefficient of variation is on the order of one (e.g. an exponential distribution of mutational effects on fitness), so the power is not very large (see Table 1 and Keightley, 1994). With such a distribution of mutational effects it is the nearly neutral mutations, with selection coefficients close to $1/(2N_e)$, that do the most damage to the population, because strongly selected mutations rarely become fixed and more weakly selected mutations have relatively little impact on fitness (Lande, 1994; Lynch, Conery & Bürger, 1995a, b).

With high initial fitness, even for extremely small populations it may take hundreds of generations for fixation of new mildly deleterious mutations to cause extinction. For sufficiently large populations, advantageous, compensatory and reverse mutations will completely prevent the erosion of fitness by deleterious mutations. Thus it is only for small populations with low fitness that the extinction risk from fixation of new deleterious mutations is a serious concern within the typical 100-year time scale of conservation planning. However, for populations of moderate size, with $N_e$ up to few thousand, fixation of new mutations could substantially decrease their *long-term* viability (Lande, 1995).

## DISCUSSION

The primary anthropogenic causes of species declines cascade through a series of ecological and genetic effects that are finally expressed, and can be evaluated, in population dynamics and extinction risk. Land development causes habitat loss and fragmentation, which, along with overexploitation and artificial introductions of exotic species, produces population declines and small population effects, intensifying metapopulation dynamics. Demographic and genetic factors affecting small populations are involved in positive feedback loops with population decline, termed 'extinction vortices' by Gilpin & Soulé (1986).

Management for recovery of an endangered species already reduced to small and/or fragmented populations requires consideration of all of the potential risk factors described above, as well as their interactions. Small-population effects are usually more a symptom than a cause of impending extinction, and treating them without addressing the underlying causes of population decline will not prevent extinction (Lande, 1988b; Caughley, 1994). The scaling laws for mean time to extinction under different risks (Fig. 2.1 and Table 2.1) support the idea that deterministic population declines of anthropogenic origin are generally of much greater importance than stochastic factors as the main causes of species declines prior to their becoming endangered. This is especially important because it is often possible to ascertain the causes of deterministic declines and to reverse them through restoration and management actions (Caughley & Gunn, 1996).

Habitat destruction and fragmentation restrict dispersal, and eliminate for many species what was the most important mechanism for population persistence in response to long-term climatic alterations: change of geographic distribution (Pease *et al.*, 1989; Peters & Lovejoy, 1992; see also Huntley, this volume). In response to previous periods of global warming and cooling associated with glacial cycles, species often changed their geographic range while maintaining essentially the same phenotype except perhaps for changes in body size (e.g. Coope, 1979; Smith, Betancourt & Brown, 1995). Species restricted to isolated habitat fragments and reserves must instead rely either on their limited physiological tolerances, or on evolutionary adaptation *in situ*, to survive rapid global warming in the coming centuries. A small proportion may be aided by accidental or deliberate artificial transport. Persistence of many species during the next millennium will therefore come increasingly to depend on maintaining ample genetic variation for adaptive evolution, and on having natural or artificial opportunities for dispersal.

Despite heightened public awareness and concern about environmental issues, national and international efforts at conservation and restoration remain largely inadequate, as most nations promote continued human population growth, more land development, increased resource exploitation and anthropogenic global warming. Although politicians and societies rarely make plans on time scales longer than decades, conservation biologists must increasingly plan on time scales of centuries, millennia, and longer, if our attempts to preserve some fraction of existing biodiversity are to have any lasting effect.


## ACKNOWLEDGEMENTS

I thank B-E. Sæther, J. Mallet and an anonymous reviewer for comments on the manuscript. This work was supported by NSF grant DEB–9225127.

### References

Allee, W. C., Emerson, A. E., Park, O., Park, T. & Schmidt, K. P. (1949). *Principles of animal ecology*. Saunders, Philadelphia.

Allendorf, F. W. & Waples, R. S. (1996). Conservation and genetics of salmonid fishes. In *Conservation genetics: case histories from nature*: 238–280. (Eds Avise, J. C. & Hamrick, J. L.). Chapman & Hall, New York.

Andreassen, H. P., Halle, S. & Ims, R. A. (1996). Optimal width of movement corridors for root voles: not too narrow and not too wide. *J. Appl. Ecol.*, **33**, 63–70.

Andrewartha, H. G. & Birch, L. C. (1954). *The distribution and abundance of animals*. University of Chicago Press, Chicago.

Arnold, S. J. (1995). Monitoring quantitative genetic variation and evolution in captive populations. In *Population management for survival and recovery: analytical methods and strategies in small populations*: 295–317. (Eds Ballou, J., Gilpin, M. & Foose, T. J.). Columbia University Press, New York.

Atkinson, I. (1989). Introduced animals and extinctions. In *Conservation for the twenty-first century*: 54–75. (Eds Western, D. & Pearl, M. C.). Oxford University Press, New York & Oxford.

Beddington, J. R. & May, R. M. (1977). Harvesting populations in a randomly fluctuating environment. *Science*, **197**, 463–5.

Brown, J. H. & Kodric-Brown, A. (1977). Turnover rates in insular biogeography:

effect of immigration on extinction. *Ecology*, **58**, 445–9.

Burkey, T. V. (1989). Extinction in nature reserves: the effect of fragmentation and the importance of migration between reserve fragments. *Oikos*, **55**, 75–81.

Burkey, T. V. (1995). Extinction rates in archipelagoes: implications for populations in fragmented habitats. *Conserv. Biol.*, **9**, 527–41.

Bürger, R. & Lande, R. (1994). On the distribution of the mean and variance of a quantitative trait under mutation-selection-drift balance. *Genetics*, **138**, 901–12.

Bürger, R. & Lynch, M. (1995). Evolution and extinction in a changing environment: a quantitative-genetic analysis. *Evolution*, **49**, 151–63.

Caughley, G. (1994). Directions in conservation biology. *J. Anim. Ecol.*, **63**, 215–44.

Caughley, G. & Gunn, A. (1996). *Conservation biology in theory and practice.* Blackwell Science, London.

Charlesworth, D. & Charlesworth, B. (1987). Inbreeding depression and its evolutionary consequences. *A. Rev. Ecol. Syst.*, **18**, 237–68.

Clark, C. W. (1973). The economics of overexploitation. *Science*, **181**, 630–4.

Clark, C. W. (1990). *Mathematical bioeconomics.* (2nd edn). Wiley, New York.

Coope, G. R. (1979). Late Cenozoic fossil Coleoptera: evolution, biogeography, and ecology. *Annu. Rev. Ecol. Syst.*, **10**, 247–67.

Crow, J. F. & Kimura, M. (1970). *An introduction to population genetics theory.* Harper & Row, New York.

DeMauro, M. M. (1993). Relationship of breeding system to rarity in the Lakeside Daisy (*Hymenoxys acaulis var. glabra*). *Conserv. Biol.*, **7**, 542–50.

Doak, D. (1989). Spotted owls and old growth logging in the Pacific Northwest. *Conserv. Biol.*, **3**, 389–96.

Dobson, A. P. & May, R. M. (1986). Disease and conservation. In *Conservation biology: the science of scarcity and diversity*: 345–365. (Ed. Soulé, M. E.). Sinauer, Sunderland, MA.

Dobzhansky, Th. (1970). *Genetics of the evolutionary process.* Columbia University Press, New York.

Endler, J. (1977). *Geographic variation, speciation, and clines.* Princeton University Press, Princeton. (*Monogr. Popul. Biol.* No. 10.)

Ewens, W. J., Brockwell, P. J., Gani, J. M. & Resnick, S. I. (1987). Minimum viable population sizes in the presence of catastrophes. In *Viable populations for conservation*: 59–68. (Ed. Soulé, M. E.). Cambridge University Press, Cambridge.

Falconer, D. S. & Mackay, T. F. C. (1996). *Introduction to quantitative genetics.* (4th edn). Longman, London.

FEMAT (1993). *Forest ecosystem management: an ecological, economic, and social assessment..* Report of the Forest Ecosystem Management Assessment Team. US Government Printing Office, Washington, DC.

Frankham, R. (1995a). Inbreeding and extinction: a threshold effect. *Conserv. Biol.*, **9**, 792–9.

Frankham, R. (1995b). Effective population size/adult population size ratios in wildlife: a review. *Genet. Res.*, **66**, 95–107.

Franklin, I. R. (1980). Evolutionary change in small populations. In *Conservation*

*biology: an evolutionary–ecological perspective*: 135–149. (Eds Soulé, M. E. &
Wilcox, B. A.). Sinauer, Sunderland, MA.

Gilpin, M. E. & Soulé, M. E. (1986). Minimum viable populations: processes of
species extinction. In *Conservation biology: the science of scarcity and diversity*:
19–34 (Ed. Soulé, M. E.). Sinauer, Sunderland, MA.

Goodman, D. (1987*a*). The demography of chance extinction. In *Viable populations
for conservation*: 11–34. (Ed. Soulé, M. E.). Cambridge University Press,
Cambridge.                                    ⸱

Goodman, D. (1987*b*). How do any species persist? Lessons for conservation
biology. *Conserv. Biol.*, **1**, 59–62.

Grant, P. R. & Price, T. D. (1981). Population variation in continuously varying
traits as an ecological genetics problem. *Am. Zool.*, **21**, 795–811.

Groombridge, B. (Ed.) (1992). *Global biodiversity: status of the earth's living
resources*. Chapman & Hall, London.

Hanski, I. & Gilpin, M. E. (Eds). (1997). *Metapopulation biology*. Academic Press,
London.

Hanski, I. & Gyllenberg, M. (1993). Two general metapopulation models and the
core-satellite species hypothesis. *Am. Nat.*, **142**, 17–41.

Hanski, I., Poyry, J., Pakkala, T. & Kuussaari, M. (1995). Multiple equilibria in
metapopulation dynamics. *Nature, Lond.*, **377**, 618–21.

Hedrick, P. W. (1995). Gene flow and genetic restoration: the Florida panther
as a case study. *Conserv. Biol.*, **9**, 996–1007.

Hedrick, P. W. (1996). Bottleneck(s) or metapopulation in cheetahs. *Conserv.
Biol.*, **10**, 897–9.

Hess, G. (1996). Disease in metapopulation models: implications for
conservation. *Ecology*, **77**, 1617–32.

Jiménez, J. A., Hughes, K. A., Alaks, G., Graham, L. & Lacy, R. C. (1994). An
experimental study of inbreeding depression in a natural habitat. *Science*, **266**,
271–3.

Keightley, P. D. (1994). The distribution of mutation effects on viability in
*Drosophila melanogaster*. *Genetics*, **138**, 1315–22.

Keller, L. F., Arcese, P., Smith, J. N. M., Hochachka, W. M. & Stearns, S. C. (1994).
Selection against inbred song sparrows during a natural population
bottleneck. *Nature, Lond.*, **372**, 356–7.

Kierstead, H. & Slobodkin, L. B. (1953). The sizes of water masses containing
plankton bloom. *J. Mar. Res.*, **12**, 141–7.

Lacy, R. C., Petric A. & Warneke, M. (1993). Inbreeding and outbreeding in captive
populations of wild animal species. In *The natural history of inbreeding and
outbreeding: theoretical and empirical perspectives*: 352–374. (Ed. Thornhill, N.
W.). University of Chicago Press, Chicago.

Lande, R. (1987). Extinction thresholds in demographic models of territorial
populations. *Am. Nat.*, **130**, 624–35.

Lande, R. (1988*a*). Demographic models of the northern spotted owl (*Strix
occidentalis caurina*). *Oecologia*, **75**, 601–7.

Lande, R. (1988*b*). Genetics and demography in biological conservation. *Science*,
**241**, 1455–60.

Lande, R. (1993). Risks of population extinction from demographic and environmental stochasticity and random catastrophes. *Am. Nat.*, **142**, 911–27.

Lande, R. (1994). Risk of population extinction from fixation of new deleterious mutations. *Evolution*, **48**, 1460–9.

Lande, R. (1995). Mutation and conservation. *Conserv. Biol.*, **9**, 782–91.

Lande, R. (1998c). Demographic stochasticity and Allee effect on a scale with isotropic noise. *Oikos* (in press).

Lande, R. & Barrowclough, G. F. (1987). Effective population size, genetic variation, and their use in population management. In *Viable populations for conservation*: 87–123. (Ed. Soulé, M. E.). Cambridge University Press, Cambridge.

Lande, R., Engen, S. & Sæther, B-E. (1994). Optimal harvesting, economic discounting and extinction risk in fluctuating populations. *Nature, Lond.*, **372**, 88–90.

Lande, R., Engen, S. & Sæther, B-E. (1995). Optimal harvesting of fluctuating populations with a risk of extinction. *Am. Nat.*, **145**, 728–45.

Lande, R., Engen, S. & Sæther, B-E. (1998). Extinction times in finite metapopulation models with stochastic local dynamics. *Oikos* (in press).

Lande, R., Sæther, B-E. & Engen, S. (1997). Threshold harvesting for sustainability of fluctuating resources. *Ecology*, **78**, 1341–50.

Lande, R. & Schemske, D.W. (1984). The evolution of self-fertilization and inbreeding depression in plants. I. Genetic models. *Evolution*, **39**, 24–40.

Lande, R., Schemske, D. W. & Schultz, S. T. (1994). High inbreeding depression, selective interference among loci, and the threshold selfing rate for purging recessive lethal mutations. *Evolution*, **48**, 965–78.

Lande, R. & Shannon, S. (1996). The role of genetic variability in adaptation and population persistence in a changing environment. *Evolution*, **50**, 434–7.

Levin, D. A., Francisco-Ortega, J. & Jansen, R. K. (1996). Hybridization and the extinction of rare plant species. *Conserv. Biol.*, **10**, 10–16.

Levins, R. (1970). Extinction. In *Some mathematical problems in biology*: 77–107. (Ed. Gerstenhaber, M.). American Mathematical Society, Providence, RI.

Lewontin, R. C. & Birch, L. C. (1966). Hybridization as a source of variation for adaptation to new environments. *Evolution*, **20**, 315–36.

Lopez, M. A. & Lopez-Fanjul, C. (1993a). Spontaneous mutation for a quantitative trait in *Drosophila melanogaster*. I. Response to artificial selection. *Genet. Res.*, **61**, 107–16.

Lopez, M. A. & Lopez-Fanjul, C. (1993b). Spontaneous mutation for a quantitative trait in *Drosophila melanogaster*. II. Distribution of mutant effects on the trait and fitness. *Genet. Res.*, **61**, 117–26.

Lovejoy, T. E. *et al.* (1986). Edge and other effects of isolation on Amazon forest fragments. In *Conservation biology: the science of scarcity and diversity*: 257–285. (Ed. Soulé, M. E.). Sinauer, Sunderland, MA.

Ludwig, D., Hilborn, R. & Walters, C. (1993). Uncertainty, resource exploitation, and conservation: lessons from history. *Science*, **260**, 17, 36.

Lynch, M., Conery, J. & Bürger, R. (1995a). Mutational meltdown in sexual populations. *Evolution*, **49**, 1067–80.

Lynch, M., Conery, J. & Bürger, R. (1995b). Mutation accumulation and the extinction of small populations. *Am. Nat.*, **146**, 489–518.

Lynch, M. & Lande, R. (1993). Evolution and extinction in response to environmental change. In *Biotic interactions and global change*: 234–250. (Eds Kareiva, P. M., Kingsolver, J. G. & Huey, R. B.). Sinauer, Sunderland MA.

MacArthur, R. H. & Wilson, E. O. (1967). *The theory of island biogeography*. Princeton University Press, Princeton.

Mackay, T. F. C., Lyman, R. F. & Jackson, M. S. (1992). Effects of *P* element insertion on quantitative traits in *Drosophila melanogaster*. *Genetics*, **130**, 315–32.

Maruyama, T. & Kimura, M. (1980). Genetic variation and effective population size when local extinction and recolonization of subpopulations are frequent. *Proc. Natl Acad. Sci. USA*, **77**, 6710–14.

May, R. M. (1976). Harvesting whale and fish populations. *Nature, Lond.*, **263**, 91–2.

May, R. M., Beddington, J. R., Horwood, J. W. & Shepherd, J. G. (1978). Exploiting natural populations in an uncertain world. *Math. Biosci.*, **42**, 219–52.

McKelvey, K., Noon, B. R. & Lamberson, R. H. (1993). Conservation planning for species occupying fragmented landscapes: the case of the northern spotted owl. In *Biotic interactions and global change*: 424–450. (Eds Karieva, P. M., Kingsolver, J. G. & Huey, R. B.). Sinauer, Sunderland MA.

Myers, R. A., Bridson, J. & Barrowman, N. J. (1995). Summary of worldwide spawner and recruitment data. *Can. tech. Rep. Fish. aquat. Sci.* No. 2024: 1–327.

Nehlsen, W., Williams, J. E. & Lichatowich, J. A. (1991). Pacific salmon at the crossroads: stocks at risk from California, Oregon, Idaho and Washington. *Fisheries*, **16**, 4–21.

ODEC (1991). *The state of the environment*. Organization for Economic Co-operation and Development, Paris.

Okubo, A. (1980). *Diffusion and ecological problems: mathematical models*. Springer-Verlag, Berlin.

Pease, C.M., Lande, R. & Bull, J. J. (1989). A model of population growth, dispersal and evolution in a changing environment. *Ecology*, **70**, 1657–64.

Peters, R. L. & Lovejoy, T. E. (Eds) (1992). *Global warming and biological diversity*. Yale University Press, New Haven & London.

Pimm, S. L. (1991). *The balance of nature? Ecological issues in the coservation of species and communities*. University of Chicago Press, Chicago.

Quinn, J. F. & Hastings, A. (1987). Extinction in subdivided habitats. *Conserv. Biol.*, **1**, 198–209.

Ralls, K. & Ballou, J. D. (1983). Extinction: lessons from zoos. In *Genetics and conservation: a reference for managing wild animal and plant populations*: 164–184. (Eds. Schonewald-Cox, C. M., Chambers, S. M., MacBryde, B. & Thomas, W. L.). Benjamin/Cummings, Menlo Park, CA.

Ratner, S., Lande, R. & Roper, B. B. (1997). Population viability analysis of spring chinook salmon in the South Umpqua river, Oregon. *Conserv. Biol.*, **11**, 879–89.

Redford, K. H. (1992). The empty forest. *BioScience*, **42**, 412–22.

Richter-Dyn, N. & Goel, N. S. (1972). On the extinction of a colonizing species. *Theoret. Popul. Biol.*, **3**, 406–33.

Robinson, S. K., Thompson, F. R. III, Donovan, T. M., Whitehead, D. R. & Faaborg, J. (1995). Regional forest fragmentation and the nesting success of migratory birds. *Science*, **267**, 1987–90.

Rosenberg, A. A., Fogarty, M. J., Sissenwine, M. P., Beddington, J. R. & Shepherd, J. G. (1993). Achieving sustainable use of renewable resources. *Science*, **262**, 828–9.

Roush, R. T. & McKenzie, J. A. (1987). Ecological genetics of insecticide and acaricide resistance. *A. Rev. Ent.*, **32**, 361–80.

Seehausen, O., van Alphen, J. & Witte, F. (1997). Cichlid fish diversity threatened by eutrophication that curbs sexual selection. *Science*, **277**, 1808–11.

Simmons, M. J. & Crow, J. F. (1977). Mutations affecting fitness in *Drosophila* populations. *A. Rev. Genet.*, **11**, 49–78.

Smith, F. A., Betancourt, J. L. & Brown, J. H. (1995). Evolution of body size in the woodrat over the past 25,000 years of climate change. *Science*, **270**, 2012–14.

Soulé, M. E. (1980). Thresholds for survival: maintaining fitness and evolutionary potential. In *Conservation biology: an evolutionary–ecological perspective*: 151–169. (Eds Soulé, M. E. & Wilcox, B. A.). Sinauer, Sunderland, MA.

Stokes, T. K., McGlade, J. M. & Law, R. (1993). *The exploitation of evolving resources*. Springer-Verlag, Berlin. (*Lect. Notes Biomath.* **99**.)

Thomas, J. W., Forsman, E. D., Lint, J. B., Meslow, E. C., Noon, B. R. & Verner, J. (1990). *A conservation strategy for the northern spotted owl*. US Government Printing Office, Washington, DC.

Vitousek, P. M. (1988). Diversity and biological invasions of oceanic islands. In *Biodiversity*: 181–189. (Ed. Wilson, E. O.). National Academy Press, Washington, DC.

Wayne, R. K. (1996). Conservation genetics in the Canidae. In *Conservation genetics: case histories from nature*: 75–118. (Eds Avise, J. C. & Hamrick, J. L.). Chapman & Hall, New York.

Wright, S. (1940). Breeding structure of populations in relation to speciation. *Am. Nat.*, **74**, 232–48.

Wright, S. (1969). *Genetics and the evolution of populations. 2. The theory of gene frequencies*. University of Chicago Press, Chicago.

Young, T. P. (1994). Natural die-offs of large mammals: implications for conservation. *Conserv. Biol.*, **8**, 410–18.

# 3

# Integrating endangered species protection and ecosystem management: the Cape Sable seaside-sparrow as a case study

AUDREY L. MAYER AND STUART L. PIMM

## INTRODUCTION

We should construct a global conservation system that will encompass as many species as possible in protected areas. Such areas, 'parks' for short, should require as little time, effort, and money to manage as is possible. How large must a park be to maintain its original species complement or for its ecosystem processes to be self-sustaining? This is an ecological question, but the answer comes as a statement of what is politically feasible. We will show that areas larger than 10 000 km² (roughly a square of one degree of latitude and longitude) are few. In our experience, such large parks are likely to be famous flagships of their countries' efforts to protect the natural environment. We concentrate on one of these rich and famous parks, and the way in which natural events and human activities affect (*Ammodramus maritimus mirabilis*), the Cape Sable seaside-sparrow a species found only within its boundaries.

Everglades National Park and its adjacent conservation areas cover 10,000 km² and encompass most of southern Florida. In the western hemisphere, few parks are larger or enjoy anywhere near as much prestige and associated financial resources. Nonetheless, we show that the Park and its adjacent areas will probably retain their species only through constant vigilance and active, informed ecosystem management.

### Parks in the western hemisphere

Currently, protected areas encompass ~ 5% of the earth's land surface, so perhaps the current rates of biological extinction should not surprise us (Ryan, 1992). In industrial nations such as the United States, national parks are often islands surrounded by a sea of agriculture, pasture, and urban development. Even the largest of parks suffer invasions by exotic species and disturbance due to heavy tourism (Houston, 1971). Roads and trails through a park increase the vulnerability of its interior to 'edge effects', eliminating some of the advantages of large size. In less-industrialized countries, the park is surrounded by areas that are sometimes pristine habitats, but more often degraded by fires, clear-cutting and agriculture.

This 'parks as islands' metaphor suggests an obvious calculation. In archipelagos of oceanic islands, the number of species scales as area raised to the $1/4$ power. This is the familiar species ($S$) to area ($A$) relationship $S = cA^{1/4}$, where $c$ is a constant (Rosenzweig, 1995). Protect only 5% of the area and one might lose $\sim 50\%$ of the planet's species.

Two factors mitigate this bleak prospect. First, some species will survive in the human-dominated 95%. The number of survivors will depend on a complex of factors. These include the degree of protection of the park's surrounding matrix and the survival of the particular species within it. For many areas with burgeoning human populations (developing countries and regions like Florida) parks may represent the best hope for protecting biodiversity.

Secondly, we might be judicious in our choice of the 5%, protecting those areas rich in otherwise vulnerable species. Extinctions concentrate in 'hot spots' – areas of many species with small geographical ranges (Myers, 1990; Pimm et al., 1995; see also Myers, this volume). For example, the great majority of the world's $\sim 1100$ bird species deemed likely to become extinct soon have geographical ranges less than $50\,000\,\mathrm{km}^2$ (Collar, Crosby & Stattersfield, 1994). Protecting such range-restricted species in their special places may save more than 50% of the planet's biodiversity.

A third factor exacerbates the potential loss of species from the 5% of protected land. Unlike oceanic islands, parks, particularly small ones, are surrounded by areas whose land-use practices may have a severe impact on their flora and fauna. Examining these impacts is this chapter's major theme.

We start by asking how many parks there are? Table 3.1 catalogues the area protected by parks, the total number of parks and the number of large parks in each country in the western hemisphere.

The amount of land set aside in parks does not increase significantly with the size of the country (World Resources Institute, 1994). Wealth and aggressive conservation policies are likely key factors. Although Ecuador is only 2% of the size of North America, its proportion of land classified as

**Table 3.1.**
*Parks and other protected areas in the western hemisphere*

| North and Central America | Total area of country (km²) | Area protected (km²) | Number of parks | Number of parks over 10 000 km² |
|---|---|---|---|---|
| Trinidad, Tobago | 5130 | 180 | 9 | 0 |
| Jamaica | 10 830 | 20 | 1 | 0 |
| El Salvador | 20 720 | 190 | 5 | 0 |
| Belize | 22 800 | 2910 | 10 | 0 |
| Haiti | 27 560 | 100 | 3 | 0 |
| Dominican Republic | 48 380 | 10 480 | 18 | 0 |
| Costa Rica | 51 060 | 6210 | 25 | 0 |
| Panama | 75 990 | 13 280 | 15 | 0 |
| Guatemala | 108 430 | 8330 | 17 | 0 |
| Cuba | 109 820 | 8940 | 57 | 0 |
| Honduras | 111 890 | 5430 | 38 | 0 |
| Nicaragua | 118 750 | 9520 | 21 | 0 |
| Mexico | 1 908 690 | 98 970 | 60 | 2 |
| United States | 9 166 600 | 984 560 | 937 | 21 |
| Canada | 9 220 970 | 494 480 | 411 | 12 |

*Source:* World Resources Institute, 1994. Countries are ordered by increasing size.

| South America | Total area in country (km²) | Area protected (km²) | Number of parks | Number of parks over 10 000 km² |
|---|---|---|---|---|
| Surinam | 156 000 | 7360 | 13 | 0 |
| Uruguay | 174 810 | 320 | 8 | 0 |
| Guyana | 196 850 | 590 | 1 | 0 |
| Ecuador | 276 840 | 111 360 | 15 | 1 |
| Paraguay | 397 300 | 14 830 | 19 | 0 |
| Chile | 748 800 | 137 150 | 65 | 5 |
| Venezuela | 882 050 | 275 340 | 104 | 5 |
| Colombia | 1 038 700 | 93 910 | 79 | 2 |
| Bolivia | 1 084 380 | 92 500 | 26 | 4 |
| Peru | 1 280 000 | 41 760 | 22 | 2 |
| Argentina | 2 736 690 | 93 360 | 100 | 2 |
| Brazil | 8 456 510 | 277 420 | 214 | 4 |

'protected' (40%) is over twice that in the United States and Canada combined (16%). Large parks are few. Outside the United States and Canada, there are only 21 of them.

Large parks are surely better than small ones for species. By decreasing edge effects, large parks may also be better able to preserve their flora and fauna in the midst of encroaching environmental degradation and human activity. Our key question is: even given their size, are these flagships up to the task?

We now turn to Everglades National Park and Big Cypress National Preserve. These constitute a 'flagship' park surrounded by ocean on one front and the south Florida urban sprawl on the other. In particular, we examine the ability of this park to maintain the Cape Sable seaside-sparrow. This bird does not migrate, the park encompasses its entire range and its individuals hold territories typical of such a small species. Can the park allow sparrows to survive within it while humanity monopolizes its surroundings?

## EVERGLADES NATIONAL PARK AND BIG CYPRESS
## NATIONAL PRESERVE

The comic designation of the two epochs in southern Florida, BC ('before canals') and AD ('after drainage'), betrays the seriousness of the hydrological transformation that has occurred there (Brown, 1948). Before canals, the 'River of Grass' was a 28 205 km$^2$ shallow river, extending from Lake Okeechobee in central Florida south to Florida Bay (Fig. 3.1; Light & Dineen, 1994). At its peak flow in the wet season, it averaged 64 km wide and 0.5 m deep (US Dept. of the Interior, 1994). The relatively flat terrain (0 to 6 m above sea level) allowed the water to flow in a vast sheet across the landscape, at up to 0.6 m per minute (Rosendahl & Rose, 1982).

The natural hydrology proved disastrous to fledgling agricultural endeavours (Douglas, 1988). The wet-season rains flooded many fields and villages. Their inhabitants had constructed them on seemingly 'high' ground in the dry season. To promote development in southern Florida, Congress passed the Swamplands Act of 1850. It paved the way for the construction of over 2200 km of canals and levees, and over 40 water structures, gates and pumps over the next 140 years (Light & Dineen, 1994). In the 1930s, the construction of massive levees that impound Lake Okeechobee delivered the most profound change to the natural hydrology of southern Florida. These projects have concentrated the flow of water into narrow, flooded tracts while leaving other areas unnaturally dry (US Dept. of the Interior, 1994).

The original expanse of Everglades is now divided into three land-use areas. Three park areas, Everglades National Park (6113 km$^2$), Big Cypress

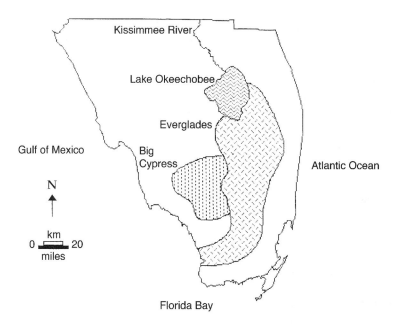

Fig. 3.1. The historic drainage of the Everglades watershed, flowing uninterrupted from Lake Okeechobee to the Gulf of Mexico and Florida Bay.

National Preserve (2306 km²), and Biscayne National Park (734 km²), preserve about 30% of the original extent of the Everglades for recreational and educational use (Fig. 3.2) (US Dept. of the Interior, 1994). Three 'Water Conservation Areas' north of the national parks encompass over 3550 km². These protect another 37% of the original expanse of the Everglades and the national parks from run-off from the 'Everglades Agricultural Area' (2830 km²) downstream of Lake Okeechobee. They bear little resemblance to the original habitat (US Dept. of the Interior 1994). In sum, these protected areas, though large, are embedded in greatly modified surroundings.

## ENDANGERED AND THREATENED SPECIES IN SOUTH FLORIDA

Everglades National Park, Big Cypress National Reserve and Biscayne National Park support over 1640 vertebrate species and 650 plant species (National Park Service 1996). Of these, 56 are listed as Federally Endangered or Threatened. Another 29 species are currently being considered for feder-

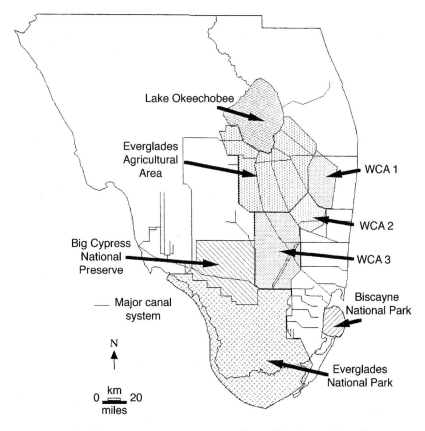

Fig. 3.2. The three Water Conservation Areas filter polluted water from the Everglades Agricultural Area before it flows into Biscayne and Everglades National Parks and Big Cypress National Preserve.

al listing status (US Dept. of the Interior, 1994). These species depend on the mosaic of habitat types, including pinelands, mangrove forests, cypress swamps and vast seasonally flooded prairies. Some of these habitats, such as the prairies, are highly dynamic, and can change rapidly in response to changes in hydrology (Nott *et al.*, 1998).

Over 400 species of migratory birds depend on habitats in the region (US Fish and Wildlife Service, 1996), and are greatly affected by changes in hydrology (Kushlan, 1979). Several species, such as the wood stork (*Mycteria americana*), snail kite (*Rostrhamus sociabilis plumbeus*) and Cape Sable seaside-sparrow have experienced precipitous declines in the last decade. Critical to our discussion is whether our large parks offer enough protection from natural and human-caused disturbances. Alternatively, is active management essential to save these species from extinction?

As a case study, we describe our work on the ecology of the Cape Sable seaside-sparrow and the factors inimical to its continued survival. As we discovered, proper management can negate some effects. We can ameliorate others only by providing a large enough area for the sparrow to overcome adversity on its own.

## THE CAPE SABLE SEASIDE-SPARROW

The Cape Sable seaside-sparrow's habitat preferences are unique among the seaside-sparrows. They occupy seasonally inundated freshwater marshes and not the saltwater marshes used by other seaside-sparrows. The closest relative of the Cape Sable race was the dusky seaside-sparrow. This became extinct in 1991 because of habitat loss (Post & Greenlaw, 1994).

The range of the Cape Sable seaside-sparrow is fragmented and it occupies parts of that range episodically. Howell (1932) found the first populations on Cape Sable, a peninsula in the south-west corner of Everglades National Park. In 1935, a hurricane flooded the prairies on the Cape with a 4 m saltwater storm surge. Eventually, this inundation caused major vegetational changes, destroying suitable sparrow habitat. In short, the sparrow is a freshwater sparrow, not a seaside sparrow, and it no longer occurs on Cape Sable.

Later populations, found in Everglades National Park and Big Cypress National Preserve to the north, have disappeared and reappeared with regularity. Werner (1975) and Bass & Kushlan (1982) conducted extensive helicopter surveys of Everglades National Park and Big Cypress National Preserve. Until then, the range of the Cape Sable seaside-sparrow was unknown.

### Current distribution (1981–1996)

Since 1992, we have continued an extensive helicopter survey first conducted by Bass & Kushlan (1982). Before 1993, the total sparrow population was divided into six subpopulations. Two core subpopulations (A, in the

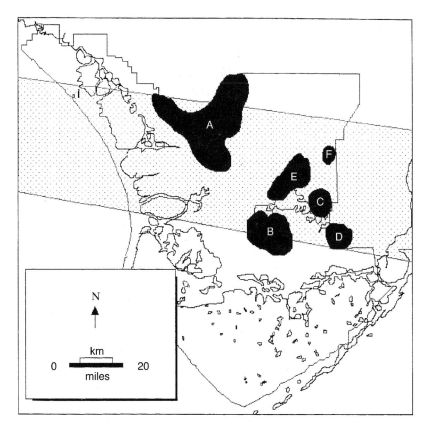

Fig. 3.3. The path of Hurricane Andrew (shaded area) passed over almost all of the six subpopulations of Cape Sable seaside-sparrows (darkened areas).

north-west section of Everglades National Park, and B, in the south-east section) held the majority of the sparrows. Four other peripheral subpopulations, C–F, held small and variable numbers (Fig. 3.3). In 1992, Hurricane Andrew passed directly over subpopulation A, and the 1993 survey revealed the near-extinction of that subpopulation. As of 1996, that subpopulation remains at 16% of its 1992 abundance. Subpopulation B has remained approximately constant. Two of the four peripheral subpopulations (C to F) became extinct between 1992 and 1995, but were recolonized by small numbers in 1996. Peripheral subpopulation E has fluctuated in size since 1992.

### Hypotheses for the sparrow's decline

We have evaluated four factors that might explain these changes in population: chance population fluctuations, hurricanes, fire and hydrology (Curnutt et al., 1998; Nott et al., 1998). Each one could cause the extinction of the sparrow. We cannot mitigate chance and hurricanes (apart from the costly process of transplanting individuals back into abandoned areas). We can manage fire and hydrology, but can we do so wisely?

Extinctions due to random fluctuations in populations have a higher probability of occurring in small populations (Pimm, 1991). Of the six subpopulations, four are peripheral, smaller populations that have experienced several local extinctions and recolonizations. We first asked whether the duration of local extinction in some of the smaller subpopulations was longer than one should expect by chance alone.

We applied a population dynamics model developed by Curnutt, Pimm & Maurer (1996) for grassland sparrows in North America. This model used population variability data for 10 grassland sparrow species, obtained over 20 years for the North American Breeding Bird Survey. It estimates empirically the chance that a population of a given average size would be absent by chance alone for periods of 1, 2, 3 ... $n$ years.

The model concluded that a three-year disappearance of birds from subpopulation C was unlikely to be due to chance alone. Three-year extinctions of similarly sized populations of grassland birds happened in fewer than 5% of the cases. In contrast, because subpopulations D and F were smaller, their extinctions were not significantly unusual. Finally, the large drop in subpopulation A from 1992 to 1993 had few precedents among the many small bird species for which we have long-term population counts (Fig. 3.3).

We then explored whether hurricanes could better explain the unusual declines. Hurricane Andrew in 1992 swept over almost all of the subpopulations. It flooded none of the area, however. The storm was a relatively dry one, it passed east to west, and the storm surge affected only coastal areas. Our survey in 1993 found the greatest loss (83%) in subpopulation A (Fig. 3.3), while other subpopulations were less affected. Subpopulation A has not recovered and has continued to decline. From the details of the local declines between 1992 and 1993 and the lack of recovery afterward, we conclude that Hurricane Andrew was not the principal cause of the sparrow's decline. Given the intensity of the storm, however, it seems likely that some (and perhaps many) birds did perish in it.

Hydrology has the most profound effects on sparrow habitat. During

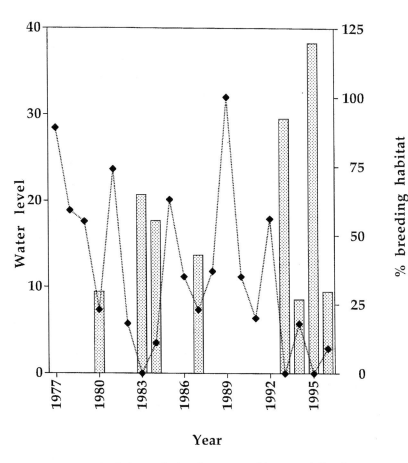

Fig. 3.4. Water depth during the breeding season (histogram, left scale, cm above Mean Sea Level) varies considerably from year to year. In wet years, there is almost no dry habitat in which the sparrows can breed (diamonds, right scale, percentage of maximum habitat possible).

the breeding season (March through June), above-ground water levels higher than 10 cm halt breeding activity. High water floods nests directly. It also leads to higher rates of nest predation (Lockwood *et al.*, 1997). An increase in the length of the period of flooding (the hydroperiod) also favours sawgrass (*Cladium jamaicense*) (Nott *et al.*, 1998). Sparrows do not inhabit areas dominated by sawgrass. Although natural rainfall alters water levels and their duration, water management practices control most of the hydrological dynamics in Everglades National Park.

The decline of the north-west core population (A) coincided with large water releases in 1993, 1994 and 1995 from several floodgates to the north. Nott *et al.* (1998) obtained hydrological data on water levels, rainfall, and water releases from the floodgates at the north end of the Park. Statistical analyses demonstrated that water releases were crucial in determining the water levels in the sparrow's habitat (Fig. 3.4). Rainfall was not so important. Simply, managed water flows were most responsible for the bird's precipitous decline in subpopulation A.

Fire also affects the sparrows and their habitat. Sparrows abandon an area for several years after a fire, until suitable habitat has regrown (Werner, 1975). Curnutt *et al.* (1998) mapped fire frequency for areas that support relatively stable populations, and compared these maps to population changes found on our helicopter survey. Sparrow density was highest in sites that burned once or twice in a 10-year period, and approached zero in sites that burned seven or more times in that period.

The extinctions of subpopulations C and F are probably due to the high frequency of fires started by human activities along the Park's border. The generally drier nature of these areas is due, in turn, to water management policies that move water to the west of Shark River Slough. In short, management floods the western areas of the sparrow's range and overdrains the eastern ones.

We can only manage for chance and hurricanes by protecting enough habitat to support a large sparrow population. Invariably, this would mean increasing the size of the park. For some parks, such as Everglades National Park, increasing the park into the degraded agricultural areas has proved expensive and politically difficult. In this respect, Everglades National Park is much like an oceanic island.

We cannot manage fire and hydrology, however, by simply providing an island that is large enough. Allowing only lightning-ignited fires to burn would approximate the natural fire regime and this is the current policy. The ability to prevent unplanned human ignitions, including arson, is clearly limited. The hydrology of the Everglades cannot simply be left alone, as it will never return to its pre-drainage flows. Water management must actively pursue water release programmes that resemble this natural flow. This hydrological influence also affects the frequency and intensity of fire in the park.

## ECOSYSTEM MANAGEMENT AND CONSERVING ENDANGERED SPECIES

### Parks as islands

The entire range of the Cape Sable seaside-sparrow exists within the boundaries of Everglades National Park and Big Cypress National Preserve – there is no habitat elsewhere. Because of this, it is tempting to visualize the park as an island surrounded by unsuitable habitat. Many other parks are similar and this metaphor is certainly not a new one (Shafer, 1990).

All populations vary in numbers over time. This variation may bring a small population down to a level from which it cannot recover, whereas a larger one may survive the crisis. Obviously, islands of once more extensive habitat cannot each support populations as numerous as those of the original habitat; thus island populations are at greater risk of extinction. Moreover, immigrants will rescue nearby populations more often than isolated populations on the verge of extinction. These are the two familiar mechanisms that explain why islands have fewer species than mainlands, and why parks, when isolated, might be expected to lose species.

The Cape Sable seaside-sparrow offers an excellent illustration of these risks. Its population is fragmented into six isolated subpopulations of different sizes, whose numbers vary over time. The small, peripheral subpopulations declined to zero for a few years, and were recolonized by sparrows dispersing from neighbouring populations. As the total sparrow population declines within the Park, the chances of extinction for small subpopulations increase, and colonization from other subpopulations decreases.

Another threat to small, isolated populations is catastrophic disturbance. A hurricane may have a major impact on a sparrow population and so push it closer to extinction. If the disturbance has not drastically altered the vegetation or landscape, sparrows from less-affected populations can recolonize the area. Large numbers of individuals spread over a large area is the natural defence against disturbance-caused extinction.

Such examples are not unique to Everglades National Park. For large mammal species in western North America, Newmark (1987, 1995) found even 10 000 km² parks were too small to support a full complement of the historic assemblage. Only the Kootenay-Banff-Jasper-Yoho park assemblage, which covers almost 21 000 km², had no mammal extinctions since delineation of park boundaries. Unfortunately, the success of this park may not be completely attributable to its large size, but may also depend on the relatively pristine condition of the surrounding area. Newmark (1995) found that survival of large carnivores in the western parks relied upon habitat adjacent to the park.

### The Park is not an island

Unlike true islands, where the surrounding ocean poses little threat to the islands' species, isolated parks have to contend with threats that penetrate the park's boundary. For Everglades National Park, these involve water and fire.

Water plays a key role for the sparrow. The South Florida Water Management District controls the area's hydrology through a vast system of canals, gates and levees. As ecological knowledge accumulates, the Water Management District alters water distribution and delivery rates to the park. From the sparrow's point of view, Everglades National Park is not an island: it links too tightly to the sources of water and fires that surround the park.

In general, the Water Management District must contend with several sources of adversity (US Dept. of the Interior 1994). Drainage and flood control have dried and otherwise degraded historic wetlands, increasing fire frequency on the park's eastern boundaries. Freshwater diverted into estuaries on either side of the park increases siltation, disrupting the saline balance of the waters and affecting fisheries and other marine systems in Biscayne National Park. Human pressures, such as increased urban sprawl (Miami and Homestead), agricultural demands for water, polluted runoff and mining for limestone prevent the Water Management District from effecting optimal water delivery programmes. And changes in hydrology and hydroperiod have significantly changed vegetation and associated animal communities in the park.

Kushlan (1979) found a similar dependence on adjacent land in two wading bird species in Everglades National Park. Although overall the community of wading birds in the park had dropped to 20% of its historic level, the decline was not equal among all species. In particular, the white ibis (*Eudocimus albus*), which has established breeding colonies outside park boundaries, did not experience as precipitous a decline as the wood stork (*Mycteria americana*). The wood stork remains dependent on breeding habitat in Everglades National Park. Water flow alteration and diversion by water management activity have severely altered its habitat. Even at

10 000 km², the 'legal' boundary of the Everglades–Big Cypress–Biscayne park trio may not be large enough to encompass its 'biological' boundary (Newmark, 1985). This was most certainly the entire watershed from Lake Okeechobee to Florida Bay.

Worldwide, flagship parks have a long, idiosyncratic list of external threats that jeopardize the survival of their unique species (Burton 1991). Oil spills constantly threaten the Northern Yukon National Park in Canada (10 169 km²). Flooding from hydropower projects and deforestation by wealthy ranchers and poverty-stricken squatters jeopardize the immeasurable biodiversity in Amazonia National Park (10 000 km²) in Brazil. In Russia, the Baikal Region National Park (15 640 km²) must contend with oil spills and pollution in the air, soil, and water. And in the Serengeti National Park and Ngorongoro Conservation Area in Tanzania (31 339 km²), cattle grazing and possible railroad construction compete with the impressive megafauna for water and other scarce resources.

## CONCLUSIONS

Flagship parks are few. Even the largest areas are not large enough to be indifferent to the ecosystem processes that surround them. Endangered species – like the Cape Sable seaside-sparrow – provide clues to how we must manage those processes. Thus, in the Everglades National Park, where roughly speaking the west is sometimes too wet and the east is probably always too dry, redistribution of water from the west to the east would aid the sparrow's recovery. Such a redistribution would restore the water flows to something like their natural condition.

Outside influences make it impossible to treat this park as an island unaffected by its surroundings. The Cape Sable seaside-sparrow cannot survive natural disturbances in the face of profound hydrological alteration, even though the park boundaries protect the entire population. The sparrow's response to changes in water management practices can be a good indicator of our ability to approximate the original water flow and timing. Good ecosystem management is essential for the sparrow's survival. And the sparrow's survival is a measure of the quality of that management.

More generally, we cannot assume that, even if we design our parks to be technically large enough to support viable populations of the megafauna, the parks will no longer require our services (see also Bond, this volume). We must continually track the species within, paying close attention to dramatic declines that may correlate with human activity inside or outside park boundaries.


## ACKNOWLEDGEMENTS

We would like to thank the National Biological Service, the National Park Service, the United States Army Corps of Engineers, and the United States Fish and Wildlife Service for funding for our research in Everglades National Park. Also, we extend our gratitude to those who provided invaluable service in the field: Karla Balent, Tom Brooks, John Curnutt, Tabby Fenn, Nancy Fraley, Stephen Killeffer, Julie Lockwood, Lisa Manne, M. Philip Nott, Gareth Russell and Ester Stanton. Without the vision of Marty Fleming and Sonny Bass our work would never have been started. Their support, and that of Jon Moulding, made it possible.


References
Bass, O. L., Jr. & Kushlan, J. A. (1982). *Status of the Cape Sable Sparrow*. Report T-672, South Florida Research Center, Everglades National Park. Homestead, Florida.
Brown, A. H. (1948). Haunting heart of the Everglades. *Nat. Geogr. Mag.*, **93**, 145–73.
Burton, R. (1991). *Nature's last strongholds*. Oxford University Press, New York.
Collar, N. J., Crosby, M. J. & Stattersfield, A. J. (1994). *Birds to watch* **2**. *The world list of threatened birds*. BirdLife International, Cambridge, UK.
Curnutt, J. L., Mayer, A. L., Brooks, T. M., Manne, L., Bass, O. L., Jr, Fleming, D. M. & Pimm, S. L. (1998). Population dynamics of the endangered Cape Sable Seaside-sparrow. *Anim. Conserv.*, **1**, 11–21.
Curnutt, J. L., Pimm, S. L. & Maurer, B. (1996). Population variability of sparrows in space and time. *Oikos*, **76**, 131–44.
Douglas, M. S. (1988). *The Everglades: river of grass*. Pineapple Press, Inc. Sarasota, FL.
Houston, D. B. (1971). Ecosystems of national parks. *Science*, **172**, 648–51.
Howell, A. H. (1932). *Florida bird life*. Coward-McCann, Inc. NY.
Kushlan, J. A. (1979). Design and management of continental wildlife reserves: lessons from the Everglades. *Biol. Conserv.*, **15**, 281–90.
Light, S. S. & Dineen, J. W. (1994). Water control in the Everglades: a historical perspective. In *Everglades: the ecosystem and its restoration*: 47–84. (Eds Davis, S. M. and Ogden, J. C.). St. Lucie Press, Delray Beach, FL.
Lockwood, J. L., Fenn, K. H., Curnutt, J. L., Rosenthal, D., Balent, K. L. & Mayer, A. L. (1997). Life history of the Endangered Cape Sable seaside-sparrow. *Wilson Bull.*, **109**, 720–31.
Myers, N. (1990). The biodiversity challenge: expanded hot-spots analysis.

*Environmentalist*, **10**, 243–56.

National Park Service (1996). *NPFauna and NPFlora for the U.S. National Park Service.* (WWW). Available on **http://ice.ucdavis.edu/US_National_Park_Service/**. (27 August 1996).

Newmark, W. D. (1985). Legal and biotic boundaries of western North American national parks: a problem of congruence. *Biol. Conserv.*, **33**, 197–208.

Newmark, W. D. (1987). A land-bridge island perspective on mammalian extinctions in western North American Parks. *Nature, Lond.*, **325**, 430–2.

Newmark, W. D. (1995). Extinction of mammal populations in western North American national parks. *Conserv. Biol.*, **9**, 512–26.

Nott, M. P., Bass, O. L., Jr, Fleming, D. M., Killeffer, S. E., Fraley, N., Manne, L., Curnutt, J. L., Brooks, T. M., Powell, R. & Pimm, S. L. (1998). Water levels, rapid vegetational changes, and the Endangered Cape Sable seaside-sparrow. *Anim. Conserv.*, **1**, 23–32.

Pimm, S. L. (1991). *The Balance of nature? Ecological issues in the conservation of species and communities.* University of Chicago Press, Chicago.

Pimm, S. L., Russell, G. J., Gittleman, J. L. & Brooks, T. M. (1995). The future of biodiversity. *Science*, **269**, 347–50.

Post, W. & Greenlaw, J. S. (1994). Seaside sparrow (*Ammodramus maritimus*). *Birds N. Am.* No. 127, 1–28.

Rosendahl, P. C. & Rose, P. W. (1982). Freshwater flow rates and distribution within the Everglades marsh. In *Proceedings of the national symposium on freshwater inflow to estuaries, coastal ecosystems project* (Eds Cross, R. D. & Williams, D. L.) US Fish and Wildlife Service, Washington, DC.

Rosenzweig, M. L. (1995). *Species diversity in space and time.* Cambridge University Press, Cambridge.

Ryan, J. C. (1992). *Life Support: Conserving biological diversity.* WorldWatch Institute, Washington, DC. (*Worldwatch Pap.* No. 108).

Shafer, C. L. (1990). *Nature reserves: island theory and conservation practice.* Smithsonian Institution Press, Washington, DC.

US Dept. of the Interior (1994). *The impact of federal programs on wetlands 2. A report to Congress by the Secretary of the Interior.* US Department of the Interior, Washington, DC.

US Fish and Wildlife Service (1996). *Endangered is not forever: a recovery plan for the threatened and endangered species of south Florida.* South Florida Ecosystem Office, Vero Beach, FL.

Werner, H. W. (1975). *The biology of the Cape Sable sparrow.* Report to US Fish and Wildlife Service, Everglades National Park, Homestead, Florida.

World Resources Institute (1994). *World resources 1994–1995.* World Resources Institute, Washington, DC.

# 4

# The dynamic response of plants to environmental change and the resulting risks of extinction

BRIAN HUNTLEY

## INTRODUCTION

In order to gain an understanding of how plants, or indeed any other group of organisms, respond to environmental change, evidence must be synthesized from different sub-disciplines of ecology and used as the basis for the construction of models. These models then can be used to assess the impact of a given environmental change upon a species and the consequent risk of extinction for that species.

The first issue that must be addressed is the way in which the environment determines the distribution and abundance of species in the group being examined. In particular, which environmental variables are involved and how do they operate? To a large extent such questions are the stuff of what has conventionally been termed biogeography, although in general biogeographers provide only hypotheses as to the determinants of species' range limits upon the basis of observed coincidences or correlations with particular values of environmental variables that *a priori* are considered likely to be of importance (Dahl, 1951; Hintikka, 1963; Conolly & Dahl, 1970). Experimental tests of these hypotheses come from autecological studies of individual species (Woodward & Pigott, 1975; Pigott, 1975, 1981; Pigott & Huntley, 1981); such experimental tests, however, are many fewer than the number of hypotheses that have been constructed upon the basis of the biogeographical data. Indeed, as Sykes, Prentice & Cramer (1996) recently noted, we remain woefully ignorant of the ecophysiological characteristics that determine the range limits even of some of the forest dominants of northern Europe.

In the case of terrestrial higher plants, three classes of macroclimatic variable are commonly invoked by biogeographers to account for species' overall distribution patterns. In general terms, these are the degree of winter cold, the growing-season warmth and the availability of moisture. Whereas individual range limits, or parts of those limits, have often been correlated with a threshold value of a climatic variable representative of one of these three general classes (Conolly & Dahl, 1970), defining the overall limits to a species' range will generally require consideration of at least two, and more often all three, of these classes of variable (Hintikka, 1963). Huntley, Berry *et al.* (1995) recently demonstrated the success with which a climate response model may be constructed for a variety of higher plant species using the mean temperature of the coldest month, the annual temperature sum above 5°C and the annually integrated ratio of actual to potential evapotranspiration as the three macroclimatic variables. Sykes *et al.* (1996) adopted an alternative approach to modelling the performance and distribution of a variety of north European tree species. Although they used a similar combination of three macroclimatic variables, they modified the annual temperature sum by subtracting an element that was ineffective because it preceded the time when the species chilling requirement had been satisfied and integrated the ratio of actual to potential evapotranspiration only during the period when temperature was above a threshold for assimilation/growth by the species in question.

The success with which such static modelling of plant species' distributions in relation to a limited number of macroclimatic variables can be performed has led Beerling, Huntley & Bailey (1995), Huntley, Berry *et al.* (1995) and Sykes *et al.* (1996) all to argue not only that species' overall geographical ranges are principally determined by the macroclimate, but that, in addition, species distributions are, as others have argued upon the basis of palynological and palaeoecological evidence (Webb, 1986; Huntley, Bartlein & Prentice, 1989; Prentice, Bartlein & Webb, 1991), in equilibrium with contemporary climatic conditions. Although such studies have been performed principally for higher plants, it can be argued that their results are also applicable to invertebrates as well as to many smaller vertebrates (Nix & Switzer, 1991); only in the case of large-bodied vertebrates may the organism perhaps achieve a degree of independence from the direct controlling influence of climate.

This evidence of the primacy of climate in determining the geographical distributions of a majority of organisms leads to an inevitable conclusion that we should expect organisms to respond to a change in climate. This response, however, may be either primarily spatial or primarily evolutionary (Huntley, Cramer *et al.*, 1997*a*), or else some combination of the two. An organism that did not exhibit one or both of these forms of response would in the short term experience reduction of its geographical range; any major climate change would have the potential to lead to its extinction (Fig. 4.1, colour plate). In order to assess the extent to which organisms tend to exhibit spatial or evolutionary responses, or else become extinct, in the face of major climate changes, we may examine the palaeoecological record for the late-Quaternary period, which has been characterized by repeated major cyclical fluctuations in global climate. Given the insights thus to be gained from Quaternary palaeoecological data, we then can consider the appropriate modelling approaches that will enable us to simulate the likely response of species to the climate changes that are forecast to result from anthropogenic alterations in the composition of the global atmosphere and in the character of the global land surface (Houghton *et al.*, 1996). Only then can the risks of extinction be assessed and the ecological consequences of such extinctions considered.

## PALAEOECOLOGICAL EVIDENCE

Until relatively recently rather few workers have exploited the ability of palaeoecological evidence to provide insight into ecological processes that operate over time scales of centuries to millennia; indeed many ecologists remain woefully ignorant of the potential of palaeoecology, whilst many Quaternary scientists who generate palaeoecological data lack the ecological background to apply these data to contemporary ecological problems. Davis (1989) drew attention to the core position of palaeoecology with respect to the current problems of 'global change' and their ecological consequences. Since that time many important contributions have followed from other palaeoecologists; however, the key conclusions have not changed.

The first of these conclusions is that species have exhibited a spatial response to past climate changes (Huntley & Webb, 1989). The evidence supporting this conclusion is derived from the past spatial distributions of species recorded by the Quaternary fossil record. This evidence is overwhelming and relates to many different groups of organisms whose Quaternary fossils can readily be found and identified, including plants (Bernabo & Webb, 1977; Davis, 1983; Huntley & Birks, 1983), vertebrates (Graham, 1992, 1997; FAUNMAP Working Group, 1996), molluscs (Preece, 1997) and beetles (Ashworth, 1997; Morgan, 1997). The magnitude of these spatial responses is in many cases such that species' past and present geographical distributions do not overlap. Mapping of dated fossil occurrences has made it possible to estimate the rates at which these spatial responses were achieved (Huntley & Birks, 1983; Huntley 1998, 1989, 1991*b*; Huntley & Webb, 1989), revealing that these rates are often much faster than might be inferred from small-scale contemporary studies of the species' population biology.

A second, complementary conclusion is that at least some species have exhibited adaptive evolutionary responses to past climate changes (Smith, Betancourt & Brown, 1995; Rousseau, 1997). Although only rather few examples of morphological evolution are available to support this conclusion, it seems likely that they reflect a much more widespread phenomenon that operates principally upon physiological and other characteristics that are not recorded by the fossil record. However, as Bennett (1990) has argued, the relatively frequent reversal of the direction of the selective force, as Quaternary climates have fluctuated on time scales much less than those conventionally considered to be required for major adaptive evolution, has for most species precluded evolution as their primary response. Those well-documented examples of evolutionary responses exhibit two important characteristics that support his argument. First, the species exhibit cyclical changes in response to the cyclical climatic changes (Smith *et al.*, 1995; Rousseau, 1997), and second, the extreme morphological forms found in the fossil record typically are within the range of forms found today when the species' entire geographical/environmental range is examined (Rousseau, 1997). Thus these evolutionary responses principally reflect selection amongst genotypes already present within the initial population; the evolution of new alleles and hence of novel genotypes is much too infrequent for this to have played a significant role in species response to climate changes on the relatively short time scales of the Quaternary and certainly cannot be expected to contribute more than marginally to species' responses to forecast anthropogenic climate changes. Figure 4.2 (colour plate) illustrates schematically how perhaps we best may view the combination of migratory and evolutionary responses of a species to a climate change. In the example illustrated there is also a shift in the range of genotypes represented; this is not intended to imply the evolution of new alleles but simply the selection of novel combinations of alleles under novel climatic conditions.

The third conclusion to emerge from the palaeoecological record is that of the individualism of species. Species that at one time and under the conditions then prevailing co-occur to form a recognizable species assemblage or 'community' may, following a climatic change, no longer co-occur.

Such individualism of response by terrestrial plants to Quaternary environmental changes was commented upon by West as long ago as 1964 (West, 1964); more recently various palaeoecologists have drawn attention to individualism as a fundamental characteristic of the response of many groups of organisms to environmental changes (Graham & Grimm, 1990; Huntley, 1991b). Two principal factors underlie these individualistic responses; first, no two species have precisely the same climatic tolerances/requirements, and second, as climate changes some combinations of conditions are no longer available whereas other novel combinations of conditions are newly available. Figure 4.3 (colour plate) illustrates such a scenario of individualistic responses by two species to the same overall environmental change. The consequence of species' individualistic responses to environmental change is that communities or species assemblages will dissociate and reform as a consequence of climate change rather than maintaining their integrity (West, 1964; Graham & Grimm, 1990; Graham, 1992, 1997; Huntley, 1996).

The fourth conclusion from the palaeoecological record is that times of rapid environmental change during the Quaternary have often been associated with episodes of extinction (Stuart, 1993; Sher, 1997; Huntley, Cramer et al., 1997b). Thus, the last deglaciation coincides with the extinction of many large vertebrates both in North America (Lundelius et al., 1983) and in northern Eurasia (Stuart, 1982, 1993; Sher, 1997). Although such extinctions might be argued simply to reflect the rapidity and/or the magnitude of the environmental change at that time, there is little or no evidence to suggest that this change was more rapid or of larger magnitude than previous glacial terminations. However, a consequence of such large and rapid environmental changes, which involve independent changes in the climate and other environmental variables, may be the occurrence of spatio-temporal restrictions or even discontinuities in the occurrence of particular combinations of conditions. Novel combinations of conditions may arise during such periods of rapid change; these may or may not satisfy the requirements/tolerances of any particular species. Those species that experience a severe spatio-temporal restriction in the availability of conditions that satisfy their requirements/tolerances will have an enhanced likelihood of extinction because of their reduced population size. Species that suffer from spatio-temporal discontinuities in the availability of conditions that satisfy their requirements/tolerances almost certainly will become extinct (Fig. 4.4, colour plate). Sher (1997) has recently argued that the extinction of mammoths and a range of associated vertebrates during the last glacial termination may exemplify the effects of restriction, the 'steppe-tundra' biome that they occupied becoming severely reduced in extent to the point where no spatially extensive areas persisted into the Holocene. The second situation, discontinuity, is likely to be the cause of the Pleistocene extinction in Europe of some of those genera of trees, e.g. *Tsuga*, that have persisted in North America and eastern Asia, although here too the very restricted area of forest biomes in Europe during Pleistocene glacial maxima probably played a major role (Huntley, 1993).

To summarize, the Quaternary palaeoecological record indicates that organisms have adjusted to the major environmental changes that have characterized that period predominantly by means of spatial responses, although coupled with evolutionary responses that have principally involved selection amongst pre-existing genotypes. Individualistic responses predominate, with the result that species' assemblages or communities dissociate and new assemblages form as a result of environmental changes. Although species' extinctions have been associated with the most rapid and extreme changes, these are less likely to reflect a failure to exhibit an evolutionary or spatial response than to result from a spatio-temporal restriction or discontinuity in the availability of the conditions required by the species.

## STATIC AND DYNAMIC MODELLING OF SPATIAL RESPONSES

Given the predominant role of spatial responses to environmental changes, a key area to be addressed by modelling activities must be these responses. Two complementary approaches can be applied to this problem, using static and dynamic models (Prentice & Solomon, 1991) respectively. The static modelling approach utilizes the climate response models developed by biogeographers to describe the present relationship between macroclimate and species' distributions (Mitchell, 1991; Gignac, Vitt & Bailey, 1991; Gignac, Vitt, Zoltai, et al., 1991; Beering et al., 1995; Huntley, Berry et al., 1995; Sykes et al., 1996). Species' potential future geographical ranges are simulated using forecast changes in climate (e.g. Mitchell, 1983; Hansen et al., 1988; Manabe & Wetherald, 1987; Schlesinger & Zhao, 1989). Such simulations provide the means to assess the spatial extent of the adjustments that species must make if they are to maintain their geographical ranges in equilibrium with given scenarios of climate change. Both the spatial displacement of range boundaries and the extent of the overlap between present and potential future ranges can then be estimated (Huntley, 1995b; Huntley, Berry et al., 1995). A number of examples of such simulations have been published (e.g. Huntley, 1995b; Huntley, Berry, et al., 1995; Beering et al., 1996). Although the results clearly depend heavily upon the particular future climate scenario being examined, the general pattern that emerges is one of range margin shifts of between a few hundred and two thousand kilometres. Especially for species with relatively more restricted present ranges, the extent of the overlap between present and potential future ranges is often very small or even zero (Huntley, 1995b, in press; Huntley, Berry et al., 1995). Placed into a palaeoecological context, these potential range shifts are of similar magnitude to those seen during the Holocene as species have responded to the ongoing climate changes of the last 10 000 years (Huntley & Birks, 1983; Prentice, Bartlein, et al., 1991; Sykes et al., 1996).

In order to assess the extent to which species may be able to achieve such spatial responses, the rate at which the environment may in future change must be considered and compared with the rate at which species are able to adjust their geographical ranges. Present forecasts indicate that climate change over the next century is likely to be at a rate at least an order of magnitude faster than climate changes during the recent past (Houghton et al., 1996). In order to maintain equilibrium with such rapid changes species' spatial responses need to be an order of magnitude faster than in the past. The extent to which this may be attainable may be explored by using dynamic models of the process of migration. The MIGRATE model (Collingham, 1995; Collingham, Hill & Huntley, 1996) is an example of one such model that offers a number of advantages over previous modelling approaches based upon mathematical descriptions of the process of diffusion (Hengeveld, 1988, 1989, 1990; Van den Bosch, Hengeveld & Metz, 1992). In particular, MIGRATE uses biologically meaningful and in general measurable parameters and is spatially explicit so that it can simulate migration across realistic heterogeneous landscapes. Experiments using parameter values appropriate for the small-leaved lime (Tilia cordata Mill.) reveal that such trees are unlikely to be capable of migration at rates much faster than those observed in the Quaternary record; even achieving such rates requires 1% of propagules to be dispersed with a root-mean-square displacement of 9.7 km (Collingham, 1995; Huntley, 1998). Furthermore, in many regions human destruction of habitat markedly reduces the rate of migration that can be attained (Collingham, 1995; Collingham et al., 1996; Huntley, 1998), rendering even less attainable an equilibrium spatial response to likely climate changes of the near future.

Combining the results from static and dynamic modelling of species' spatial response to climate change leads to the inevitable conclusion that many species will be unable to respond sufficiently rapidly to maintain their geographical range in equilibrium with the changing climate (Huntley, 1995b, in press). Predicting the ecological consequences of the resulting disequilibrium in any detail is more difficult. Some species may initially persist throughout all or most of their present range if the changed conditions are not sufficiently altered to prevent their survival. This will be more likely for long-lived organisms than for annual or short-lived organisms that depend upon frequent regeneration, the regeneration process often being more climatically demanding than is persistence of mature individuals (Summerfield, 1973; Pigott, 1975, 1981, 1992; Grubb, 1977; Pigott & Huntley, 1981). Such species persisting in disequilibrium will, however, become increasingly susceptible to eradication by extreme events and will be unable to replace themselves following an episode of disturbance. Other species, including many short-lived organisms, may be eradicated rapidly from much of their present range yet be capable of expanding into newly suitable areas only much more slowly. The overall net effect is likely to be one of a reduction in the taxonomic diversity of many ecosystems and the opportunistic expansion of species that have an inherently high migration rate, generally as a result of a short generation time, a high output of propagules and effective long-distance dispersal, whether by natural means or because they are able to benefit from accidental dispersal by human agencies.

## THE RISKS OF EXTINCTION

The palaeoecological record shows that species' extinction risk has, in the past, been higher during times of rapid environmental change. The same mechanisms will operate during the period of rapid anthropogenic climate change predicted for the next century and beyond. However, the extreme rapidity of these predicted changes adds an additional extinction mechanism that further enhances species' risk of extinction. As discussed above and described elsewhere (Huntley, 1995a,b, 1998), a pronounced disequilibrium is likely to develop between many species' actual and potential ranges as a result of their inability to achieve a sufficiently rapid spatial response (Fig. 4.5, colour plate). This will lead to population reduction and, in extreme cases, to a spatio-temporal discontinuity in the species' range. The former will enhance the species' risk of extinction; the latter almost inevitably will lead to extinction.

The direction and magnitude of the predicted climate change adds yet further to the risk of extinction for many species, because it will lead to global conditions warmer than at any time during the recent geological past. The resulting combinations of climate and latitude will have no parallel during the period that has seen the evolution as species of most of the world's present biota. Thus, whereas species may carry the genetic material that has enabled them to survive the differing combinations of climate and latitude during the Quaternary, when the major departures of global conditions from those of today have been global cooling during glacial stages, they may lack the genetic capability to adapt to the new combinations of conditions that will arise in the near future. If this is the case, then even some of those with the ability to achieve sufficiently rapid spatial responses may be prevented from doing so by their inability to adapt genetically to the new combinations of conditions. Once again this will lead to population reduction and consequent enhanced risk of extinction.

Although it is clear that many species are thus likely to be at risk of extinction as a consequence of anthropogenic climate change, we are unable to quantify this risk in any sytematic way at present, for several reasons. Foremost amongst these are, first, our ignorance of the biological characteristics of the vast majority of the world's biota that will determine their ability to achieve the required spatial and evolutionary responses and, second, the uncertainty that remains with respect to the magnitude and rate of the predicted anthropogenic climate change. It is essential, nonetheless, that we attempt to make some kind of estimate of the proportion of species that are at risk. Whilst recognizing that any such estimate will have many shortcomings, we cannot plan appropriate conservation measures without knowing at least in broad terms the magnitude of the problem that we face. Such an estimate can be made upon the basis of the limited palaeoecological evidence and modelling results available to date.

The palaeoecological record for Europe documents the extinction of many tree genera during Quaternary glacial stages. Huntley has argued that this most probably resulted from the severe reduction in the area of forest biomes in Europe during glacial stages. The present European flora contains *ca.* 20% fewer tree genera than do the floras of the comparable areas of eastern and western North America (Huntley, 1993). This reduction, however, was not the consequence of a single episode but has accumulated throughout the Pleistocene. In contrast, during the last glacial stage, seven of the eight herbivores with body masses > 600 kg and three of the four carnivores with body masses > 50 kg formerly present in Europe became extinct, most of them apparently during the last glacial termination (Stuart, 1982). Thus we must conclude that the risk of extinction is likely to vary systematically among major groups of organisms. However, the extreme rate and apparently unprecedented direction of the predicted change, viewed in the context of the Quaternary, render it likely that at least some groups of organisms may suffer extinction rates > 80%, although other groups may experience little or no extinction. To some extent we can identify those groups or types of organism most at risk. Huntley, Cramer *et al.* (1997*b*: 494–495), for example, list the following series of characteristics that they argue will increase a taxon's risk of extinction as a consequence of rapid climate change: large body size; low levels of both of intra- and inter-population genetic variation; spatially limited geographical distribution; habitat specialization; resource specialization; a relatively low position in the trophic pyramid; absence of behavioural flexibility; and adaptations to cold conditions.

The modelling results available to date are limited. However, some general patterns begin to emerge when the results are examined for those species whose responses to predicted climate have been simulated using static models by Huntley (1995*b*), Huntley, Berry *et al.* (1995), Sykes *et al.* (1996), McDonald (1994), and Beerling *et al.* (1995). When considered alongside the results from dynamic modelling (Collingham, 1995; Collingham *et al.* 1996; Huntley, 1998), the following conclusions emerge. First, despite the uncertainty that still remains as to the magnitude of the forthcoming global warming (Houghton *et al.*, 1996), the magnitude of the associated regional climate changes in an area such as Europe will lead to large shifts, by between a few hundred and almost two thousand kilometres, in the boundaries of species' potential ranges. Second, the extent of the overlap between species' present and potential future ranges is often small, even for quite extensively distributed species. This is most acute for species that at present occupy restricted geographical ranges; unless their present spatial restriction masks greater overall climatic potential, some of which they may be newly able to realize under the changed conditions of the future, then many such restricted species will be at risk of extinction if they are unable to migrate at a sufficient rate. Third, even across homogeneously suitable habitat, species' migration rates are insufficient to maintain their ranges in equilibrium with climate changes of the predicted rate; habitat fragmentation and reduction as a result of human activities will exacerbate this problem. Many species may achieve migration rates much less than one tenth of those needed to maintain equilibrium with the changing climate.

The inevitable conclusion to be drawn from the palaeoecological evidence and the modelling results available to date is that, at least amongst the higher latitude biota that have been the principal focus of these studies, the risk of extinction of a substantial part of that biota during the coming few centuries is very high if anthropogenic climate change of the predicted magnitude is allowed to occur. Although it may be tempting to suggest that globally the problem will be less severe, tropical biota being at less risk and at the same time accounting for a large fraction of global biodiversity, this almost certainly is incorrect. Although there remains much greater uncertainty as to the patterns of change in precipitation, as opposed to temperature, associated with 'global warming', it is certain that some tropical areas, perhaps many, will suffer marked changes in their precipitation regime. This will result in shifts in the boundaries between the tropical biomes, these boundaries being determined principally by the extent to which a seasonal drought occurs (Prentice, Cramer et al., 1992; Haxeltine, 1996; Haxeltine & Prentice, 1996). When coupled to the physiological consequences of the increased atmospheric carbon dioxide concentration, many parts of the tropics will experience a change in their predominant biome as a consequence of 'global change' (Haxeltine, 1996). Add to this the vulnerability of tropical montane biotas in the face of warming, and it becomes apparent that many tropical species also are at risk of extinction. Given, in addition, the magnitude of human impacts upon tropical ecosystems (Kirschbaum et al., 1996), tropical biota are probably subject to a similar magnitude of risk to biota in the temperate zone.


## DISCUSSION

Given that the theme of this symposium is one of conservation, it is pertinent to ask what strategy might be adopted in order to minimize the loss of biodiversity that 'global change' threatens to bring about? First, and most importantly, the inevitable conclusion must be that conserving global biodiversity requires the rate and magnitude of anthopogenic changes of the global environment to be reduced substantially below those currently predicted for the coming centuries. Without such measures, many species are at risk of extinction and the global loss of biodiversity is likely to be substantial – it may even match in magnitude the mass extinctions of the geological record. Second, because, even if stringent measures were taken immediately to limit climate change, the changes already brought about in global atmospheric composition have committed the world to a significant degree of warming over the next century, it is necessary to plan conservation measures that will facilitate the spatial and evolutionary responses of species to these inevitable changes. Facilitating species' spatial response requires a new approach to the conservation and protection of species in the wider landscape and the development of connected networks of reserves and other areas set aside for wildlife (Huntley, 1991a, 1995a, in press). This requires the needs of wildlife to be taken into account in landscape planning and, in many of the landscapes heavily modified by man, may require large areas to be set aside for the practice of 'creative conservation'. Facilitating species' evolutionary response requires steps to be taken urgently to limit the extent to which species' populations are depleted as a result of habitat loss, persecution, etc. Reduction in the size of a species' population inevitably tends to lead to loss of intraspecific genetic diversity (Prentice, 1997); this, as well as the reduced population in itself, renders the species more vulnerable to stochastic extinction.

## ACKNOWLEDGEMENTS

I am grateful to the organizers of the Zoological Society symposium *Conservation in a changing world* for the invitation to prepare this paper. The ideas presented herein owe much to discussions with numerous colleagues, especially those who participated in the NATO Advanced Research Workshop *Past and future rapid environmental changes: the spatial and evolutionary responses of terrestrial biota*. The modelling work described was supported by the Natural Environment Research Council through a grant under its TIGER (Terrestrial Initiative in Global Environmental Research) programme, award number GST/02/636, and a CASE studentship GT4/92/TLS/9 co-sponsored by the Institute of Terrestrial Ecology, Monks Wood. A grant from the Publications Board of the University of Durham made possible the publication of the colour figures.

## References

Ashworth, A. C. (1997). The response of beetles to Quaternary climate changes. In *Past and future rapid environmental changes: the spatial and evolutionary responses of terrestrial biota:* 119–28. (Eds Huntley, B., Cramer, W., Morgan, A. V., Prentice, H. C. & Allen, J. R. M.). Springer-Verlag, Berlin. (*NATO ASI Ser. I: Global envir. Change* **47**).

Beerling, D. J., Huntley, B. & Bailey, J. P. (1995). Climate and the distribution of *Fallopia japonica*: use of an introduced species to test the predictive capacity of response surfaces. *J. Vegn Sci.,* **6**, 269–82.

Bennett, K. D. (1990). Milankovitch cycles and their effects on species in ecological and evolutionary time. *Paleobiology,* **16**, 11–21.

Bernabo, J. C. & Webb, T., III. (1977). Changing patterns in the Holocene pollen record from northeastern North America: a mapped summary. *Quaternary Res., NY,* **8**, 64–96.

Collingham, Y. C. (1995). *The development of a spatially explicit landscape-scale model of migration and its application to investigate the response of trees to climate change.* PhD thesis: University of Durham.

Collingham, Y. C., Hill, M. O. & Huntley, B. (1996). The migration of sessile organisms: a simulation model with measurable parameters. *J. Vegn Sci.,* **7**, 831–46.

Conolly, A. P. & Dahl, E. (1970). Maximum summer temperature in relation to the modern and Quaternary distributions of certain arctic-montane species in the British Isles. In *Studies in the vegetational history of the British Isles:* 159–223. (Eds Walker, D. & West, R. G.). Cambridge University Press, Cambridge.

Dahl, E. (1951). On the relation between summer temperature and the distribution of alpine vascular plants in the lowlnds of Fennoscandia. *Oikos,* **3**, 22–52.

Davis, M. B. (1983). Holocene vegetational history of the eastern United States. In *The Holocene. Late-Quaternary environments of the United States.* **2**: 166–181. (Ed. Wright, H. E., Jr.). University of Minnesota Press, Minneapolis.

Davis, M. B. (1989). Insights from paleoecology on global change. *Bull. Ecol., Soc. Am.,* **70**, 220–8.

FAUNMAP Working Group (1996). Spatial response of mammals to late Quaternary environmental fluctuations. *Science,* **272**, 1601–6.

Gignac, L. D., Vitt, D. H. & Bayley, S. E. (1991). Bryophyte response surfaces along ecological and climatic gradients. *Vegetatio,* **93**, 29–45.

Gignac, L. D., Vitt, D. H., Zoltai, S. C. & Bayley, S. E. (1991). Bryophyte response surfaces along climatic, chemical, and physical gradients in peatlands of western Canada. *Nova Hedwigia,* **53**, 27–71.

Graham, R. W. (1992). Late Pleistocene faunal changes as a guide to understanding effects of greenhouse warming on the mammalian fauna of North America. In *Global warming and biological diversity:* 76–87. (Eds Peters, R. L. & Lovejoy, T. E.). Yale University Press, New Haven.

Graham, R. W. (1997). The spatial response of mammals to Quaternary climate changes. In *Past and future rapid environmental changes: the spatial and evolutionary responses of terrestrial biota:* 153–62. (Eds Huntley, B., Cramer, W., Morgan, A. V., Prentice, H. C. & Allen, J. R. M.). Springer-Verlag, Berlin. (*NATO ASI Ser I: Global envir. Change* **47**).

Graham, R. W. & Grimm, E. C. (1990). Effects of global climate change on the patterns of terrestrial biological communities. *Trends Ecol. Evol.*, **5**, 289–92.

Grubb, P. J. (1977). The maintenance of species-richness in plant communities: the importance of the regeneration niche. *Biol. Rev.*, **52**, 107–45.

Hansen, J. E., Fung, I. Y., Lacis, A. A., Rind, D., Lebedeff, S., Ruedy, R., Russell, G. & Stone, P. (1988). Global climate changes as forecast by the Goddard Institute for Space Studies three dimensional model. *J. geophys. Res.*, **93**, 9341–64.

Haxeltine, A. (1996). *Modelling the vegetation of the Earth.* PhD thesis: Lund University.

Haxeltine, A. & Prentice, I. C. (1996). BIOME3: an equilibrium biosphere model based on ecophysiological constraints, resource availability and competition among plant functional types. *Global biogeochem. Cycles*, **10**, 693–710.

Hengeveld, R. (1988). Mechanisms of biological invasions. *J. Biogeogr.*, **15**, 819–28.

Hengeveld, R. (1989). *Dynamics of biological invasions.* Chapman and Hall, London.

Hengeveld, R. (1990). *Dynamic biogeography.* Cambridge University Press, Cambridge.

Hintikka, V. (1963). Uber das Grossklima einigr Pflanzenareale in zwei Klimakoordinatensystemen dargestellt. *Annls bot. Soc. zool. bot. fenn. 'Vanamo'*, **34**, 1–64.

Houghton, J. T., Meira Filho, L. G., Callander, B. A., Harris, N., Kattenberg, A. & Maskell, K. (eds) (1996). *Climate change 1995: the science of climate change.* Cambridge University Press, Cambridge.

Huntley, B. (1988). Glacial and Holocene vegetation history: Europe. In *Vegetation history*: 341–383. (Eds Huntley, B. & Webb, T., III). Kluwer Academic Publishers, Dordrecht.

Huntley, B. (1989). European post-glacial vegetation history: a new perspective. In *Proceedings of the XIX international ornithological congress.* **1**, 1060–77. (Ed. Ouellet, H.). University of Ottawa Press, Ottawa.

Huntley, B. (1991a). Historical lessons for the future. In *The scientific management of temperate communities for conservation*: 473–503. (Eds Spellerberg, I. F., Goldsmith, F. B. & Morris, M. G.). Blackwell Scientific Publications, Oxford.

Huntley, B. (1991b). How plants respond to climate change: migration rates, individualism and the consequences for plant communities. *Ann. Bot.*, **67**, 15–22.

Huntley, B. (1993). Species-richness in north-temperate zone forests. *J. Biogeogr.*, **20**, 163–80.

Huntley, B. (1995a). How vegetation responds to climate change: evidence from palaeovegetation studies. In *The impact of climate change on ecosystems and species: environmental context*: 43–63. (Eds Pernetta, J., Leemans, R., Elder, D. & Humphrey, S.). IUCN, Gland, Switzerland.

Huntley, B. (1995b). Plant species' response to climate change: implications for the conservation of European birds. *Ibis* **137** (suppl. 1), S127–38.

Huntley, B. (1996). Quaternary palaeoecology and ecology. *Quaternary Sci. Rev.*, **15**.

Huntley, B. (1998). Species distribution and environmental change: considerations from the site to the landscape scale. In *The scientific basis of ecosystem management for the third millennium. The first Sibthorp papers.* (Eds Holgate, M., Maltby, E., Acreman, M. & Weir, A.) (in press).

Huntley, B., Bartlein, P. J. & Prentice, I. C. (1989). Climatic control of the distribution and abundance of beech (*Fagus* L) in Europe and North America. *J. Biogeogr.*, **16**, 551–60.

Huntley, B., Berry, P. M., Cramer, W. P. & McDonald, A. P. (1995). Modelling present and potential future ranges of some European higher plants using climate response surface. *J. Biogeogr.*, **22**, 967–1001.

Huntley, B. & Birks, H. J. B. (1983). *An atlas of past and present pollen maps for Europe: 0-13000 B.P.* Cambridge University Press, Cambridge.

Huntley, B., Cramer, W., Morgan, A. V., Prentice, H. C. & Allen, J. R. M. (Eds) (1997a). *Past and future rapid environmental changes: the spatial and evolutionary responses of terrestrial biota.* Springer-Verlag, Berlin. (*NATO ASI Series I: Global envir. Change*, **47**.)

Huntley, B., Cramer, W., Morgan, A. V., Prentice, H. C. & Allen, J. R. M. (1997b). Predicting the response of terrestrial biota to future environmental changes. In *Part and future rapid environmental changes: the spatial and evolutionary responses of terrestrial biota*: 487–504. (Eds Huntley, B., Cramer, W., Morgan, A. V., Prentice, H. C. & Allen, J. R. M.). Springer-Verlag, Berlin. (*NATO ASI Ser I: Global envir. Change* **47**.)

Huntley, B. & Webb, T., III (1989). Migration: species' response to climatic variations caused by changes in the earth's orbit. *J. Biogeogr.*, **16**, 5–19.

Kirschbaum, M. U. F., Fischlin, A., Cannell, M. G. R., Cruz, R. V. O., Galinski, W. & Cramer, W. R. (1996). Climate change impacts on forests. In *Climate change 1995: impacts, adaptations and mitigation of climate change*: 95–129. (Eds Watson, R. T., Zinyowerea, M. C. & Moss, R. H.). Cambridge University Press, Cambridge.

Lundelius, E. L., Jr., Graham, R. W., Anderson E., Guilday, J., Holman, J. A., Steadman, D. W. & Webb, S. D. (1983). Terrestrial vertebrate faunas. In *The late Pleistocene. Late-Quaternary environments of the United States.* **1**, 311–353. (Ed. Porter, S. C.). University of Minnesota Press, Minneapolis.

Manabe, S. & Wetherald, R. T. (1987). Large-scale changes in soil wetness induced by an increase in carbon dioxide. *J. atmos. Sci.*, **44**, 1211–35.

McDonald, A. P. (1994). *The response to global warming of plants restricted to north-western Britain.* MSc thesis: University of Durham.

Mitchell, J. F. B. (1983). The seasonal response of a general circulation model to changes in $CO_2$ and sea temperatures. *Q. Jl R. met. Soc.*, **109**, 113–52.

Mitchell, N. D. (1991). The derivation of climate surfaces for New Zealand, and their application to the bioclimatic analysis of the distribution of kauri (*Agathis australis*). *Jl R. Soc. N. Z.*, **21**, 13–24.

Morgan, A. V. (1997). Fossil Coleoptera assemblages in the Great Lakes Region of North America: past changes and future prospects. In *Past and future rapid environmental changes: the spatial and evolutionary responses of terrestrial biota*: 129–142. (Eds Huntley, B., Cramer, W., Morgan, A. V., Prentice, H. C. & Allen, J. R. M.). Springer-Verlag, Berlin. (*NATO ASI Ser. I: Global envir.*

*change,* **47**.)

Nix, H. A. & Switzer, M. A. (1991). Rainforest animals: atlas of vertebrates endemic to Australia's wet tropics. *Kowari,* **1**, 112.

Pigott, C. D. (1975). Experimental studies on the influence of climate on the geographical distribution of plants. *Weather,* **30**, 82–90.

Pigott, C. D. (1981). Nature of seed sterility and natural regeneration of *Tilia cordata* near its northern limit in Finland. *Annals bot. fenn.,* **18**, 255–63.

Pigott, C. D. (1992). Are the distributions of species determined by failure to set seed? In *Fruit and seed production*: 203–216. (Eds Marshall, C. & Grace, J.). Cambridge University Press, Cambridge.

Pigott, C. D. & Huntley, J. P. (1981). Factors controlling the distribution of *Tilia cordata* at the northern limts of its geographical range. III. Nature and causes of seed steriligy. *New Phytol.,* **87**, 817–39.

Preece, R. C. (1997). The spatial response of non-marine Mollusca to past climate changes. In *Past and future rapid environmental changes: the spatial and evolutionary responses of terrestrial biota*: 163–178. (Eds Huntley, B., Cramer, W., Morgan, A. V., Prentice, H. C. & Allen, J. R. M.). Springer-Verlag, Berlin. (*NATO ASI Ser. I: Global envir. Change,* **47**.)

Prentice, H. C. (1997). Variation in plant populations: history and chance or ecology and selection. In *Past and future rapid environmental changes: the spatial and evolutionary responses of terrestrial biota*: 343–356. (Eds Huntley, B., Cramer, W., Morgan, A. V., Prentice, H. C. & Allen, J. R. M.). Springer-Verlag, Berlin. (*NATO ASI Ser. I: Global envir. Change,* **47**.)

Prentice, I. C., Bartlein, P. J. & Webb, T., III (1991). Vegetation and climate change in eastern North America since the last glacial maximum. *Ecology,* **72**, 2038–56.

Prentice, I. C., Cramer, W., Harrison, S. P., Leemans, R., Monserud, R. A. & Solomon, A. M. (1992). A global biome model based on plant physiology and dominance, soil properties and climate. *J. Biogeogr.,* **19**, 117–34.

Prentice, I. C. & Solomon, A. M. (1991). Vegetation models and global change. In *Global changes of the past*: 365–383. (Ed. Bradley, R. S.). UCAR/Office for Interdisciplinary Earth Studies, Boulder.

Rousseau, D-D. (1997). The weight of internal and external constraints on *Pupilla muscorum* L. (Gastropoda: Stylommatophora) during the Quaternary in Europe. In *Past and future rapid environmental changes: the spatial and evolutionary responses of terrestrial biota*: 303–318. (Eds Huntley, B., Cramer, W., Morgan, A. V., Prentice, H. C. & Allen, J. R. M.). Springer-Verlag, Berlin. (*NATO ASI Ser. I: Global envir. Change,* **47**.)

Schlesinger, M. E. & Zhao, Z-C. (1989). Seasonal climatic changes induced by doubled $CO_2$ as simulated by the OSU atmospheric GCM/mixed-layer ocean model. *J. Clim.,* **2**, 459–95.

Sher, A. (1997). Late-Quaternary extinction of large mammals in northern Eurasia: A new look at the Siberian contribution. In *Past and future rapid environmental changes: the spatial and evolutionary responses of terrestrial biota*: 319–340. (Eds Huntley, B., Cramer, W., Morgan, A. V., Prentice, H. C. & Allen, J. R. M.). Springer-Verlag, Berlin. (*NATO ASI Ser. I: Global envir. Change,* **47**.)

Smith, F. A., Betancourt, J. L. & Brown, J. H. (1995). Evolution of body size in the woodrat over the past 25,000 years of climate change. *Science*, **270**, 2012–14.

Stuart, A. J. (1982). *Pleistocene vertebrates in the British Isles*. Longman, London.

Stuart, A. J. (1993). The failure of evolution: Late Quaternary mammalian extinctions in the Holarctic. *Quaternary Int.*, **19**, 101–7.

Summerfield, R. J. (1973). Factors affecting the germination and establishment of seedlings of *Narthecium ossifragum* in mire ecosystems. *J. Ecol.*, **61**, 387–98.

Sykes, M. T., Prentice, I. C. & Cramer, W. (1996). A bioclimatic model for the potential distributions of north European tree species under present and future climates. *J. Biogeogr.*, **23**, 203–33.

Van den bosch, F., Hengeveld, R. & Metz, J. A. J. (1992). Analyzing the velocity of animal range expansion. *J. Biogeogr.*, **19**, 135–50.

Webb, T., III (1986). Is vegetation in equilibrium with climate? How to interpret late-Quaternary pollen data. *Vegetatio*, **67**, 119–30.

West, R. G. (1964). Inter-relations of ecology and Quaternary palaeobotany. *J. Ecol.*, **52**, (Suppl.), 47–57.

Woodward, F. I. & Pigott, C. D. (1975). The climatic control of the altitudinal distribution of *Sedum rosea* (L.) Scop and *S. telephium* L. I. Field observations. *New Phytol.*, **74**, 323–34.

# Ecological and evolutionary importance of disturbance and catastrophes in plant conservation

WILLIAM J. BOND

## INTRODUCTION

Conservation, for many, means the protection of nature from disruptive threats to the natural balance, especially threats initiated by humans. However some species and some ecosystems can only be conserved by frequent disturbance. For these, the notion of nature in 'balance' is a mistaken distortion leading to actions that have endangered disturbance-dependent species. Human-induced, and other large-scale disturbances such as fire are pervasive influences on biotic communities. Changing patterns of disturbance constitute a major threat to many plant species. This is well understood in some systems, such as fire-prone shrublands and forests. In others, it is poorly understood or not recognized at all. One example is the decline of extremely well protected pockets of 'primary' eastern North American forests. It now appears that regeneration of the 'climax' oaks in these forests depended on burning by native Americans. The long exclusion of fire, first by European settlers, then by latter-day conservationists, has led to the senescence of disturbance-dependent species (Botkin, 1990; Lorimer, Chapman & Lambert, 1994). This pattern of over-protection leading to decline of disturbance-dependent plant species is most common in industrialized countries. In non-industrial countries, population pressures are such that protection from human exploitation is the most immediate need. However, here too the impact of human and other disturbance in generating patterns of diversity is poorly recognized and controversial.

In this chapter, I have focused on the importance of disturbance in plant conservation by asking:

1. How does disturbance influence the distribution of major vegetation formations? It would be convenient if we could identify disturbance-

dependent vegetation formations, at a global scale, since these are most likely to require active intervention for their continued existence.

2. What is the evolutionary history of disturbance-dependent formations? The evolutionary significance of disturbance in the evolution of new biotas has been comparatively neglected. However, some of the richest floras of the world may owe their existence to the opening of vegetation, by large-scale disturbance, since late Tertiary times.

3. How can plant species' response to disturbance be included in conservation assessments of threatened species? The demography of plants has several peculiar features which affect the application of extinction models derived for vertebrates. Chief among these are the great longevity of some plants, and great variation in tolerance to disturbance. I suggest that information on how individuals persist through disturbance is an essential starting point for species-specific assessments of extinction threats.

## THE IMPORTANCE OF DISTURBANCE IN THE DISTRIBUTION OF VEGETATION

Botanists were slow to recognize the importance of disturbance in shaping vegetation. Fire is an extremely widespread and influential disturbance, yet for the first three-quarters of this century there has been a widespread antipathy to burning natural ecosystems. In the 1920s, for example, leading botanists in South Africa agreed that the biggest threat to the conservation of the flora was the 'scourge of fire'. For reasons that today seem inexplicable, they failed to notice that thousands of plant species are unable to complete their life cycle if left unburnt (Le Maitre & Midgley, 1992; Bond & van Wilgen, 1996). Fire suppression was practised until the 1970s when policy-makers began to realize that the vegetation was 'designed' to burn.

Many ecologists have argued that open formations (without closed tree canopies and/or where the dominant tree species recruit only in large openings) owe their character and geographic extent to regular disturbance by fire or vertebrate herbivory (Sauer, 1950; Stewart, 1956; Jackson, 1968; Wells, 1962, 1970; Booysen & Tainton, 1984). Formations with dense grass (mesic grasslands, savannas), shrub (Mediterranean-type shrublands), or flammable tree cover (some eucalypt and conifer forests) appear to be disturbance-dependent formations. The physiognomic consequences of disturbance by fire, herbivores or human activities are:

- to reduce vegetation height (tall forests to shorter ones, woodlands to shrublands);
- to replace woody vegetation by grasslands;
- to promote flammable species or communities (low litter decomposition rates, more xeromorphic leaves, finer twigs/branches);
- to reduce biomass.

Thus disturbance-dependent communities are of lower stature and more open than predicted from the climatic potential of an area. For example, high rainfall is usually associated with tall forests, yet shrub-dominated fynbos vegetation in South Africa spans a rainfall gradient from 400 m to > 3000 mm, where it is probably maintained by frequent fire (Moll, McKenzie & McLachlan, 1980). Reduction of disturbance, such as by fire suppression, should allow vegetation to reach its climatic potential through replacement of grassland by woody plants, shrublands by trees and wood-lands by tall forests. Evidence for the importance of disturbance, such as fire, has been based on the frequent occurrence of alternative flammable and fire-free vegetation types in fire-prone landscapes and experimental demonstration of transitions between the two when fire is excluded (for reviews see Peet, 1992; Bond & van Wilgen, 1996). Relictual closed forest patches in savanna and shrubland landscapes may represent the climatic potential but the regional open vegetation cover is a product of the disturb-ance regime. Vertebrate exclosure experiments have demonstrated similar transformation from open to closed vegetation in many areas when herbi-vory is suppressed (Crawley, 1983; Owen-Smith, 1989).

There is still great uncertainty as to the scale over which disturbance holds sway over climate in generating major vegetation patterns. What proportion of British heathlands, for example, could support conifer forests or deciduous woodlands if fires, or sheep grazing, were suppressed and tree seed sources still available? What proportion of the 20% of the world's land surface covered by savanna has the potential to form closed woody forma-tions if disturbance were to be excluded? For many conservation problems, the scales are more local and the threats of a shift from one structural formation to another with changing disturbance are easier to assess.

## EVOLUTIONARY ORIGINS OF DISTURBANCE-DEPENDENT VEGETATION

The evolutionary origins of open, angiosperm-dominated vegetation are comparatively recent in geological terms. Closed woody formations dominated world vegetation for over 50 million years from the beginning of the Tertiary until mid-Miocene times (Wolfe, 1985). Open savanna and grassland formations first became widespread some 10–12 million years ago and by the late Miocene open formations covered large areas of the earth (Wolfe, 1985). The spread of open vegetation continued to the present with pure grasslands appearing as recently as the Pleistocene some 2 million years ago (Janis, 1993). Similar changes from closed to open formations were occurring in Mediterranean regions from the Pliocene to the Pleistocene. Fire-prone sclerophyll shrublands replaced taller ancestral forests in South Africa (Linder, Meadows & Cowling, 1992), California (Axelrod, 1975, 1989) and the Mediterranean basin (Herrera, 1992). Australia's distinctive fire-prone woodlands and open forests also began to replace rainforest as the dominant vegetation from the Miocene though eucalypts only became prominent in the Pleistocene (Kershaw, Martin & McEwen Mason, 1994).

The opening of Tertiary vegetation is usually attributed to the development of drier and cooler climates. However, although climate may have triggered the changes, analogies with modern landscapes suggest that the process was aided and abetted by the evolution of agents promoting disturbance, especially large mammalian herbivores, highly flammable plants such as C4 grasses and shrubs and hominid fire-users, tool makers and cultivators. Studies of charcoal in marine sediments support the argument for major changes in the importance of fire in late Tertiary vegetation (Herring, 1985). Charcoal fluxes in north Pacific marine sediments began to increase from about 10 million years ago to reach levels two orders of magnitude higher than early Tertiary sediments by the late Pleistocene (Herring, 1985). As yet, we don't know just where vegetation was becoming prone to fire because terrestrial sources of charcoal in marine sediments are mixed by wind (Verardo & Ruddiman, 1996). In Australia, however, terrestrial deposits of charcoal have been studied in conjunction with the pollen record of vegetation change. They show a dramatic increase in charcoal coinciding with the replacement of rainforest by open formations, with the same pattern repeated at different times in different localities (Kershaw *et al.*, 1994).

The evolution of large mammals, adapted to open conditions, followed the evolution of grassy formations (Janis, 1993). Either alone, or in combination with fire, modern analogies suggest that these grazing herds would have contributed further to the opening of forest formations (Owen-Smith, 1989; Dublin, Sinclair & McGlade, 1990). The final set of actors in the trio of major modern disturbance agents appeared with the evolution of hominids. Hominids have contributed to the disappearance of closed formations since at least the late Pleistocene through manipulation of fire (Brain & Sillen, 1988), development of tools that could fell trees, and the recent invention of agriculture. The relative role of climate versus disturbance in structuring major vegetation patterns is far from settled, either now or during the events of the late Tertiary. However, there is enough contemporary evidence of major vegetation change when disturbance regimes are altered to suggest a long history of major disturbance events influencing the evolution of modern biotas.

## EVOLUTIONARY INNOVATION IN DISTURBANCE-DEPENDENT VEGETATION

An expected consequence of major ecological change should be adaptive radiation of taxa, in this case to exploit the new open disturbance-dependent formations. There are several indications of diversification of open formation taxa in plants but few formal analyses of the problem. Herrera (1992) used fossil evidence and distribution records to show that Mediterranean shrubland floras are made up of both ancient lineages and new genera that appeared in the Pleistocene. Despite their younger age, the modern genera are richer in species, suggesting diversification into the new open habitats. Large species-rich genera are also characteristic of the extremely speciose fire-prone fynbos flora of South Africa whereas South African forest floras have high genus-to-family ratios but low species-to-genus ratios (Linder et al., 1992). Californian chaparral is also dominated by large species-rich shrub genera (Arctostaphylos and Ceanothus) and high speciation rates have been attributed to the evolution of novel fire life histories (Wells, 1969). In Australia, Eucalyptus and Acacia, both extremely species-rich genera characteristic of fire-prone vegetation, become common in the pollen record only in charcoal-rich deposits of the Pleistocene (Kershaw et al., 1994). It would be interesting to analyse savanna tree floras for comparable patterns of diversification from the few taxa that escaped the forest to survive the frequent fires and browsing pressures of open habitats.

## DISTURBANCE AND PROTECTED AREAS

A major challenge for conservation is both to recognize, and to simulate, the disturbance regimes under which ecosystems evolved. Disturbance processes caused by fire, large vertebrates and human activities are difficult to maintain in fragmented landscapes, yet may be critically necessary for maintaining diversity within protected areas. Management of disturbance processes is frequently controversial and highly political. In the Mediterranean basin, for example, goats have been widely maligned for their 'destructive' effect since at least since Plato's time, culminating in an EC ban on subsidies for goat herders in 1992. Yet goats help to maintain a rich herbaceous flora by opening the woody overstorey, and exclusion of goats results in a uniform, species-poor shrubland (Seligman & Perevolotsky, 1994). The biological uniformity of these densely wooded areas excludes many local species of native fauna and flora (Naveh, 1971) which fortunately persist in the unprotected adjacent areas. Even the oft-quoted ecosystem degradation attributed to goats is open to question (Seligman & Perevolotsky, 1994).

Proponents of the argument that goats are beneficial need to show whether goats are substitutes for wild ungulates or fire, and whether their browsing promotes rare species or just enhances the diversity of weedy species. Nevertheless, this example illustrates the difficulty in maintaining disturbance processes to help to conserve biodiversity. Manipulation of disturbance regimes is often philosophically distasteful (because 'unnatural'), expensive (e.g. prescribed burning), and politically or legally risky (litigation if elephants leave the park, or fire burns adjoining properties). Managing disturbance becomes even more difficult in fragmented areas. Leach & Givnish (1996), for example, showed that prairie remnants had lost from 8 to 60% of the original plant species over a 32- to 52-year period of fire suppression caused by landscape fragmentation. They attributed these losses to the lack of burning, rather than to small population effects because local extinction was greatest in short, small-seeded plants and legumes. These traits are associated with early successional, open vegetation maintained by fire. In South Africa, natural fynbos fragments, surrounded by non-flammable forests for much of the Holocene, had 40–80% fewer species than continuous fynbos habitats. The greatest losses were of species most dependent on frequent fires, especially short-growth forms (Bond, Midgley & Vlok, 1988). No comparable losses were observed on limestone fynbos fragments surrounded by vegetation which burns regularly (Cowling & Bond, 1991). Using fire to maintain fire-dependent species in small protected areas is not easy. Besides the practical difficulties of safely burning small areas, burning can increase the risk of recruitment failure, even for fire-dependent species (Burgman & Lamont, 1992) or provide opportunities for invasion by alien species (Hobbs, 1991; Hobbs & Huenneke, 1992).

## INCORPORATING DISTURBANCE RESPONSE IN APPRAISALS OF THREATENED PLANT SPECIES

If changes in disturbance processes are a very general problem in the conservation of protected areas, what can be usefully done to guide conservation actions? There is a very large literature on fire, mammal herbivory and human exploitation of ecosystems, little of which deals with conservation concerns (Hobbs & Huenneke, 1992). Research on fire and grazing practices in grasslands and savannas, including those in areas protected for wildlife, has generally been aimed at promoting productivity rather than diversity. There is growing concern over species losses caused by these practices (Mentis & Bailey, 1990; Howe, 1994). We have little in the way of general principles for managing disturbance for diversity or for reduction of extinction risks.

However, there is a large literature on plant responses to disturbance (Noble & Slatyer, 1980; Whelan, 1995; Bond & van Wilgen, 1996) which could usefully be incorporated into assessing extinction threats for plant species. The problem is enormous. In South Africa, a global hot spot for plant species, 3435 species are considered to be threatened with global extinction, including 58 taxa assumed to be extinct and 250 endangered (Hilton-Taylor, 1996). Not surprisingly, very few of these species have been studied in any detail or targeted for specific management efforts. Here I briefly consider how response to disturbance might be incorporated into the study of threatened plant species so as to help to set priorities for species conservation.

Research on plant conservation biology generally follows the pattern described by Caughley (1994) of 'two separate fronts with little overlap'. The 'small population paradigm', concerned with the risks of extinction inherent in small population size, has stimulated a growing number of studies on conservation genetics (Young, Boyle & Brown, 1996) and a small set of studies of the demography of threatened plants (Menges, 1990;

Burgman & Lamont, 1992; Schemske *et al.*, 1994; Bradstock *et al.*, 1996). Contrasted with this are studies in the 'declining population paradigm' which focus on processes by which populations are driven to extinction by agents external to them. These include many studies on the impact of invasive plants and animals, disruption of reproductive mutualisms, changes in the disturbance regime, and the effect of various forms of environmental pollution. Studies in both paradigms are bedevilled by unusual demographic features of plants. Common problems in the demographic analysis of plants include the following:

- episodic recruitment and mortality, occurring after rare, sporadic events;
- long generation times (see below);
- persistent seedbanks which further prolong generation time but are difficult to quantify;
- considerable size-dependent differences in mortality and fecundity.

An important consequence of long generation times and episodic population change for 'small population' studies is that there are very few long-term data sets from plant populations providing means or variances of population growth rates comparable to vertebrate populations. Indeed, the risks of small population size may generally be less than in vertebrates because of the buffering effects of long generations, dormant seedbanks and/or high reproductive potential. Useful extinction models for small populations of plants have been developed (Menges, 1990; Burgman & Lamont, 1992; Bradstock *et al.*, 1996) but only for a few short-lived species.

Studies of underlying causes of extinction, such as reduction in pollinators, face similar demographic problems in assessing the overall effect on plant populations (Bond, 1994). Reduction of pollinators leading to a reduction in the number of seeds produced may have negligible effects on the persistence of a long-lived clonal species. I suggest that consideration of the probability of persistence of established individuals is a useful starting point for plant ecologists wishing to study extinction threats for plants. Because disturbance is a key mortality agent, plant persistence in the face of disturbance gives an indication of the rate at which a population may decline. Disturbance often does not kill plants but, by resetting succession, helps to maintain disturbance-dependent species.

### The persistence niche

The persistence niche concerns those aspects of plant biology that influence the persistence of established individuals. It complements the concept of the regeneration niche proposed by Grubb (1977). Differences in persistence are important for plant conservation because they determine generation time and what constitutes a 'catastrophe' for a plant species. Plants vary enormously in their longevity (from $< 10^0$ years to $> 10^4$ years; Harper & White, 1974; Loehle, 1988). It is very difficult to study plant population dynamics in any meaningful way in species whose lifespan is measured in centuries or millennia. When, for example, should one become concerned at the lack of seedling regeneration in a population of 1000-year-old baobabs? Although some plants have the potential to live for very long periods, this may only happen in the absence of catastrophic disturbance. Many trees, especially very long-lived conifers, are killed outright by disturbances such as fire. Other plant species survive major disturbance by sprouting and may also be very long-lived. They include diverse growth forms not obviously associated with great longevity such as ferns, grasses, herbs, shrubs and trees. The most famous examples are clonal species (Cook, 1983) which spread vegetatively producing 'populations' that are the asexual progeny of a single seed. Sprouting behaviour is not restricted to clonal species but is also very common in non-clonal shrubs and trees affording different degrees of 'immortality' to individual plants.

Persistence by sprouting varies among species, among age classes within a species, and across different types and intensities of disturbance. This variation can be usefully summarized in survivorship profiles of individuals, analogous to survivorship curves of populations. These indicate the probability of survival for a given size class for a given disturbance (Hodgkinson, 1986; Bond & van Wilgen, 1996; Fig. 5.1). For threatened species in decline, the response of mature individuals to disturbance is of key importance. This information is seldom available in taxonomic keys or even in detailed compilations of ecological data such as that of Grime, Hodgson & Hunt (1988) for components of the British flora. However, the data are not difficult to obtain from post-disturbance inventory (e.g. Kauffman 1991 for fire in tropical forests; Bellingham, Tanner & Healey, 1994; Zimmermann *et al.*, 1994 for sprouting after hurricane damage).

### Persistence and regeneration

Persistence properties of plant species may be correlated with regeneration properties because of allocation trade-offs. Resource allocation trade-offs between growth and reproduction have been widely studied in plants (e.g.

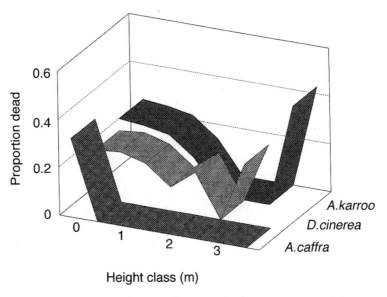

0.6

0.4

0.2

0

Proportion dead

0

1

2

3

A.karroo

D.cinerea

A.caffra

Height class (m)

Fig. 5.1 An example of survivorship curves for three savanna trees. The graph indicates the probability of mortality for different size classes after experimental clipping to ground level. *Acacia karroo* and *Dichrostachys cinerea* are weak persisters and lose the capacity to sprout once they become large trees. Both produce numerous seedlings and can become problematic invaders of grassy savannas. *Acacia caffra* sprouts vigorously, when injured, retaining this ability as trees. This species is a strong persister but seldom recruits from seedlings and is not invasive. (From K. Maze & W. Bond, unpublished data.)

Tilman, 1988), forming the basis of life-history classifications such as the Competitor–Stress tolerator–Ruderal system of Grime (1979). However, the implications of resource allocation for persistence, other than for clonal species, are less well known. Plants that allocate resources to below-ground reserves for sprouting after injury would be expected to allocate fewer resources to above-ground growth or reproduction. Good persisters should be poor seedling recruiters and vice versa. This pattern holds true for clonal plants which seldom regenerate from seedlings and colonize space primarily from vegetative spread (Cook, 1983; Eriksson, 1989). Trade-offs in non-clonal plants are perhaps best known from fire-prone shrublands through comparisons of congeneric pairs of sprouting and non-sprouting shrubs (Keeley, 1977; Bellairs & Bell, 1990; Pate, Froend *et al.*, 1990; Pate, Meney & Dixon, 1991; Le Maitre & Midgley, 1992). Strongly sprouting species tend to produce fewer surviving seedlings than non-sprouters. In some cases, this is due to reduced allocation to reproductive function, such as reduced seed numbers (Bellairs & Bell, 1990). However, early allocation of resources to below-ground reserves in sprouter seedlings is correlated with reduced above-ground growth, and poorer survival rates, than those of non-sprouters (Thomas & Davis, 1989; Pate, Froend et al., 1990; Hansen, Pate & Hansen, 1991). Sprouter–non-sprouter comparisons have rarely been made outside these shrubland systems. Kruger, Midgley & Cowling (1997) found that multi-stemmed sprouting species growing in southern African closed evergreen forests produced fewer seedlings than single-stemmed, weakly or non-sprouting species. If these patterns prove general, sprouting behaviour would be a useful predictor of the frequency of seedling regeneration and relative colonizing ability of threatened species. Metapopulation theory would be most applicable to non-sprouters since rates of colonization are more likely to be comparable to rates of extinction. Local extinction of strongly sprouting populations would be much less likely to be restored by colonization of seedlings in time frames relevant for conservation management.

### The persistence niche and the identification of population decline

IUCN categories for threatened species status now include explicit consideration of population trajectories over time (IUCN, 1994; see also Mace & Lande, 1991). Species with declining populations should clearly receive priority attention. Population size structure is a useful indicator of population trajectories and has been widely used by foresters for assessing the status of forest trees. Inverse J-shaped curves of the frequency of trees in stem diameter classes (Fig. 5.2) are considered indicative of healthy populations with plenty of regeneration. However, interpretation of size structure changes if the persistence niche is included. The absence of new recruits is of much less concern in persistent species, especially those that are vigorous sprouters. Indeed, vigorous sprouters often have very poor seedling recruitment, as discussed above. A great deal of effort can be wasted on studying regeneration problems in such species when the lack of regeneration is not, in the medium term, a problem at all.

### Causes of population decline

For many plant species, 'small population' methods are inappropriate starting points for studying extinction risk. Strong persisters should show low

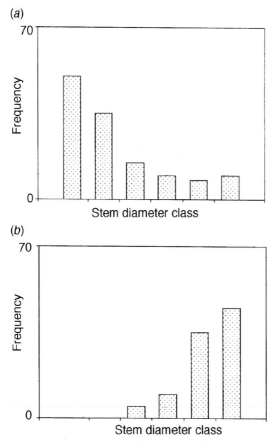

Fig. 5.2 Interpretation of stem class distributions and population status of trees depends on the persistence niche. (*a*) Stable, or growing, population structure with adequate recruitment; (*b*) declining population with poor recruitment *or* stable population of a strongly persistent sprouter *or* population with episodic recruitment.

variance in population size over long time periods. They are buffered against the usual problems associated with small populations because of their long generation times. Though such species may appear near immortal, they are not. But the kinds of threats they face are different from those most emphasized in population vulnerability analyses. Table 5.1 shows a tentative hierarchy of threats associated with different persistence modes. The frequencies of the different persistence modes is poorly known for most vegetation types and no generalizations can be made from available data. Even communities with superficially similar physiognomic structure

**Table 5.1**

*A suggested protocol that incorporates the persistence niche in population vulnerability analyses for plants. The protocol is in the form of a key that suggests most profitable lines of study to ameliorate problems for a threatened species*

............................................................................................................................................

1. NON-SPROUTERS: Mature individuals do not sprout under current or anticipated range of disturbances
Juveniles well represented in populations:

> *Demographic problems a minor threat? Changes in ecosystem properties may be important (e.g. eutrophication, changes in hydrology, pollution, etc.)*

Juveniles under-represented in populations:

Recruitment episodic:  *Explore likely events that trigger recruitment. If these are disturbance related, are the necessary disturbances occurring?*

Recruitment continuous:  *Explore causes of poor recruitment such as pollinator failure, 'small population' effects.*

2. SPROUTERS: Mature individuals typically sprout after most disturbance
Mature individuals sprout without external disturbance (e.g. after tree-fall of an old trunk, examples: *Tilia, Ginkgo*):

> *Very persistent species, often with poor regeneration and poor colonizers. Lack of regeneration is not a problem in the medium term. Most important threats likely to be external habitat modification or habitat destruction*

Sprouting stimulated by disturbance such as fire, hurricane damage, felling but senescent individuals die without sprouting:

Plants become moribund after long periods without disturbance:

> *Dieback may necessitate manipulation of disturbance frequency*

Plants threatened with overtopping or likely to be outcompeted by other species (typically weak sprouters or non-sprouters) in the absence of disturbance:

> *Manipulate disturbance regime to favour threatened sprouter*

Population is declining even though disturbance frequency is adequate and without obvious competitors:

> *Investigate survival responses to different types, seasons and intensities of disturbance*

............................................................................................................................................

may have very different persistence properties. For example, non-sprouters made up 48% of a sample of 4418 species from South African fynbos (Le Maitre & Midgley, 1992) whereas all Chilean matorral shrub species sprout (Keeley, 1986).

Typical threats associated with different persistence modes are discussed briefly below.

Short-lived non-sprouting or weakly sprouting species are appropriate subjects for 'small population' type analysis. Their demographic behaviour is closest to animal analogues for which the methods were first developed. Some of the more successful applications of vulnerability analysis in plants come from just such examples (Menges, 1990; Burgman & Lamont, 1992; Bradstock *et al.*, 1996). Weak persisters should also respond quickest to deterministic causes of extinction, such as loss of pollinators or changes in disturbance intensity. In southern African game parks, it is the weakly sprouting trees, such as species of *Acacia* and *Commiphora*, that are eliminated from areas accessible to elephants. Strongly sprouting species, such as *Colophospermum mopane*, survive heavy browsing as multi-stemmed shrubs (W. Bond and J. Midgley, unpublished observations).

Long-lived non-sprouters make poor subjects for population genetic or demographic studies of small population effects because of their long generation time ( > 3000 years in conifers such as the bristle-cone pine). For such species, increased mortality of established plants should be a key concern, especially after rare catastrophic disturbance.

Among woody sprouting species, the most strongly persistent are those that can replace trunks that have died by basal sprouting – in the absence of external disturbance. A notable example is *Ginkgo biloba*, the maidenhair tree, which still persists in parts of south-west China (Tredici, 1992). This woodland species has basal swellings which bud out new sprouts continually replacing old, dying trunks. Individuals would be near immortal if habitat remained unchanged. *Tilia cordata*, the lime tree, is a well-studied example from Britain (Pigott, 1993). Northern populations of this species appear to have had no seedling recruitment since the climate cooled some 5000 years ago! Though a trunk may senesce and die, the individual plant persists by continuously replacing dead shoots with basal sprouts. There is little information on the abundance of such species in nature but, at least in southern African forests, they seem to be very rare. Populations of these disturbance-independent sprouters are heavily dominated by old established individuals and seedling recruitment is very rare. Because of this, strong persisters are likely to be poor colonizers. Chief threats are habitat destruction or habitat modification leading to the death of mature plants. Loss of any mature individual is a warning sign since recruitment is so rare.

Plants that sprout only after external disturbance are far commoner. Population decline in such species is, again, usually due to increased mortality of mature plants rather than regeneration failure. The appropriate problem to study is therefore factors influencing mortality and not pollination, dispersal, genetic or other problems influencing seedling additions. The interaction between disturbance and survival is the most efficient way of understanding the causes of population decline.

There are several causes of population decline through increased mortality of adult sprouters (Table 5.1). Some species become moribund in the absence of disturbance. This is a well-known phenomenon for tussock grass species occurring when grazing or burning is excluded for long periods (e.g. Tainton & Mentis, 1984; Tilman & Wedin, 1991). Some woody plants, such as aspen, show a similar negative growth response to the absence of disturbance. The solution to this kind of problem is to re-introduce typical disturbances (e.g. fire, grazing) at appropriate frequencies.

Sprouting species are often poor competitors for light. Midgley (1996) has noted that sprouters are typically shorter than conspecific neighbours. Multi-stemmed woody sprouters can be overtopped by single-stemmed competitors and are replaced by them in the absence of frequent disturbance. Manipulation of the disturbance regime to maintain the early successional status required by threatened sprouter species will often be necessary.

Population declines of sprouter species may occur even though disturbances in protected areas are still occurring at appropriate frequencies. In such cases, the type, season and intensity of disturbance may be the cause of the problem. This is often the case in fire-prone systems where prescribed fires are usually burnt under 'safe' conditions – that is, at seasons and weather conditions which promote low-intensity fires. These conditions are often quite different from the kinds of fires under which a particular vegetation type developed and can result in dramatic decline in sensitive species (see Bond & van Wilgen, 1996 for examples).

## CONCLUSIONS

The small population paradigm has greatly stimulated development of theory in conservation biology. However, the methods and models were developed by zoologists and may be less appropriate for plants. Terrestrial animals do not have the enormous variation in generation time seen in plants nor the extraordinary persistence of individuals in the face of injury. Recruitment is naturally an important focus of organisms with comparatively short life spans, as is stochastic variation in mortality. In plants, factors influencing individual persistence can be of great importance but overlooked because they fall outside the ambit of typical demographic studies. The body of methods developed for assessing population viability are appropriate for relatively short-lived weak persisters but may merely divert attention from the key concern of survival, especially in relation to changes in the disturbance regime, in strong persisters.

Disturbance is a key process maintaining plant diversity. I have argued that changes in disturbance regimes were major factors in the evolution of modern biotas in the late Tertiary. We are emerging from a long period when we were philosophically inclined to exclude disturbances, especially fire and human activity, from protected areas (Pickett, Parker & Fiedler, 1992). Disturbance processes are among the first, and most important, to change in remnant protected areas. Formal recognition of their importance in viability assessments would help in providing early warning of their conservation consequences.


## ACKNOWLEDGEMENTS

Thanks to Jeremy Midgley, Kristal Maze and Lawrence Kruger for their helpful contributions. Thanks, too, to the Foundation for Research and Development and the University of Cape Town for their support.


### References

Axelrod, D. I. (1975). Evolution and biogeography of Madrean-Tethyan sclerophyll vegetation. *Ann. Mo. bot. Gdn*, **62**, 280–334

Axelrod, D.I. (1989). Age and origin of chaparral. In *The California chaparral: paradigms reexamined*. (Ed. Keeley, S. C.). *Sci. Ser. Nat. Hist. Mus. Los Angeles Cty*, **34**, 7–19.

Bellairs, J. M. & Bell, D. T. (1990). Canopy-borne seed store in three Western Australian plant communities. *Aust. J. Ecol.*, **15**, 299–305.

Bellingham, P. J., Tanner, E. V. J. & Healey, J. R. (1994). Sprouting of trees in Jamaican montane forests, after a hurricane. *J. Ecol.*, **82**, 747–58.

Bond, W. J. (1994). Do mutualisms matter? Assessing the impact of pollinator/disperser disruption on plant extinctions. *Phil. Trans. R. Soc. Lond.* B, **344**, 83–90

Bond, W. J., Midgley, J. & Vlok, J. (1988). When is an island not an island? Insular effects and their causes in fynbos shrublands. *Oecologia*, **77**, 515–21.

Bond, W.J. & van Wilgen, B. (1996). *Fire and plants*. Chapman and Hall, New York & London.

Booysen, P. de V. & Tainton, N. M. (Eds) (1984). Ecological effects of fire in South African ecosystems. *Ecol. Stud. Anal. Synth.*, **48**, 1–426.

Botkin, D. B. (1990). *Discordant harmonies: a new ecology for the twenty-first century.*

Oxford University Press, New York & Oxford.

Bradstock, R. A., Bedward, M., Scott, J. & Keith, D. A. (1996). Simulation of the effect of spatial and temporal variation in fire regimes on the population viability of a *Banksia* species. *Conserv. Biol.*, 10, 776–84.

Brain, C. K. & Sillen, A. (1988). Evidence from the Swartkrans cave for the earliest use of fire. *Nature, Lond.*, 336, 464–6.

Burgman, M. A. & Lamont, B. B. (1992). A stochastic model for the viability of *Banksia cuneata* populations: environmental, demographic and genetic effects. *J. appl. Ecol.*, 29, 719–27.

Caughley, G. (1994). Directions in conservation biology. *J. Anim. Ecol.*, 63, 215–44.

Cowling, R. M. & Bond, W. J. (1991). How small can reserves be? An empirical approach in Cape fynbos. *Biol. Conserv.*, 58, 243–56.

Cook, R. E. (1983). Clonal plant populations. *Am. Sci.*, 71, 244–53.

Crawley, M. J. (1983). *Herbivory: the dynamics of animal–plant interactions.* Blackwell, Oxford. (*Stud. Ecol.*, 10)

Dublin, H. T., Sinclair, A. R. E. & McGlade, J. (1990). Elephants and fire as causes of multiple stable states in the Serengeti–Mara woodlands. *J. Anim. Ecol.*, 59, 1147–64.

Eriksson, O. (1989). Seedling dynamics and life histories in clonal plants. *Oikos*, 55, 231–8.

Grime, J. P. (1979). *Plant strategies and vegetation processes.* John Wiley, Chichester.

Grime, J. P., Hodgson, J. G. & Hunt, R. (1988). *Comparative plant ecology. A functional approach to common British species.* Unwin-Hyman, London.

Grubb, P. (1977). The maintenance of species richness in plant communities: the importance of the regeneration niche. *Biol. Rev.*, 52, 107–45.

Hansen, A., Pate, J. S. & Hansen, A. P. (1991). Growth and reproductive performance of a seeder and a resprouter species of *Bossiaea* as a function of plant age after fire. *Ann. Bot.*, 67, 497–509.

Harper, J. L. & White, J. (1974). The demography of plants. *A. Rev. Ecol. Syst.*, 5, 419–63.

Herrera, C. M. (1992). Historical effects and sorting processes as explanations for contemporary ecological patterns: character syndromes in Mediterranean woody plants. *Am. Nat.*, 140, 421–46.

Herring, J. R. (1985). Charcoal fluxes into sediments of the North Pacific Ocean: the Cenozoic record of burning. In *The carbon cycle and atmospheric CO2: natural variations Archaean to present*: 419–422. (Eds Sundquist, E. T. & Broecker, W. S). American Geophysical Union, Washington DC (*Geophys. Monogr.* 32.)

Hilton-Taylor, C. (1996). *Red data list of southern African plants. Strelitzia* 4. National Botanical Institute, Pretoria.

Hobbs, R. J. (1991). Disturbance a precursor to weed invasion in native vegetation. *Plant Prot. Q.*, 6, 99–104.

Hobbs, R. J. & Huenneke, L. F. (1992). Disturbance, diversity and invasion: implications for conservation. *Conserv. Biol.* 6, 324–37.

Hodgkinson, K.C. (1986). Responses of rangeland plants to fire in water-limited environments. In *Rangelands: a resource under siege*: 437–441. (Eds Joss, P. J.,

Lynch, P. W. & Williams, O. B.). Cambridge University Press, Cambridge.

Howe, H. F. (1994). Managing species diversity in tallgrass prairie: assumptions and implications. *Conserv. Biol.*, **8**, 691–704.

IUCN (1994). *IUCN Red List categories.* IUCN, Gland, Switzerland.

Jackson W. D. (1968). Fire, air, earth and water—an elemental ecology of Tasmania. *Proc. ecol. Soc. Aust.*, **3**, 9–16.

Janis, C. M. (1993). Tertiary mammal evolution in the context of changing climates, vegetation, and tectonic events. *A. Rev. Ecol. Syst.*, **24**, 467–500.

Kauffman, J. B. (1991). Survival by sprouting following fire in tropical forests of the eastern Amazon. *Biotropica*, **23**, 219–24.

Keeley, J. E. (1977). Seed production, seed populations in soil, and seedling production after fire for two congeneric pairs of sprouting and nonsprouting chaparral shrubs. *Ecology*, **58**, 820–9.

Keeley, J. E. (1986). Resilience of mediterranean shrub communities to fires. In *Resilience in Mediterranean-type ecosystems*: 95–112. (Eds Dell, B., Hopkins, A. J. M. & Lamont, B. B.). Junk, Dordrecht.

Kershaw, A. P., Martin, H. A. & McEwen Mason, J. R. C. (1994). The Neogene: a period of transition. In *History of the Australian vegetation: Cretaceous to Recent*: 299–327. (Ed. Hill, R. S.). Cambridge University Press, Cambridge.

Kruger, L. M., Midgley, J. J. & Cowling, R. M. (1997). Sprouters versus seeders in South African forest trees; a model based on forest canopy height. *Funct. Ecol.*, **11**, 101–5.

Leach, M. K. & Givnish, T. J. (1996). Ecological determinants of species loss in remnant prairies. *Science*, **273**, 1555–8.

Le Maitre, D. C. & Midgley, J. J. (1992). Plant reproductive ecology. In *The ecology of fynbos: nutrients, fire and diversity*: 135–174. (Ed. Cowling, R. M.). Oxford University Press, Cape Town.

Linder, H. P., Meadows, M. E. & Cowling, R. M. (1992). History of the Cape flora. In *The ecology of fynbos: nutrients, fire and diversity*: 113–134. (Ed. Cowling, R. M.). Oxford University Press, Cape Town.

Loehle, C. (1988). Tree life history strategies: the role of defenses. *Can. J. For.*, **18**, 209–22.

Lorimer, C. G., Chapman, J. W. & Lambert, W. D. (1994). Tall understorey vegetation as a factor in the poor development of oak seedlings beneath mature stands. *J. Ecol.*, **82**, 227–37.

Mace, G. M. & Lande, R. (1991). Assessing extinction threats: towards a reevaluation of IUCN threatened species categories. *Conserv. Biol.*, **5**, 148–57.

Menges, E. S. (1990). Population viability analysis for an endangered plant. *Conserv. Biol.*, **4**, 41–62.

Mentis, M. T. & Bailey, A. W. (1990). Changing perceptions of fire management in savanna parks. *J. Grassland Soc. sth. Afr.*, **7**: 81–85.

Midgley, J. J. (1996). Why the world's vegetation is not totally dominated by resprouting plants; because resprouters are shorter than reseeders. *Ecography*, **19**, 92–5.

Moll, E. J., McKenzie, B. & McLachlan, D. (1980). A possible explanation for the lack of trees in the fynbos, Cape Province, South Africa. *Biol. Conserv.*, **17**, 221–8.

Naveh, Z. (1971). The conservation of ecological diversity of Mediterranean ecosystems through ecological management. In *The scientific management of plant and animal communities for conservation*: 603–622. (Eds Duffey, E. & Watt, A. S.). Blackwell, Oxford.

Noble, I. R. & Slatyer, R. O. (1980). The use of vital attributes to predict successional changes in plant communities subject to recurrent disturbances. *Vegetatio*, **43**, 5–21.

Owen-Smith, N. (1989). Megafaunal extinctions: the conservation message from 11,000 years B.P. *Conserv. Biol.*, **3**, 405–12.

Pate, J. S., Froend, R. H., Bowen, B. J., Hansen, A. & Kuo, J. (1990). Seedling growth and storage characteristics of seeder and resprouter species of Mediterranean-type ecosystems of S.W. Australia. *Ann. Bot.*, **65**, 585–601.

Pate, J. S., Meney, K. A. & Dixon, K. W. (1991). Contrasting growth and morphological characteristics of fire-sensitive (obligate seeder) and fire-resistant (resprouter) species of Restionaceae (S. hemisphere restiads) from south-western Australia. *Aust. J. Bot.*, **39**, 505–25.

Peet, R. K. (1992). Community structure and ecosystem function. In *Plant succession: theory and prediction*: 103–151. (Eds Glenn-Lewin, D. C., Peet, R. K. & Veblen, T. T.), Chapman & Hall, London.

Pickett, S. T. A., Parker, V. T. & Fiedler, P. L. (1992). The new paradigm in ecology: implications for conservation biology above the species level. In *Conservation Biology. The theory and practice of nature conservation, preservation and management*: 65–88. (Eds Fiedler, P. L. & Jain, S. K.), Chapman & Hall, New York & London.

Pigott, C. D. (1993). Are the distributions of species determined by failure to set seed? In *Fruit and seed production*: 203–216. (Eds Marshall, C. & Grace, J.), Cambridge University Press, Cambridge.

Sauer, C. O. (1950). Grassland climax, fire and man. *J. Range Mgmt*, **8**, 117–21.

Schemske, D. W., Husband, B. C., Ruckelshaus, M. H., Goodwillie, C., Parker, I. M. & Bishop, J. G. (1994). Evaluating approaches to the conservation of rare and endangered plants. *Ecology* **75**, 584–606.

Seligman, N. G. & Perevolotsky, A. (1994). Has intensive grazing by domestic livestock degraded Mediterranean Basin rangelands? In *Plant–animal interactions in Mediterranean-type ecosystems*: 93–104. (Eds Arianoutsou, M. & Groves, R. H.). Kluwer, Dordrecht.

Stewart, O. C. (1956). Fire as the first great force employed by man. In *Man's role in changing the face of the earth*: 115–133. (Ed. Thomas, W. L.), University of Chicago Press, Chicago.

Tainton, N. M. & Mentis, M. T. (1984). Fire in grassland. In *Ecological effects of fire in South African ecosystems*: 115–147. (Eds Booysen, P. de V. & Tainton, N. M.), Springer-Verlag, Berlin. (*Ecol. Stud. Anal. Synth.*, **48**.)

Thomas, C. M. & Davis, S. D. (1989). Recovery patterns of three chaparral shrub species after wildfire. *Oecologia*, **80**, 309–20.

Tilman, D. (1988). *Plant strategies and the dynamics and structure of plant communities*. Princeton University Press, Princeton, New Jersey.

Tilman, D. & Wedin, D. (1991). Oscillations and chaos in the dynamics of a perennial grass. *Nature, Lond.*, **353**, 653–5.

Tredici, P. D. (1992). Natural regeneration of *Ginkgo biloba* from downward growing cotyledonary buds (basal chichi). *Am. J. Bot.*, **79**, 522–30.

Verardo, D. J. & Ruddiman, W. F. (1996). Late Pleistocene charcoal in tropical Atlantic deep-sea sediments: climatic and geochemical significance. *Geology*, **24**, 855–7.

Wells, P. V. (1962). Vegetation in relation to geological substratum and fire in the San Luis Obispo quadrangle, California. *Ecol. Monogr.*, **32**, 79–103.

Wells, P. V. (1969). The relation between mode of reproduction and extent of speciation in woody genera of the California chaparral. *Evolution*, **23**, 264–7.

Wells, P. V. (1970). Post-glacial vegetational history of the Great Plains, new evidence reopens the question of the origin of treeless grasslands. *Science*, **167**, 1574–82.

Whelan, R. J. (1995). *The ecology of fire*. Cambridge University Press, Cambridge.

Wolfe, J. A. (1985). Distribution of major vegetational types during the Tertiary. In *The carbon cycle and atmospheric CO2: natural variations Archaean to present*: 357–375. (Eds Sundquist, E. T. & Broecker, W. S. American Geophysical Union, Washington, D.C. (*Geophys. Monogr.* **32**.)

Young, A., Boyle, T. & Brown T. (1996). The population genetic consequences of habitat fragmentation for plants. *Trends Ecol. Evol.*, **11**, 413–18.

Zimmerman, J. K., Everham, E. M., Waide, R. B., Lodge, D. J., Taylor, C. M. & Brokaw, N. V. L. (1994). Responses of tree species to hurricane winds in subtropical wet forest in Puerto Rico: implications for tropical tree life histories. *J. Ecol.*, **82**, 911–22.

$$\left(6\right)$$

# Butterfly distributional patterns, processes and conservation

CHRIS D. THOMAS, DIEGO JORDANO, OWEN T. LEWIS, JANE K. HILL,
ODETTE L. SUTCLIFFE AND JEREMY A. THOMAS

## INTRODUCTION

Conservation requires an understanding of how species are distributed, and the population processes that maintain distributions at small and large scales (e.g. Lawton, 1995). This chapter examines these patterns in temperate butterflies, concentrating on large-scale patterns of density and distribution, regional population dynamics, the spatial structure of populations, the role of metapopulation dynamics in regional persistence, and the role of habitat isolation in population survival. We develop an integrated approach to species distributions in which the niche theory of species distributions (Hengeveld & Haeck, 1982; Brown, 1984) is used to understand habitat patterns and some aspects of population dynamics in different parts of geographic ranges, and metapopulation theory (Hanski, 1982, 1985; Gilpin & Hanski, 1991) is used to understand which of these habitats will be populated. As suitable breeding habitats become increasingly localized at natural margins and through habitat fragmentation, metapopulations fail to persist where the rate of local extinction exceeds the rate of colonization, and where too high a fraction of the population is lost during migration between habitat patches. Landscape fragmentation that decreases patch areas and increases distances between habitats can convert 'core' landscapes into 'marginal' ones, and 'marginal' landscapes into 'uninhabitable' ones, and so lead to regional extinctions and increasingly localized distributions throughout geographic ranges. Whenever possible, rare and endangered species should be protected where they are still relatively common, and where large networks of suitable habitat still survive. These conditions are most likely to be met in core regions of species distributions.

## PATTERNS OF DENSITY AND DISTRIBUTION

Hengeveld and Haeck (1982) and Brown (1984) suggested that the environ-mental and resource requirements (niche) of each species interact with environmental gradients across the earth's surface to shape the species, distribution. Distributions will be limited by different factors or combina-tions of factors at different margins, but we show a simplified version in Fig. 6.1 based on a simple thermal gradient. In any one region, there is a distribution of microclimates, some of which will be suitable (solid and shaded), and some of which will be unsuitable (open) for a given species. 'Suitable' indicates that mean $r > 0$ and 'unsuitable' that mean $r < 0$ ($r$ is the habitat-specific intrinsic rate of population increase). In the species core, there is a close correspondence between species requirements and gross climate, such that suitable thermal environments cover a high frac-tion of the land surface, giving the *potential* for the organism to be wide-spread. It is still limited by other factors, such as host plants, and may be quite localized even in core regions. The core is usually, but not always, towards the geographic centre of a species' distribution (Lawton, 1995). In contrast, only a small proportion of the land surface is likely to meet a species' thermal requirements in marginal regions (Fig. 6.1). Here, patches of suitable microclimates may be small and widely separated from one an-other. It has also been suggested that the most suitable habitats in the core of a range are likely to support higher population densities than those at the margin, but this is not inevitable because other factors may be more im-portant determinants of local density once some minimum set of climatic and resource requirements has been met. Thus, moving from the centre to the margin of a distribution, a species is expected to inhabit progressively fewer localities and perhaps to exist at lower local densities where present (e.g. Hengeveld & Haeck, 1982; Brown, 1984; Svensson, 1992).

The range margins of many European butterfly species correlate with climatic variables, rather than with the limits of their host plants (Dennis, 1993), and marginal populations tend to be restricted to locations with spe-cific microclimates (J. A. Thomas, 1993; Gutiérrez & Menéndez, 1995). At northern margins, populations are often associated with warm microcli-mates, such as south-facing hillsides, sheltered woodland clearings (J. A. Thomas, 1993), or frost-free areas (Jordano, Retamosa & Fernández Haeger, 1991). At southern margins, European species typically occur in relatively cool or especially moist microclimates, such as at high elevations, in wetlands, or on north-facing slopes (personal observations). That species

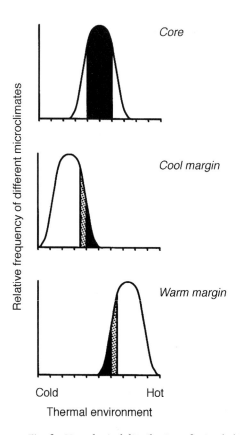

Fig. 6.1 Hypothetical distribution of microhabitats available at the core and two margins of the geographic range of one species. Solid areas indicate microhabitats that fulfil the species' thermal requirements. Shading indicates local adaptations to marginal climates by marginal populations.

use relatively warm microhabitats where the general climate is cool, and cool or moist microclimates where the general climate is warm, suggests that the actual set of local climatic conditions which permit net population growth are narrower than would be imagined from examining gross climates across entire geographic distributions. These observations are consistent with the main premise of the niche model, that species have environmental requirements that limit their distributions at small and large spatial scales.

Many butterfly species in Britain become more (or less) localized as one moves northwards. Using data from Heath, Pollard and Thomas (1984), we

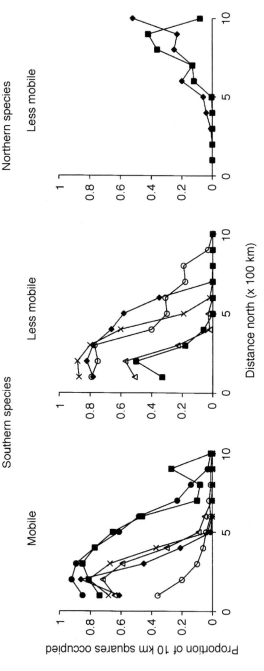

Fig. 6.2 Proportions of 10 km grid squares in each 100 km latitudinal band occupied by selected species that reach latitudinal limits in Britain. Reduced occupancy in the southernmost and northernmost bands may be due to peninsular effects. The southernmost latitudinal band is restricted to the relatively maritime south-west of England, where summer temperatures are on average cooler than in the next 100 km band to the north. Mobile southern species; ● *Inachis io*, ■ *Anthocharis cardamines*, × *Polygonia c-album*, Δ *Celastrina argiolus*, ◆ *Gonepteryx rhamni*, ○, *Colias croceus*. Less mobile, southern species; ■ *Aricia agestis*, × *Pyronia tithonus*, Δ *Melanargia galathea*, ◆ *Ochlodes venata*, ○ *Aphantopus hyperantus*.
Less mobile, northern species; ■ *Erebia aethiops*, ◆ *Coenonympha tullia*.

quantified patchiness in distribution by calculating the proportion of 10 km grid squares occupied by different species in 100 km-wide latitudinal bands, with band 1 corresponding to southern England, and band 10 to northern Scotland. We ignored species which were clearly more widely distributed in either the east or west of Britain, and species for which data are unreliable, such as those found in forest canopies or for which there are identification problems. For most species which reach their range margin within Britain, a declining fraction of squares is occupied 200–500 km south of the northern margin, indicating patchiness well within the absolute range margin (Fig. 6.2). This appears to be a real distributional phenomenon (rather than a function of recording effort, or peculiarities of British landscapes) because different species reach their range margin at different latitudes, and the few northern species which occur in Britain show the reverse pattern, becoming increasingly localized at their southern margin (Fig. 6.2). These results are consistent with the niche model predictions.

Using published data from transect counts of butterflies made throughout Britain (Pollard, Hall & Bibby, 1986), we found limited evidence for declines in local densities nearer range margins, although this trend does exist (Table 6.1). Larger sample sizes might reveal greater significance, but the overall picture is of extreme variation in local density in all parts of species distributions, including in core regions. The clearest trends and only significant results were obtained for mobile species (Table 6.1), as might have been expected. Mobile species may 'average the environment' over relatively wide areas, and occur at lower densities in regions where suitable breeding areas are localized (at range margins). In contrast, less mobile species can remain within suitable localized environments, and attain high local densities even where the surrounding landscape is inhospitable. Further evidence for this interpretation comes from the effects of niche breadth (measured as the number of habitats each species can occupy) on local density. Relatively immobile species showed no effect of niche breadth on local density, but there was an effect for mobile species (Table 6.2). Local densities of immobile species would not be expected to be influenced greatly by surrounding habitats, whereas densities of more mobile species could be influenced by a range of habitats in the surrounding countryside.

The relationship between distributional extent and density is of great importance in conservation, because species which are localized and also occur at low densities may be the most vulnerable. As in many other studies

**Table 6.1**

*Pearson correlations (r) between local abundance-where-present (ln butterflies per 100 m) and distance north (in km; 0 = most southern 100 km grid line)*

| Species | Density | | | |
|---|---|---|---|---|
| | Maximum | | Mean | |
| **Mobile populations** | | | | |
| Celastrina argiolus | − 0.150 | (33) | − 0.199 | (53) |
| Gonepteryx rhamni | − 0.287[*] | (51) | − 0.217 | (60) |
| Inachis io | − 0.281[**] | (71) | − 0.459[***] | (76) |
| Polygonia c-album | − 0.400[**] | (46) | − 0.262[*] | (58) |
| **Less mobile populations** | | | | |
| Aphantopus hyperantus | 0.206 | (47) | 0.254 | (53) |
| Aricia agestis | − 0.141 | (20) | − 0.029 | (24) |
| Erynnis tages | − 0.132 | (24) | − 0.265 | (28) |
| Melanargia galathea | − 0.230 | (25) | − 0.063 | (31) |
| Ochlodes venata | − 0.146 | (58) | − 0.231 | (66) |
| Pyronia tithonus | − 0.062 | (61) | − 0.091 | (63) |

[*] $P < 0.05$; [**] $P < 0.01$; [***] $P < 0.001$.

All species included are southern. Two analyses are shown. 'Maximum' uses highest density section of transect, in a single year, 'Mean' uses density averaged over the entire transect, and up to 10 years. Numbers of sample localities are given in brackets.

of abundance–distribution relationships (e.g. Gaston & Lawton, 1990), local population density from transect counts across Britain was positively correlated with regional distribution, in our case measured as the number of 10 km squares occupied in Britain (Table 6.2(a)). This result held for all species, and for relatively immobile and mobile species separately (Table 6.2(b),(c)), but with mobile species occurring at significantly lower local densities than less mobile species. This also suggests that mobile species are 'averaging' environments over relatively large regions which include areas of poor and non-habitat.

The number of 10 km squares occupied is just one measure of species distribution, so we also considered worldwide distributions, scoring each species on a seven-point scale from European endemic through to cosmopolitan (distributed across more than three continents). We obtained the opposite relationship, with European endemics occurring at relatively high local densities, and geographically widespread species occurring at lower densities (Table 6.2). This pattern held for relatively sedentary species, but not for mobile species (Table 6.2); however, most mobile species have wide distributions, so this last test lacked statistical power. We have no evidence

**Table 6.2**

*Correlations between distributional variables and density*

| | Density | |
|---|---|---|
| | Maximum | Mean |
| **(a) All species** $N = 46$ | | |
| Geographic range[a] | − 0.266 | − 0.400[**] |
| Number of habitats[a] | 0.229 | 0.183 |
| Number of occupied 10 km[b] grid squares in Britain | 0.296[*] | 0.365 |
| **(b) Species with less mobile populations** $N = 34$ | | |
| Geographic range[a] | − 0.295 | − 0.425[*] |
| Number of habitats[a] | 0.305 | 0.050 |
| Number of occupied 10 km[b] grid squares in Britain | 0.473[**] | 0.390[*] |
| **(c) Species with mobile populations** $N = 12$ | | |
| Geographic range[a] | − 0.030 | − 0.041 |
| Number of habitats[a] | 0.577[*] | 0.609[*] |
| Number of occupied 10 km[b] grid squares in Britain | 0.782[**] | 0.798[**] |

[a] Spearman correlations; [b] Pearson correlations; [*] $P < 0.05$; [**] $P < 0.01$; [***] $P < 0.001$.

Geographical range is on an ordinal scale, with a larger number indicating a more extensive worldwide distribution (from Higins & Riley 1980). Number of 'habitats' was the number (1 to 12) of categories that each species occupies, from the following list (mainly from Heath *et al.*, 1984; Pollard *et al.*, 1986; Emmet & Heath, 1990; J. A. Thomas & Lewington, 1991): agricultural, coastal, calcareous grassland, acid/neutral grassland, heathland, moorland, scrub, wetland, closed-canopy deciduous woodland, open woodland, coniferous woodland.

to distinguish between several possible explanations for this pattern, in-cluding that (i) endemics may be better adapted to European climate or habitats, (ii) there could be a hidden relationship between mobility and range size within our coarse 'immobile' population category, or (iii) more widespread species might accumulate more parasitoids and pathogens.

Whatever the reason, species with relatively narrow geographic distribu-tions can occur at high density within their range. We are uncertain whether this result can be extended to species with very narrow distribu-tions because no butterfly species is entirely restricted to Britain. However, races that are restricted to Britain are consistent with the pattern. *Plebejus argus caernensis* and *Hipparchia semele thyone* on limestone in North Wales, and *Papilio machaon britannicus* on remnant fenland in East Anglia, are localized and occur at high densities (Dennis, 1977; C. D. Thomas, 1993; Dempster, 1995). Endemics in the Atlas Mountains in Morocco tend to be localized, but with no obvious diminution of density (C. D. Thomas & Mallorie, 1985a,b), and tropical butterflies with narrow distributions are also relatively localized in human-modified landscapes (C. D. Thomas, 1991a; Hill, Hamer et al., 1995; Hamer et al., in press). Endemic races and species appear to be at risk by virtue of being localized within their narrow geographical ranges, rather than because they occur at lower local densities than other species.

Most species with narrow distributions restricted to Europe now occur in montane habitats, even though many of them would probably have been widespread during glacial periods (most of the past million years) (Dennis, 1993). Some of these species may have distributions that resemble those depicted in Fig. 6.1, with the environmental gradient associated with a change of altitude, rather than latitude. Such a species may be quite widely distributed at relatively high elevations, but most of the European land surface is at low elevation, and the species' geographic distribution is necessarily small. These are endemics with small core regions. For other endemics, ideal environments may not exist anywhere under present-day combinations of climate and habitats, even if such conditions are widespread during glacial periods. The entire distribution may look like one of the marginal graphs in Fig. 6.1. In both cases, the underlying environmental tolerances, or fundamental niches, of restricted species may be no narrower than those of widespread species; what distinguishes many of them from more widespread species may simply be that a lower percentage of the land surface currently fulfils their environmental requirements.

Given that species margins and the entire ranges of endemic species both tend to be characterized by localized populations, it is worth examining patterns of regional extinction in relation to range margins. The pattern is worrying. For British butterflies, the percentage loss of 10 km squares this century has tended to be highest for species with narrow distributions in Britain (Fig. 6.3; C. D. Thomas 1994a); i.e. for those closest to their range margins (this has partially reversed for some species recently, probably in response to climatic warming: Pollard & Eversham, 1995, cf. Parmesan, 1996, and the restoration of rabbit grazing on calcareous grasslands: J. A. Thomas, 1991; C. D. Thomas & Jones, 1993). Within species, percentage declines have been highest close to range margins (Heath et al., 1984). What is happening at a population level may be rather different. At the margin, there are few local populations per 10 km grid square, whereas in core areas there are many more. Therefore, the same percentage loss of local populations throughout a range may result in the loss of populations from entire grid squares near the margins, but not in core regions (C. D. Thomas & Abery, 1995). If many endemic species also have few local populations per unit area, they too can be expected to suffer substantial contractions of range in response to habitat degradation.

Conservation efforts are likely to be most cost-effective in regions where many large populations still exist, usually in the distributional core. For restricted species with small core regions, or none at all, more careful and detailed assessment is likely to be necessary. Global priorities should be to identify and conserve (i) locations which contain many species with narrow distributions, and (ii) parts of the world which support unusual numbers of species core regions.

## ENVIRONMENTAL STOCHASTICITY, POPULATION DYNAMICS AND SPECIES MARGINS

Conservation strategies also require knowledge of how population sizes and distributions change within any part of the range. Using transect counts of British butterflies, Pollard and Yates (1993) and Sutcliffe, Thomas and Moss (1996) found that populations of a single species tend to fluctuate in synchrony over hundreds or even thousands of kilometres; Hanski and Woiwod (1993) reached the same conclusion for aphids and moths. With the exception of a few migrant species, there is no possibility that the movements of individuals synchronize populations over such vast areas, so synchrony must be attributed to correlated climates. Dispersal can also synchronize dynamics, but usually over shorter distances. For butterflies, this appears to take place up to 0.5 km in very immobile species, like *P. argus* (C. D. Thomas, 1991*b*), to 1–4 km for most relatively sedentary and 'intermediate' species, through to 4–10 km for mobile species, and perhaps beyond for this last group (Sutcliffe, Thomas & Moss, 1996). This extra synchrony is on top of widespread climate-induced synchrony.

Given that climatic extremes are often implicated in population extinction, and that climate causes widespread population synchrony, climatic extremes could potentially remove species from regions as large as $10^4$ to $10^6$ km$^2$. This seems to be rare, which implies that populations may not all behave identically in response to environmental extremes. The niche model (Fig. 6.1) predicts that populations are likely to be relatively buffered

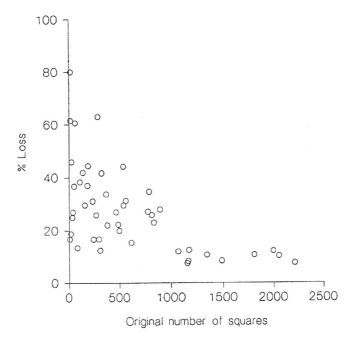

Fig. 6.3 Relationship between number of 10 km grid squares occupied
by different butterfly species in Britain, and percentage decline (from C. D.
Thomas 1994*a*, courtesy of Intercept Ltd.). Percentage loss is 1970–82
distributed divided by 1940–82 distribution (see C. D. Thomas 1994*a*
for further details).

in central parts of the species distribution. In a hot–dry year (we could talk
about any other environmental extreme), individuals may shift into cooler–
moister microhabitats nearby; populations already in relatively cool microhabitats may increase, while those in relatively hot microclimates decline.
In a cold year, the pattern is reversed. Whatever extreme environmental
event takes place, it is likely to be accommodated because populations may
potentially shift back and forth along locally available environmental gradients.

The buffering effect of different microclimates/habitats has been
shown most clearly in a study of grasshoppers, where local populations
which occupied heterogeneous patches (long and short grass) survived better than those in simpler habitats (all short or all long; Kindvall, 1995,
1996). In normal years, warm, short-grass microhabitats were favoured,
but populations fared better in long grass in a drought year. In woodland
ringlet butterflies, *Aphantopus hyperantus*, local populations which occurred

in habitats of intermediate shade fluctuated in close synchrony, but populations in sunny habitats did not fluctuate in close synchrony with those in relatively deep shade (Sutcliffe, Thomas, Yates & Greatorex-Davies, 1997). Several other butterfly examples also suggest that habitat heterogeneity may be important to persistence (Singer, 1972; Ehrlich *et al.*, 1980; Weiss, Murphy & White, 1988; Bourn & Thomas, 1993; C. D. Thomas, Singer & Boughton, 1996). These heterogeneous local dynamics appear to be nested within large-scale patterns of synchrony, and this may help to explain why climatic events which extirpate populations over wide areas rarely result in the extinction of every population in a region (Sutcliffe, Thomas, Yates *et al.*, 1996).

At their geographical margins, populations become increasingly localized in favourable microclimates (J. A. Thomas, 1993), and there is much less buffering. At the cool margin of a species' distribution, populations have nowhere to go in a cold year, and are likely to contract to the warmest available microhabitat (if any). In contrast, they may expand in numbers and spatial extent in warm years. At the warm margin, the species may contract in hot years and increase in cool or moist years. This lack of buffering leads to the prediction that populations will boom and bust near geographic range margins, both in absolute numbers and spatial extent, whereas core populations will be more stable. The same predictions have also been derived from possible differences in density-dependence processes between core and marginal populations (Hanski, Turchin *et al.*, 1993). Analysis of transect count data has confirmed that butterfly populations tend to fluctuate more at the margins than towards the core (J. A. Thomas, Moss & Pollard, 1994), and this is associated with an expansion of spatial extent in years of high abundances (O. L. Sutcliffe, C. D. Thomas & D. Moss, unpublished observations). In summary, the niche model successfully predicts differences in spatial dynamics towards range margins, as well as predicting changes in distributional patterns.

## METAPOPULATIONS AND HABITAT NETWORKS

Patchy distributions of potential breeding areas for a given species are generated by microclimatic requirements, host plant distributions and growth form, refuges to avoid natural enemies, and other physical and biotic features of the environment. We will subsume all these factors into 'habitat' in this section. As previously described, the niche model predicts that patchi-

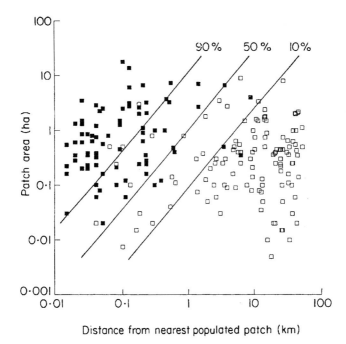

Fig. 6.4 Distribution of *Hesperia comma* skipper butterflies in relation to habitat patch area and isolation, in southern England. ■ Populated patches, □ vacant patches. Fitted lines give probabilities of patch occupancy in relation to area and isolation. From C. D. Thomas & Jones (1993), courtesy of Blackwell Science.

ness will occur throughout a species' range, but patches are predicted to be larger and closer together in core regions, and smaller and more widely spaced towards range margins. The next question is 'what proportion of these habitat patches will be occupied?'

Metapopulation theory provides one approach to this problem (Gilpin & Hanski, 1991; Hanski & Gilpin, 1997). In metapopulations, local populations occur in networks of habitat patches, connected by some relatively low level of dispersal. Each local population may be prone to extinction, but metapopulations persist provided that the rate of extinction does not exceed that of colonization. The equilibrium proportion of habitat patches occupied is determined by the rates of extinction and colonization which, in stable habitat networks, are determined largely by patch areas and distances between patches. Local populations in small habitat patches are prone to stochastic extinction because small patches contain few individuals and lack habitat heterogeneity. Empty habitat patches are most likely to be col-

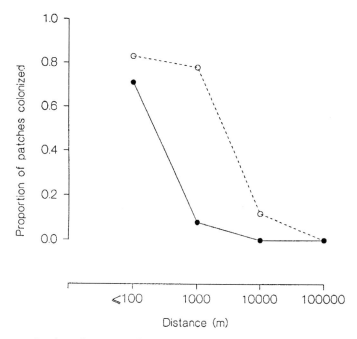

Fig. 6.5 Colonization of empty habitat in relation to distance from the nearest existing population of *Plebejus argus* (●, over 7 years) and *Hesperia comma* (○, over 9 years). 1000 represents distances of 101 to 1000 m, etc. From C. D. Thomas (1994*a*) courtesy of Intercept Ltd.

onized if they are close to large source populations. These dynamic processes of extinction and colonization produce a pattern that patches are likely to be populated if they are large and close together, and vacant if they are small and isolated.

For butterflies, these dynamics have been reviewed elsewhere (C. D. Thomas & Hanski, 1997), and only a brief summary follows. Studies of butterfly metapopulations consistently show that large and non-isolated habitat patches are most likely to be populated, and small and isolated patches are likely to be empty (Fig. 6.4). Much the same is true of many other taxa (Hanski & Gilpin, 1997). Where information is available, these patterns have been shown to be generated by relatively high rates of extinction from small and isolated patches, and relatively high rates of colonization of empty patches that are near to existing population sources (Fig. 6.5; C. D. Thomas & Hanski, 1997). The same patterns are obtained when one compares whole patch networks rather than individual patches; occupancy increases with average patch areas, and decreases with increasing average isolation (Hanski, Pakkala *et al.*, 1995; Hansky, Pöyry *et al.*, 1995). Below a certain mean patch area, and below a certain density of habitat patches in the landscape, butterfly metapopulations collapse. The closer patch networks are to these thresholds of area and isolation, the more unstable metapopulation dynamics become, potentially switching between alternative quasi-stable states of high and low patch occupancy, causing unstable dynamics at geographic margins and in some fragmented landscapes (Gyllenberg & Hanski, 1992; Hanski, Pöyry *et al.*, 1995). Even when patch networks meet the threshold requirements of mean patch area and isolation, there may be an additional requirement for some absolute amount of habitat to be present within each patch network. Studies of several butterfly species show that surviving metapopulations of butterflies usually occupy at least 15 to 20 habitat patches, whereas regions with fewer than ten patches are rarely populated. Again, this is roughly in accord with theoretical predictions of metapopulation models (Thomas & Hanski, 1997). No empirical or theoretical guidelines should be used in place of detailed assessment of a particular system; many more patches are needed if patches are small or dynamics are synchronous, but one enormous patch might occasionally suffice, especially if it is deliberately managed as a nature reserve to maintain continuity of high quality and heterogeneous habitat for a species.

These regional dynamics are nested within larger-scale distributions. Brown (1984) emphasized that the interaction of environmental gradients and species niches determines the distribution of suitable habitats, and the distribution of suitable habitats dominates species distributions at small scales (where individuals may be able to sample all potential habitats) and at very large scales (where the continental distribution of habitats determines the overall geographic range). In contrast, Hanski's (1982, 1985, 1991) core:satellite metapopulation hypothesis has emphasized the consequences of extinction and colonization dynamics at an intermediate scale. Although there has been some confusion in the literature, these two approaches are fully compatible. The niche model helps to generate the patchy distribution of habitats, and the metapopulation model is used to understand which will be populated.

Thus, patches will almost all be populated towards the centre of a species' distribution where patches are large and close together, and probably of higher overall quality (core), a relatively low and potentially unstable fraction will be populated near the range margin where patches are smaller and more widely spaced (satellite), and none of the habitat will be occupied

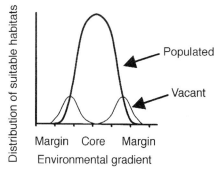

Fig. 6.6 Expected distribution of populated and vacant habitats in relation to position in the species range. The total distribution of habitats is obtained by adding the curves together. A high fraction of habitat is populated at the range core, with an increasing fraction of suitable habitat being empty towards the range margins.

where it is even more widely scattered, beyond the range margin (Fig. 6.6). These patterns are seen empirically in butterflies; the lower the proportion of the landscape that is occupied by suitable habitats, the lower the proportion of those suitable habitats is occupied. In terms of conservation, modern habitat fragmentation which decreases patch areas and increases spacing may be converting core regions into marginal or uninhabitable ones. But, detailed patterns are species-specific. Some species have specific adaptations (e.g. to rare host plants) which cause them to be extremely localized even at the centres of their distributions.

## VARIATIONS ON THE METAPOPULATION THEME

The conceptual basis of the metapopulation approach is that each local population has partial independence, that local extinction is determined predominantly by local birth and death, and that the main role of migration is to establish new local populations in empty patches. Following initial colonization, migration is typically assumed to have little impact on within-patch dynamics. In the remainder of this chapter, we will argue that patch-specific rates of emigration and immigration are also important determinants of local density and persistence. Despite this and other variations on the metapopulation theme, they do not modify the main message that it is difficult for populations to persist in regions where habitat patches are small and scattered.

Population biologists must ask how individuals as well as populations respond to habitat patchiness. The answer is complicated by the enormous range of mobility exhibited by different species; monarchs *Danaus plexippus* and painted ladies *Cynthia cardui* are transcontinental migrants, whereas silver-studded blues *Plebejus argus* and black hairstreaks *Strymonidia pruni* rarely fly further than 20–30 m per generation (C. D. Thomas, Thomas & Warren, 1992). In very mobile butterflies, each female may visit many potential habitat patches scattered across the landscape, and behaviourally decide where to lay her eggs. This sort of system is what Harrison (1991, 1994) termed a 'patchy population'. Others are not so mobile and many, most or all individuals may remain within one habitat patch; these are described as metapopulations or separate populations. Mobility and patch spacing vary continuously, so there is a continuum in spatial structure from practically no local reproduction in the natal habitat patch (patchy populations), through substantial local reproduction (metapopulations), to all reproduction in the natal patch (separate populations). This is well illustrated by studies of butterfly 'metapopulations', which have revealed exchange rates of individuals between nearby patches ranging from 1.4% to 30 or 40%, and these studies do not include investigations of isolated populations or of truly mobile species (C. D. Thomas & Hanski, 1997).

Exchange rates vary greatly because they are generated by the interaction of population mobility and spatial structure of the landscape. For example, habitat patches vary in isolation, and isolated habitat patches receive relatively few immigrants (Harrison, Murphy & Ehrlich, 1988; C. D. Thomas & Hanski, 1997; Hill, Thomas & Lewis, 1996). Patches also vary in area, and large patches usually generate and receive relatively large numbers of migrants (Hill, Thomas *et al.*, 1996; Sutcliffe, Thomas & Peggie, 1997). However, as patch area increases, local population size (proportional to patch $r^2$) increases faster than the numbers of emigrants and immigrants (proportional to $r$), which results in lower per capita emigration and immigration rates for larger patches (Fig. 6.7; Hill, Thomas *et al.*, 1996). Thus, small patches which are close together have a stream of individuals entering and leaving them, whereas larger and more isolated patches patches in the same population system may retain most individuals (Hill, Thomas *et al.*, 1996; Sutcliffe, Thomas & Peggie, 1997). In the remainder of this chapter, we use the term metapopulation rather loosely to describe these complex, spatially structured population systems. The important point is that birth, death, emigration and immigration may all be important determinants of local population size, and hence local persistence. The rela-

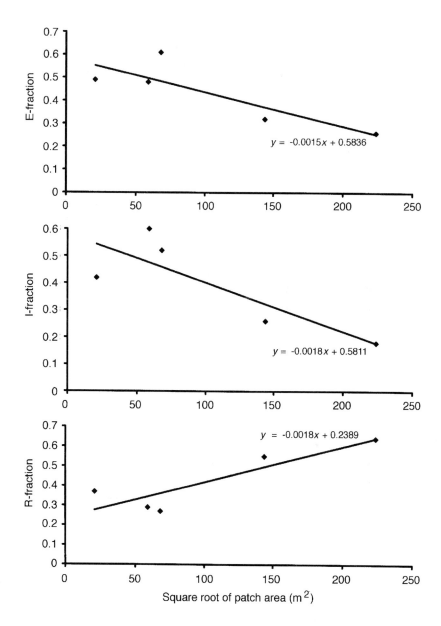

Fig. 6.7 Per capita emigration (E-fraction), immigration (I-fraction) and residence (R-fraction) by *Aphantopus hyperantus* in relation to patch area, from mark–release–recapture within one metapopulation. Fractions differed significantly among patches ($P < 0.001$). From Sutcliffe, Thomas & Peggie (1997), courtesy of Springer-Verlag.

tive importance of these factors will depend on the species and landscape in question.

As an aside, the habitat matrix may be dynamic itself, and dominate the dynamics of butterfly species associated with transient successional vegetation or when habitats suffer from continuing attrition (Warren, 1987; J. A. Thomas, 1991; C. D. Thomas, 1994a,b, 1995; C. D. Thomas & Hanski, 1997). So, the habitat matrix is one driving force in spatial change, as is the changing distribution of suitable microhabitats caused by environmental stochasticity (above). These two factors generate a shifting topography of rates of population increase, and decrease (in sink habitats), in any landscape. Thus, the 'traditional' metapopulation dynamics of stochastic local extinctions and recolonizations must be superimposed on a potentially dynamic habitat matrix. When habitat dynamics drive butterfly spatial change, as they usually do in Britain, all of the general conclusions concerning the need for substantial habitat networks still hold. In fact, they are reinforced. Where species occupy ever more precise microhabitats at their range margins, they are likely to be especially susceptible to subtle changes in the vegetation and microclimate, e.g. slight changes of grazing which bring about rapid changes in local microclimates at ground level.

## DISPERSAL AND ISOLATION

Fragmented landscapes often contain small groups of habitat patches and isolated habitats; of these, local populations are usually restricted to groups of patches (C. D. Thomas, Thomas et al., 1992). Metapopulation models of stochastic extinction and colonization provide part of the explanation for why butterflies are restricted to patch networks, but not all of it. Stochastic metapopulation and single-population models predict that some isolated populations may take many years to become extinct. Why do we not observe more recently isolated populations waiting to go extinct?

In conventional models, extinction of isolated populations, and of local populations within metapopulations, takes place when local birth rates fail to match local death rates (Hanski & Gilpin, 1997). Few metapopulation models consider the balance of immigration and emigration from individual patches. If migration is considered, it is usually regarded as a 'good thing' because it promotes colonization and a few immigrants reduce the probability that small populations will become extinct (the rescue effect; Brown & Kodric-Brown, 1977; Hanski, 1991). Emigration and immigration rates can also be important determinants of local population size.

In contrast, in the early to mid-1980s, emigration was thought to increase extinction risk in single isolated populations because the drain of emigrants could lead to population collapse (e.g. Game, 1980; Buechner, 1987; Stamps, Buechner & Krishnan, 1987). This is analagous to harvesting a natural population because emigrants which are not replaced by immigrants are equivalent to individuals which have been culled: if too high a number or fraction of the population is culled, the population may decline and become extinct (e.g. Crawley, 1992). That emigration could directly cause population collapse does have a parallel in metapopulation models – if metapopulation-wide levels of dispersal are set too high, for example, because distances between habitat patches are high, the metapopulation will collapse when birth within local populations cannot sustain high system-wide mortality during migration (Lande, 1988; Hanski & Zhang, 1993). Given that migration in isolated and fragmented landscapes may have both positive and negative effects, an important task is to identify the circumstances under which dispersal enhances or threatens population and metapopulation persistence.

In this section, we consider two butterflies, *Plebejus argus* and *Hesperia comma*. Within each metapopulation of these species, there is considerable variation in degree of isolation. Some local populations are low tens of metres from their nearest neighbour, whereas others are isolated by hundreds of metres (in the case of *P. argus*) or a few kilometres (in the case of *H. comma*) (C. D. Thomas & Harrison, 1992; C. D. Thomas, Thomas *et al.*, 1992; C. D. Thomas & Jones, 1993). Although all patches may generate emigrants, rates of immigration can be expected to vary substantially; in the central part of each metapopulation, numbers of immigrants into a patch may nearly match (and sometimes exceed) numbers of emigrants, but numbers of emigrants will greatly exceed numbers of immigrants in semi-isolated local populations at the margins of a metapopulation. We consider here whether emigration acts as a drain on isolated and semi-isolated local populations at the margins of metapopulations, and whether this process could be an important determinant of species distributions in fragmented landscapes, and at range margins.

### Model for isolated populations

Emigrants lost from truly isolated populations are not replaced by immigrants. In a population with discrete generations, population changes can be described by

$$N_{t+1} = RN_t \, e^{r(1-RN_t/K)} \tag{1}$$

where $N_t$ is the number of individuals in generation $t$, $r$ is the intrinsic rate of population increase, and $K$ is the carrying capacity in the absence of emigration. $R$ can be thought of as the proportion of individuals which are resident within the population (those which do not emigrate), but strictly it is the average fraction of reproductive effort that individuals emerging or being born into a patch make in their natal patch.

Equilibrium population size is $(K/R)(1 + [\ln R]/r)$ with extinction when $[\ln R]/r < -1$. The population goes extinct when local breeding success fails to replace the fraction lost to emigration. Even when $[\ln R]/r > -1$, depression of local population size by emigration can make isolated populations more susceptible to demographic and environmental stochasticity, and $[\ln R]/r$ values close to $-1$ will reduce rates of population recovery following environmental extremes.

### Parameterizing the model

We parameterized $K$, $r$ and $R$ for *H. comma* and *P. argus*. Values for $K$ were estimated by multiplying area by the mean density in large patches where emigration would be low. Densities were measured using standard transect counts which are correlated with actual population density (J. A. Thomas 1983): 490 adults $ha^{-1}$ for *H. comma* in patches $\geq 14$ ha in 1982 (J. A. Thomas, Thomas et al., 1986); 2128 adults $ha^{-1}$ for *P. argus* in patches $\geq 5$ ha in 1983 (C. D. Thomas, 1983).

For intrinsic rates of population increase, $r = 0.92$ was used for *H. comma*, the empirical value obtained from fixed transect counts used to monitor the natural expansion of a population following colonization of a large area of previously unoccupied habitat, Old Winchester Hill in Hampshire, England, from an extant population on Beacon Hill (C. D. Thomas & Jones, 1993; M. Finnemore, unpublished data). In the absence of comparable data for *P. argus*, $r = 1.17$ was used, based on population expansion of a related butterfly, *Lysandra bellargus*, following its introduction to good-quality habitat, also at Old Winchester Hill (J. A. Thomas, unpublished data).

Reliably estimating the area-dependent fractions of individuals which remain in ($R$) or emigrate from ($M$) local populations was more difficult. Mark–Release–Recapture (MRR) consistently reveals higher *per capita* rates of emigration from small than from larger patches, including in *H. comma* (Hill, Thomas et al., 1996) and *A. hyperantus* (Fig. 6.7; Sutcliffe,

Thomas & Peggie, 1997). However, emigrants were recorded only when they immigrated successfully into other patches, so we failed to detect mortality during dispersal and individuals that left the entire study area. We underestimated true emigration rates. Thus, we adopted a second approach. We obtained data on the distribution of distances moved by *H. comma* from MRR (Fig. 6.8; Hill, Thomas *et al.*, 1996). To obtain a distribution of distances moved by *P. argus*, observations of their distribution were made over two weeks, following release at a single point in May/June 1993, at Llanymynech Hill, Powys, UK (Fig. 6.8).

We then simulated the proportion of individuals which would be expected to emigrate, *M*, from patches of different areas. We 'placed' butterflies at random positions within a habitat patch, and allowed them to 'fly' at a random angle for a distance chosen at random from the empirical distribution of dispersal distances given in Fig. 6.8. Parameter *M* was the mean fraction of butterflies leaving the patch (10 replicates for each area). The results show a strong relationship between patch area and emigration, with high proportions of individuals lost from small patches (Fig. 6.8). We were pleased by the qualitative similarity between MRR and the simulation, and also by the quantitative difference (higher estimates of emigration from the simulation). Using the simulation approach, emigration (*M*) was negatively related to patch area, allowing us to parameterize residence (*R*) in Equation 1 in relation to patch area ($R = 1 - M$).

We assumed patch boundaries to be fully permeable in the simulation, which may lead to an overestimate of the emigration fraction. However, the empirically measured distribution of distances moved in Fig. 6.8 shows *net* displacement: the actual tracks followed by these butterflies before they were recaptured may have been complex, and some of those recorded as having low displacement may have encountered a patch boundary and have turned back as a result. Opposing this, the underestimated proportion of individuals recorded in the longest distance classes in Fig. 6.8 (because of individuals that leave the entire study area) is likely to lead to an underestimate of the emigration fraction. Unfortunately, we cannot tell which bias is the greater. Direct observations of *H. comma* individuals that we followed suggest that even the simulated emigration rates may be conservative. Notwithstanding some uncertainty concerning the exact level of emigration, per capita emigration rates are clearly higher from relatively small patches, so the predictions that follow should be qualitatively robust, even if they are not quantitatively exact.

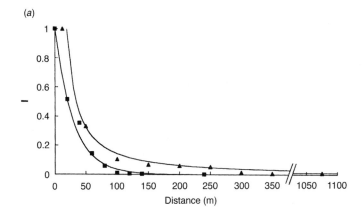

(a)

(b)

Fig. 6.8 (a) The distribution of dispersal distances of *Hesperia comma* ▲, $n = 133$ movements) and *Plebejus argus* (■, $n = 637$ movements). Fitted dispersal functions:

*H. comma*: $\ln I = -4.69 - 1.19 \ln D$, $F_{1,8} = 230.23$, $P < 0.0001$, $r^2 = 0.98$
*P. argus*: $\ln I = -31.94 D$, $F_{1,8} = 334.32$, $P < 0.0001$, $r^2 = 0.98$

weighted regressions, where $I$ is the fraction of individuals reaching $\geq$ distance $D$ in km.

(b) Estimated fractions of emigrants ($M$) of *H. comma* (▲) and *P. argus* (■), in relation to $\text{Log}_{10}$ patch area ($A$, in ha). Patches used in simulations were square. Fitted lines were:

*H. comma*: $\ln(\text{Arcsin}\sqrt{M}) = 3.834 - 0.416 \ln\sqrt{A}$; $F_{1,5} = 4584$, $P < 0.0001$, $r^2 = 0.999$
*P. argus*: $\text{Arcsin}\sqrt{M} = 35.024 + 14.280 \ln\sqrt{A}$; $F_{1,8} = 1441$, $P < 0.0001$, $r^2 = 0.995$.

## Model predictions

Using the parameter values described, we could then use Equation 1 to estimate the relationship between habitat patch area and predicted equilibrium population size. Equation 1 predicted that the minimum area that can be populated is about 0.63 ha for *H. comma*, and 0.052 ha for *P. argus* (Fig. 6.9), with the more sedentary nature of *P. argus* being the main reason why it can survive in smaller patches. On Fig. 6.9, we have also plotted the actual measured population sizes for both butterfly species in habitat patches around the margins of existing metapopulations (where immigration rates will be very low, or zero). The match between predicted and actual population sizes is striking. For *H. comma*, four vacant patches above the threshold were populated historically, but became extinct during an unfavourable period for *H. comma* when habitats were temporarily overgrown; i.e., when habitat quality dramatically declined (J. A. Thomas, Thomas *et al.*, 1986; C. D. Thomas & Jones, 1993; Hanski & Thomas, 1994). These sites may yet be recolonized as part of normal metapopulation dynamics. For *P. argus*, the populated site below the threshold was extinct by 1990. Given that there will be variation in habitat quality between patches, and that emigration rates will depend on additional factors such as the nature of the surrounding vegetation, we are encouraged by the accuracy of the model predictions.

Our results suggest that isolated patches of good potential breeding habitat can fail to be populated because emigration rates are too high for local breeding success (plus low levels of immigration, if any) to replace. This effect of emigration is consistent with the widespread observation that isolated populations are prone to extinction (Brown & Kodric-Brown, 1977; Hanski, 1991; Hanski, Pakkala *et al.*, 1995; Sjögren, 1991; Sjögren Gulve, 1994; Ouberg, 1993; C. D. Thomas & Jones, 1993). Patches of habitat below the critical threshold size will be inhabited only when they are close to sources of immigrants which offset losses to emigration.

We conclude that the immigration:emigration balance of different habitat patches may be an important determinant of regional distribution, and has important implications for conservation. (i) Populations within nature reserves may decline or become extinct if populations are eliminated elsewhere, removing sources of immigrants. (ii) Reduction of area or deterioration of local habitat quality that reduces $R$ or local breeding success can potentially decrease $[\ln R]/r$ to $< -1$, resulting in deterministic extinction. For insects and vertebrates which are more mobile than the two butterflies

(a)

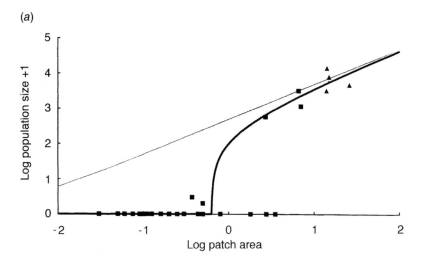

(b)

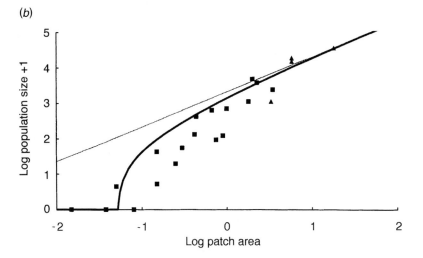

Fig. 6.9 Predicted and actual population sizes in relation to $Log_{10}$ patch area (ha) for (a) *H. comma* and (b) *P. argus*. Thin line = *K*, the predicted population size in the absence of emigration. Thick line = predicted patch occupancy and population sizes according to Equation 1. One has been added to all measured and predicted population sizes, so that zero values can be plotted. (a) ■ Measured *H. comma* population sizes on chalk (soft limestone) hills in a 150

we studied, or which have lower intrinsic rates of increase, thresholds may often exceed the areas of habitat fragments, nature reserves and national parks in modern landscapes (e.g. Stamps *et al.*, 1987). In this case, metapopulations must be conserved in networks of habitat patches and reserves (e.g. Caughley, 1994; C. D. Thomas, 1994*a,b*). (iii) Successful population establishment following colonization may only take place in relatively large habitat patches, as has been found in *H. comma* (C. D. Thomas & Jones, 1993), and species recovery programmes which involve translocations may fail if released individuals are dissipated too widely.

Imagine now an entire metapopulation which is isolated from other metapopulations. The same principle can operate at this scale. We just need to consider the fraction of individuals resident in the entire metapopulation (emigrants from patches that arrive in other patches within the metapopulation are treated as residents; those that leave the entire metapopulation or die in transit between patches are treated as emigrants from the system). If patches are small, with high emigration rates, and scattered so that there are low immigration rates, metapopulation-wide losses to migration may be too high for local breeding success within populated patches to support (see Hanski & Zhang, 1993). Consideration of the balance of emigration: immigration leads to two general conclusions, that conservation must be of large areas that are individually well above the habitat threshold area, or of metapopulations where patches are close together, and migrant mortality is low. The more mobile a species, the greater the importance of mortality during migration as a determinant of regional abundance and persistence, leading to the prediction that mobile species will be relatively prone to declines in local population density towards range margins (as seen in Table 6.1) and in other marginal landscapes. Metapopulations and regional populations of more mobile species may collapse very

Caption for Fig. 6.9 (*cont.*)

by 100 km region of south-east England in 1991; ▲ additional sites monitored in 1982 and used to estimate *K* density. Patches were 0.6 to 5 km from the nearest (other) population*.
(*b*) ■ Measured *P. argus* population sizes on limestone hills in a 20 by 10 km region of north Wales in 1983; ▲ sites used to estimate *K* density. Patches were 0.06 to 0.8 km from the nearest (other) population*.
* Habitat patches which are sufficiently isolated that immigration is likely to have negligible effects on local density, but not so isolated that sites could not be colonized in time by occasional migrants; based on dispersal distances and observed colonization distances. Less and more isolated habitat patches are not included.

rapidly beyond a certain level of habitat fragmentation, with the last populations going deterministically extinct because losses to migration are too high. In conclusion, habitat fragmentation that causes habitat patches to be smaller and further apart is likely to increase the ratio of emigration to immigration, and may contribute to reduced densities and persistence in naturally and anthropogenically fragmented landscapes.

## CONCLUSIONS

Niche models give insight into the distributions of suitable breeding habitats within landscapes, and metapopulation and patch-migration models give insight into which of these will be populated. Effective conservation often requires an understanding of both. We need to establish the habitat needs of rare and endangered species, evaluate the distribution (in space and time) of habitats and resources, and measure or infer the mobility of individuals and populations in relation to habitat networks. Much still needs to be learned about the details of spatially structured populations, but the message is usually similar if we want to develop conservation strategies. The most important principle is that the best chances of long-term success are likely to come from maintaining populations in areas where they are doing relatively well, in high-quality habitats (including any need for habitat heterogeneity), and in regions where there are many large breeding areas connected by dispersal. Patches should be close enough that colonization of empty habitat is rapid and that mortality during migration is low. These circumstances are most likely to be found near the core of a species' distribution, although some very substantial and persistent metapopulations can be found where extensive patch networks survive close to range margins. This sounds obvious, but it is frequently the opposite of conservation practice, where enormous effort is routinely taken to protect the last population of quite widespread species in regions where they are marginal. Regional conservation should prioritize the conservation of species/habitats for which that region is internationally important (see Williams, this volume), and deal with marginal areas of widespread species only if there are resources to spare.

An important caveat is that climate change may cause some marginal areas to become core regions, and core regions to become margins (Parmesan, 1996). A second caveat is that quite degraded landscapes may still be of great importance to global conservation – when it is all that is left. Conservation biologists and managers should not abandon degraded landscapes simply because they have lost their megavertebrates. Habitat fragments that seem small to vertebrate ecologists may support strong and persistent local populations of many insect species, as they do for some plants (Turner & Corlett, 1996). These may be of considerable importance in regions with high levels of endemism. None the less, conservation of populations in degraded landscapes is likely to be harder and more expensive than conserving them in less damaged regions.

Despite an increasing appreciation of the patterns and processes of local and regional extinction in butterflies and other insects, we do not know the number or proportion of species that are threatened by global extinction. Most insect species considered at risk of global extinction are localized endemics, with island species being most heavily represented on red lists. For example, 22 out of 28 swallowtail species listed as 'endangered' or 'vulnerable' live on islands (Collins & Morris, 1985). Whether the much larger numbers of localized continental insect species are also at risk of global extinction remains unknown. These species are potentially susceptible to habitat loss throughout their geographical ranges, and they may also be threatened by climate change. The level of threat may depend on whether these species have small distributional cores (where they may be quite 'safe'), or whether their distributions are all marginal (ideal climates/habitats do not currently exist). It will never be possible to evaluate the threats to every localized species, but there is a clear need for detailed studies of example taxa. More optimistically, it is feasible to identify global patterns of butterfly diversity and endemism. Because endemics can often be found together on islands and in mountain ranges, effective conservation of substantial habitat networks over a relatively small proportion of the earth's surface may protect a disproportionate number of endangered species (e.g. Groombridge, 1992; Gaston & Williams, 1996; Williams, this volume).

## ACKNOWLEDGEMENTS

We thank R. Wilson, M. Brookes, M. Crawley, Y. Graneau, I. Hanski, W. Kunin, J. Lawton, J. Mallet, J. Prendergast and O. Rose for various contributions. We were supported by NERC grants GR3/A9107 and GST/04/1211.

## References

Bourn, N. A. D. & Thomas, J. A. (1993). The ecology and conservation of the brown argus butterfly *Aricia agestis* in Britain. *Biol. Conserv.*, **63**, 67–74.

Brown, J. H. (1984). On the relationship between abundance and distribution of species. *Am. Nat.*, **124**, 255–79.

Brown, J. H. & Kodric-Brown, A. (1977). Turnover rates in insular biogeography: effects of immigration on extinction. *Ecology*, **58**, 445–9.

Buechner, M. (1987). Conservation in insular parks: simulation models of factors affecting the movement of animals across park boundaries. *Biol. Conserv.*, **41**, 57–76.

Caughley, G. (1994). Directions in conservation biology. *J. Anim. Ecol.*, **63**, 215–44.

Collins, N. M. & Morris, M. G. (1985). *Threatened swallowtail butterflies of the world.* IUCN, Gland.

Crawley, M. J. (1992). Population dynamics of natural enemies and their prey. In *Natural enemies: the population biology of predators, parasites and diseases*: 40–89. (Ed. Crawley, M. J.). Blackwell Scientific Publications, Oxford.

Dempster, J. P. (1995). The ecology and conservation of *Papilio machaon* in Britain. In *Ecology and conservation of butterflies*: 137–149. (Ed. Pullin, A. S.). Chapman & Hall, London.

Dennis, R. L. H. (1977). *The British butterflies: their origin and establishment.* Classey, Faringdon.

Dennis, R. L. H. (1993). *Butterflies and climate change.* University Press, Manchester.

Ehrlich, P. R., Murphy, D. D., Singer, M. C., Sherwood, C. B., White, R. R. & Brown, I. L. (1980). Extinction, reduction, stability and increase: the responses of checkerspot butterfly (*Euphydryas*) populations to the California drought. *Oecologia*, **46**, 101–5.

Emmet, A. M. & Heath, J. (Eds) (1990). *The moths and butterflies of Great Britain and Ireland Hesperidae – Nymphalidae. The butterflies*, **7**(1). Harley Books, Colchester.

Game, M. (1980). Best shapes for nature reserves. *Nature, Lond.*, **287**, 630–2.

Gaston, K. J. & Lawton, J. H. (1990). Effects of scale and habitat on the relationship between regional distribution and local abundance. *Oikos*, **58**, 329–35.

Gaston, K. J. & Williams, P. H. (1996). Spatial patterns of taxonomic diversity. In *Biodiversity: a biology of numbers and difference*: 202–229 (Ed. Gaston, K. J. Blackwell Science, Oxford.

Gilpin, M. & Hanski, I. (Eds) (1991). *Metapopulation dynamics: empirical and theoretical investigations.* Academic Press, London.

Groombridge, B. (Ed.) (1992). *Global biodiversity: status of the Earth's living resources.* Chapman & Hall, London.

Gutiérrez, D. & Menéndez, R. (1995). Distribution and abundance of butterflies in a mountain area in the northern Iberian peninsula. *Ecography*, **18**, 209–16.

Gyllenberg, M. & Hanski, I. (1992). Single-species metapopulation dynamics: a structured model. *Theor. Pop. Biol.*, **42**, 35–61.

Hamer, K. C., Hill, J. K., Lace, L. A. & Langan, A. M. (1998). Ecological and biogeographical effects of forest disturbance on tropical butterflies of Sumba, Indonesia. *J. Biogeogr.* (in press).

Hanski, I. (1982). Dynamics of regional distribution: the core and satellite species hypothesis. *Oikos*, **38**, 210–21.

Hanski, I. (1985). Single-species spatial dynamics may contribute to long-term rarity and commonness. *Ecology*, **66**, 335–43.

Hanski, I. (1991). Single-species metapopulation dynamics: concepts, models and observations. *Biol. J. Linn. Soc.*, **42**, 17–38.

Hanski, I. A & Gilpin, M. E. (1997). *Metapopulation biology: ecology, genetics, and evolution.* Academic Press, San Diego.

Hanski, I., Pakkala, T., Kuussaari, M. & Lei, G. (1995). Metapopulation persistence of an endangered butterfly in a fragmented landscape. *Oikos*, **72**, 21–8.

Hanski, I., Pöyry, J., Pakkala, T. & Kuussaari, M. (1995). Multiple equilibria in metapopulation dynamics. *Nature, Lond.*, **337**, 618–21.

Hanski, I. & Thomas, C. D. (1994). Metapopulation dynamics and conservation: a spatially explicit model applied to butterflies. *Biol. Conserv.*, 68, 167–80.

Hanski, I., Turchin, P., Korpimäki, E. & Hentonnen, H. (1993). Population oscillations of boreal rodents: regulation by mustelid predators leads to chaos. *Nature, Lond.*, **364**, 232–5.

Hanski, I. & Woiwod, I. P. (1993). Spatial synchrony in the dynamics of moth and aphid populations. *J. Anim. Ecol.*, **62**, 656–68.

Hanski, I. & Zhang, D.-Y. (1993). Migration, metapopulation dynamics and fugitive co-existence. *J. theor. Biol.*, **163**, 491–504.

Harrison, S. (1991). Local extinction in a metapopulation context: an empirical evaluation. *Biol. J. Linn. Soc.*, **42**, 73–88.

Harrison, S. (1994). Metapopulations and conservation. In *Large scale ecology and conservation biology*: 111–128. (Eds Edwards, P. J., May, R. M. & Webb, N.). Blackwell Scientific Publications, Oxford.

Harrison, S., Murphy, D. D. & Ehrlich, P. R. (1988). Distribution of the Bay checkerspot butterfly, *Euphydryas editha bayensis*: evidence for a metapopulation model. *Am. Nat.*, **132**, 360–82.

Heath, J., Pollard E. & Thomas, J. A. (1984). *Atlas of butterflies in Britain and Ireland.* Viking, Harmondsworth.

Hengeveld, R. & Haeck, J. (1982). The distribution of abundance. I. Measurements. *J. Biogeogr.*, 9, 303–16.

Higgins, L. G. & Riley, N. D. (1980). *A field guide to the butterflies of Britain and Europe.* (4th edn). Collins, London.

Hill, J. K., Hamer, K. C., Lace, L. A. & Banham, W. M. T. (1995). Effects of selective logging on tropical forest butterflies on Buru, Indonesia. *J. appl. Ecol.*, **32**, 754–60.

Hill, J. K., Thomas, C. D. & Lewis, O. T. (1996). Effects of habitat patch size and isolation on dispersal by *Hesperia comma* butterflies: implications for metapopulation structure. *J. Anim. Ecol.*, **65**, 725–35.

Jordano, D., Retamosa, E. C. & Fernández Haeger, J. (1991). Factors facilitating the continued presence of *Colotis evagore* (Klug, 1829) in southern Spain. *J. Biogeogr.*, **18**, 637–46.

Kindvall, O. (1995). The impact of extreme weather on habitat preference and survival in a metapopulation of the bush cricket *Metrioptera bicolor* in Sweden. *Biol. Conserv.*, **73**, 51–8.

Kindvall, O. (1996). Habitat heterogeneity and survival in a bush cricket metapopulation. *Ecology*, **77**, 207–14.

Lande, R. (1988). Demographic models of the northern spotted owl (*Strix occidentalis caurina*). *Oecologia*, **75**, 601–7.

Lawton, J. H. (1995). Population dynamic principles. In *Extinction rates*: 147–163. (Eds Lawton, J. H. & May, R. M.). Oxford University Press, Oxford.

Ouberg, N. J. (1993). Isolation, population size and extinction: the classical and metapopulation approaches applied to vascular plants along the Dutch Rhine-system. *Oikos*, **66**, 298–308.

Parmesan, C. (1996). Climate and species' range. *Nature, Lond.*, **382**, 765–6.

Pollard, E. & Eversham, B. C. (1995). Butterfly monitoring 2 – interpreting the changes. In *Ecology and conservation of butterflies*: 23–36. (Ed. Pullin, A. S.). Chapman & Hall, London.

Pollard, E., Hall, M. L. & Bibby, T. J. (1986). *Monitoring the abundance of butterflies, 1976–1985*. Nature Conservancy Council, Peterborough.

Pollard, E. & Yates, T. J. (1993). *Monitoring butterflies for ecology and conservation. The British butterfly monitoring scheme*. Chapman & Hall, London.

Singer, M. C. (1972). Complex components of habitat suitability within a butterfly colony. *Science*, **176**, 75–7.

Sjögren, P. (1991). Extinction and isolation gradients in metapopulations: the case of the pool frog (*Rana lessonae*). *Biol. J. Linn. Soc.*, **42**, 135–47.

Sjögren Gulve, P. (1994). Distribution and extinction patterns within a northern metapopulation of the pool frog, *Rana lessonae*. *Ecology*, **75**, 1357–67.

Stamps, J. A., Buechner, M. & Krishnan, V. V. (1987). The effects of edge-permeability and habitat geometry on emigration from patches of habitat. *Am. Nat.*, **129**, 533–52.

Sutcliffe, O. L., Thomas, C. D. & Moss, D. (1996). Synchrony and asynchrony in butterfly population dynamics. *J. Anim. Ecol.*, **65**, 85–95.

Sutcliffe, O. L., Thomas, C. D. & Peggie, D. (1997). Area-dependent migration by ringlet butterflies generates a mixture of patchy population and metapopulation attributes. *Oecologia*, **109**, 229–34.

Sutcliffe, O. L., Thomas, C. D., Yates, T. J. & Greatorex-Davies, J. N. (1997). Correlated extinctions, colonizations and population fluctuations in a highly correlated ringlet butterfly metapopulation. *Oecologia*, **109**, 235–41.

Svensson, B. W. (1992). Changes in occupancy, niche breadth and abundance of three *Gyrinus* species as their respective range limits are approached. *Oikos*, **63**, 147–56.

Thomas, C. D. (1983). *The ecology and status of* Plebejus argus *(Lepidoptera: Lycaenidae) in north-west Britain*. MSc thesis: University of Wales, Bangor.

Thomas, C. D. (1991a). Habitat use and geographic ranges of butterflies from the wet lowlands of Costa Rica. *Biol. Conserv.*, **55**, 269–81.

Thomas, C. D. (1991b). Spatial and temporal variability in a butterfly population. *Oecologia*, **87**, 577–80.

Thomas, C. D. (1993). The silver-studded blue, *Plebejus argus* L. In *The conservation biology of Lycaenidae (butterflies)*: 97–99. (Ed. New, T. R.). IUCN, Gland. (*Occ. Pap. IUCN SSC* 8.)

Thomas, C. D. (1994*a*). Local extinctions, colonizations and distributions: habitat tracking by British butterflies. In *Individuals, populations and patterns in ecology*: 319–336. (Eds Leather, S. R., Watt, A. D., Mills, N. J. & Walters, K. F. A.) Intercept Ltd., Andover.

Thomas, C. D. (1994*b*). Extinction, colonization and metapopulations: environmental tracking by rare species. *Conserv. Biol.*, **8**, 373–8.

Thomas, C. D. (1995). Ecology and conservation of butterfly metapopulations in the fragmented British landscape. In *Ecology and conservation of butterflies*: 46–63. (Ed. Pullin, A. S.). Chapman & Hall, London.

Thomas, C. D. & Abery, J. C. G. (1995). Estimating rates of butterfly decline from distribution maps: the effect of scale. *Biol. Conserv.*, **73**, 59–65.

Thomas, C. D. & Hanski, I. (1997). Butterfly metapopulations. In *Metapopulation biology: ecology, genetics and evolution*: 359–86 (Eds Hanski, I. & Gilpin, M. E.). Academic Press, London.

Thomas, C. D. & Harrison, S. (1992). Spatial dynamics of a patchily-distributed butterfly species. *J. Anim. Ecol.*, **61**, 437–46.

Thomas, C. D. & Jones, T. M. (1993). Partial recovery of a skipper butterfly (*Hesperia comma*) from population refuges: lessons for conservation in a fragmented landscape. *J. Anim. Ecol.*, **62**, 472–81.

Thomas, C. D. & Mallorie, H. C. (1985*a*). Rarity, species richness and conservation: butterflies of the Atlas mountains in Morocco. *Biol. Conserv.*, **33**, 95–117.

Thomas, C. D. & Mallorie, H. C. (1985*b*). On the altitudes of Moroccan butterflies. *Entomologists' mon. Mag.*, **121**, 253–56.

Thomas, C. D., Singer, M. C. & Boughton, D. A. (1996). Catastrophic extinction of population sources in a 'source-pseudosink' butterfly metapopulation. *Am. Nat.*, **148**, 957–75.

Thomas, C. D., Thomas, J. A. & Warren, M. S. (1992). Distributions of occupied and vacant butterfly habitats in fragmented landscapes. *Oecologia*, **92**, 563–7.

Thomas, J. A. (1983). A quick method of estimating butterfly numbers during surveys. *Biol. Conserv.*, 27, 195–211.

Thomas, J. A. (1991). Rare species conservation: case studies of European butterflies. *Symp. Br. Ecol. Soc.*, **31**, 149–97.

Thomas, J. A. (1993). Holocene climate changes and warm man-made refugia may explain why a sixth of British butterflies possess unnatural early-successional habitats. *Ecography*, **16**, 278–84.

Thomas, J. A. & Lewington, R. (1991). *The butterflies of Britain and Ireland*. Dorling Kindersley, London.

Thomas, J. A., Moss, D. & Pollard, E. (1994). Increased fluctuations of butterfly populations towards the northern edges of species' ranges. *Ecography*, **17**, 215–20.

Thomas, J. A., Thomas, C. D., Simcox, D. J. & Clarke, R. T. (1986). Ecology and declining status of the silver-spotted skipper butterfly (*Hesperia comma*) in Britain. *J. appl. Ecol.*, **23**, 365–80.

Turner, I. M. & Corlett, R. T. (1996). The conservation value of small isolated fragments of lowland tropical forest. *Trends Ecol. Evol.*, **11**, 330–3.

Warren, M. S. (1987). The ecology and conservation of the heath fritillary butterfly, *Mellicta athalia*. III. Population dynamics and the effect of habitat management. *J. appl. Ecol.*, **24**, 499–513.

Weiss, S. B., Murphy, D. D. & White, R. R. (1988). Sun, slope and butterflies: topographic determinants of habitat quality for *Euphydryas editha*. *Ecology*, **69**, 1486–96.

# Continent-wide conservation priorities and diversification processes

JON FJELDSÅ AND CARSTEN RAHBEK

## INTRODUCTION

The conservation of key areas for biodiversity may conflict with poverty-driven pressures to convert these habitats to agriculture, or with national development strategies where forest resources are converted to cash to support rapid industrialization. The success of conservation efforts therefore depends on how precisely we can identify unique biological communities which would be damaged by new development initiatives, and how well we can advise planners about designation of land for conservation or for development.

Identification of fully representative networks of target areas for conservation requires good data about how biodiversity is distributed (see Williams this volume). However, urgency and the prohibitive costs of complete charting force us to search for acceptable compromises between accuracy and the use of proxy data. In the present study the generality of the results can be evaluated by comparing four families of birds which differ in their ecological requirements. Our study covers South America, which is the richest continent biologically, and includes the single richest biome (at the species level): the Amazon rainforest. This biome often features as the top priority on the global conservation agenda. The Amazon basin has just over 1000 species of breeding birds and alpha diversities of up to 233 species per square kilometre (Terborgh *et al.*, 1990). However, as shown by Rahbek (1995, 1997), the magnitude of this species pool is partly a result of the enormous area of the biome (see also Terborgh, 1973; Mares, 1992).

We will evaluate the myths about Amazonia as a focal area for conservation by examining the variation in species richness and endemism in a 1° grid system for each family and will identify fully representative minimum sets of areas which include all species.

Fortunately, the majority of South American species are sufficiently widespread that they can be conserved at low cost, e.g. in areas with low human population densities. However, the cost of conservation rises as we try to protect a complete species assortment (Magrath et al., 1995), which includes unique species assemblies in many areas with high human populations. Balmford & Long (1994) demonstrated, world-wide, that avian endemism is positively correlated with the current annual deforestation rate. As will be shown, some of the most remarkable aggregates of endemic species in South America are immediately adjacent to centres where human civilizations flourished in the past and in areas where the remaining patches of natural vegetation are now under intense pressure from dense human populations. Although the causes for this correlation between endemism and human populations are still unexplored, we intuitively believe that local ecoclimatic conditions, which played a key role in the biological diversification process, also provided an important life-support system for humans.

We believe that balanced conservation strategies require good understanding of ecosystem functions that underlie geographical variation in species richness and endemism. The results will therefore be discussed with reference to a model hypothesis for continent-wide diversification (Fjeldså, 1994; Fjeldså & Lovett, 1997; Fjeldså et al., 1997).

## MATERIALS AND METHODS

For our analysis we used the WORLDMAP computer program (version 3.18/3.19). This is a PC-based graphical tool designed for fast, interactive assessment of priority areas for conserving biodiversity (Williams, 1994; Williams, Gibbons et al., 1996 and Williams, Prance et al., 1996 for applications; see also Williams this volume). The program accommodates distributional data for large numbers of species. Relative differences in endemism are expressed as a rarity score that is calculated for each grid cell as the sum of the inverse range sizes of all species present (see Usher, 1986, and Williams, 1994, for details).

Baseline maps for South American birds were prepared over a 10-year period by R. S. Ridgely and W. L. Brown and were kindly placed at our disposal by the Academy of Natural Sciences of Philadelphia. These maps include verified records and an assumed range boundary (demarcating breeding and non-breeding ranges; this was a consensus of several persons with long field experience in South America). We revised all maps, including data from 18 years of fieldwork in the Andes by the first author and N. Krabbe (see Fjeldså and Krabbe, 1990) and other expedition teams from the Zoological Museum, University of Copenhagen, the databases of BirdLife International (ICBP, 1992; Collar *et al.*, 1992; Wege & Long, 1995) and the databases on Brazilian birds of J. M. Cardosa da Silva, and from the primary literature (hundreds of references). The revised maps are conservative (i.e. much more detailed than the generalized maps published in Ridgely & Tudor, 1989, 1994) as the range boundaries are kept close to the documented records. However, we regard species as continuously present between collecting points when the available habitat maps (and numerous satellite images) suggest fairly uniform intervening habitat (unless absences of records from well-studied sites suggest discontinuities).

We regard the 1° grid scale (approximately 12 000 km²) used as the finest resolution permissible considering the collecting gaps which exist in certain parts of the continent. We emphasize that our resolution is quite unique and probably the finest that is possible for an entire continent which spans the tropical zone (compare, e.g. with other previous analyses of South American birds using area plots of 272 000 km² and 611 000 km²: Cotgreave & Harvey, 1994 and Gaston & Blackburn, 1995, respectively).

In this paper we analyse breeding distribution data for four monophyletic groups (see Sibley & Ahlquist, 1990 for phylogenies; Sibley & Monroe, 1990, 1993 for taxonomy) with altogether 913 species: (i) parrots (Psittacidae, 118 species), which are mainly forest-adapted frugivores; (ii) ovenbirds and woodcreepers (Furnariidae, incl. Dendrocolaptinae; 226 species), which are insectivorous birds of scrub and open land, with some subgroups of scansorial forest birds; (iii) New World flycatchers (Tyrannidae *sensu lato*, incl. Cotinginae and Piprinae, 456 species), which comprise flycatching and foliage-gleaning insectivores as well as frugivores and which inhabit a wide habitat range; and (iv) wrens (South American clades Troglodytinae and Polioptilinae of Certhiidae; 54 species), which are mainly insectivores of the forest understorey. Additional families were analysed by Fjeldså and Rahbek (1997).

Among several analytical options in WORLDMAP, we examined patterns of species richness and endemism, and identified conservation priorities using the principles of complementarity of species ranges (see Austin & Margules, 1986; Williams, Gibbons *et al.*, 1996; Williams, Prance *et al.*, 1996; and Williams, this volume). This was done family by family.

In order to suggest realistic conservation areas in terms of holding viable populations, we now assume that a species is 'safe' if present in at least three grid cells. We identified irreplaceable grid cells, new flexible grid cells, and flexible grid cells from ties (see Williams, 1994 for details). The first two make up the near-minimum set of areas needed to keep all species. Irreplaceable grid cells are identified as those with species whose total range falls within 1–3 grid cells. New, flexible grid cells are those areas that could be exchanged for other areas, although this may require larger sets of areas than the minimum set. Flexible areas from ties are the most likely alternatives to identified flexible grid cells if biodiversity management is impossible in the latter owing to conflicts with other interests.

The near-minimum set of grid cells needed to cover all species (Figs. 7.1–7.4(c)) was supplemented with two Gap Analyses of the entire data set, where we pre-selected areas where the birds can be regarded as currently safe (Fig. 7.5; see Butterfield, Csuti & Scott, 1994 for assumptions and limitations). The first of these analyses considers existing protected areas (IUCN 1992, and new reserves in Harcourt & Sayer, 1996). The reserve areas differ greatly in extent and legal status, and in how well the biological resources are managed. Many areas were established to support indigenous people, others mainly because of cultural heritage, scenic landscapes and low levels of conflict with other interests. Owing to lack of detailed data (species lists and information about the management) for some of these reserves, we assume that the birds are well protected in grid cells which satisfy one of the following criteria: (i) formal protection of at least one third of the grid cell's area, (ii) three nominally different reserves, or (iii) an ongoing conservation project providing effective protection of the biologically most unique parts of the grid cell. We identified 263 such grid units, hereafter referred to as the 'existing network of well-protected areas'.

The second analysis considers human population pressures. Unfortunately, information on these is hard to quantify. Demographic data are published for political units and are difficult to convert into grids. Furthermore, different human populations practise widely different types of land management, some of which may be sustainable, others highly destructive. Pressures on nature driven by poverty, by opportunistic colonization along new roads, by individual enterprises, or by regional development policies, are known mainly in qualitative terms, as quantitative data are inconsistent and often outdated. Rather than using available human population statistics we therefore used all 1:500 000 and 1:1 000 000 maps for South America (from Defense Mapping Agency Aerospace Center, St Louis, MO) to identify grid cells which will encompass a rectangle, corresponding to one third of the cell's area, in which there is no indication of infrastructure (buildings, roads, airstrips, powerlines, etc.). Unfortunately, many map sheets for the Amazon–Guianas are old (1980–85); these were supplemented with information from more recent maps on infrastructure, deforestation, mining activities, etc. We defined a set of 343 grid cells which for convenience we refer to as 'low human population areas'. The small communities which exist in these areas will generally have a low impact, and we therefore consider that biodiversity has a high chance to persist in these areas even without specific conservation investments.


## RESULTS

### Distribution patterns for parrots

This group shows high species richness (Fig. 7.1(a), colour plate) in certain parts of the Amazon-Guianas, with a peak density of 28 species along the Amazonian midflow in Pará. This peak is caused by a combination of endemics, isolated populations of species which also live in other parts of the continent, intrusion of some species from the Guianan coastal savannahs, and two cases of parapatry (related species replacing each other on opposite river banks). The species richness is low in some of the Amazonian floodplains andLis generally high in the Andean foothills. Endemism (Fig. 7.1(b), colour plate) is high in many areas along the periphery of the continent, with the peak values on the Espirito Santo coast and in the Colombian Cordillera Central. Unlike in the following groups, the endemism is high locally in the Brazilian highland and in the Pantanal.


### Distribution patterns for ovenbirds and woodcreepers

This group (Fig. 7.2(a),(b), colour plate) is widely represented in all ecoregions, with the highest species richness in the humid parts of the Andes (peak richness of 68 species at 0–1° S, 77–78° W) and a considerable diversity also in most of the Amazon basin and the Guianas, and locally in the Atlantic forests. Among the Amazonian taxa, woodcreepers and some ovenbirds of the genera *Xenops* and *Philydor* inhabit all kinds of forest, while most *Automolus* and *Sclerurus* species are restricted to *terra firme* forest. Many species (e.g. of the ovenbird genera *Synallaxis*, *Certhiaxis*, *Cranioleuca*) are widespread but patchily distributed in riparian habitat (in the

Amazon and in depressions in the Cerrado region) but generally absent from floodplains with strongly meandering rivers. Most Amazonian congeners have broadly overlapping ranges, but the woodcreepers include some cases of replacement across major rivers. There are no narrowly endemic species in the Amazon area but a few species have small but disjunct ranges along the periphery of the basin. Vicariance patterns are more typical along the eastern Brazilian Andean track (Silva, 1995), with many examples of tiny ranges. Thus, endemism is marked in most parts of the Andes and in the Atlantic Forest (Fig. 7.2(b), colour plate).

### Distribution patterns for New World flycatchers

New World flycatchers (Fig. 7.3(a),(b) are well represented in all ecoregions but with the highest species richness in the evergreen tropics, notably along the eastern slope of the tropical Andes (peak value of 158 species at 0–1° S 77–78° W in Ecuador, and nearly identical numbers in some grid cells southwards to Bolivia), in the eastern sub-Andean zone, in the Guianas and in Pará. High endemism in a number of isolated grid cells in Fig. 7.3(b) is in most cases due to a single collection of an enigmatic species, most of these in notoriously difficult genera.

### Distribution patterns for wrens

This group (Fig. 7.4(a),(b) showed high species richness in most parts of the tropical evergreen forest zones and into the drier zone of northern Colombia, with peak density (19 species) at 6–7° N and 72–73° and 76–77° W in the Colombian Andes. Endemism is very high in the north-west of the continent, with a peak also in the southern Atlantic forest.

### Overall species richness

Combining all groups, the highest species richness (Fig. 7.5(a)) is along the eastern slope of the tropical Andes region rather than in the Amazon basin.

Caption for Fig. 7.3 (*opposite*)

Fig. 7.3 Variation in species richness (a) and endemism (b) for 456 New World flycatchers, including cotingas, manakins etc., Tyrannidae *sensu lato*, with the near-minimum set of irreplaceable and flexible areas needed to cover all species (c).

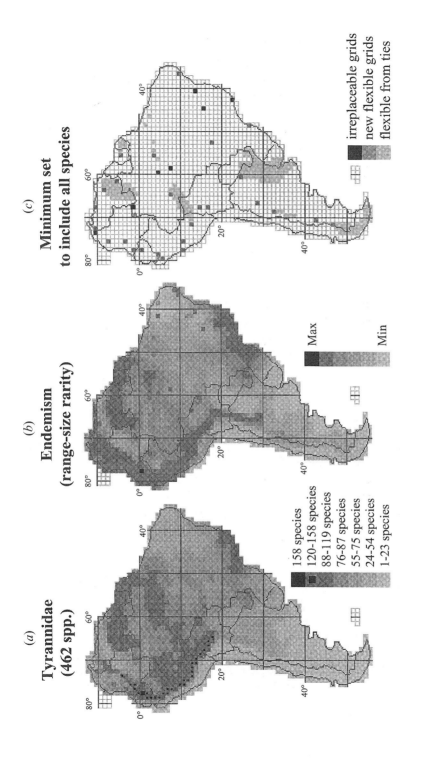

*(a)*
**Tyrannidae
(462 spp.)**

158 species
120-158 species
88-119 species
76-87 species
55-75 species
24-54 species
1-23 species

*(b)*
**Endemism
(range-size rarity)**

Max

Min

*(c)*
**Minimum set
to include all species**

irreplaceable grids
new flexible grids
flexible from ties

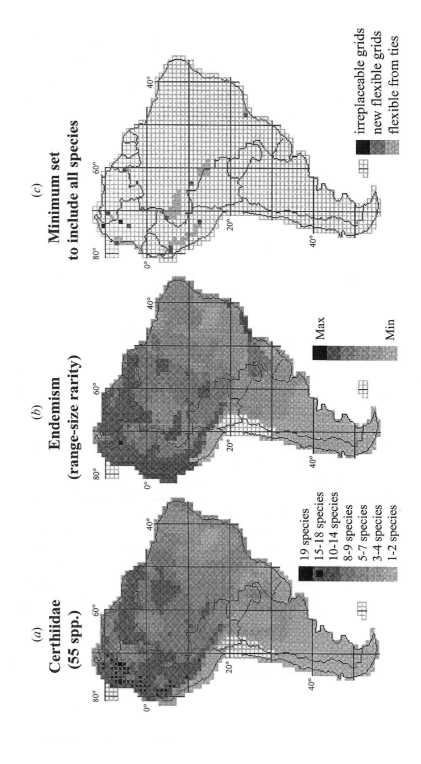

*(a)*
**Certhiidae (55 spp.)**

19 species
15-18 species
10-14 species
8-9 species
5-7 species
3-4 species
1-2 species

*(b)*
**Endemism (range-size rarity)**

Max

Min

*(c)*
**Minimum set to include all species**

irreplaceable grids
new flexible grids
flexible from ties

This pattern is found also for other taxonomic groups (Fjeldså & Rahbek, 1997) and it appears that the absolute peak value of avian beta diversity is at 0–1° S, 77–78° W (the Sumaco Volcano and adjacent foothills, Ecuador, with altogether 267 species). However, the level of species richness is fairly uniform all the way along the eastern slope of the Andes to 18° S. All groups share high species richness in areas with incipient mountain folding in the upper Amazon basin (Cordillera Divisorial and Alto do Moa, Alto de Iquitos and Alto de Fitzcarrald) and along the lower Amazon in Pará (207 species) and in the Guianan Tepuis (up to 183 species).

### The avian diversity of pre-selected protected and 'low human population' areas

The networks of areas which we considered well protected or as being 'low human population' areas (labelled 'existing areas' in Fig. 7.5(b,(c) comprise large numbers of grid cells in the Amazon area, notably in the Brazilian frontier zones towards its neighbouring countries, and in southern Chile. Overall, the overlap between the two sets of 263 and 343 grid cells is 191 grid cells. The main differences between the two networks comprise very extensive 'low human population' areas in some parts of the Amazon–Guianas areas, very few large 'low human population' areas in the tropical Andes region and Argentina and a total lack of such areas in south-east Brazil.

A number of small reserves has been established in recent years in important endemic bird areas along the Brazilian Atlantic coast, and there are also many small reserves in areas with high endemism in Colombia. Overall, however, the protected areas have low levels of endemism (compare Tables 7.1 and 7.2). Many of the larger reserves in the Andes are situated where endemism is decidedly low compared with nearby areas (see Fig. 6 in Fjeldså & Rahbek, 1997). As an example, the high part of the Manu National Park in Peru is characterized by large numbers of widespread species, whereas the number of restricted-range species rises markedly immediately west of the park boundary. Among the 40 largest Andean conservation areas, only four (Sierra Nevada in Mérida, Venezuela; Santa

Caption for Fig. 7.4 (*opposite*)

Fig. 7.4 Variation in species richness (*a*) and endemism (*b*) for 54 species of wrens Certhidae (viz. Troglodytinae and Polioptilinae), with the near-minimum set of irreplaceable and flexible areas needed to cover all species (*c*).

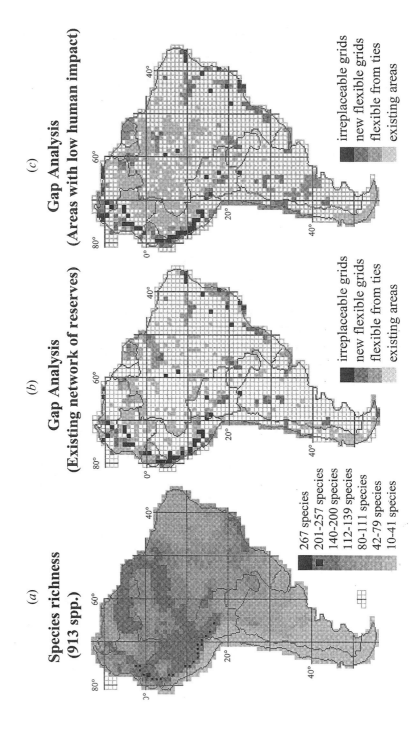

*(a)*
**Species richness**
**(913 spp.)**

267 species
201-257 species
140-200 species
112-139 species
80-111 species
42-79 species
10-41 species

*(b)*
**Gap Analysis**
**(Existing network of reserves)**

irreplaceable grids
new flexible grids
flexible from ties
existing areas

*(c)*
**Gap Analysis**
**(Areas with low human impact)**

irreplaceable grids
new flexible grids
flexible from ties
existing areas

Marta in Colombia; Podocarpus in Ecuador; Huascarán in Peru) cover local peak concentrations of endemic species.

The 'low human population' areas are rich in species but have an even lower level of endemism than the protected areas (Table 7.1). The combination of high endemism and virtual absence of people in the Andes is found in only four grids: in the Colombian Chocó, the Cordillera Colán and the northern Cordillera Vilcabamba (Peru), and to the north of Cordillera Tunari (Bolivia).

### Comparison of minimum sets

The near-minimum set of grid units needed for three representations of all 118 parrots (Fig. 7.1(c), colour plate) is three irreplaceable and 21 flexible areas, with only three flexible sites in the Amazon basin (we will not discuss here whether this criterion is realistic for long-term survival of large parrots). This reflects wide distributions and large extent of range overlaps between the 50 Amazonian species. All 226 ovenbirds and woodcreepers could be covered in five irreplaceable and 45 flexible cells, with four of the latter in the Amazon basin (Fig. 7.2(c), colour plate). All 462 New World flycatchers could be covered in seven irreplaceable and 26 flexible cells (Fig. 7.3(c)). The two irreplaceable sites in the Amazon basin are needed for *Pipra villasboasi* and *Todirostrum senex*, both of which are known from a single site (Fig. 7.3(c)). The 54 wrens could be covered in six irreplaceable (all in the Andes) and 19 flexible cells (Fig. 7.4(c)).

To reach the goal of representation of each species in three grid cells the pre-selected reserves and 'low human population' areas had to be supplemented with the following numbers of new conservation areas: for parrots, 10 or 16 irreplaceable and 28 or 37 flexible cells, respectively; for ovenbirds and woodcreepers, 20 or 28 irreplaceable cells (16 or 21 in the Andes) and 40 or 57 flexible cells (only two, in Pará, needed for the Amazon basin); for New World flycatchers, 15 irreplaceable and 37 or 55 flexible cells (with two irreplaceable and two flexible areas in the Amazon basin); for wrens, seven or eight irreplaceable and four or six flexible sites.

Caption for Fig. 7.5 (*opposite*)

Fig. 7.5. Near-minimum sets of new irreplaceable and flexible areas for conserving all species of parrots, ovenbirds, New World flycatchers and wrens in at least three areas, identified in relation to pre-selected 'existing network of well-protected areas' (b) and 'low human population areas' (c). Overall species richness is also shown (a).

**Table 7.1**
*Average species richness and endemism score with standard deviation, for all grid cells, and for the two subsets of pre-selected areas used for the Gap Analyses (i.e. grid cells belonging to the set of 'existing network of well-protected areas' and 'low human population areas', respectively)*

|  | Species richness | Endemism |
| --- | --- | --- |
| All grid cells | 93.5 (± 49.8) | 0.9 (± 1.1) |
| Gap Analyses (reserves) | 107.1 (± 53.9) | 1.3 (± 1.5) |
| Gap Analyses ('low human population areas') | 118.6 (+ 47.0) | 0.9 (± 1.1) |

**Table 7.2**
*Species richness and endemism score (with standard deviation) for all grid cells and for the subsets of suggested conservation areas (near-minimum sets for three representations of all species)*

|  | Species richness | Endemism |
| --- | --- | --- |
| All grid cells | 93.5 (± 49.8) | 0.9 (± 1.1) |
| No constraints | 118.9 (± 55.2) | 2.8 (± 2.1) |
| Gap Analyses (reserves pre-selected) | 111.0 (± 55.1) | 2.9 (± 2.1) |
| Gap Analyses ('low human population areas' pre-selected) | 111.6 (± 51.5) | 3.0 (± 2.0) |

The table compares the optimal near-minimum set found without any areas being pre-selected ('No constraints') with new conservation areas needed to supplement the existing network of well-protected areas (reserves pre-selected) and the pre-selected 'low human population areas'.

The near-minimum sets (Figs. 7.1–7.4) showed little redundancy between /the families, as only Nevado Santa Marta (10–11° N, 73–74° W) was needed for all four families. Other areas shared by two or three families were mainly in the Andes and in south-east Brazil. However, there was absolutely no overlap between families in irreplaceable and flexible sites in the Amazon basin. Because of the near-absence of species with very small distributions in the Amazon basin, the minimum sets are biased to boundaries where different sets of species meet, e.g. ecotones towards adjacent highlands, or major rivers where opposite banks are occupied by different allospecies. Because most Amazonian species range well into the 'low human population' hinterlands (away from rivers or ecotones), very few new

**Table 7.3**

*The number of areas needed in order to protect all 913 species in at least three areas, based on complementarity of species ranges. 'No constraints' is the optimal near-minimum set found without any areas being pre-selected*

|  | Pre-selected areas | Irreplaceable areas | Flexible areas | Total near-minimum set |
|---|---|---|---|---|
| No constraints | 0 | 64 | 113 | 177 |
| Gap Analysis (reserves) | 263 | 47 | 62 | 372 |
| Gap analyses ('low human population areas') | 343 | 57 | 78 | 478 |

conservation areas are needed in the Amazon area according to the Gap Analyses. The attention is shifted, instead, to surrounding areas with slightly lower species richness but higher endemism (Table 7.2).

The minimum set for all four families combined in one analysis would be 64 irreplaceable and 113 flexible areas (Table 7.3) if the goal of three representations of each species is to be reached. When pre-selecting a network of protected areas (Fig. 7.5(b)) or 'low human population' areas (Fig. 7.5(c)), 47 irreplaceable and 62 flexible sites or 57 irreplaceable and 78 flexible sites would be needed, respectively. Because of the low endemism of the pre-selected areas (Tables 7.1 and 7.2) and the partial overlap between the two pre-selected networks, the needs for new conservation investments are nearly the same whether we pre-select formally protected areas or 'low human population' areas. The overlap between the 109 and 135 grid cells, which constitute the two near-minimum sets of new conservation investments (Figs 7.5(b) and (c)), is 92 grid cells. Comparing Tables 7.1 and 7.2 it is evident that the proposed new conservation areas are characterized by very high endemism compared with the formally protected and 'low human population' areas ($P < 0.0001$ for both sets using Student's $t$-test), whereas the variation in species richness is not significant.

The key problem for conserving the avian diversity in South America is that aggregates of narrowly endemic species are found in regions which are inhabited, and many of which are immediately adjacent to centres of past civilizations or centres of high population density today (Fig. 7.6).

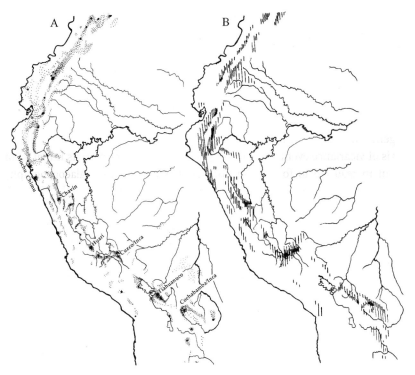

Fig. 7.6. A comparison of human populations and avian endemism in the tropical Andes region. In (A) stippling shows areas with dense human settlement and infrastructure (based on 1 : 500 000 maps from Defense Mapping Agency Aerospace Center, St Louis, MO), dots show larger towns, * marks centres of past civilizations (I. Schjellerup pers. comm.). In (B) areas with high mean endemism are shaded, with peak densities black (based on a preliminary data set for Andean birds, in WORLDMAP, with 15' × 15' resolution).

## DISCUSSION

### A model hypothesis for landscape processes moulding the biogeographic patterns

There is a considerable amount of literature that reviews past and current processes that affect the distribution of biodiversity in South America. Much attention has been given to the role of assumed habitat changes caused by the interaction between general global cooling since the Pliocene and climatic oscillations forced by orbital changes (see Bartlein & Prentice, 1989; Bennett, 1990; Hooghiemstra et al., 1993). Thus, Haffer (1974) explained the tremendous number of Amazonian species in terms of isolation in ecological 'refuges' which were permanently forested during cold/dry Pleistocene episodes (see also Whitmore & Prance, 1987). However, the age of species had been inferred from assumptions about a Pleistocene speciation mechanism, and little attention had been given to whether the patterns were modified by post-speciation redistribution in accordance with current carrying capacity. Use of DNA data to assess the genetic divergence of taxa (e.g. Amorim, 1991; Fjeldså, 1994) and more rigorous analysis of vicariance events did not support the refuge theory in its initial form but instead led to formulation of new hypotheses: the palaeogeography hypothesis, the gradient hypothesis, the river hypothesis and the river-refuge hypothesis (for reviews see Haffer, 1997; Tuomisto & Ruokalainen, 1997). The detailed knowledge that has been obtained during recent years about marine ingressions, tectonically induced flooding cycles and landscape turnover on the floodplains (Salo, 1988; Hanagarth, 1993; Kalliola, Puhakka & Danjoy, 1993) suggests that current patterns of species richness to a large extent reflect the levels of functional heterogeneity of different areas. Thus, most floodplain species are relatively rare but present over considerable areas as they find patches of suitable habitat that arise locally as a result of the migration of river meanders. The species richness peak in Pará is a mosaic of forest, grasslands, cultivation and wetlands, and is furthermore characterized by the highest interannual ecoclimatic variability in the whole Amazon basin (J. Fjeldså & E. Lambin, unpublished data set based on 10 years' meteorological satellite images).

A new model hypothesis for continent-wide diversification (Fjeldså, 1994; Fjeldså & Lovett, 1997) was based on a comparison of distribution patterns of species of different ages (based on the large data set of DNA–DNA hybridizations by Sibley & Ahlquist 1990), and this is now being evaluated by speciation studies using DNA sequence data (Roy *et al.*, 1997). Maybe the most significant finding is that hydrologically unstable floodplains (specific parts of the Amazon basin, Llanos, Choco and Mesopotamia) are dominated by widespread species that represent deep phylogenetic branches. In groups which diversified during the Pleistocene, more than 80% of the species present in the Amazon area also exist outside it (in gallery forests in the Cerrados, in the Guianas or in the Andes), and so need not be Amazonian by origin. The Amazon floodplains may therefore be seen as an area where taxa of potentially diverse origins accumulate, rather than as a centre of Pleistocene diversification.

The enormous species richness of South America was probably the result of an intensive speciation burst in the Pliocene and Pleistocene in the tropical Andes and in adjacent sub-Andean forelands (Fjeldså 1994). In antbirds, maybe the most typical Amazonian forest group, the *ca.* 50 species with particularly small ranges (mostly members of the speciose genera *Thamnophilus*, *Herpsilochmus*, *Myrmotherula*, *Cercomacra* and *Grallaria*) form local aggregates in areas characterized by incipient geological uplift (Altos de Fitzcarrald, Moa and Iquitos, and along the Andes), with a few others in white-sands habitats in upper Río Negro and along the southern boundary of the Amazon basin. These areas are unaffected by floodplain dynamics and so remain stable.

The highest endemism in continental faunas is associated with montane cloudforest (Long, 1994; see also Stotz, this volume). Undoubtedly a large proportion of the speciation events in the montane areas can be directly associated with physical barriers. However, marked local assemblies of endemic species may also reflect intrinsic properties of certain areas. It has been documented (Stebbins & Major, 1965 for the Californian flora; Fjeldså, 1995 for Andean birds; Fjeldså & Lovett, 1997 for African birds and plants) that places with peak concentrations of local component taxa of strongly diversified groups also have several biogeographic relics. These latter would seem to indicate low local rates of extinction and low rates of ecological change (see Best, 1992; Fjeldså, 1995; Fjeldså *et al.*, 1997 for ecoclimatic support). The most important single factor may be local moderation of climatic extremes leading to persistent mist formation and development of cloudforests that secure a predictable water supply into adjacent montane basins. It needs to be assessed to what extent productivity and soil sustainability is also enhanced by the complex biological communities that evolved here (see Tilman & Downing, 1994).

This interpretation differs from traditional refuge concepts as local climatic moderation can persist through shifting global climates only within regions with a marked topography (Vrba, 1993). Furthermore, the assumptions about palaeoecological barriers between centres of endemism can be replaced by assumptions about ecoclimatic disturbance favouring high species turnover and low chance of dispersal of specialist species between widely disjunct stable places.

**The Gap Analysis seen in the light of continent-wide biogeographic process**

It is apparent that the existing network of protected areas has not been planned in a way that explicitly considered biogeographic patterns and processes. Many species were redundantly conserved in reserves situated in regions with virtually no people. Unfortunately, such areas have few endemics and so few species to lose (Table 7.1). It is evident from Figs. 7.1–7.6 and Tables 7.1–7.3 that the most unique local aggregates of species are found outside currently protected and 'low human population' areas, and often in places that are under strong human pressure.

Considerable investments are therefore still needed to form fully representative and adequate networks of conservation areas (Table 7.3). A realistic conservation strategy should consider the ecoclimatic conditions and processes that determine endemism and human settlement.

There is considerable circumstantial evidence to suggest that areas which were stable in ecoclimatic terms have fragile biological communities, in contrast to regions which were characterized by violent ecoclimatic changes (boreal and arid regions, inland areas sometimes extensively flooded, etc.). These latter communities may bounce back rapidly after a disturbance. Unpredictable conditions may lead to opportunistic habits, boom-and-burst breeding and erratic dispersal. It follows that intense conservation efforts may be less needed on hydrologically unstable plains than in places which remain unaltered over geological time.

The uniqueness of the Amazon area as a whole, and its value for maintaining hydrologic and climatic stability is indisputable. However, because its species pool is partly a consequence of area, habitat turnover and wide species distributions, precise goals for concentrated management are difficult to identify. The identification of conservation targets is also sensitive to the algorithms and data used (compare Figs. 7.1–7.5). Furthermore, global persistence of species is indeed possible despite considerable amounts of local extinction. We should therefore consider management alternatives that are based on macropolitical decisions rather than on site-specific actions. It seems that the most realistic way to conservation of Amazonian biodiversity is through economic planning which considers the total economic values of the environment (climatic and hydrological buffering, tourism, option values of biodiversity etc.; see also Myers, this volume).

The centres of endemism discussed in this paper seem to a much larger extent to be threatened by dense rural populations, which often have few alternatives. In much of the tropical Andes, the highest population pressures are found just below the mist zone at 3000–3500 m. Many local populations have already virtually destroyed the natural vegetation in this zone, and this leads to soil degradation, reduced water catchment functions and irregular water supply in the valleys below. As illustrated in Fig. 7.6, the centres for development of earlier civilizations in the Andes (Mochu, Chimu, Chavín, Huari, Inca, Tiahuanuco, and Taironov around Nevado Santa Marta in northern Colombia) were immediately adjacent to local peak concentrations of endemism. There is strong evidence that even very early human cultures exerted strong pressures on the Andean habitats. However, Earls (1991) argues that famines and social tensions resulting from the degradation of the ecosystems were the driving forces for the development of the Andean cultures. Unfortunately, the environmental regulations under the Inca Empire were suddenly stopped by the Conquista, when Spanish landlords enforced new and ecologically very inappropriate landuse methods. Many areas that may initially have been covered by species-rich montane forests now appear as eroded and dry wastelands. In some districts so little cloudforest is left that important water catchment functions may now have been irreversibly lost. The situation is particularly severe in many parts of the Colombian Andes, in southwestern Ecuador, and in the montane basins of northern and central Peru and Cochabamba, Bolivia, where only tiny remnants of natural vegetation are left. High risks of global extinction of species are therefore closely linked with the loss of ecosystem services that severely affect human living conditions.

Although the cost of a fully representative network of conservation areas will be high, this investment is indeed relevant, as it relates directly to ecosystem functions that are also important for man. The distinctions made in this paper between specific places where new species arise and areas where species accumulate suggest that a balanced biodiversity management strategy for South America should comprise the following two kinds of actions.

*For extensive areas where high biological diversity is maintained on a large geographical scale*

These areas are important for the sheer multitude of life forms and genetic diversity. However, since this diversity is maintained by functional heterogeneity operating over vast areas, it is unclear how well the biodiversity can be maintained inside a fixed network of conservation sites (see also Balmford, Mace & Ginsberg, this volume). We suggest that priority should mainly be given to actions for refining and enforcing international agreements on forests, climate change, and tariffs and trade (see also Myers, this volume): national development policies based on principles of ecological economics and sustainability (see Glowka *et al.*, 1994); and adaptations of land tenure systems to local market situations (see Beaumont & Walker 1996).

Special attention may be needed to the upper (sub-Andean) and lower parts of the Amazon Basin and Rondonia, to unique wetland areas (such as the Pantanal) and to areas of natural grassland, of which very little is left.

*For areas with high endemism*

Because of their small size and high concentration of unique taxa, the risk of global loss of biodiversity is high in these areas; important ecosystem services may also be irreversibly lost. Among the new conservation actions suggested by the Gap Analyses, the top priorities should be massive support to sound land management in western Ecuador and in various highlands and montane basins elsewhere in the tropical Andes region. Investments are strongly needed to permit regeneration of the unique natural mist vegetation above the Peruvian coastal desert. Concentrated actions are also needed in Bahía and in the Atlantic forests of south-east Brazil. The actions must be rapid and intensive and must comprise strict protection of key elements of ecosystems as well as intensive support for improved use of areas that are already densely inhabited. Key sites for endemic species are often on ridges separating humid zones and rainshadow basins with dense human populations; in these cases the protection of elfin and cloud forest patches will be extremely valuable, and the allocation of water will be an extremely critical factor.

## ACKNOWLEDGEMENTS

This analysis was possible only because of long-term economic support from the Danish Natural Science Research Council (currently grant No. 11-0390), and good collaboration with a number of people. P. Williams kindly provided the WORLDMAP software and did a great extra service by programming according to our specific wishes. For provision of distributional data we thank mainly R. Ridgely and the Academy of Natural Sciences of Philadelphia, but also BirdLife International, N. Krabbe, S. Maijer and J.M. Cardoso da Silva; for a large computerizing effort we thank Ivan Olsen and Casper Paludan. For many stimulating discussions and comments we thank P. Arctander, N. Burgess, H. de Klerk, N. Krabbe, J. Lovett, I Schjellerup and J. M. Cardoso da Silva.

## References

Amorim, D. S. (1991). Refuge model simulations: testing the theory. *Revista bras. Ent.*, **35**, 803–12.

Austin, M. P. & Margules, C. R. (1986). Assessing representativenes. In *Wildlife conservation evaluation*: 45–67 (Ed. Usher, M. B.). Chapman & Hall, London.

Balmford, A. & Long, A. (1994). Avian endemism and forest loss. *Nature, Lond.*, **372**, 623–4.

Bartlein, P. J. & Prentice, I. C. (1989). Orbital variations, climate and paleoecology. *Trends Ecol. Evol.*, **4**, 195–9.

Beaumont, P. M. & Walker, R. T. (1996). Land degradation and property regimes. *Ecol. Econ,.* **18**, 55–66.

Bennett, K. D. (1990). Milankovitch cycles and their effects on species in ecological and evolutionary time. *Paleobiology*, **16**, 11–21.

Best, B. J. (ed.) (1992). *The threatened forests of south-west Ecuador*. Biosphere Publications, Leeds, UK.

Butterfield, B. R., Csuti, B. & Scott, J. M. (1994). Modelling vertebrate distributions for gap analysis. In *Mapping the diversity of nature*: 53–68. (Ed. Miller, R. I.). Chapman & Hall, London.

Collar, N. J., Gonzaga, L. P., Krabbe, N., Madroño Nieto, A., Naranjo, L. G., Parker, T. A. & Wege, D. C. (1992). *Threatened birds of the Americas. The ICBP/IUCN Red Data Book. 3rd edition, part 2*. Smithsonian Institution Press, Washington, D.C., & International Council for Bird Preservation, Cambridge, UK.

Cotgreave, P. & Harvey, P. H. (1994). Associations among biogeography, phylogeny and bird species diversity. *Biodiv. Lett.*, **2**, 46–55.

Earls, J. (1991). *Ecologia y agronomia en los Andes*. Hisbol, La Paz.

Fjeldså, J. (1994). Geographical patterns for relict and young species of birds in Africa and South America and implications for conservation priorities. *Biodiv. Conserv.*, **3**, 207–26.

Fjeldså, J. (1995). Geographical patterns of neoendemic and older relict species of Andean forest birds: the significance of ecologically stable areas. In *Biodiversity and conservation of neotropical montane forests*: 89–102. (Eds Churchill, S. P., Balslev, H., Forero, E. & Luteyn, J. L.). The New York Botanical Garden, New York.

Fjeldså, J., Ehrlich, D., Lambin, E. & Prins, E. (1997). Are biodiversity 'hotspots' correlated with ecoclimatic stability? A pilot study using NOAA–AVHRR remote sensing data. *Biodiv. Conserv.*, **6**, 401–22.

Fjeldså, J. & Krabbe, N. (1990). *Birds of the High Andes*. Zoological Museum, University of Copenhagen & Apollo Books, Svendborg, Denmark.

Fjeldså, J. & Lovett, J.C. (1997). Geographical patterns of phylogenetic relicts and phylogenetically subordinate species in tropical Africa forest biota. *Biodiv. Conserv.*, **6**, 325–46.

Fjeldså, J. & Rahbek, C. (1997). Species richness and endemism in South American birds: implications for the design of networks of nature reserves. In *Tropical forest remnants: ecology, management and conservation of fragmented communities*: 466–482. (Eds Laurance, W.F. Bierregaard, R.). University of Chicago Press, Chicago.

Gaston, K.J. & Blackburn, T.M. (1995). Mapping biodiversity using surrogates for species richness: macro-scales and New World birds. *Proc. R. Soc. Lond. B*, **262**, 335–41.

Glowka, L., Burhenne-Guilmin, F., Synge, H., McNeely, J.A. & Gündling, L. (1994). *A guide to the Convention on Biological Diversity*. IUCN, Gland and Cambridge.

Haffer, J. (1974). Avian speciation in tropical south America: with a systematic survey of the toucans (Ramphastidae) and jacamars (Galbulidae). *Publ. Nuttall orn. Club* No. 14, 1–390.

Haffer, J. (1997). Alternative models of vertebrate speciation in Amazonia: an overview. *Biodiv. Conserv.*, **6**, 451–76.

Hanagarth, W. (1993). *Acerca de la geoecologia de las sabanas del Beni en el norest de Bolivia*. Instituto de Ecología, La Paz.

Harcourt, C. S. & Sayer, J. A. (Eds). (1996). *The conservation atlas of tropical forests. The Americas*. Simon & Schuster, New York.

Hooghiemstra, H., Milica, J. L., Berger, A. & Schackelton, N. J. (1993). Frequency spectra and paleoclimatic variability of the high-resolution 30–1450 ka Funza I pollen record (Eastern Cordillera, Colombia). *Quat. Sci. Rev.*, **12**, 141–56.

ICBP (1992). *Putting biodiversity on the map: global priorities for conservation*. ICBP, Cambridge, UK.

IUCN (1992). *Protected areas of the world: a review of national systems. 4. Nearctic and Neotropical*. IUCN, Gland, Switzerland and Cambridge, UK.

Kalliola, R., Puhakka, M. & Danjoy, W. (1993). *Amazonia Peruana. Vegetacion húmeda tropical en el llano subandino*. ONERN, Lima.

Long, A. (1994). The importance of tropical montane cloud forests for endemic and threatened birds. In *Tropical montane cloud forests*, 79–106. (Eds Hamilton, L. S., Juvik, J. O. & Scatena, F. N.). Springer-Verlag, New York. (*Ecol. Stud. Anal. Synth.*, **110**.)

Magrath, W. B., Peters, C., Kishor, N. & Kishor, P. (1995). *The economic supply of biodiversity in West Kalimantan: preliminary results*. World Bank, Asia Technical Department, Washington, DC.

Mares, M. A. (1992). Neotropical mammals and the myth of Amazonian biodiversity. *Science*, **255**, 976–9.

Rahbek, C. (1995). The elevational gradient of species richness: a uniform pattern? *Ecography*, **18**, 200–5.

Rahbek, C. (1997). The relationship among area, elevation, and regional species richness in Neotropical birds. *Am. Nat.*, **149**, 875–902.

Ridgely, R.S. & Tudor, G. (1989). *The birds of South America. 1. The oscine passerines*. Oxford University Press, Oxford.

Ridgely, R. S. & Tudor, G. (1994). *The birds of South America. 2. The suboscine passerines*. Oxford University Press, Oxford.

Roy, S. M., Silva, J. M. C., Arctander, P., García-Morena, J. & Fjeldså, J. (1997). The role of montane regions in the speciation of South American and African birds. In *Avian molecular evolution and systematics*: 325–343. (Ed. Mindell, D. P.). Academic Press, New York.

Salo, J. (1988). *Rainforest diversification in the western Amazon basin: the role of river dynamics*. PhD Dissertation: Department of Biology, University of Turku, Finland.

Sibley, C. G. & Ahlquist, J. E. (1990). *Phylogeny and classification of birds. A study in molecular evolution.* Yale University Press, New Haven, Connecticut.

Sibley, C. G. & Monroe, B. L., Jr. (1990). *Distribution and taxonomy of birds of the world.* Yale University Press, New Haven, Connecticut.

Sibley, C.G. & Monroe, B.L., Jr. (1993). *A supplement to 'Distribution and taxonomy of birds of the world'.* Yale University Press, New Haven, Connecticut.

Silva, J. M. C. da (1995). Biogeographic analysis of the South American Cerrado avifauna. *Steenstrupia*, **21**, 49–67.

Stebbins, G.L. & Major, J. (1965). Endemism and speciation in the California flora. *Ecol. Monogr.*, **35**, 1–35.

Terborgh, J. (1973). On the notion of favorableness in plant ecology. *Am. Nat.*, **107**, 481–501.

Terborgh, J., Robinson, S. K., Parker, T., III, Munn, C. A. & Pierpont, N. (1990). Structure and organization of an Amazonian forest bird community. *Ecol. Monogr.*, **60**, 213–38.

Tilman, D. & Downing, J. A. (1994). Biodiversity and stability in grasslands. *Nature, Lond.*, **367**, 363–5.

Tuomisto, H. & Ruokalainen, K. (1997). The role of ecological knowledge in explaining biogeography and biodiversity in Amazonia. *Biodiv. Conserv.*, **6**, 347–58.

Usher, M. B. (Ed.) (1986). *Wildlife conservation evaluation.* Chapman & Hall, London.

Vrba, E. S. (1993). Mammal evolution in the African Neogene and a new look at the Great American Interchange. In *Biological relationship between Africa and South America*: 393–432. (Ed. Goldblatt, P.). Yale University Press, New Haven.

Wege, D. C. & Long, A. J. (1995). *Key areas for threatened birds in the Neotropics.* BirdLife International, Cambridge, U.K. (*Bird Life Conserv. Ser.*, **5**.)

Whitmore, T. C. & Prance, G. T. (Eds). (1987). *Biogeography and quaternary history in tropical America.* Clarendon Press, Oxford.

Williams, P. H. (1994). *WORLDMAP. Priority areas for biodiversity. Using version 3.* Privately distributed, London, UK.

Williams, P., Gibbons, D., Margules, C., Rebelo, A., Humphries, C. & Pressey, R. (1996). A comparison of richness hotspots, rarity hotspots and complementary areas for conserving diversity using British birds. *Conserv. Biol.*, **10**, 155–74.

Williams, P. H., Prance, G. T., Humphries, C. J. & Edwards, K. S. (1996). Promise and problems in applying quantitative complementary areas for representing the diversity of some Neotropical plants (families Dichapetalaceae, Lecythidaceae, Caryocaraceae, Chrysobalanaceae and Proteaceae). *Biol. J. Linn. Soc.*, **58**, 125–57.

# 8

# Endemism and species turnover with elevation in montane avifaunas in the neotropics: implications for conservation

DOUGLAS F. STOTZ

## INTRODUCTION

Species diversity has played a major role in attracting conservation attention to certain parts of the globe. This is especially true for the lowland
rainforests of Amazonia, where most major groups of organisms show tre-
mendously high levels of diversity. Conservationists cannot specify conservation priority regions further in the tropics for most groups of organisms,
because too little is known about their distributions. But, birds are an exception (see Stotz *et al.*, 1996; Fjeldå & Rahbek, this volume). Although new
species are still discovered at the rate of about two per year (Vuilleumier,
LeCroy & Mayr, 1992), and increased knowledge of the biology of species
still changes the taxonomic rank of others every year (e.g. Stotz, 1990; Willis, 1992; Bierregaard, Cohn-Haft & Stotz, in press), the vast majority of
avian diversity has been catalogued. Knowledge of the distribution and ecology of individual species continues to be refined, but our understanding of
these parameters for tropical birds is extensive.

Recent studies of patterns of distribution and endemism among neotropical birds (e.g. Fjeldså, 1994; Stotz *et al.*, 1996) have focused on montane regions (the humid Andes in particular) as important for avian
diversity and especially for avian endemism (see also Fjeldså & Rahbek, this
volume). Montane forests have much higher levels of endemism than do
lowland forests, even though diversity at a single site is much lower at the
montane sites. Here I describe more detailed patterns of avian diversity and
endemism along elevational gradients in the neotropics. I then explore the
historical and ecological processes that have helped create these patterns,
and consider the implications of these gradients for conservation.

## METHODS

The analyses presented here are based on the databases of Parker, Stotz and Fitzpatrick (1996), especially the databases on ecology and distribution (Databases A and B, respectively). I restricted analyses to the breeding distributions of birds only, and did not include elevational and geographical ranges occupied solely during the non-breeding season. I created lists of species for five of the major montane areas and associated lowlands in the neotropics. These were the eastern slope of the eastern Andes of Colombia, the eastern slope of the Peruvian Andes from Cuzco and Puno, the Caribbean slope and lowlands in Mexico from Veracruz to the Isthmus of Tehuantepec, the Caribbean slope and lowlands in Costa Rica, and the mountains and coastal lowlands of south-eastern Brazil from Rio de Janeiro to Paraná. Lists of taxa for these regions were generated from the ecology database (Parker *et al.*, 1996: Database A) by selecting the relevant zoogeographic regions (Northern Andes and Northern Amazonia for eastern Colombia, Central Andes and Southern Amazonia for eastern Peru, Madrean Highlands and Gulf–Caribbean Slope for southern Mexico, Chiriqui–Darien Highlands and Gulf–Caribbean Slope for Costa Rica, and Atlantic forest for south-eastern Brazil; see Parker *et al.*, (1996) for details of the limits of these regions) and then limiting the habitats to be analysed.

These zoogeographic regions are too broad for analysis, so I removed species not known as breeders in the country analysed by using Database B (Distribution by Country: Parker *et al.*, 1996). I then visually inspected the lists to remove any remaining species that are not known to occur in the specified habitats along the elevational transect being analysed. I used Paradox (Borland International, 1992) to analyse the remaining sets of species.

In the following analyses, zoogeographic regions and zoogeographic subregions refer to the units delineated by Parker *et al.* (1996) in which the neotropical region is subdivided into 22 zoogeographic regions and these regions are further subdivided into a total of 56 subregions. Endemism as discussed below is in reference to these units. I consider a taxon endemic if it is restricted to a single zoogeographical region or subregion, although this means that endemic species may have geographical ranges wider than the more limited elevational transects used in these analyses.

In analyses of threatened birds, I use conservation priority ranks in Parker *et al.* (1996) to categorize species. Birds ranked as 1 or 2 by Parker *et al.*, are treated as 'threatened', and birds ranked as 3 are considered 'vulnerable'. These three ranks combined are treated as 'at risk'. Similar analyses were performed using the threatned and near-threatened (considered equivalent to Category 3 of Parker *et al.*) lists of Collar, Gonzaga *et al.*, (1992). Although these rankings are not identical – in particular the near-threatened category of Collar, Gonzaga *et al.* is much less inclusive than Category 3 of Parker *et al.* – the results are qualitatively very similar, so I present only the results of the analysis based on the rankings of Parker *et al.* (1996).

## RESULTS

In the five major montane regions in the neotropics, species richness among birds decreases with increasing elevation in *terra firme* forest (Fig. 8.1). However, all regions show a slight rise in species richness along their lower slopes. The lowest peak in species richness occurs at 700 m in the Atlantic forest region, and the highest peak occurs at 1300 m in the Madrean highlands.

When all habitats are included in the analysis, the species richness peak

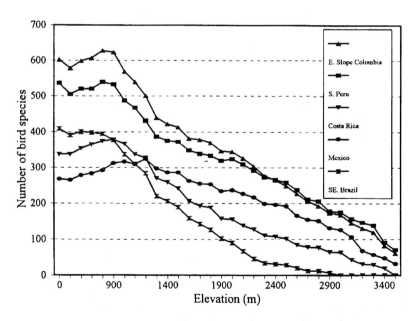

Fig. 8.1 Species richness of *terra firme* forest avifaunas vs. elevation by region in neotropics.

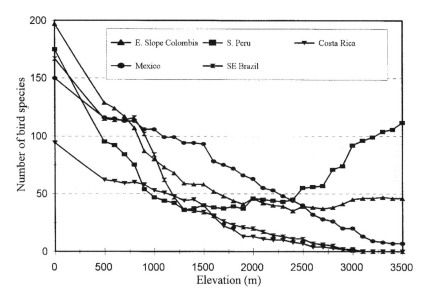

Fig. 8.2 Species richness of non-forest avifaunas vs. elevation by region in neotropics.

at intermediate elevations disappears, and species richness declines with elevation through the forested portions of the montane slopes. Open habitats, including secondary formations, other forest habitats and aquatic habitats all contribute substantial numbers of species in the lowlands, but are poorly represented on the forested slopes (Fig. 8.2). Except in the Peruvian Andes, there is a monotonic decline in the species richness of the avifaunas in these habitats. In Peru, the extensive grassland, scrub and aquatic habitats associated with the altiplano above treeline, and with some dry inter-montane valleys, result in a bimodal pattern of species richness. The larger peak is in the lowlands, but there is also a significant peak above treeline in the open habitats of the altiplano.

We can look at the overall pattern of species richness in the montane forest avifaunas as composed of two parts: a set of lowland species that disappear as one moves up slope (Fig. 8.3), and a group of purely montane species that occur only along the slopes above the lowlands. The pattern of species richness of the lowland birds is consistent across the five montane regions (Fig. 8.3), varying only in the number of species found at the base of the montane slopes. By 1800 m, the number of lowland species that remain is about equal among regions, and is about 20% of the total number in the lowlands.

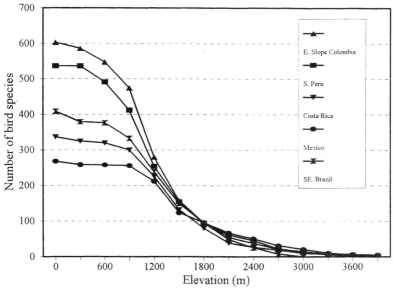

Fig. 8.3 Species richness of *terra firme* forest avifaunas vs. elevation by region in neotropics – lowland species only.

In contrast, the purely montane avifauna components vary distinctly in pattern (Fig. 8.4). First, the total number of species varies widely among the different regions. While in the lowland species the richest region has about twice as many species as the poorest, the montane component of the richest region (eastern Colombia) has roughly 10 times as many species as that in the poorest region (south-eastern Brazil). In addition, the peaks of species richness vary dramatically among regions, from about 800 m in the mountains of southeastern Brazil to 2100 m in the Andes of south-eastern Peru. Besides differences in the placement of the peak, there are also differences in how broad the peak is: broadest in the highlands of Mexico, and narrowest in south-eastern Brazil. Endemic bird species show patterns similar to the overall diversity patterns, except in eastern Peru, where the peak is strongly shifted to higher elevations, with the peak at 3000 m (Fig. 8.5).

The montane avifauna consists of birds with overlapping but non-congruent elevational ranges. Turnover in species composition is relatively rapid. In the Andes of Peru, about 50% of the avifauna turns over with every 500 m gain in elevation (Fig. 8.6). There are three areas of relatively rapid turnover. One occurs where the lowland avifauna is largely replaced by a montane one, between 700 and 1100 m. The second occurs between

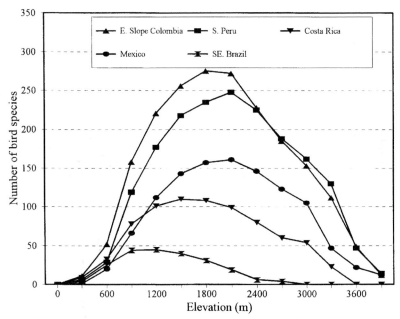

Fig. 8.4 Species richness of *terra firme* forest avifaunas vs. elevation by region in neotropics – strictly montane species.

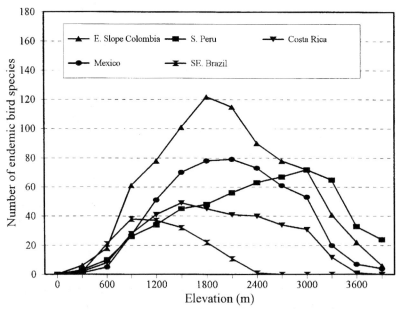

Fig. 8.5 Species richness of *terra firme* forest avifaunas vs. elevation by region in neotropics – montane endemic species only.

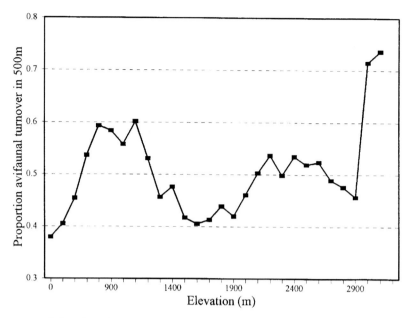

Fig. 8.6 Avifaunal turnover with elevation on east slope of Andes in southern Peru. Turnover is measured as one minus the proportion of species occurring within the 500 m interval from the indicated elevation upward that occur at the indicated elevation and 500 m above.

2100 and 2600 m, and the third occurs above 3000 m, as the treeline approaches.

The average width elevational range for purely montane species is 1330 m. This width increases up to 2600 m, and then declines (Fig. 8.7). The largest number of species with narrow elevational ranges is found on the lower slopes, below 2000 m. The width of mean elevational ranges varies substantially among regions: south-eastern Brazil has the narrowest mean width, and Mexico has the widest (Table 8.1; $t$-test comparisons among pairs of regions are significant at $P < 0.01$ for all comparisons except between Peru and Columbia, $t = 0.11$, $P > 0.50$). Species with narrow elevational ranges are more likely to be endemic than are species with broader elevational ranges (Table 8.2).

Endemism is strongly related to risk of extinction in birds. A species of bird that is endemic to a single zoogeographic region or subregion is much more likely to be at risk of extinction than one that is more widespread (Fig. 8.8). Among montane species, this tendency is even stronger if the elevational range is also narrow. Yet surprisingly, the elevational distribution of

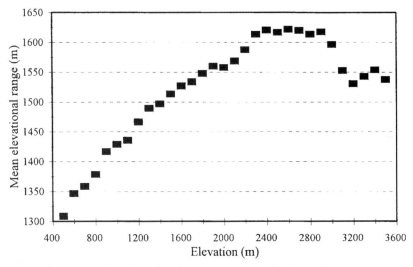

Fig. 8.7 Mean width of elevational range vs. elevation for all strictly montane bird species.

bird species at risk does not track the distribution of endemics (compare Fig. 8.9 and Fig. 8.5). In all montane regions except south-eastern Brazil, these vulnerable species are more common at lower elevations than endemics are. The difference is especially striking in eastern Peru, where the peak of threatened species is at 1500 m, while that for endemics is at 3000 m. Even among endemics, a greater proportion of birds at risk is at the lower elevations (G-test, $P > 0.05$).

## DISCUSSION

### Where does diversity peak?

Rosenzweig (1992, 1995) argues that habitat selection by organisms is an evolved response to high diversity; it allows more organisms to coexist at a single site. He suggests that habitat selection is a consequence of high diversity, not a cause of it. There is some evidence to support this view, at least in part. Several authors have shown that habitat selection by birds is affected by the presence of closely related competitors (Terborgh, 1985). Further, certain types of habitat specialization are found only in high-diversity areas like the Amazon basin (Remsen & Parker, 1983). According to

**Table 8.1**

*Width of elevational distributions of montane birds by region*

| | Number of species | Mean (m) | Standard deviation |
|---|---|---|---|
| Southern Mexico | 190 | 1754 | 547 |
| Costa Rica | 161 | 1481 | 524 |
| Eastern Columbia | 535 | 1303 | 517 |
| Eastern Peru | 413 | 1307 | 512 |
| South-eastern Brazil | 57 | 1075 | 472 |

**Table 8.2**

*Width of elevational distribution of neotropical montane birds versus number of zoogeographic regions occupied*

| | Number of species | Mean (m) | Standard deviation |
|---|---|---|---|
| 1 sub-region | 517 | 1199 | 541 |
| 1 region, not restricted to subregion | 167 | 1418 | 489 |
| 2–3 regions | 357 | 1466 | 514 |
| 4–6 regions | 45 | 1606 | 594 |

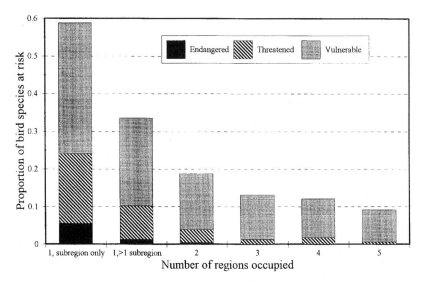

Fig. 8.8 Threat status of birds in relation to range size. Threat status of birds restricted to one subregion, to one region but more than one subregion, and to two regions are significantly more at risk than more widespread species (*t*-tests, $P < 0.01$ for all comparisons). There are no significant differences in threat status among birds found in three, four, or five + regions.

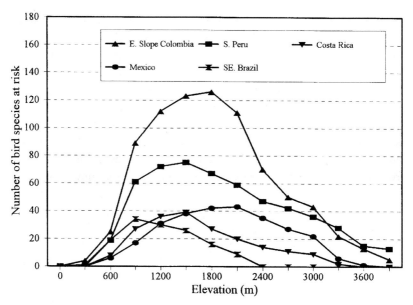

Fig. 8.9 Species richness of birds at risk in *terra firme* forest vs. elevation by region in neotropics.

this view, *all* habitats must be considered together for an appropriate analysis of diversity patterns along elevational gradients. When all habitats are considered, single-site diversity peaks in the lowlands.

However, the high level of habitat diversity that underlies this great number of species in the lowlands has a basis in physical parameters of the environment. The habitats exploited by the additional species do not exist on the slopes of mountain ranges. For example, oxbow lakes and other riverine habitats are an important element of the habitat diversity in lowland Amazonia (Remsen & Parker, 1983). They provide aquatic habitats, as well as a variety of successional vegetation used by a number of bird species. These habitats, and nearly all the species associated with them, are absent on the slopes of the Andes. Birds associated with aquatic habitats are incapable of occurring on the Andean slopes. Similarly, within Amazonia, a site that lacks oxbow lakes or slow-moving rivers will also be lacking the same set of aquatic bird species. Habitat diversity as such has an enormous effect on single-site bird diversity; it is not simply an artefact of how we interpret the coexistence of species.

One might argue that the bird diversity peak at intermediate elevations in *terra firme* forests reflects the lumping of separate gradients in these regional analyses. If species-area curves are steeper in the montane areas than in the lowlands, the regional approach could result in increased diversity on the slopes, even if single sites are actually less diverse. Although Rahbek (1995) did not find evidence that species–area curves were different on the slopes than in the lowlands, the areas he examined were all in the range of thousands of square kilometres, and the shape of the curve at smaller scales is uncertain. Certainly, at the scale at which habitat diversity is expressed, the species-area curve would be shallower on the montane slopes at any particular elevation than in the lowlands. In addition, data from a gradient studied in detail in south-eastern Peru shows a peak in species richness of *terra firme* birds at about 700 m (see Stotz *et al.*, 1996: Fig. 3.5). This is somewhat below the peak for eastern Peru in the regional analysis (900 m). This study also found that when all habitats were included, species richness peaked in the lowlands. Similarly, a study in south-eastern Brazil (A. Aleixo, J. M. E. Vielliard, W. R. Silva & D. F. Stotz, unpublished data) found that bird species richness in humid forests increased between sea level and 850 m; unfortunately this study had no comparable data for higher elevations.

### Why are there elevational gradients in species richness?

Regardless of where one considers the peak to exist, the overall pattern of species richness among birds in the neotropical montane areas shows a basic pattern of declining diversity with elevation. A number of theories have been proposed to account for such gradients. I will focus on two of these ideas.

#### Rapoport's rule

Stevens (1989) observed that a common pattern along latitudinal gradients was that the latitudinal range of organisms was greater at higher than at lower latitudes. He suggested that this pattern, which he termed 'Rapoport's rule' because E. Rapoport had noticed and commented on the pattern in a variety of taxa (Rapoport, 1982), resulted from species at higher latitudes being tolerant of wider amplitudes in climatic variables, because they face greater climatic variability within a single latitude than do species at more tropical latitudes. He argued that this climatic tolerance enables organisms of higher latitudes to occupy a wider latitudinal range than do tropical species.

According to Stevens, then, the latitudinal gradient in diversity results from tropical latitudes containing a set of both narrow-ranging and wide-ranging species, while higher latitudes contain only species that are wide-ranging. Stevens suggests that in the high diversity sites, these wide-ranging species often occupy population sinks.

Stevens (1992) later extended this idea to elevational gradients, arguing that the commonly observed decline in diversity with elevation was associated with wider elevational ranges among organisms that occupy the lower-diversity high elevations. Again, he suggested that species occurring in the low-diversity sites (in this case, high elevations) were tolerant of broader climatic regimes and so were able to occupy a broader elevational range. The gradient in species richness results from these wide-ranging elements adding extra species to the narrowly distributed species of the lower elevations. In both papers, Stevens presents a series of datasets that demonstrate the gradient in diversity and the pattern of range sizes he uses to develop his hypotheses.

In the montane gradients of the neotropics, birds show the basic pattern of species richness that Stevens is attempting to explain, i.e. decreasing species richness with increasing elevation (Fig. 8.1). However, they do not demonstrate increasing mean elevational range with decreasing diversity (e.g. Fig. 8.10 for eastern Peru). Of the five montane regions examined, only south-eastern Brazil shows a consistent increase in elevational range with decreasing species richness. This pattern in south-eastern Brazil sheds light on the general pattern along elevational gradients. The avifauna of the mountains of south-eastern Brazil consists primarily of a lowland element that attenuates in diversity upslope, with only a small element of montane species (Fig. 8.3 and 8.4). Because the lowland element dominates, and because lowland birds that occur at high elevations of necessity have wide elevational ranges, mean range size increases with increasing elevation, and with it decreasing diversity. Figure 8.7, showing a peak of elevational range of montane species at 2600 m, is not completely relevant to this discussion because it lumps all the gradients together, and since it excludes lowland species, it is not directly associated with overall measures of either diversity or elevational range. It does, however, indicate that within the strictly montane element of the avifauna, Stevens' extension of Rapoport's rule to elevational gradients does not conform with the data. The peak diversity sites (ca 2000 m) have an intermediate mean elevational range, while the lowest diversity of the montane element of the avifauna (at the base of the slope) has the narrowest elevational range. The overall

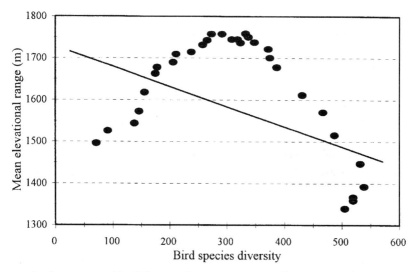

Fig. 8.10 Mean width of elevational range vs. species richness in *terra firme* avifauna of southern Peru on eastern slope of Andes. Each point represents the species richness and mean elevational range at 100 m intervals. The black line represents the predicted relationship based on Stevens (1992).

relationship between species richness and elevational range is positive, although not significantly so (Spearman rank correlation = 0.32; 0.10 > $P$ > 0.05), contrary to the prediction of a negative relationship by Stevens. This indicates that any tendency that neotropical birds show toward following Rapoport's rule for elevation is due entirely to the increase in average elevational range with elevation of lowland taxa.

The pattern shown by neotropical avifaunas along elevational gradients is the converse of that suggested by Stevens to explain Rapoport's rule. It is the *lowland* species with wide elevational ranges that are swamping a depauperate montane fauna high on the slopes, rather than wide-ranging montane forms increasing the diversity of lowland sites. Of the examples that Stevens (1992) provides of elevational gradients that demonstrate Rapoport's rule, in at least half the pattern seems to be explained primarily by the attenuation of lowland groups. Further, many others do not actually show the monotonic decline in diversity that Stevens seeks to explain (see Rahbek, 1997 for more discussion). This suggests that the mechanism suggested by Stevens is not an important determinant of diversity patterns along elevational gradients. If most of the wide-ranging species are lowland rather than montane, this suggests that the population sink dynamics that

Stevens (1992) proposes that species should exhibit at the edge of their elevational ranges, should occur not in the highly diverse, low-elevation sites, but instead in lower-diversity, high-elevation sites.

### Area effects

Rosenzweig (1992, 1995) has suggested that elevational diversity gradients and latitudinal diversity gradients have decidedly different mechanisms at their base. He suggests that latitudinal gradients in species richness are basically the result of area effects. Large contiguous areas of tropical land are climatically similar while, at higher latitudes, only small areas share the same climatic conditions. He suggests that this has allowed the build-up of substantially higher diversity in the tropical regions than in more temperate areas, creating a diversity gradient through both an increase in speciation rates and a decrease in extinction rates. In contrast, he considers diversity along elevational gradients to be a reflection of underlying patterns of primary productivity. Specifically, he finds many elevational gradients with intermediate peaks in diversity (like that demonstrated by *terra firme* birds). He explains this as a tendency of organisms to peak at intermediate levels of productivity, for which he provides a number of empirical examples, and theoretical justification.

Rosenzweig's explanation of elevational diversity gradients is difficult to evaluate, in part because our knowledge of the patterns of primary productivity in the tropics is decidedly poor. Additionally, although the pattern of species richness among *terra firme* birds shows an intermediate peak, the peak shifts to the lowlands when all habitats are included. There is still some question as to which is the appropriate diversity gradient to consider (see above). However, since Rosenzweig has argued that habitat selection is a response to high diversity, it would seem that he would favour the gradient with all habitats and no intermediate elevation peak.

More to the point, the elevational gradient in species richness strongly reflects area effects. The humid lowlands of the neotropics have an enormous extent and an enormous number of species associated with them. The decrease in diversity with increasing elevation is largely due to the loss of this lowland avifauna. Furthermore, the magnitude of the purely montane component of the avifaunas also reflects the available area of humid forest in the particular montane region. The small and isolated mountains of south-eastern Brazil have the lowest purely montane diversity. The mountains of Central America are somewhat higher in diversity and larger in area. The Andes have much larger areas of humid forest and they have a substantially larger montane avifauna. The mountains of Mexico have a relatively large area, yet moderate diversity; however, much of this region falls outside the tropics geographically, vegetationally and in the biogeographic relationships of the avifauna.

Productivity certainly plays a role in the elevational diversity gradient. However, the strong effect of area in creating a huge lowland avifauna (within an admittedly very productive environment) mirrors the area effects that Rosenzweig (1992) uses to explain latitudinal gradients in species richness. This lowland avifauna, whose attenuation upslope dominates the diversity gradient even in those regions with a significant montane avifauna, as well as our lack of data on the actual relationship of productivity to elevation, makes it difficult to evaluate directly the relationship of productivity to diversity. Rahbek (1997) attempted to consider the effects of area on elevational diversity gradients by dividing the Andean gradation into elevational slices. He also concluded that area had a dominant effect on the pattern of species richness with elevation in neotropical birds and found that the relationship of productivity to species richness remained to be determined.

### Conservation implications of elevational patterns and processes

Since the range size of an organism is closely connected with the perceived threat that it faces (see above and ICBP, 1992), we might expect that the elevational pattern of endemic birds (Fig. 8.5) and threatened birds (Fig. 8.9) would mirror one another. However, this is not the case: threatened birds on montane slopes are clearly skewed downward in distribution compared to endemics. Why is this so?

Endemism, while an important factor in making a species vulnerable, is, perhaps with the exception of some island species, not sufficient by itself to place a species at risk among birds. Birds have relatively large ranges. Except for a handful of species, even range-restricted continental taxa had original distributions on the order of thousands of square kilometres. Although Collar, Crosby and Stattersfield (1994) suggest that as many as a quarter of the threatened species of birds are threatened by small range or population size alone, only 23 of the nearly 300 neotropical species that they consider threatened are shown to be threatened by range size along (Collar, Crosby et al., 1994: Appendix 1). An additional threat usually exists for a bird to be at risk of extinction. For the vast majority of tropical birds, that threat is habitat destruction. In the montane humid forest regions in the neotropics, habitat destruction has been strongly concentrated on the lower slopes, especially below 1500 m. That is where most agriculture in the Andean countries is concentrated, especially coffee and cocoa cultivation. Since, in addition, montane bird species on these lower slopes have narrower than average elevational ranges, these species are even more vulnerable to habitat destruction.

In large part, the amount and pattern of deforestation, combined with the elevational ranges of the birds in the region, determines the relative threat to the avifauna. Although there is extensive deforestation on the lower and middle slopes of the Mexican mountains, many of the birds still fare relatively well: the broad elevational ranges of the birds in the Madrean highlands allow them to maintain significant populations above the areas hardest hit by deforestation. In eastern Peru, eastern Colombia and Costa Rica, birds of high-elevation areas are substantially less at risk than those on the lower slopes. In Costa Rica, the high-elevation avifauna is largely protected by national parks; in Colombia and Peru, it is protected by the unsuitability of the land at higher elevation for agriculture. The less dramatic skew to lower elevations for threatened species in Colombia results from the more extensive deforestation at mid-elevations there than elsewhere in the neotropical mountains. In south-eastern Brazil, nearly all forest below 800 m has been destroyed. Most remaining forest is at higher elevations. However, most birds at these elevations cover the entire gradient, including the lowlands. Nearly all purely montane species are restricted to the largely deforested lower slopes. These birds, along with the endemic species restricted to lowland forests, constitute the most endangered avifauna in the New World.

The deforestation that dominates the lower slopes of the neotropical mountains has effects beyond threatening species that are restricted to those elevational zones. Elevational migrants that cross these areas may have their movements disrupted by such deforestation. Unlike most latitudinal migrant birds, many species of elevational migrants in the neotropics are intolerant of non-forest habitats (Stiles, 1988; Powell & Bjork, 1995; Stotz et al. 1996), so deforestation can limit the ability of these species to use distinct breeding and wintering grounds. Further, these migrants are dominated by frugivorous and nectarivorous species (Stiles, 1988; Levey & Stiles, 1992; Stotz et al., 1996). The disruption of their movement patterns may provoke ecosystem-wide consequences because of the loss or alteration of their pollination and dispersal services.

Much of the diversity on lower montane slopes is composed of lowland species that climb to higher elevations. Many of these species may be maintained at these higher elevations through immigration from lower elevations (see above). The loss of continuity with low-elevation forest could result in the loss of substantial numbers of species on these lower slopes. There is little empirical evidence to evaluate this idea; however, I have analysed the list of Scott & Brooke (1985) from Serra dos Orgãos National Park in Rio de Janeiro, Brazil. This park extends from *ca.* 2250 m down to *ca.* 800 m in elevation. Below this elevation, the slopes are nearly completely deforested. Scott & Brooke (1985) found virtually all the high-elevation forest bird species expected at the site; however, 22 forest birds that occur in the lowlands or only along the lower slopes of the mountains in southeastern Brazil, and extend commonly upslope at least to 800 or 1000 m elsewhere in Rio de Janeiro and São Paulo, were not encountered. At a similar forest site at 850 m in São Paulo, where forest is continuous with lowland forests, 19 of these 22 species were found (pers. obs.). These data are consistent with the suggestion advanced above that the populations of these birds at the upper edges of their elevational ranges are population sinks. They are maintained by interchange with populations lower on the slopes, and when contact among these populations is interrupted, the high-elevation populations disappear.

Although we understand the patterns of diversity and endemism among birds rather well, an important issue in planning conservation in montane regions in the neotropics is whether patterns of diversity and endemism among taxonomic groups correspond. If they do, conservation plans based on a single group (for example, the well-known birds) could act as an umbrella for most biodiversity. At relatively large scales, patterns of endemism among classes of terrestrial organisms (mainly vertebrate and vascular plant data) seem to agree rather well (ICBP, 1992; Balmford & Long, 1995; Biodiversity Support Program *et al.*, 1995). However, at more local scales, agreement is harder to find. For example, Prendergast *et al.* (1993) found little agreement among diversity patterns in various groups in Great Britain. They also found that the distribution of 'rare' species showed little agreement with distributional patterns for the same group as a whole, or with rare species of other taxa.

More geographically relevant are the papers of Patterson *et al.* (in press) and Graham (1990), who found substantive differences among diversity patterns in bats and birds along different elevational gradients in the Peruvian Andes. The largest difference was that, while birds had substantial numbers of species restricted to montane elevations, nearly all bats occurred at lowland elevations and the montane fauna was essentially a lowland fauna that attenuated upslope (much like the bird pattern in south-eastern Brazil). Patterson *et al.* (in press) further found that rodents exhibited yet a third pattern, even more distinct than bats and birds, with almost complete turnover of species in at least three distinct bands. However, they did find that, if all mammals were considered together, the pattern did begin to approach that of birds.

The extent of overlap of *diversity* patterns among groups may be effectively irrelevant to considerations of tropical conservation, however. It is clear that *endemic* taxa are the ones most likely to be threatened with extinction. Diversity patterns are usually dominated by widespread taxa of little conservation interest. Among birds, the high diversity in the Amazonian lowlands means much less from a conservation perspective than do the numerous endemics found on the montane slopes of the Andes. Comparisons of patterns of *endemism* among groups would be a much more useful exercise for pointing out the regions in immediate need of conservation action and protection.

## CONCLUSIONS

The elevational distributions of birds in the neotropical mountains and the processes that underlie them have relevance to conservation activities, not just in the neotropics, but throughout the tropical biomes of the world. There are four major conclusions of this work which have broad importance for tropical conservation:

(i)   Threats to the environment, in particular agricultural development, are not evenly distributed elevationally, but are concentrated on lower montane slopes; thus, although endemism is an important predictor of a bird's risk of extinction, endemism alone cannot be used to focus conservation attention.

(ii)  Middle- and high-elevation forests act as population sinks for wide-ranging lowland species, so that these species may be lost from montane areas that have been isolated from lowland forests through agricultural development.

(iii) This isolation of montane forests from lowland forests may also disrupt elevational migration of forest birds, putting these birds at risk. Since these migrants are dominated by nectarivorous and frugivorous birds, this can have important consequences for forest ecosystems through the loss of their services as pollinators and seed dispersal agents.

(iv) Congruence in patterns of endemism among taxonomic groups is more relevant to conservation than the lack of congruence that has been found in patterns of diversity across some taxonomic groups. Because of their shared history, such congruence is expected to be more often encountered among endemics than among species as a whole. Because of the relatively high risk faced by endemic taxa, these patterns of congruence can help to shape effective conservation activities.

### References

Balmford, A. & Long, A. (1995). Across-country analyses of biodiversity congruence and current conservation effort in the tropics. *Conserv. Biol.*, **9**, 1539–1547.

Bierregaard, R. O., Jr., Cohn-Haft, M. & Stotz, D. F. (1997). A cryptic species of *Cercomacra* antbird, with the description of a new subspecies. *Orn. Monogr.* **48**, 111–28.

Biodiversity Support Group, Conservation International, The Nature Conservancy, Wildlife Conservation Society, World Resources Institute & World Wildlife Fund (1995). *A regional analysis of geographic priorities for biodiversity conservation in Latin America and the Caribbean.* Biodiversity Support Program, Washington, DC.

Borland International (1992). *Paradox: Version 4.0.* Borland International, Scott's Valley, CA.

Collar, N. J., Crosby, M. J. & Stattersfield, A. J. (1994). *Birds to watch 2: the world list of threatened birds.* BirdLife International, Cambridge, UK.

Collar, N. J., Gonzaga, L. P., Krabbe, N., Madroño Nieto, A., Naranjo, L. G., Parker, T. A., III & Wege, D. C. (1992). *Threatened birds of the Americas: the ICBP/ IUCN Red data book.* (3rd edn, part 2). Smithsonian Institution Press, Washington, DC.

Fjeldså, J. (1994). Geographical patterns for relict and young species of birds in Africa and South America and implications for conservation priorities. *Biodiv. Conserv.*, **3**, 207–26.

Graham, G. L. (1990). Bats versus birds: comparisons among Peruvian volant vertebrate faunas along an elevational gradient. *J. Biogeogr.*, **17**, 657–68.

ICBP (1992). *Putting biodiversity on a map: priority areas for global conservation.* International Council for Bird Preservation, Cambridge, UK.

Levey, D. J. & Stiles, F. G. (1992). Evolutionary precursors of long-distance migration: resource availability and movement patterns in Neotropical landbirds. *Am. Nat.*, **140**, 447–76.

Parker, T. A., III, Stotz, D. F. & Fitzpatrick, J. W. (1996). Ecological and distributional databases. In *Neotropical birds: ecology and conservation*: 118–436. (Eds

Stotz, D. F., Fitzpatrick, J. W., Parker, T. A., III & Moskovits, D. K.). University of Chicago Press, Chicago, IL.

Patterson, B. D., Stotz, D. F., Solari, S., Fitzpatrick, J. W. & Pacheco, V. (1998). Contrasting patterns of elevational zonation of vertebrates in the Andes of SE Peru. *J. Biogeogr.* (in press).

Powell, G. V. N. & Bjork, R. (1995). Implications of intratropical migration on reserve design: a case study using *Pharomachrus mocinno. Conserv. Biol.*, **9**, 354–62.

Prendergast, J. R., Quinn, R. M., Lawton, J. H., Eversham, B. C. & Gibbons, D. W. (1993). Rare species, the coincidence of diversity hotspots and conservation. *Nature, Lond.*, **365**, 335–7.

Rahbek, C. (1995). The elevational gradient of species richness: a uniform pattern? *Ecography*, **18**, 200–5.

Rahbek, C. (1997). The relationship among area, elevation, and regional species diversity in Neotropical birds. *Am. Nat.*, **149**, 875–902.

Rapoport, E. H. (1982). *Areography: geographical strategies of species.* Pergamon, New York, NY.

Remsen, J. V., Jr. & Parker, T. A., III. (1983). Contribution of river-created habitats to bird species richness in Amazonia. *Biotropica*, **15**, 223–31.

Rosenzweig, M. L. (1992). Species diversity gradients: we know more and less than we thought. *J. Mammal*, **73**, 715–30.

Rosenzweig, M. L. (1995). *Species diversity in space and time.* Cambridge University Press, Cambridge, UK.

Scott, D. A. & Brooke, M. de L. (1985). The endangered avifauna of southeastern Brazil: a report on the BOU/WWF Expeditions of 1980/81 and 1981/82. In *Conservation of tropical forest birds*: 115–139. (Eds Diamond, A. W. & Lovejoy, T. E.). International Council for Bird Preservation, Cambridge. (*Tech. Publ. ICBP*, **4**.)

Stevens, G. C. (1989). The latitudinal gradient in geographical range: how so many species coexist in the tropics. *Am. Nat.*, **133**, 240–56.

Stevens, G. C. (1992). The elevational gradient in altitudinal range: an extension of Rapoport's latitudinal rule to altitude. *Am. Nat.*, **140**, 893–911.

Stiles, F. G. (1988). Altitudinal movements of birds on the Caribbean slope of Costa Rica: implications for conservation. *Mem. Calif. Acad. Sci.*, **12**, 243–58.

Stotz, D. F. (1990). The taxonomic status of *Phyllomyias reiseri. Bull. Br. Orn. Club*, **110**, 184–7.

Stotz, D. F., Fitzpatrick, J. W., Parker, T. A., III & Moskovits, D. K. (1996). *Neotropical birds: ecology and conservation.* University of Chicago Press, Chicago, IL.

Terborgh, J. (1985). Habitat selection in Amazonian birds. In *Habitat selection in birds*: 311–38. (Ed. Cody, M. L.). Academic Press, Orlando, FL.

Vuilleumier, F., LeCroy, M. & Mayr, E. (1992). New species of birds described from 1981 to 1990. *Bull. Br. Orn. Club*, **112A** (Suppl.), 267–309.

Willis, E. O. (1992). Three *Chamaeza* antthrushes in eastern Brazil (Formicariidae). *Condor*, **94**, 110–16.

**Fig. 4.1** Alternative responses to climate change.

The rectangular area represents an arbitrary geographical space within which the ellipses represent either the geographic range of a species or the area of intersection between geographical space and climate space within which the species' initial climatic requirements/tolerances are met. An initial situation (A) is shown in which the species is in equilibrium with climate so that its area of occurrence coincides with the area within which its present climatic requirements/tolerances are met (green ellipse). The other three diagrams represent alternative situations following a major climate change such that the area within which the species' initial climatic requirements/tolerances are met no longer overlaps the species' initial range but instead is represented by the additional ellipse in the upper right-hand corner of the geographic space.

In the first of these (B) the species has responded to the climatic change spatially, by migrating so as to maintain its range in equilibrium with the changing climate; its new range thus coincides with the area within which its initial climatic requirements/tolerances are now met (green ellipse) and it is no longer present in its initial range (empty ellipse). The second case (C) represents an evolutionary response; the species has evolved new climatic requirements/tolerances enabling it to sustain its original geographic range (lavender ellipse), which no longer overlaps the area within which its initial climatic requirements/tolerances are now met (yellow ellipse). The third case (D) represents failure to exhibit a spatial or an evolutionary response; the area within which the species' initial climatic requirements/tolerances are now met (yellow ellipse) no longer overlaps its original geographical range (empty ellipse), within which it is now extinct.

**Fig. 4.2** Combined spatial and evolutionary response to climate change.

As in Fig. 4.1, the rectangular area represents an arbitrary geographical space. The shaded ellipses represent the geographical range of a species that is in equilibrium with climate and thus is occupying the area of intersection between geographical space and climate space within which its climate requirements/tolerances are met. The empty ellipses represent the species' range before/after a climate change, reflecting the element of spatial response indicated by the unshaded arrow in B. The varying shades, from purple to green, within the ellipses representing the species' occupied geographical range indicate the varying genotype of the species, which exhibits climatically related clinal variation within its area of occurrence.

In the first case (A) the species' range is in the 'south-west' of the geographical area and 'purple' genotypes are predominant. In contrast, following the climatic change (B) the species' geographical range is 'north-eastern' and 'green' genotypes predominate. Note that the more extreme 'purple' genotypes are absent in B and the more extreme 'green' genotypes absent in A; this reflects a shift in the position in climate space, as well as in geographical space, of the intersection between the two within which the species' climatic requirements/tolerances are met. The species' response to this changed intersection has been evolutionary and is indicated by the shaded arrow in B. Note also that the genotype of individuals within the geographical area occupied both before and after the climatic change has also changed, being toward the 'green' end of the range in A, but being replaced by genotypes more toward the 'purple' end of the range in B.

**Fig. 4.3** Individualistic responses of two species to a climate change.

As in the previous figures the rectangles represent an arbitrary geographical space and the shaded ellipses represent the geographical ranges of two species that are in equilibrium with climate and thus are occupying the area of intersection between geographical space and climate space within which their climatic requirements/tolerances are met. The shading within the ellipses reflects the genotypes of the species, each species exhibiting clinal variation in relation to climate. The empty ellipses in each case represent the geographical range of the other species. The geographical distributions of the first species are shown in A and B whereas those of the second are shown in A′ and B′. In the initial situation (A and A′) the two species exhibit overlapping distributions although their climatically determined clinal variation patterns are orthogonal to one another. Following climate change (B and B′) each species exhibits a combination of spatial and evolutionary responses as a consequence of which their geographical ranges no longer overlap. This reflects the failure of the climate conditions jointly favourable both to the more 'blue' genotypes of the first species and to the more 'red' genotypes of the second any longer to intersect the geographical space. Instead, the more extreme 'green' genotypes of the first and 'blue' genotypes of the second, which occupy distinct climatic conditions, are now favoured in different parts of the geographical space.

**Fig. 4.4** Alternative mechanisms of extinction as a consequence of climate change. Three alternative extinction mechanisms are illustrated by the sequence of panels. Time advances from the top panel downwards, as indicated by the arrow. As time advances, the climate of the geographical area represented by the rectangle changes progressively. This climate change impacts upon the location and/or extent of the geographical area within which each species' climatic requirements/tolerances are met. These areas are represented by the ellipses, which are shaded if the species is occupying them and empty with a dashed outline if the species is absent.

Species A (green) experiences a progressive and severe reduction in its potential range from time $t$ to time $t+3$ followed by an increase at times $t+4$ and $t+5$. The extreme reduction of its range at time $t+3$, however, renders it extremely susceptible to stochastic extinction as a consequence of extreme environmental events or random population fluctuations; thus it has become extinct before the subsequent increase in its potential range at time $t+4$.

Species B (red) experiences progressive but less severe range reduction from time $t$ to time $t+3$. However, at time $t+3$, a second discrete area of potential range becomes available in a different part of the overall geographical space. By time $t+4$ the original component of the potential range has disappeared; the new component, however, has increased in extent and does so again at time $t+5$. The species nonetheless becomes extinct because it is unable to achieve the long-distance dispersal necessary to cross the spatial discontinuity between the two component parts of its potential range at time $t+3$.

Species C (blue) experiences a progressive but moderate range reduction from time $t$ to time $t+3$. At time $t+2$, however, no part of the geographical space offers climatic conditions that satisfy its requirements/tolerances and it thus has no potential range. Although suitable conditions are once again available at time $t+4$ and the area of its potential range increases once again thereafter, it has become extinct at time $t+3$ as a consequence of the temporal discontinuity in its potential range.

**Fig. 4.5** Schematic representation of the consequences of a rapid climate change. Once again the rectangle represents a geographical space, the four panels representing successive situations along a time-series that advances downwards, as indicated by the arrow. The ellipses again represent the range of a species that initially, at time $t$, is occupying fully its potential climatically determined range, as indicated by the shading of the entire ellipse.

Climate changes progressively at times $t+1$ to $t+3$ so that the species' potential range steadily shifts north-eastwards; this potential range is indicated by the ellipse with the dashed outline. The species migrates north-eastwards in response to this climate change, which makes new areas of potential range available along the north-eastern sector of its previously occupied range. However, the species' migration rate is insufficient to maintain its advancing range margin in equilibrium with climate. At the same time, climatic conditions in parts of its original range no longer satisfy requirements/tolerances and consequently it dies out in those areas. The overall consequence is a reduction in the area occupied by the species, as indicated by the shaded area at each time step, so that by time $t+3$ it has suffered a severe reduction in range and hence also in population. Even if no further climate change occurred after time $t+4$, the species has been rendered vulnerable to extinction because its population has been severely reduced. If climate change continued at the same rate for one more time step then the species would become extinct as a result of its failure to migrate at a sufficient rate to continue to occupy any part of its potential range.

Fig. 4.1

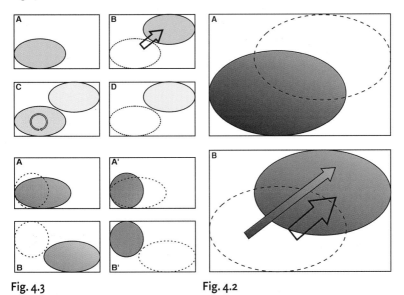

Fig. 4.3

Fig. 4.2

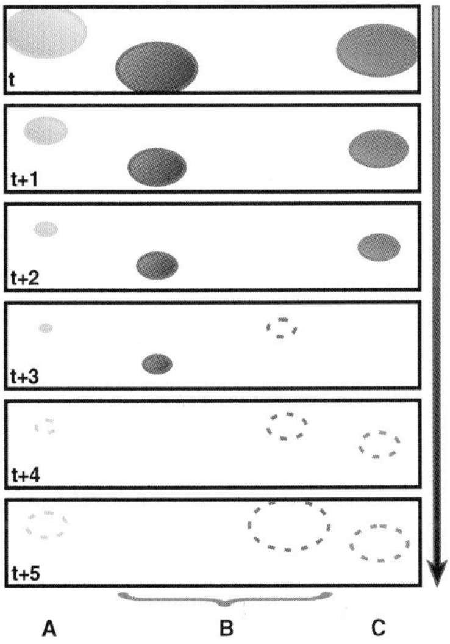

A          B          C

Fig. 4.4

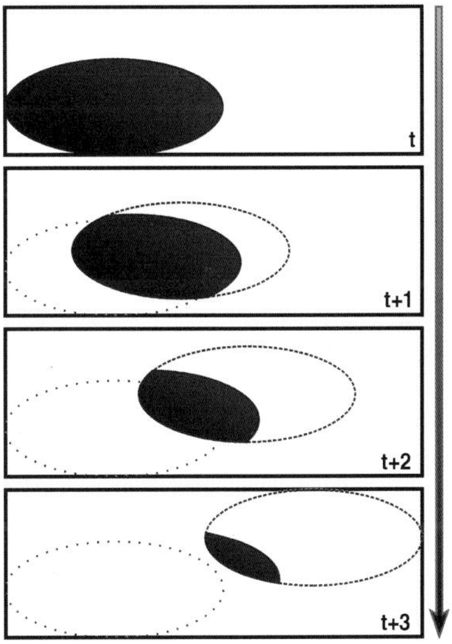

Fig. 4.5

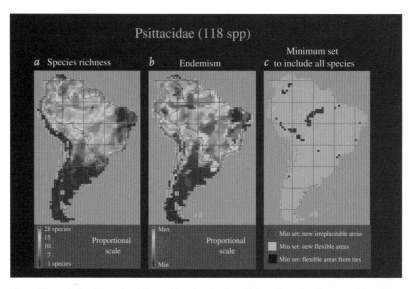

**Fig. 7.1** The variation in species richness (*a*) and endemism (*b*) for 118 species of parrots, Psittacidae, with the near-minimum set of irreplaceable and flexible areas needed to cover all species (*c*).

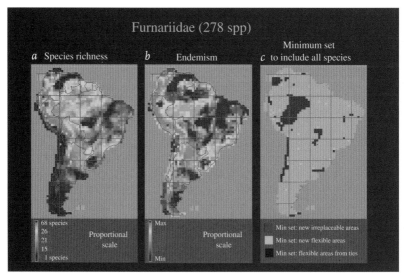

**Fig. 7.2** The variation in species richness (*a*) and endemism (*b*) for 274 ovenbirds and woodcreepers, Furnaridae, with the near-minimum set of irreplaceable and flexible areas needed to cover all species (*c*).

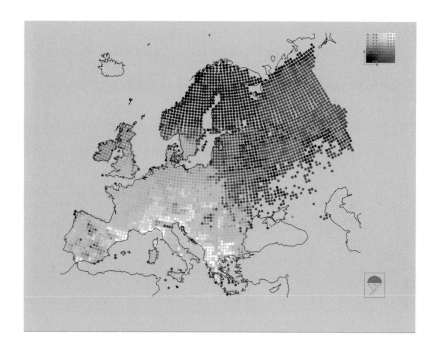

**Fig. 10.2** The geographical pattern of deviations from any 'indicator' relationship of diversity between two groups of organisms can be visualized by overlaying the two diversity maps in two separate colours (Williams 1996a). Here, increasing intensity of blue is used to represent increasing species and subspecies richness of Pinaceae (pines, first, spruces, larches) and increasing intensity of green is used for increasing species and subspecies richness of Fagaceae (oaks, beeches and chestnut). Consequently, black grid cells on the map show low richness for both; white shows high richness for both; and shades of grey show intermediate and linearly covarying richness for both (these covarying scores lie on the diagonal of the colour key, to the upper right of the map). In contrast, areas of the map with highly saturated blue cells show an excess of richness for Pinaceae over Fagaceae, and areas with highly saturated green show an excess of Fagaceae over Pinaceae (Spearman correlation coefficient $rho = -0.33$, $P < 0.0005$). The colour classes are arranged to give even frequency distributions of richness scores along both axes (at least within the constraints imposed by tied richness scores), between the observed maximum and minimum (non-zero) scores. For a review of similar colour systems see Brewer (1994), and for an example of a three-dimensional plot see Williams (1993a). Data are taken from joint work with Chris Humphries, Raino Lampinen, Tapani Lahti and Pertti Uotila, for 'native' records for $50 \times 50$ km grid cells from the *Atlas Florae Europaeae*.

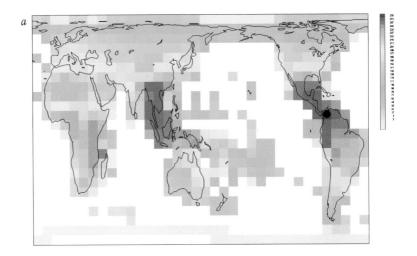

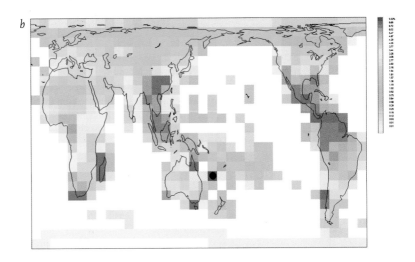

**Fig. 10.3** Maps combining (*a*) family richness and (*b*) family range-size rarity (showing concentrations of narrow endemism) of terrestrial and freshwater seed plants, amphibians, reptiles and mammals world-wide on an equal-area grid map (grid-cell area *c*. 611 000 km$^2$, for intervals of 10° longitude). Range-size rarity is measured by summing the inverse of the range sizes for each family in a grid cell. Maximum scores are shown in red with a white spot, other scores are divided into 32 colour-scale classes of approximately equal size by numbers of grid cells. Although the numerical values differ, the frequency classes (with nearly equal areas) remain comparable among maps. After Willams, Gaston & Humphries (1997).

# 9

# Indicator taxa for biodiversity assessment in the vanishing tropics

SACHA SPECTOR AND ADRIAN B. FORSYTH

## INTRODUCTION

Information on the distribution of biological diversity is the basis of conservation planning and priority-setting and is sorely needed in the many tropical countries now building protected-area systems. Biodiversity surveys provide this fundamental information needed for protected area justification and design, and for development of management plans. In response, many international conservation organizations such as The Nature Conservancy, Conservation International, and the World Wildlife Fund, and scientific institutions such as the Smithsonian and the Field Museum of Chicago are expanding their biodiversity assessment programmes. Multi- and bilateral agencies such as the World Bank and United States Agency for International Development (USAID) require biodiversity assessments for setting investment priorities and for monitoring integrated conservation and development programmes.

The demand for biodiversity information greatly exceeds the delivery capacity of the scientific institutions and scientists that work in the tropics. In the tropics the flora and fauna are too diverse for all-taxa inventories. Nor is it possible to monitor the fate of all taxa. Indicator taxa which serve as surrogates for the entire biota are therefore needed for both biodiversity assessment and ecological monitoring (Kremen, 1992; Norton & Ulanowicz, 1992; Pearson & Cassola, 1992; Kremen, Merenlender & Murphy, 1994). This is especially true for invertebrates, which are estimated to make up as much as 90% of biodiversity at the species level (Disney, 1986; Kim, 1993; Samways, 1993, 1994).

Insects show promise as biodiversity indicators because of their abundance, habitat specialization, response to small-scale habitat heterogeneity (Hill, 1996; Niemela, Haila & Puntilla, 1996) and important roles in ecosystem function (Didham et al., 1996). Although aquatic biodiversity surveys and monitoring programmes often include insects (Buikema, Nieder-lehner & Cairns, 1982), terrestrial surveys in the tropics rarely include insects other than butterflies. Instead, plants and birds are used as surrogates for overall biodiversity (Dinerstein *et al.*, 1995; Wege & Long, 1995; Stotz, Fitzpatrick & Moskvits, 1996). However, recent work by Basset *et al.* (1996), Gaston & Hudson (1994), and Oliver, Beattie & York (in press) suggests that plants and vertebrates do not accurately predict patterns of insect biodiversity. Given their species richness and ecological importance, any comprehensive biodiversity assessment should include insects (Rosenberg, Danks & Lehmkuhl, 1986; Brown, 1992; Hammond, 1992; New, 1995).

The enormous species richness of insects presents technical and financial obstacles to any effort that seeks a comprehensive survey of the fauna. For example, a proposed all-taxa biological inventory project proposed for Costa Rica estimated the cost of surveying just the Hymenoptera alone at greater than $26 million (L. Masner pers. comm.). This constraint begs the question of which subset of insect taxa should be utilized for biodiversity surveys. Brown (1992) suggested that there were 10 neotropical insect groups, including chrysomelid and curculionid beetles, various Hymenoptera, myrid bugs, tabanid and asilid flies, odonates, and various butterfly families 'already near to optimum usefulness'. But what makes these taxa good indicators and how much effort is required before these taxa can be compared across tropical localities?

This chapter presents a brief account of our efforts to develop an insect indicator taxon. We review some of the criteria used in selecting indicator taxa and discuss them in the light of our work using dung beetles (Coleoptera: Scarabaeidae: Scarabaeinae). We illustrate some of the issues surrounding the use of indicator taxa, primarily with data from a single survey of a large protected area in eastern Bolivia that we conducted in January 1997. We also include observations drawn from surveys that we have conducted in some 14 localities in Amazonia and the tropical Andes, ranging from Colombia to Bolivia. Since funding for tropical conservation and science is scarce, we discuss the utility of such surveys and the costs associated with developing an indicator taxon in the tropics.

## INDICATOR TAXA : A PRIMER

The ideal indicator taxon is hard to find. It must possess an ensemble of traits rarely found in one taxon. Noss (1990), Kremen (1992), Pearson &

Cassola (1992), Halffter & Favila (1993) and Pearson (1994) review the attributes of ideal indicator taxa. We summarize these below and suggest additional factors which, based on our experience, require consideration.

## Taxonomic issues

The enormous diversity of many insect taxa makes their use as indicators impossible. Many taxa need revision and contain numerous undescribed species and genera, making the identification of specimens a major hurdle. Pearson & Cassola (1992) consequently argue that one criterion for indicator taxa should be that they are sufficiently stable taxonomically to permit accurate and consistent identification. They equate this stability with a low rate of species invalidation through synonymy in the taxonomic literature. However, we suggest that availability of taxonomic expertise is of equal importance. If there are no active researchers of a particular taxon, there will certainly be few synonymies, falsely indicating taxonomic stability. More practically, the degree of synonymy in a taxon will hardly matter if there is no one to identify the material sampled. Thus, as important as the state of a taxon's taxonomy is the state of its taxonomists. This issue will become increasingly pressing as the ranks of taxonomists continue to dwindle (Gaston & May, 1992). No one should embark on biodiversity surveying without substantial taxonomic resources.

Given this taxonomic challenge, are short cuts in order or is aiming for species-level data worthwhile and necessary? Use of morphospecies (Beattie, 1992; Oliver & Beattie, 1993; Beattie & Oliver, 1994) or higher taxonomic levels (Balmford, Green & Murray, 1996; Balmford, Jayasuriya & Green, 1996) reduces the time, effort and costs required by surveys. However, higher taxonomic levels are plagued by a lack of equivalency. For example, a single beetle genus such as *Agra* (Coleoptera: Carabidae), which includes more than 2000 species, may well exhibit greater genetic and ecological diversity than that of entire bird families. Species, on the whole, are more equivalent across taxa in the amount of genetic and ecological diversity they represent. Morphospecies and higher taxa surveys also do not yield the data necessary to draw conclusions about the species-level endemism of a fauna or flora. As a result, they are less likely to place the components of the community in any clear biogeographic context. Politically, much biodiversity conservation legislation and protection such as listing under CITES or the United States Endangered Species Act is directed at the species level, making identification of taxa to the species level important. Thus, while these shortcut methods are useful in some contexts, they do not address the goal of identifying and conserving unique taxa.

Specimen and information management is also critical for enhancing the utility of biodiversity assessments. As specimens are incorporated into museum collections, they are normally dispersed according to a phylogenetic curation scheme. Valuable ecological data on species co-occurrence, habitat specialization and relative abundance is lost in the process. This phenomenon is particularly troublesome when species in a study are merely identified as 'morphospecies 1, 2, 3'. If no site-specific synoptic collection is maintained, the potential for later cross-matching of morphospecies from different sites is greatly reduced. Ability to relocate particular specimens and collections is also important in light of the frequency of misidentification, even by specialists, or where taxonomy is tentative, which may be the case for a large fraction of tropical taxa. Few tropical (indeed any) museums have specimen tracking systems that enable ecological data to be extracted. Failure to archive surveys properly generally results in a great and often irreversible loss of information.

### Sampling

The efficiency with which a significant fraction of an indicator taxon can be captured is a crucial issue for biodiversity surveys. Butterflies, for example, have often been suggested as ideal indicators (Brown, 1992; Hammond, 1992), yet to survey a tropical butterfly community adequately takes on the order of years rather than days or months. One of the most diverse lepidopteran communities in the neotropics (found at Explorer's Inn, Madre de Dios Province, Peru) required 10 years of periodic collecting to encounter the majority of species (Lamas, 1994). In such cases a subset of the taxon should be selected.

The ideal taxon should also be amenable to sampling that yields a portrait of community composition based on relative or absolute abundance data. Presence/absence or other qualitative data are not adequate for conservation priority-setting that considers centres of population density (Angermeier & Winston, 1997; see chapters by Williams and by Nicholls, this volume). In the case of dispersive insects, a large proportion of any sample may be composed of 'tourist species' – species represented by one or two specimens that are probably not derived from resident breeding populations. This is especially problematic for sites where high altitudinal relief places entirely different habitats and faunas in immediate proximity to one another and increases the probability of encountering species outside their breeding range. Tourist species confound attempts to estimate how well the resident community in an area has been sampled. Monitoring for environmental change also demands more sensitive information about shifts in relative abundance than a species' presence or absence.

Most survey data are not comparable to other survey results because of a lack of standard sampling methodologies. While a trapping method always has inherent biases, efforts should be taken so that these biases are consistent across sampling events and surveys. Sampling consistency is difficult to achieve for mobile taxa such as Lepidoptera or tiger beetles (Coleoptera: Cicindelidae). Unequal sample size is another factor that can reduce the strength of between-site comparisons and lead to erroneous conclusions about priority areas for biodiversity (Fagan & Kareiva, 1997). Long-term monitoring particularly requires simple and standard trapping methods that remove the effect of an individual's experience and expertise at hand-capturing the taxon and permit clear quantification of sampling effort.

### Biogeographic distribution

Broadly distributed taxa are preferred as indicators. Taxa with restricted ranges may be appropriate for monitoring specific sites, but they are not useful for making the broad-scale biodiversity comparisons that determine conservation investments by major donors such as the World Bank, USAID and international conservation agencies. Gaining insights into the biogeographic patterns of the taxon that are necessary for regional priority-setting depends on regional rather than local data.

### Responses to habitat degradation

Habitat loss or degradation is perhaps the paramount issue in biodiversity conservation. One of the primary uses of indicator taxa in this context is for monitoring of environmental change. Biodiversity assessment should also give attention to identifying areas where species are likely to be habitat specialists or otherwise exceptionally sensitive to habitat degradation (Kremen, Colwell *et al.*, 1993). To provide this information, indicator taxa must be sensitive to environmental disturbance. However, highly sensitive taxa in which all species go locally extinct in response to minimal disturbance are less useful than those which provide information over a range of disturbance regimes. Useful indicators of habitat alteration must therefore be capable of displaying a gradient of responses to a gradient of environmental change.

The response of most proposed indicator taxa (*sensu* Brown, 1992) to habitat change is poorly known. Not all insects decline in diversity or abundance as a result of environmental degradation (but see Kremen (1992) and Dorvillè (1996) for examples of insect indicators that react negatively to habitat disruption). Litter-inhabiting ants, for example, exhibit no clear response to conversion of primary forest to second-growth and plantations in parts of Africa (Belshaw & Bolton, 1993). Likewise, litter ant communities in the Atlantic forest of Brazil show much overlap with those of adjacent grasslands (Majer, Delabie & McKenzie, 1997). Baz & Garcia-Boyero (1995) found that butterfly diversity increased as the patchiness of forest fragments increased, while Blair & Launer (1997) report that butterfly diversity peaks in moderately disturbed sites in California. Likewise, Spitzer *et al.* (1997) found that, in Vietnam, butterfly diversity was greater near large clearings and villages than in primary forest. Other groups, such a passalid beetles, may also be most diverse in disturbed or regenerating habitat (J. Schuster, pers. comm.). Thus, high diversity and endemism in a survey cannot be accepted as a measure of high conservation value without an understanding of the ecological nature of the community.

### Ecological and economic criteria

Conservation-driven biodiversity assessments normally address issues of concern to project managers and donors. In this context, taxa that are important ecological or economic keystones may merit greater priority than those that are not. Indicator taxa, then, should have well-understood natural histories and be involved in ecosystem services such as pollination, nutrient cycling or seed dispersal. These characteristics can be incorporated into survey designs and be considered when drawing conclusions from data.

### Correlation with other groups

If indicators are to act as surrogates for the entire biota, then their geographic patterns of species richness and endemism should closely reflect those of other taxa. However, Prendergast *et al.* (1993), Oliver *et al.* (in press) and others show that the patterns of richness of different taxa often do not coincide. Even within higher taxa, patterns of diversity may be dissimilar. Becalloni & Gaston (1995) attempted to use Ithomiinae butterfly richness as an measure of overall butterfly diversity but this approach has not been entirely successful (B. Robbins pers. comm.). Complementarity analyses of protected areas, which measure the degree to which a proposed area contributes species unrepresented in other protected areas, generally find that focal taxa often do not overlap. For example, Kitching (1996) found that in Thailand the minimum set of areas need to represent hawkmoth and tiger beetle species richness was very different (14 areas for hawkmoths and 34 for tiger beetles). Greater efforts in the future must be devoted to establishing what proposed indicator groups actually indicate.

## A CASE STUDY OF NEOTROPICAL DUNG BEETLES

After considering a number of the insect taxa used or advocated as indicators by others, including butterflies, orchid bees (Apidae: Euglossini), ants (Hymenoptera: Formicidae), and tiger beetles (Coleoptera: Cicindelidae), we chose to look at a subfamily of dung beetles (Coleoptera: Scarabaeidae: Scarabaeinae). Dung beetles can be readily and quantitatively sampled with a standard protocol (Lobo, Martin-Piera & Veiga, 1988), have a manageable taxonomy and a community of active taxonomists, are globally distributed, have a well-known natural history (Halffter & Edmunds, 1982; Hanski & Cambefort, 1991), respond dramatically and unambiguously to habitat modification (Howden & Nealis, 1975; Klein, 1989) and play a keystone role in nutrient recycling and seed dispersal in forest ecosystems (Peck & Forsyth, 1982; Klein, 1989; Yokoyama et al., 1991; Halffter & Favila, 1993; Nestel, Dickschen & Altirei, 1993, Andreson, 1994; Hill, 1996). Most of the scarabaeine beetle community biomass is derived from the nutrients it obtains from digesting mammalian dung. Thus, biomass of the dung beetle community should correlate with mammalian biomass and ecosystem productivity. In short, the Scarabaeinae appeared to be an ideal indicator taxon for biodiversity assessment and ecological monitoring.

We attempted to test this hypothesis with a series of surveys of dung beetle communities. The most recent of these, discussed in this paper, took place in the Parque Nacional Noel Kempff Mercado (PNNKM) in eastern Bolivia (Fig. 9.1). PNNKM is an immense protected area of more than a million hectares that includes tropical dry forest, humid forests, gallery

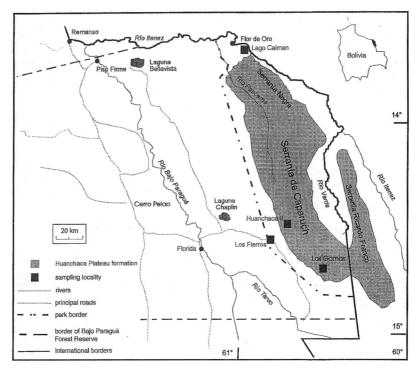

Fig. 9.1 Map of Bolivia showing position of Parque Nacional Noel Kempff Mercado and the four survey localities.

forests, savannas and cerrado habitats. This area was chosen because previous work by Timothy Killeen of the Missouri Botanical Garden and Robin Foster of the Field Museum had established that the park supports one of the greatest plant habitat diversities in the world (Killeen, Schulenberg & Awbrey, in press). This offered an ideal situation for analysing the relationship between the diversity of plant habitats and associated faunal assemblages.

Our goals were to quantify our ability to adequately sample the scarabaeine beetle fauna, to establish its degree of habitat specialization, and to assess the community's biogeographic and biodiversity significance at the regional or continental scale (by comparing our results to sites we had previously surveyed in other areas of Amazonia). We were also interested in how forces such as fire and global warming, by affecting the relative balance of open cerrado-like habitats versus forests in the park, would impact indicator biodiversity and influence park management. Lastly, we sought to examine scarabaeine communities in neotropical savanna habitats, where dung beetle faunas are particularly poorly known (Halffter & Favila, 1993).

## Methods

We used pitfall traps baited with human dung, a method that has been widely tested and utilized by ourselves and others (Howden & Nealis, 1975; Lobo et al., 1988; Klein, 1989; Halffter & Favila, 1993: trap design D). Traps consisted of 16 oz plastic cups buried in the ground so that the soil was even with the rims of the cups. The traps were baited with 20–30 g of human dung wrapped in a double layer of cotton cheesecloth and suspended over the centre of the trap. Traps were placed at 30 m intervals along transects which were located at least 200 m within the habitat type being sampled. Traps were checked and emptied every 24 h and rebaited each 48 h, except in open habitats where rapid desiccation of baits required rebaiting every 24 h. Specimens were preserved in alcohol and subsamples of 20 individuals per species were later dried and weighed for biomass determinations. Material was then identified and prepared for inclusion in the Smithsonian, Museo Noel Kempff Mercado and Canadian National collections.

We purposely did not attempt to sample 'non-trappable' dung beetle diversity, or specialized species with unusual habits, such as those that live in leaf-cutter ant or termite nests, bromeliad detritus, or on the feet of terrestrial snails. These species are not amenable to survey using the same quantitative and replicable sampling methods. Our own previous tests of the sampling protocol established that aerial trapping, hand collecting, use of a great variety of bait types such as carrion, fruit and natural mammal scat, and canopy fogging (T. Erwin pers. comm.) did not significantly increase the species richness of our samples or add significant new information on relative abundance.

We sampled at the scale of the conservation unit, attempting to cover as much of this vast park's altitudinal and habitat range as possible. This involved sampling at several sites, which necessitated the use of small planes and extensive backpacking. Ultimately, we sampled 18 habitats at a total of four localities, which were separated by between 2 and 150 km (Fig. 9.1; details of habitats summarized in Appendix 9.1). These habitats were identified by Timothy Killeen, who has established permanent study plots in many of the areas we sampled. The habitats ranged from well-developed mesic forest on well-drained soils to nearly treeless, seasonally inundated

Fig. 9.2 Map of South America showing locations of five Amazonian mesic forest sites for which complete lists of dung beetle species made community comparison possible.

savanna. Despite our attention to sampling broadly, our samples draw on a tiny fraction of the landscape.

We sampled a number of similar tall mesic forest types to test for faunal similarity within a habitat type. We compared these results with four other lowland Amazonian sites for which we have relatively complete faunal lists: Tambopata, Peru; Yasuni, Ecuador; Leticia, Colombia (surveyed by Howden & Nealis, 1975); and Caparu, Colombia (Fig. 9.2).

Our main field team consisted of four Bolivian undergraduate university students drawn from three separate institutions, plus a dung beetle taxonomist and two ecologists from North American institutions.

## RESULTS

### Taxonomy

In total, 94 species of scarabaeine dung beetles were found in PNNKM. With the assistance of Bruce Gill, one of the most active students of scarabaeine taxonomy, we were able to attach specific names to 64 species (68% of the 94 collected). The remaining 30 species were determined to genus and each given a unique morphospecies number. The most speciose genus, *Canthidium*, with 16 species collected, is taxonomically the least well known and several morphospecies appear to be unknown to science. In addition, new taxa were encountered even in groups that were recently revised. For example, four new species of the genus *Eurysternus* (Dalman) were collected despite Jessop's (1985) revision.

### Sampling efficiency

We captured some 10 200 dung beetles in the 18 habitats we sampled; 1233 individuals were collected of the single most abundant species, while seven species were each represented by a single specimen.

Using statistical estimators of species richness (Colwell & Coddington, 1994; Chazdon *et al.*, in press) calculated with the Estimate S software package (Colwell, 1998), we were able to estimate the total number of trappable species at a site and compare these estimates to observed trapping results. In practice, our estimate of total species richness became stable after relatively few trap-days, and in many habitats our observed species richness closely approximated estimated species richness.

(*a*)

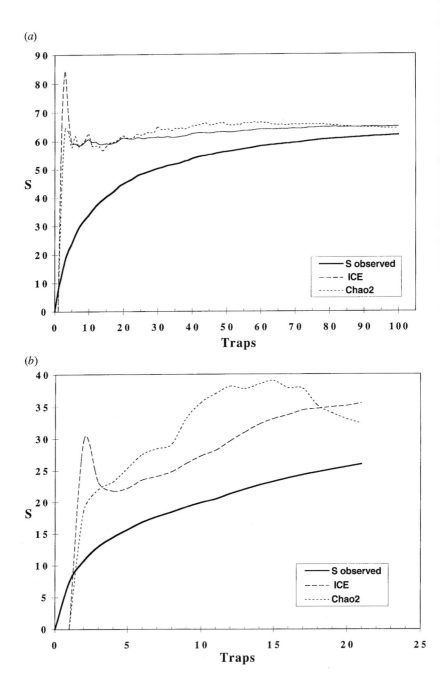

(*b*)

(c)

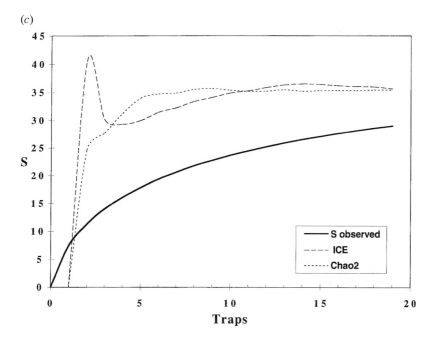

Fig. 9.3 Observed (S observed) and estimated (ICE and Chao 2) species accumulation curves for three sites. (*a*) Combined mesic forest samples at Los Fierros; (*b*) Lago Caiman dwarf semi-evergreen forest; (*c*) Los Fierros cerrado. Each point is the mean of 500 estimated values based on 500 randomizations of the trap order. ICE and Chao 2 are both incidence-based coverage estimators; see Colwell & Coddington (1994) and Chazdon *et al.* (in press) for further explanation of these two indices.

For example, analysis of the tall mesic rainforest habitats that we sampled most extensively indicated that with 45 traps we were able to encounter 85% of the estimated species richness of 64 species (Fig. 9.3(*a*)). By the 100th trap, we had collected 62 species, only two fewer than the extrapolated species richness, thus nearly exhausting our methodology's ability to encounter new species. However, it was also clear that in a number of habitats we were not able to capture completely the species richness predicted by the sample data (Fig. 9.3(*b*), (*c*)).

### Habitat specificity and response to degradation

The beetles exhibited high habitat specificity, forming distinct communities that exhibited virtually no overlap between contiguous but distinct

**Table 9.1**
*Pairwise matrix of Morisita-Horn indices of community similarity*

| | Lago Caiman-bosque alto | Los Fierros inundated forest | Los Fierros sartenjal | Los Feirros mesic forest | Los Feirros forest edge | Los Fierros dry forest | Lago Caiman liana forest | Lago Caiman dwarf forest | Lago Caiman ridge transect | Lago Caiman sertao | Lago Caiman rocky outcrop | Los Fierros cerrado | Los Fierros inundated savanna | Los Fierros north savanna | Los Fierros disturbed | Huanchaca 2 forest islands | Huanchaca 2 open savanna |
|---|---|---|---|---|---|---|---|---|---|---|---|---|---|---|---|---|---|
| Los Fierros inundated forest | 0.43 | | | | | | | | | | | | | | | | |
| Los Fierros sartenjal | 0.28 | 0.84 | | | | | | | | | | | | | | | |
| Los Feirros mesic forest | 0.25 | 0.76 | 0.87 | | | | | | | | | | | | | | |
| Los Feirros forest edge | 0.25 | 0.70 | 0.73 | 0.63 | | | | | | | | | | | | | |
| Los Fierros dry forest | 0.31 | 0.79 | 0.83 | 0.76 | 0.73 | | | | | | | | | | | | |
| Lago Caiman liana forest | 0.22 | 0.29 | 0.37 | 0.20 | 0.41 | 0.38 | | | | | | | | | | | |
| Lago Caiman dwarf forest | 0.20 | 0.31 | 0.26 | 0.26 | 0.21 | 0.39 | 0.22 | | | | | | | | | | |
| Lago Caiman ridge transect | 0.23 | 0.19 | 0.11 | 0.11 | 0.26 | 0.35 | 0.73 | 0.22 | | | | | | | | | |
| Lago Caiman sertao | 0.19 | 0.18 | 0.15 | 0.15 | 0.22 | 0.30 | 0.73 | 0.65 | 0.40 | | | | | | | | |
| Lago Caiman rocky outcrop | 0.04 | 0.07 | 0.05 | 0.02 | 0.10 | 0.11 | 0.11 | 0.30 | 0.12 | 0.25 | 0.31 | | | | | | |
| Los Fierros cerrado | 0.00 | 0.00 | 0.08 | 0.01 | 0.01 | 0.12 | 0.02 | 0.01 | 0.08 | 0.08 | 0.07 | 0.38 | | | | | |
| Los Fierros inundated savanna | 0.00 | 0.00 | 0.02 | 0.00 | 0.14 | 0.03 | 0.01 | 0.00 | 0.01 | 0.01 | 0.21 | 0.04 | 0.21 | | | | |
| Los Fierros north savanna | 0.00 | 0.00 | 0.01 | 0.00 | 0.07 | 0.01 | 0.02 | 0.00 | 0.00 | 0.00 | 0.08 | 0.02 | 0.83 | 0.44 | | | |
| Los Fierros disturbed | 0.00 | 0.01 | 0.09 | 0.01 | 0.06 | 0.06 | 0.04 | 0.01 | 0.03 | 0.01 | 0.02 | 0.03 | 0.01 | 0.30 | 0.04 | | |
| Huanchaca 2 forest islands | 0.20 | 0.23 | 0.21 | 0.25 | 0.16 | 0.26 | 0.16 | 0.12 | 0.36 | 0.12 | 0.09 | 0.16 | 0.01 | 0.00 | 0.01 | 0.01 | |
| Huanchaca 2 open savanna | 0.01 | 0.01 | 0.03 | 0.01 | 0.01 | 0.04 | 0.00 | 0.00 | 0.00 | 0.00 | 0.01 | 0.02 | 0.28 | 0.16 | 0.08 | 0.25 | 0.01 |
| Las Gamas campo cerrado | 0.16 | 0.15 | 0.15 | 0.12 | 0.22 | 0.25 | 0.16 | 0.11 | 0.10 | 0.03 | 0.05 | 0.16 | 0.01 | 0.02 | 0.06 | 0.34 | 0.08 |

All 18 habitats sampled are included. Greater values indicate higher similarity with a maximum of 1.0 for two identical communities and a minimum of 0 for completely non-overlapping communities.

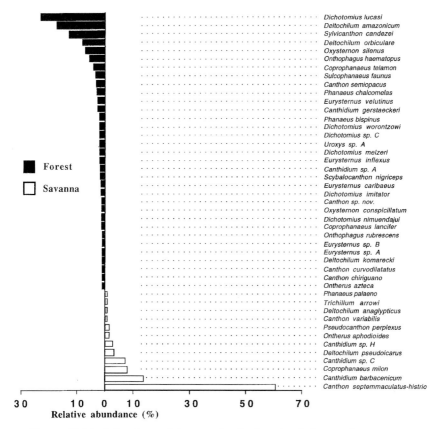

Forest

Savanna

| | Dichotomius lucasi |
| | Deltochilum amazonicum |
| | Sylvicanthon candezei |
| | Deltochilum orbiculare |
| | Oxysternon silenus |
| | Onthophagus haematopus |
| | Coprophanaeus telamon |
| | Sulcophanaeus faunus |
| | Canthon semiopacus |
| | Phanaeus chalcomelas |
| | Eurysternus velutinus |
| | Canthidium gerstaeckeri |
| | Phanaeus bispinus |
| | Dichotomius worontzowi |
| | Dichotomius sp. C |
| | Uroxys sp. A |
| | Dichotomius melzeri |
| | Eurysternus inflexus |
| | Canthidium sp. A |
| | Scybalocanthon nigriceps |
| | Eurysternus caribaeus |
| | Dichotomius imitator |
| | Canthon sp. nov. |
| | Oxysternon conspicillatum |
| | Dichotomius nimuendajui |
| | Coprophanaeus lancifer |
| | Onthophagus rubrescens |
| | Eurysternus sp. B |
| | Eurysternus sp. A |
| | Deltochilum komarecki |
| | Canthon curvodilatatus |
| | Canthon chiriguano |
| | Ontherus azteca |
| | Phanaeus palaeno |
| | Trichillum arrowi |
| | Deltochilum anaglypticus |
| | Canthon variabilis |
| | Pseudocanthon perplexus |
| | Ontherus aphodioides |
| | Canthidium sp. H |
| | Deltochilum pseudoicarus |
| | Canthidium sp. C |
| | Coprophanaeus milon |
| | Canthidium barbacenicum |
| | Canthon septemmaculatus-histrio |

30      10   0   10      30      50      70
Relative abundance (%)

Fig. 9.4 Matched abundance plot comparing the dung beetle faunas of inundated forest and inundated termite savanna at Los Fierros. Bar lengths represent the relative abundance of each species in each habitat. There is no species overlap between the two habitats.

habitats. Morisita–Horn similarity calculations based on species overlap and abundance information (Magurran, 1988) indicate that habitats most similar in terms of vegetative cover supported the most similar beetle communities (Table 9.1). For example, the tall mesic forest sites are similar to each other but differ greatly from semi-deciduous forest habitats and often show no similarity to open savanna habitats. A comparison of the faunas of a mesic forest and a termite savanna, separated by less than 100 m, showed complete turnover of the two beetle communities (Fig. 9.4).

Beetle community composition was also able to track more subtle changes in plant associations within different forest or savanna types. For example, the community found in the open, seasonally inundated termite

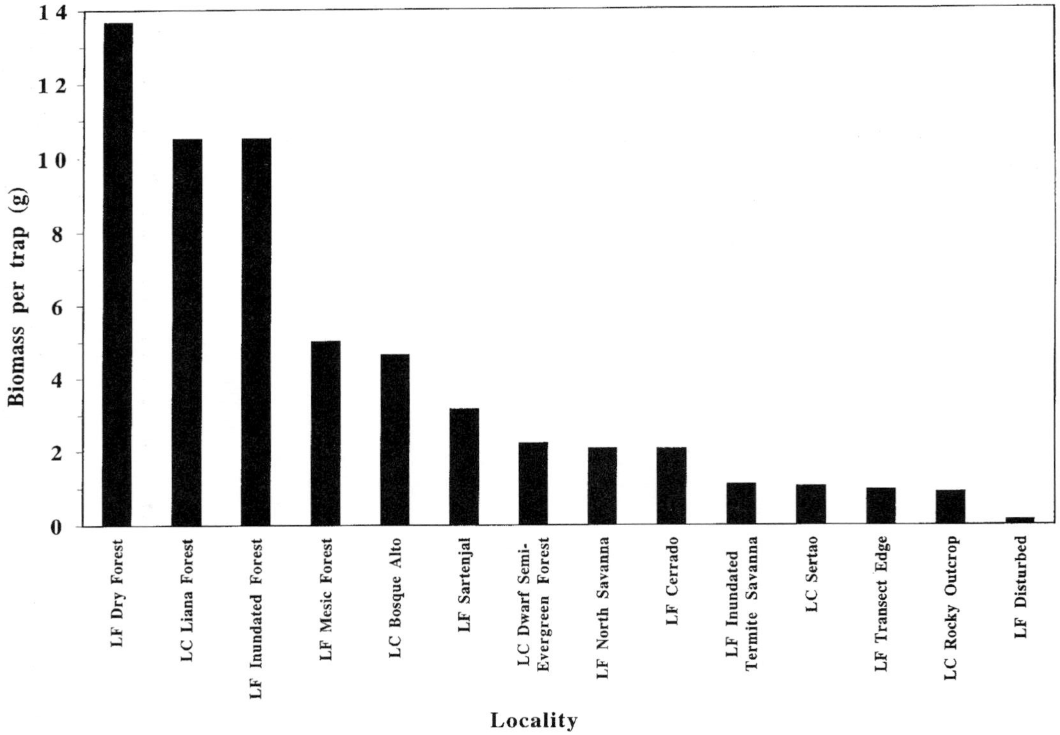

Fig. 9.5 Mean biomass per trap in 14 habitats for which biomass data were taken.

**Table 9.2**

*Similarity of dung beetle communities found at five mesic forest sites in Amazonia
(a) Pairwise matrix of Jaccard index values for five Amazonian tall mesic forest
communities (PNNKM community consists of the combined samples of all evergreen
forests at Los Fierros) and the number of species collected at each locality*

| Locality (Number of species) | Tambopata, Peru (73) | Yasuni, Ecuador (60) | Leticia, Colombia (56) | Caparu, Colombia (54) |
|---|---|---|---|---|
| PNNKM | 0.12 | 0.17 | 0.09 | 0.10 |
| Tambopata | | 0.23 | 0.15 | 0.15 |
| Yasuni | | | 0.23 | 0.18 |
| Leticia | | | | 0.12 |

Greater values indicate higher similarity with a maximum of 1.0 for two identical
communities and a minimum of 0 for completely non-overlapping communities.

*(b) Presence/absence of 13 widespread dung beetle species at five Amazonian mesic
forest sites*

| | Noel Kempff, Bolivia | Tambopata, Peru | Uasuni, Ecuador | Leticia, Colombia | Caparu, Colombia |
|---|---|---|---|---|---|
| *Eurysternus caribaeus* | + | + | + | + | + |
| *E. velutinus* | + | + | + | + | + |
| *E. foedus* | + | + | + | + | + |
| *Canthon aequinoctialis* | − | + | + | + | + |
| *C. luteicolis* | − | + | + | + | + |
| *Dichotomius podalirius* | + | + | + | − | + |
| *Deltochilum amazonicum* | + | + | + | − | + |
| *Oxysternon conspicillatum* | + | + | + | + | + |
| *O. smaragdinum* | − | + | + | + | + |
| *Coprophanaeus telamon* | + | + | + | + | + |
| *Phanaeus chalcomelas* | + | + | + | + | + |
| *Phanaeus bispinus* | + | + | + | + | + |
| *Canthidium gerstaeckeri* | + | + | − | + | + |

These 13 species account for nearly all of the community similarity between the five
sites.

savanna showed little overlap with an adjacent, better-drained termite savanna and even less with a well-drained cerrado site that supports small
trees. Likewise, upland dry forest beetle communities were dissimilar to
those found in adjacent deciduous forests.

The amount of dung beetle biomass caught per trap differed dramatically among habitats (Fig. 9.5). Biomass, on a per-trap basis, was highest in
mesic forests and lower in more open habitats with less standing woody

biomass. The group's response to habitat disturbance was also clear and unambiguous. A depauperate low-biomass beetle fauna of five species occurred in deforested areas such as airstrips and clearings. This fauna showed little overlap with the natural open savanna-cerrado habitats (Table 9.1).

### Geographic distribution

The dung beetle fauna of PNNKM showed a high amount of biogeographic differentiation. There was a distinct southern Brazilian fauna associated with the savanna–cerrado habitats and an equally distinct fauna with Amazonian forest affinities, as demonstrated by the rate of community turnover across forest–savanna edges (Fig. 9.4).

Overlap between mesic forest sites in PNNKM and four other Amazonian sites was surprisingly low based on Jaccard Index values (Table 9.2a). Furthermore, shared elements between these sites consisted almost entirely of a Pan-Amazonian complex of some 13 species that occur in most localities (Table 9.2(b)). The rest of the fauna, roughly three-quarters of the species at each locality, were unique to each locality.

### Financial considerations

The cost of this single field survey was calculated at $US 65 300 (Fig. 9.6). Personnel costs were clearly the highest fraction of the budget . Specimen preparation including sorting, identification, pinning and labelling, was also costly at $1–2 per specimen. In total, the investment in field work was 25 person–weeks. The time for sorting, pinning, labelling, and identifying specimens was equal to the field effort – every person–week spent collecting required roughly the same amount of time for specimen processing.

## DISCUSSION

### The good news

The good news is that dung beetles appear to have excellent potential as an indicator taxon. We were able to sample and identify a rich scarabaeine fauna efficiently. The total of 94 species recorded at PNNKM is the richest dung beetle fauna recorded from a single survey in the neotropics. The

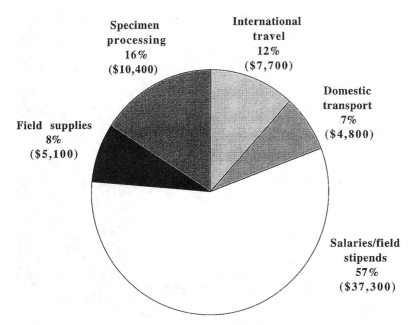

**Specimen processing 16% ($10,400)**

**International travel 12% ($7,700)**

**Domestic transport 7% ($4,800)**

**Field supplies 8% ($5,100)**

**Salaries/field stipends 57% ($37,300)**

Fig. 9.6 Proportion of total costs of survey ($US 65 000) spent on field supplies, specimen processing, international travel, domestic transport in Bolivia and salaries/field stipends.

most speciose sample previously reported from a neotropical locality is a community of 56 species found in Leticia, Colombia (Howden & Nealis, 1975).

By conducting our survey at the species level, we were able to establish that PNNKM is a 'hotspot' for the scarabaeine tribe Phanaeini. The area supports 14 species in this tribe of large, colourful and ecologically dominant dung beetles, outranking entire neotropical countries. Panama, for example, which is seven times larger than this protected area, has only 12 species. At the species level, this tribe displayed habitat specialization, especially between open and forested habitats (Fig. 9.7). Phanaeine biogeography is well known (Zunino, 1985; Edmunds, 1994) and this knowledge, coupled with spatial information on the threats to the region (Nepstad et al., 1997), enables us to make concrete conservation recommendations regarding management of the park (Forsyth et al., in press).

The high degree of habitat specialization shown by the dung beetles and their unambiguous response to deforestation makes them useful for predicting the outcome of habitat alteration as a result of factors such as fire management, road construction and logging. Habitat specialization also

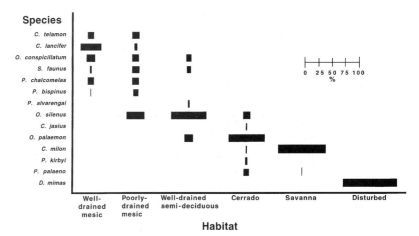

Fig. 9.7 Presence/absence and relative abundance of the 14 species in the tribe Phanaeini at five habitats. Bar lengths represent species' relative abundance as a percentage of the specimens collected in each habitat.

correlated well with broad-scale biogeographic patterns. For example, the species with known Brazilian savanna affinities do not penetrate forest habitats and species with an Amazonian distribution are not found in open habitats (Fig. 9.4). Knowledge of the rate of habitat loss of these two biomes enables us to predict that the open savanna and cerrado fauna is at much greater risk than the forest fauna.

In addition, the quantitative samples show habitat-specific shifts in community-level characteristics such as species abundance, body size, and biomass. For example, forest habitats that have the highest productivity and standing plant biomass support larger species and much higher dung beetle biomass than more open habitats (Fig. 9.5).

### The bad news

The bad news is that regional surveys using indicator taxa appear to be severely constrained by cost and scale issues. Measured against the amount of money available annually for ecological research in Bolivia, our survey was relatively costly. Moreover, many costs not incurred directly during the survey, such as time and resources still being devoted to the compilation, analysis and storage of the data and specimens, were not included in our cost estimate, nor were the costs of the previous surveys conducted in other localities which afforded us the ability to place our analysis of PNNKM's beetle fauna in a biogeographical context. Training and developing local expertise and building relationships with local scientific institutions also represented a significant additional investment of time and funds in the 3–4 years before the initiation of this survey. Nonetheless, this is a realistic estimate of most of the costs of this sort of biodiversity survey.

Much of the expenditure in this survey resulted from sampling at a relatively large scale (necessitating the use of small planes and additional field time). In many biodiversity surveys, the range of sampling is defined by the distance which a biologist can walk in half a day – a central-place foraging effort following the trails that radiate from a biological station or field camp (see Wilson & Sandoval, 1996 for examples). The results of these relatively limited surveys are often extrapolated over vast areas during priority-setting exercises. The 1° latitude/longitude grids widely utilized in descriptions of tropical diversity cover huge areas (roughly 100 km by 100 km at the Equator). Consider Pearson & Cassola's (1992) analysis of tiger beetle species richness using quadrats – at 275–350 km on a side, they contain on the order of 5–10 million hectares. This exceeds the size of the largest protected areas and in a place like Parque Nacional Alto Madidi in Bolivia would contain everything from snow-capped Andean peaks down through paramo or puna, cloudforest, montane rainforest, dry forest valleys and Amazonian forest, grasslands and wetlands. A finer scale and greater density of sampling is required for analysing complementarity of protected areas, but this is a costly prospect.

Unlike Brown (1992), we are not optimistic about the prospects that insect indicator taxa will be of much help in large-scale priority setting exercises in the near future. The majority of terrain in the Amazon basin has yet to see the attention of a single biologist, let alone a sustained effort to measure biodiversity. Surveying the Amazon basin for dung beetles using 20 sites, probably fewer than needed, would require in excess of a million dollars. A geographically comprehensive survey of any insect indicator taxon for any major tropical region is therefore unlikely to be funded.

In the short term, broadstroke efforts using so-called 'ecoregions' (Dinerstein et al., 1995) and the opinions of field biologists will continue to be used to set regional conservation investment priorities (Conservation International, 1997). Botanists working with remotely sensed information on vegetative cover combined with topographical, soil, hydrological and geological maps and modest amounts of ground-truthing (Tuomisto et al., 1995) will probably provide the best information about the conservation significance of the least known areas of the tropics. More detailed biodiversity assessments using several indicator taxa will be most useful at the local level, where they can help meet the needs of designing and managing protected areas.

The prospects for using indicator taxa in the context of regional monitoring programmes are equally grim. By nature, monitoring necessitates long-term scientific presence to detect changes in communities. Insect populations respond strongly to seasonal patterns (Begum & Oppenheimer, 1981; Nummelin, 1989) and episodic phenomena such as El Niño (Adis & Latif, 1996). This confounds analysis of population trends. Even when long-term data are available, the statistical power to detect insect population declines is weak when populations are chaotic (Van Strien *et al.*, 1997). Moreover, even large conservation projects usually only receive major funding for two to five years. Thus ambitious monitoring programmes may not be financially sustainable over the time period necessary for patterns to be detectable and statistically significant.

### The outlook

These issues may not matter to tropical conservationists. Kremen, Merenlender *et al.* (1994) surveyed the use of monitoring and evaluation by integrated conservation and development projects and found they conducted relatively little ecological monitoring in spite of their sizeable budgets. Throughout the tropics, the prospector, the logger, the road builder and the peasant farmer are almost always ahead of the conservationist in reaching pristine habitat. Conservationists may often have other more urgent needs for their funds, such as combating the anthropogenic forces that are rapidly degrading ecosystems, or making protected areas work by hiring and training park guards.

This is not to say that inventories using indicator taxa should not be attempted where financial support is available. It is clear that without more explicit data covering a wide array of possible indicator groups, our capacity to evaluate conservation priorities or monitor efficacy of management strategies will continue to be primitive. Thus, rather than avoiding this work because of its complexity and cost, the investment in closing the data gap between plants, vertebrates, and insects ought to be made now rather than later. Biodiversity assessments using indicator taxa have inherent value in the many tropical areas where conservation efforts are failing to prevent major habitat losses. If surveys are able to capture ecological data about community structure and habitat specialization they may yield information that will make restoration ecology or even restoration genetics possible.

In addition, the financial viability of indicator taxa surveys could potentially be enhanced. The possibility exists, for instance, that additional taxa could be included at minimal cost by taking advantage of fixed costs such as transport. The potential for this economy of scale was not assessed here. However, large savings seem unlikely given the fact that our largest costs related to personnel and specimen-processing, costs which would have to be duplicated for each additional taxon. Perhaps the single most important unexplored resource is the World Wide Web, which offers a way for field workers in any part of the world (where a telephone service is available) to access on-line taxonomic or museum-related information. Websites such as Otte and Nasckrecki's (1997) offer free and extremely useful tools that could substantially reduce the taxonomic constraints on biodiversity surveys. We suggest that museums place increasing priority on developing on-line databases that make in-the-field taxonomic determinations possible.

Renner and Ricklefs (1994) suggest that biodiversity inventories are a diversionary waste of time. On the contrary, we believe that biodiversity survey and rigorous development of indicator taxa are useful for immediate and long-term conservation needs. For example, a number of large protected areas in tropical countries, such as Alto Madidi and Gran Chaco in Bolivia, have been gazetted primarily on the basis of the publicity they received following biodiversity assessments. Indeed, most multilateral, bilateral and foundation donors require biodiversity assessments and monitoring. Since local biodiversity assessments will and should continue, we call for increased efforts to define those indicator taxa which can yield the maximum amount of ecological and systematic information about the vanishing tropics.

## ACKNOWLEDGEMENTS

The authors wish to thank the following people and institutions for their support of this work. T. Killeen for invaluable assistance in working in PNNKM and for providing insights into the vegetation of the park; B. D. Gill for providing taxonomic determinations of the sampled material; S. Ayzama, F. Guerra, N. Araujo, and I. Garcia for their contributions to the field work; DCNB for allowing us to conduct research in PNNKM; Fundacion de la Naturaleza for logistical support in PNNKM; Museo de Historia Natural Noel Kempff Mercado, and especially J. Ledezma, for the use of their entomological facilities; and A. Balmford, R. Capers, R. K. Colwell, K. N. Gibson, J. Ginsberg, K. Omland, D. Wagner and an anonymous reviewer for their helpful comments on earlier versions of this paper. Portions of the earlier survey work by the authors cited in this paper were part of a series of field-based training workshops supported by the John D. and Catherine T. MacArthur Foundation.

## References

Adis, J. & Latif, M. (1996). Amazonian arthropods respond to El Niño. *Biotropica* **28**, 403–8.

Andreson, E. (1994). Frugivory and primary seed dispersal by spider monkeys (*Ateles paniscus*) and howler monkeys (*Alouatta seniculus*), and the fate of dispersed seeds at Manu National Park, Peru. MSc diss.: School of the Environment, Duke University.

Angermeier, P. L. & Winston, M. R. (1997). Assessing conservation value of stream communities: a comparison of approaches based on centers of density and species richness. *Freshwat. Biol.*, **37**, 699–710.

Balmford, A., Green, M. J. B. & Murray, M. G. (1996). Using higher-taxon richness as a surrogate for species richness: I. Regional tests. *Proc. R. Soc. Lond.* B, **263**, 1267–74.

Balmford, A., Jayasuriya, A. H. M. & Green, M. J. B. (1996). Using higher-taxon richness as a surrogate for species richness: II. Local applications. *Proc. R. Soc. Lond.* B, **263**, 1571–5.

Basset, Y., Samuelson, G. A., Allison, A. & Miller, S. E. (1996). How many species of host-specific insects feed on a species of tropical tree? *Biol. J. Linn. Soc.*, **59**, 201–16.

Baz, A. & Garcia-Boyero, A. (1995). The effects of forest fragmentation on butterfly communities in central Spain. *J. Biogeogr.*, **22**, 129–40.

Beattie, A. J. (1992). Discovering new biological resources – chance or reason? *BioScience*, **42**, 290–2.

Beattie, A. J. & Oliver, I. (1994). Taxonomic minimalism. *Trends Ecol. Evol.*, **9**, 488–90.

Beccaloni, G. W. & Gaston, K. J. (1995). Predicting the species richness of neotropical forest butterflies: Ithomiinae (Lepidoptera: Nymphalidae) as indicators. *Biol. Conserv.*, **71**, 77–86.

Begum, J. & Oppenheimer, J. R. (1981). Bangladesh dung beetles (Scarabaeidae and Trogidae): seasonality, habitat, food and partial distribution. *Bangladesh J. Zool.*, **9**, 9–15.

Belshaw, R. & Bolton, B. (1993). The effect of forest disturbance on the leaf litter ant fauna in Ghana. *Biodiv. Conserv.*, **2**, 656–66.

Blair, R. B. & Launer, A. E. (1997). Butterfly diversity and human land use: species assemblages along an urban gradient. *Biol. Conserv.*, **80**, 113–25.

Brown, K. S. (1992). Conservation of neotropical environments: insects as indictors. In *The conservation of insects and their habitats*: 350–405. (Eds Collins, N. M. & Thomas, J. A.). Academic Press, New York.

Buikema, A. L., Niederlehner, B. R. & Cairns, J. (1982). Biological monitoring part IV – toxicity testing. *Water Res.*, **16**, 239–62.

Chazdon, R. L., Colwell, R. K., Denslow, J. S. & Guariguata, M. R. in press. Statistical methods for estimating species richness of woody regeneration in primary and secondary rain forests of NE Costa Rica. In *Forest biodiversity research, monitoring and modeling: conceptual background and Old World case studies.* (Eds Dallmeier, F. & Comiskey, J.). Parthenon Publishing, Paris.

Colwell, R. K. (1998). EstimateS. Statistical estimation of species richness and shared species from samples. **http://viceroy.eeb.uconn.edu/Estimate S**. June 25, 1998.

Colwell, R. K. & Coddington, J. A. (1994). Estimating terrestrial biodiversity through extrapolation. *Phil. Trans. R. Soc. Lond.* B, **345**, 101–18.

Conservation International (1997). Regional conservation analysis projects, **http:/www.conservation.org/science/cptc/consprio/!run_me!.htm**. October 19, 1997.

Didham R. K., Ghazoul, J., Stork, N. E. & Davis, A. J. (1996). Insects in fragmented forest: a functional approach. *Trends Ecol. Evol.*, **11**, 255–9.

Dinerstein, E., Olson, D. M., Graham, D. J., Webster, A. L., Primm, S. A., Bookbinder, M. P. & Ledec, G. (1995). *A conservation assessment of the terrestrial ecoregions of Latin America and the Caribbean.* The World Bank, Washington, DC.

Disney, R. H. L. (1986). Assessments using invertebrates: posing the problem. In *Wildlife conservation evaluation*: 272–292. (Ed. Usher, M. B.). Chapman and Hall Ltd., London.

Dorvillè, L. M. F. (1996). Mosquitoes as bioindicators of forest degradation in Southeastern Brazil, a statistical evaluation of published data in the literature. *Stud. Neotrop. Fauna Environ.*, **31**, 68–78.

Edmonds, W. D. (1994). Revision of *Phanaeus* Macleay, a new world genus of Scarabaeinae Dung Beetles (Coleoptera: Scarabaeidae, Scarabaeinae). *Natural History Museum of Los Angeles County. Contr. Sci.*, **443**.

Fagan, W. F. & Kareiva, P. M. (1997). Using compiled species lists to make biodiversity comparisons among regions: a test case using Oregon butterflies. *Biol. Conserv.*, **80**, 249–59.

Forsyth, A. B., Spector, S., Gill, B. D., Guerra, F. & Ayzama, S. (1998). Dung beetles (Coleoptera: Scarabaeidae: Scarabaeinae) of Noel Kempff Mercado National Park. In *A biological assessment of Parque Nacional Noel Kempff Mercado and adjacent areas, Santa Cruz, Bolivia* (Eds Killeen, T. J., Schulenberg, T. S. & Awbrey, K. M.). Conservation International, Washington, DC.

Gaston, K. J. & Hudson, E. (1994). Regional patterns of diversity and estimates of global insect species richness. *Biodiv. Conserv.*, **3**, 493–500.

Gaston, K. J. & May, R. M. (1992). Taxonomy of taxonomists. *Nature, Lond.*, **356**, 281–2.

Halffter, G. & Edmonds, W. D. (1982). *The nesting behavior of dung beetles (Scarabaeinae): an ecological and evolutive approach.* Instituto de Ecología, México, DF.

Halffter, G. & Favila, M. E. (1993). The Scarabaeinae (Insecta: Coleoptera) an animal group for analysing, inventorying and monitoring biodiversity in tropical rainforest and modified landscapes. *Biol. int.*, **27**, 15–21.

Hammond, P. (1992). Species inventory. *Global biodiversity: status of the earth's living resources*: 17–39. (Ed. Groombridge, B.). Chapman & Hall, London.

Hanski, I. & Cambefort, Y. (Eds) (1991). *Dung beetle ecology*. Princeton University Press, Princeton, New Jersey.

Hill, C. J. (1996). Habitat specificity and food preferences of an assemblage of tropical Australian dung beetles. *J. trop. Ecol.*, **12**, 449–60.

Howden, H. F. & Nealis, V. G. (1975). Effects of clearing in a tropical rain forest on the composition of the coprophagous scarab beetle fauna (Coleoptera). *Biotropica*, **7**, 77–83.

Jessop, L. (1985). An identification guide to eurysternine dung beetles (Coleoptera, Scarabaeidae). *J. nat. Hist.*, **19**, 1087–111.

Killeen, T. J., Schulenberg, T. S. & Awbrey, K. M. (Eds) (In Press). *A biological assessment of Parque Nacional Noel Kempff Mercado and adjacent areas, Santa Cruz, Bolivia*. Conservation International, Washington, DC.

Kim, K. C. (1993). Biodiversity, conservation and inventory: why insects matter. *Biodiv. Conserv.*, **2**, 191–214.

Kitching, I. J. (1996). Identifying complementary areas for conservation in Thailand: an example using owls, hawkmoths and tiger beetles. *Biodiv. Conserv.*, **5**, 841–58.

Klein, B. (1989). Effects of forest fragmentation on dung and carrion beetle communities in central Amazonia, *Ecology*, **70**, 1715–25.

Kremen, C. (1992). Assessing the indicator properties of species assemblages for natural areas monitoring. *Ecol. Appl.*, **2**, 203–17.

Kremen, C., Colwell, R. K., Erwin, T. L., Murphy, D. D., Noss, R. F. & Sanjayan, M. A. (1993). Terrestrial arthropod assemblages: their use in conservation planning. *Conserv. Biol.*, **7**, 796–808.

Kremen, C., Merenlender, A. M. & Murphy, D. D. (1994). Ecological monitoring: a vital need for integrated conservation and development programs in the tropics. *Conserv. Biol.*, **8**, 388–97.

Lamas, G. (1994). Butterflies of the Explorer Inn Reserve. In *The Tambopata-Candamo Reserved Zone of southeastern Perú: a biological assessment* **6**: 62–63. (Eds Foster, R. B., Carr, J. L. & Forsyth, A. B.). Conservation International, Washington, DC.

Lobo, J. M., Martin-Piera, F. & Veiga, C. M. (1988). Las trampas pitfall con cebo, sus posibilidades en el estudio de las comunidades coprófagas de Scaabaeoidea (Col.). I. Caracteristicas determinantes de su capacidad de captura. *Rev. Ecol. Biol. Sol.*, **25**, 77–100.

Magurran, A. E. (1988). *Ecological diversity and its measurement*. Princeton University Press, Princeton, New Jersey.

Majer, J. S., Delabie, J. H. C. & McKenzie, N. L. (1997). Ant litter fauna of forest, forest edges and adjacent grassland in the Atlantic rain forest region of Bahia, Brazil. *Insectes Soc.*, **44**, 255–66.

Nepstad, D. C., Klink, C. A., Uhl, C., Vieira, I. C., Lefebvre, P., Pedlowski, M., Matricardi, E., Negreiros, G., Brown, E. F., Amaral, E., Homma, A. & Ralker, R. (1997). Land-use in Amazonia and the cerrado of Brazil. *Ciênc. Cult. S. Paulo*, **49**, 73–86.

Nestel, D., Dickschen, F. & Altirei, M. A. (1993). Diversity patterns of soil macro-Coleoptera in Mexican shaded and unshaded coffee agroecosystems: an indication of habitat perturbation. *Biodiv. Conserv.*, **2**, 70–8.

New, T. R. (1995). *An introduction to invertebrate conservation*. Oxford University Press, New York.

Niemela, J., Haila, Y. & Puntilla, P. (1996). The importance of small-scale heterogeneity in boreal forests: variation in diversity in forest-floor invertebrates across the succession gradient. *Ecography*, **199**, 352–68.

Norton, B. G. & Ulanowicz, R. E. (1992). Scale and biodiversity policy: a hierarchical approach. *Ambio*, **21**, 244–9.

Noss, R. F. (1990). Indicators for monitoring biodiversity: a hierarchical approach. *Conserv. Biol.*, **4**, 355–64.

Nummelin, M. (1989). Seasonality and effects of forestry practices on forest floor arthropods in the Kigale Forest, Uganda. *Fauna Norv. Ser. B.*, **36**, 17–25.

Oliver, I. & Beattie, A. J. (1993). A possible method for the rapid assessment of biodiversity. *Conserv. Biol.*, **7**, 562–8.

Oliver, I., Beattie, A. J. & York, A. (in press). Spatial fidelity of plant, vertebrate and invertebrate assemblages in multiple-use forests in eastern Australia. *Conserv. Biol.*.

Otte, D. & Naskrecki, P. (1997). Orthoptera Species Online, **http: viceroy.eeb.uconn.edu/Orthoptera**. November 14, 1997.

Pearson, D. L. (1994). Selecting indicator taxa for the quantitative assessment of biodiversity. *Phil. Trans. R. Soc. Lond. B*, **345**, 75–80.

Pearson, D. L. & Cassola, F. (1992). World-wide species richness patterns of tiger beetles (Coleoptera: Cicindelidae): indicator taxon for biodiversity and conservation studies. *Conserv. Biol.*, **6**, 376–91.

Peck, S. B. & Forsyth, A. (1982). Composition, structure and competitive behaviour in a guild of Ecuadorian rainforest dung beetles (Coleoptera; Scarabaeidae). *Can. J. Zool.*, **60**, 1624–34.

Prendergast, J. R., Quinn, R. M., Lawton, J. H., Eversham, B. C. & Gibbons, D. W. (1993). Rare species, the coincidence of diversity hotspots and conservation strategies. *Nature, Lond.*, **365**, 335–7.

Renner, S. S. & Ricklefs, R. E. (1994). Systematics and biodiversity. *Trends Ecol. Evol.*, **9**, 78.

Rosenberg, D. M., Danks, H. V. & Lehmkuhl, D. M. (1986). Importance of insects in environmental impact assessment. *Envir. Mgmt*, **10**, 773–83.

Samways, M. J. (1993). Insects in biodiversity conservation: some perspectives and directives. *Biodiv. Conserv.*, **2**, 258–82.

Samways, M. J. (1994). *Insect conservation biology*. Chapman & Hall, London.

Spitzer, K., Ilavelka, J. & Leps, J. (1997). Effects of small-scale disturbance on butterfly communities of an Indochinese montane rainforest. *Biol. Conserv.*, **30**, 9–15.

Stotz, D. F., Fitzpatrick, J. W., Parker, T. A. III & Moskovits, D. K. (1996). *Neotropical birds: ecology and conservation*. University of Chicago Press, Chicago.

Tuomisto, H. Ruokolainen, K., Kalliola, R., Linna, A., Danjoy, W. & Rodriguez, Z. (1995). Dissecting Amazonian biodiversity. *Science*, **269**, 63–6.

Van Strien, A. J., Van de Pavert, R., Moss, D., Yates, T. J., Van Swaay, C. A. M. & Vos, P. (1997). The statistical power of two butterfly monitoring schemes to detect trends. *J. appl. Ecol.*, **34**, 817–28.

Wege, D. C. & Long, A. J. (1995). *Key areas for threatened birds in the neotropics.* Birdlife International, UK.

Wilson, D. E. & Sandoval, A. (Eds) (1996). *Manu: the biodiversity of southeastern Peru.* Smithsonian Institution, Washington, DC.

Yokoyama, K., Kai, H., Koga, T. & Aibe, T. (1991). Nitrogen mineralization and microbial populations in cow dung, dung balls and underlying soil affected by paracoprid dung beetles. *Soil Biol. Biochem.*, **23**, 649–53.

Zunino, M. (1985). Las relaciones taxonomicas de los Phanaeinae (Coleoptera, Scarabaeinae) y sus implicaciones biogeograficas. *Folia ent. Mex.* No. 64, 101–15.

## Appendix 9.1    Site locations and habitat descriptions

### Lago Caiman Station   13° 35'.98° S; 60° 54'.88' W

| | |
|---|---|
| Lago Caiman bosque alto | Tall, evergreen forest on deep, well-drained soils. |
| Lago Caiman liana forest | Evergreen forest with heavy liana loads, creating an uneven canopy often dominated by the liana themselves; on relatively poor soils that experience great seasonal variation in moisture regime. |
| Lago Caiman ridge transect | Transition from short, open deciduous dry forest with grassy ground cover to semi-evergreen piedmont forest, on sandy, well drained soils that transitions to rocky but more humid soils. |
| Lago Caiman sertao | Short, open deciduous forest on shallow, but relatively rich, sandy soils. |
| Lago Caiman rocky outcrop | Granitic outcrops with patches of dwarf deciduous trees and shrubs where soils are deep enough to support them. |
| Lago Caiman dwarf Semi-evergreen forest | Semi-evergreen forest with high density of narrow diameter boles, on well-drained soils of medium depth. |

### Los Fierros Station   14° 33' 28"S; 60° 55' 51" W

| | |
|---|---|
| Los Fierros mesic forest | Tall, evergreen forest on deep, well-drained soils. |
| Los Fierros sartenjal | Tall, evergreen forest regularly inundated by up to 50 cm of water from nearby river. |

| | |
|---|---|
| Los Fierros dry forest | Tall, semi-evergreen forest with heavier liana loads than the Los Fierros Mesic forest, on well drained soils. |
| Los Fierros inundated forest | Tall, evergreen forest regularly inundated (like Los Fierros Sartenjal), adjacent to savanna habitat. |
| Los Fierros forest edge | Transitional habitat separating tall, inundated forest from inundated termite savanna; short forest with most trees having very narrow diameter, regularly inundated. |
| Los Fierros inundated termite savanna | Open, grassy, regularly inundated savanna with patchy islands of shrubs and trees occurring on termite mounds |
| Los Fierros north savanna | Like termite savanna above, but less frequently inundated; higher density of shrubs between termite mounds. |
| Los Fierros cerrado | Wooded savanna with grassy ground cover interspersed with 4–6 m tall fire-adapted trees. |
| Los Fierros disturbed | Anthropogenically impacted areas immediately in and around Los Fierros station; including grassy areas and cleared areas adjacent to landing strip. |
| **Huanchaca 2 Camp** | 14° 45' 51"S; 61° 01' 58"W |
| Huanchaca 2 forest islands | Patches of tall evergreen forest surrounded by open savanna |
| Huanchaca 2 open savanna | Savanna dominated by graminoids, little or no shrub layer, no tree; on lateritic or sandy soils. |
| **Las Gamas** | 14° 48' 12"S; 60°22' 48"W |
| Las Gamas campo cerrado | Upland savanna, with shrub and open tree layers; on deep to rocky soils. |

# 10

# Key sites for conservation: area-selection methods for biodiversity

PAUL H. WILLIAMS

## INTRODUCTION

Conservation is about ensuring the persistence of value. Area selection for conservation is about the 'where first' of *in situ* conservation action rather than the 'how', and is therefore about emotive issues of values, goals and priorities. The first problem that must be faced is that values and goals are not universal, but differ among people and among situations. Therefore, values and goals ought to be made explicit and agreed as broadly as possible at the beginning of any particular area-selection exercise if conflicts are to be minimized. Area-selection methods can then be used to apply rigorous and explicit rules to determine priorities consistent with these values and goals. It is vital that this procedure is not viewed dogmatically but rather as a flexible means of exploring the consequences of using different values, rules and data so as to inform the decision-making process. The result should be a process that is focused on needs, and is transparent and accountable.

The *values* adopted by conservationists should be shared broadly by the people giving conservationists their mandate for making management decisions (Margules, 1981). Preferably such a value ought to be quantifiable (at least in relative terms) so that appropriate arguments can be presented to economists and politicians. Biodiversity value is currently one popular choice, especially following the Rio Convention (ISCBD, 1994). Any area-selection procedure for conserving biodiversity value must begin with a clear idea of what this value is and how it should be measured.

A *goal* of ensuring the best continued representation of biodiversity value within a set of areas has often been used in an attempt to approach conservation as a 'proactive' process, as opposed to 'firefighting' reactively as particular species become endangered (Groves, 1992). Resources for priority action may still be deployed in relation to perceptions of imminent threat. Representativeness in this sense therefore implies monitoring all of the valued biota (Austin & Margules, 1986), not just those parts that are currently most threatened.

Distinguishing higher from lower *priority* of areas by relative urgency for conservation management is the purpose of area-selection methods (Vane-Wright, 1996; Pressey, 1997). The need for priorities is usually unavoidable because competition with incompatible land uses limits the area available for conservation (Kirkpatrick, 1983; Pressey, 1994; Pressey & Tully, 1994). Intensity of conservation management within priority areas may vary depending upon the circumstances, from seeking to exclude some of these land uses, such as certain kinds of agriculture, to being very limited and closely integrated with current land uses.

Areas selected as priorities are usually chosen because they are necessary to meet a particular conservation goal, with no illusions that they are sufficient to meet broader goals. Analysts often begin by trying to meet minimum requirements to satisfy a particular goal. It is clearly important that minimum priority areas are then added to systematically so as to improve the prognoses for the biota (for example, these areas may conceivably be used as seed areas for future habitat restoration: Vane-Wright, 1994). However, an acceptance of priorities must recognize that this also implies that some areas and biota will be given lower priority. This is not to say that they have no conservation value, but rather that in relation to the agreed goals the actions are not as urgent.

In this chapter I review briefly (i) some of the approaches to measuring biodiversity value for use in conservation; (ii) some of the different area-selection methods; and (iii) some of the possibilities for integrating viability and threat into these methods. In the first section, biodiversity value is identified with the option value for future use or evolution of different expressible genes or phenotypic characters of organisms. From this viewpoint, the most direct measure will usually be taxonomic or phylogenetic diversity, but species richness and richness in larger biotic or environmental assemblages may be viewed as presenting a scale of surrogacy. In any practical study, the choice of surrogate from this scale will be a compromise between precision on the one hand and cost of data acquisition on the other. In the second section, approaches to maximizing the amount of biodiversity that can be represented for any given expenditure using quantitative area-selection methods are described. When the identity of the surrogate units is known in each area, or a model predicting them is known, then complementarity methods can be much more efficient than methods using scoring or hotspots of richness or rarity. The transparency of the area-selection process can also be increased by replacing combinatorial scoring methods with sequential decision methods in order to give greater public accountability. This transparency has made it much easier to justify why any particular area is selected; why it is given a particular level of priority; and precisely which parts within its local biota might deserve local management priority. In the final section, approaches to accommodating variation among areas in viability and threat are discussed, in order to avoid selecting areas with biotas that have poor prognoses for persistence. One possibility is to apply existing techniques that use niche-based models of habitat suitability in order to pre-filter data for the 'viability centres' for each species (or other surrogates). In principle, it is an approach that could be automated for datasets with large numbers of species when only general information on factors governing habitat suitability is known.

## MEASURING BIODIVERSITY VALUE FOR CONSERVATION

Biodiversity can be seen as the irreducible complexity of all life, so that no single objective measure is possible; or at least measures are only possible for particular aspects of biodiversity in relation to particular goals (Norton, 1994). Choosing any single formulation cannot include all other possible value systems, but can provide a basis from which to compare the consequences and trade-offs between this kind of value and any other. The question is then how to measure biodiversity value for conservationists, both in theory and in practice?

Leaving aside the intrinsic rights of all species, ethical arguments for conservation include responsibilities to future generations of people and obligations to the sustenance and development of human welfare in the present, both of which require some assessment of utility values. Narrow economic arguments rely on the current use value of the relatively few species presently exploited (or required for services) as particular and very small parts of biodiversity ('biospecifics', see Faith, 1997; and reply by Williams, Gaston, Humphries & Vane-Wright, 1997). But, in order to pursue properly both ethical and economic goals, a measure is required that represents the value of the broader scope of biodiversity.

People approaching the subject of biodiversity are often familiar with the diversity measures developed for ecology (e.g. introduction by Usher,

1986). These measures were initially responses to the need to be able to relate the number of species in a collection of individuals to the size of the sample, because of the difficulties inherent in sampling (for review see Magurran, 1988). Later, for some, the emphasis shifted to how the patterns of evenness in abundances among species might be interpreted in terms of resource allocation within the sampled species assemblages or 'communities'. While these measures may be important when dealing with issues such as the effect of sample size, they do not capture the sense of the difference and variety among organisms (Williams, 1993b) that is fundamental to most popular concepts of biodiversity (Gaston, 1996b).

Some people have sought to value, quantify and promote just those species with particular 'evolutionary potential' (Erwin, 1991; Brooks, Mayden & McLennan, 1992). This value for future evolution has been associated with 'species dynamo' areas, which are identified as areas that are unusually rich in closely related species, because these groups are presumed to be 'evolutionary fronts' of greater innovation. This idea may seem attractive, but it does present problems. First, there are difficulties in predicting the future course of evolution, particularly as the projected human-driven environmental changes are unlikely to reflect simply those of the past (Williams, Gaston & Humphries, 1994). Secondly, the consequences of this approach are in direct conflict with the biodiversity value of variety described below: it favours conservation of faunas with large numbers of very similar species over faunas with many divergent and disparate species. The consequence is that it could lead to focusing conservation effort on a flora consisting of several species of dandelions, in preference to a flora consisting of a dandelion and a giant redwood, which would have greater variety value.

Recently, most definitions of biodiversity have focused on the idea of the variety of organisms (for review see Gaston, 1996b). One value of this biological variety has been linked with the insurance or 'option value' it provides for maximizing future opportunities for exploitation and evolution (Reid, 1994). It is an interpretation that redirects attention away from the level of species and towards the level of their expressible genes, or towards the products of their genes, the species' expressed characters (different chemicals, morphological features, functional behaviour) (see Williams & Humphries, 1996 and references therein). It also accepts that we do not know precisely which genes or characters are going to be of value in the future, or what that value might be. The consequences of this are that first, as a form of insurance, all genes or characters should be given equal value, as a kind of fundamental 'currency' of value; and second, biodiversity con-servationists should seek to maximize the amount of this currency within the conservation 'bank'. This makes intuitive sense. For example, when difficult choices have to be made, a flora consisting of a dandelion and a giant redwood can be seen to represent a richer collection of characters in total, and so greater diversity value, than another pair of more similar spe-cies, such as a dandelion and a daisy.

### Gene or character richness

The problem with valuing the numbers of different genes or characters owned by organisms is that they cannot be counted directly. Usually data from only very small samples of characters are available, so the problem is one of how best to use this information to predict the overall character differences that are of value. Fortunately, because the valued characters are inherited or change through evolution (as homologues), it ought to be poss-ible to use our best current estimates of phylogeny, or even to use the ap-proximations expressed in taxonomic nomenclature.

Biologists have proposed a variety of phylogenetic or taxonomic measures to predict the biodiversity value of different biotas (following Vane-Wright, Humphries & Williams, 1991; for reviews see Faith, 1994; Humphries, Williams & Vane-Wright, 1995). In order to predict the ex-pected relative richness in different genes or characters of different biotas of species, these measures use knowledge of the genealogical (or hierarchi-cal) pattern of relationships among organisms, although these have to be combined with very simple models for the process of evolution of genes or characters (Williams, Gaston & Humphries, 1994). For example, at its simplest, this approach maps the changes onto a phylogenetic 'tree', so that branch lengths are proportionate to the numbers of changes (Fig. 10.1). If we can accept the assumption that the character changes in the sample are representative of all of the characters of interest, then we can predict the relative diversity value of any subset of species, such as a local biota. Thus, in choosing a set of three species from Fig. 10.1, the most diverse set would be *niavius*, *echeria* and *damocles*, because they have the largest number of character changes between them on the tree.

More often, all that is available for predicting gene or character diversity is a classification in the form of the nomenclatural hierarchy. If we are prepared to accept that this is an approximate estimate of phylogenetic pattern, then again we have to assume some model of the evolutionary

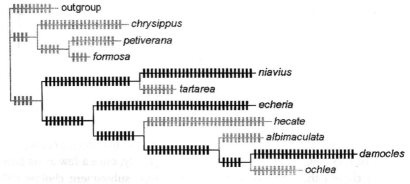

Fig. 10.1 Metric tree for African species of milkweed butterflies (family Nymphalidae) of the genera *Danaus* (1 species), *Tirumala* (2 species) and *Amauris* (7/12 species). The branching order (topology) of the tree is derived by cladistic analysis of 217 morphological and chemical characters (volatile components extracted from male scent organs). The branch lengths between each branching point on the tree are then scaled by the number of character changes within this same character sample, and these character changes are shown as vertical bars. The most diverse set of any three species according to these data would be *niavius, echeria* and *damocles,* because they have the largest number of character changes between them on the tree (shown as the black subtree) compared to any other group of three species. After Williams & Humphries (1996).

process that relates character changes to the tree. Simple and extreme possibilities for process models are, on the one hand, 'clock'-like, even rates of change; or on the other, 'punctuated equilibrium' models, where changes are associated primarily with speciation events (see Williams, Gaston & Humphries, 1994). Such models are undoubtedly crude and contentious, but the approach is still more realistic than assuming that all species are equally different. Much of the discussion surrounding the pros and cons of the different measures in effect centres on choosing among these models.

In practice, the usefulness of these measures will be limited because detailed and reliable phylogenetic information is often not available, or alternative estimates of phylogeny for the same species may yield very different measures of diversity value. Nonetheless, arguments for measuring biodiversity value as gene or character richness do at least provide a reasoned starting point, and accepting pattern as a predictor for value provides one possible key to the problem of measurement through the use of surrogacy.

## Species richness

It has been found that, when dealing with large numbers of species, species richness is usually a reasonable surrogate for available estimates of character richness (Williams & Humphries, 1996). Therefore identifying genes or characters as a fundamental currency of biodiversity value provides an additional justification for using species richness. This might be expected to work because at least some representatives of the more divergent, higher groups of organisms (which taken together are rich in different characters) will usually co-occur in many areas. Consequently, once a few areas have been chosen that include these major groups, subsequent choices will usually only add twigs with few additional characters to the phylogenetic tree, rather than adding major branches with many characters.

Unfortunately, using species richness does not solve all of the problems of data acquisition, because even a London garden has too many species for complete enumeration. Nonetheless, more work has been done on the problems of estimating richness at the level of species than at any other level (e.g. Magurran, 1988; Gaston, 1996c). Among the techniques that attempt to adjust for variations in sampling effort, those that interpolate individual species distributions (e.g. Nicholls, 1989; Busby, 1991; Aspinall, 1992; Carpenter, Gillison & Winter, 1993; Huntley et al., 1995; Margules & Redhead, 1995) remain compatible with complementarity-based area-selection methods (Williams, Prance et al., 1996; see below). In contrast, techniques for extrapolating local species richness (e.g. Palmer, 1990; Prendergast, Wood et al., 1993; Colwell & Coddington, 1994) are not, because they lose the identities of the species and with them the predictive pattern. There is also the problem that species are not always easily recognized as units (e.g. Otte & Endler, 1989).

The use of surrogates, in the broadest sense, may be applied to address three problems. First, how good is the species richness of bird faunas, for example, at predicting the character richness of bird faunas? And second, how good is it for predicting the species and character richness of other groups or even entire biotas, as an 'indicator' group? The latter, inter-group relationship (for review see Landres, Verner & Thomas, 1988; Noss, 1990; Kremen, 1992; Kremen et al., 1993; Reid et al., 1993) can be predictive under some circumstances (e.g. Beccaloni & Gaston, 1995), perhaps particularly when indicator and target organisms share similar habitat associations because of shared or similar governing factors (Gaston, 1996a). A third key question is whether complementarity within an indicator group is predictive of complementarity within other groups (Williams, 1993b; see below).

However, indicator relationships between groups cannot be assumed, because correlations for diversity measures can also be weak, absent or even negative, both at the scale of continents (Williams & Gaston, 1994; Gaston et al., 1995; Gaston, 1996a) and within countries (Ryti, 1992; Prendergast, Quinn et al., 1993; Lawton, Prendergast & Eversham, 1994; Gaston, 1996a). One familiar example is the negative correlation between two groups of European trees that have strongly differing climate preferences (Fig. 10.2: colour plate). Thus the Pinaceae (pines, firs, spruces, larches) are a dominant component of the Boreal forests of northern and eastern Europe, whereas the Fagaceae (oaks, beeches and chestnut) are a major component of the Southern-temperate forests of southern and western Europe. Nonetheless, in central Europe many species of the two groups occur in close proximity in the mountains, for example on the southern side of the Alps, although often at different altitudes. Such generally divergent patterns between some groups have long been known to natural historians.

### Higher taxon richness

It is not necessary to confine consideration of surrogacy for characters to taxa at the rank of species. The use of higher taxon richness (using, for example, genera or families) as a surrogate for gene or character richness helps to broaden the taxonomic coverage and so reduce the enormous extrapolation of using small indicator groups (Williams 1993b). For example, mapping 1000 families should represent more of biodiversity value than mapping 1000 species and be predictive of the distribution of character richness. The relationships between higher taxon richness and species richness can be relatively strong and do not depend critically on the 'naturalness' (e.g. monophyly) of higher taxa, although care is needed: (i) to select an appropriate taxonomic rank so that higher taxa are neither ubiquitous nor too expensive to survey; (ii) to avoid confounding effects of sampling area and intensity; and (iii) to avoid regional biases in taxonomy (see discussion by Gaston & Williams, 1993; Williams & Gaston, 1994; Lee, 1997).

In one recent example, family richness of seed plants and vertebrates (excluding birds) has been used in an attempt to plot the distribution of some of the most highly valued terrestrial biodiversity (Williams, Gaston & Humphries, 1997; Fig. 10.3(a): colour plate). This shows the expected latitudinal diversity gradient, with a global maximum in the tropical Americas.

**Table 10.1.** *Choosing surrogates to use in measuring biodiversity value*

| Advantage: precision as a measure of character diversity | A scale of surrogacy for a value currency of gene/character richness | | Advantage: inexpensive surveys and units more inclusive of viability-enhancing processes |
|---|---|---|---|
| | ('Ecosystem' richness ?) | | |
| Low | Environmental surrogates | Climate class richness | High |
| ⬇ | | Terrain class richness | ⬆ |
| ⬇ | | Substrate class richness | ⬆ |
| ⬇ | Environmental/assemblage surrogates | Landscape class richness | ⬆ |
| ⬇ | | Habitat class richness | ⬆ |
| ⬇ | Assemblage surrogates | 'Community' class richness | ⬆ |
| ⬇ | | Vegetation class richness | ⬆ |
| ⬇ | Taxonomic surrogates | Higher taxon richness | ⬆ |
| ⬇ | | Species/subspecies richness | ⬆ |
| High | | Taxonomic/phylogenetic subtree length | Low |
| | (Richness in gene/character currency) | | |

If greater biodiversity value is associated with richness in a currency of the characters of organisms (equivalent to expressed or expressible genes), then higher levels of biological organization (or environmental factors affecting its distribution) will have to be used in surrogate measures when surveys are extensive and resources for sampling limited (assemblages here are non-monophyletic groups of organisms; it is debatable whether ecosystems, if defined in terms of processes, can be mapped and counted). Choosing a surrogacy level from this scale is a compromise between precision of the measure on the one hand, and availability of data and cost of data compilation on the other. Higher level surrogates should have the additional advantage of implicitly integrating more of the functional processes that favour viability. After Williams (1996b).

The same data may also be used to explore range-size rarity at the rank of families (Fig. 10.3(*b*): colour plate). This picks out, in addition, many of the hotspots of endemism and threat identified by Myers (1988, 1990), for example in South Africa, Madagascar, southern Australia, New Caledonia and Chile.

### A scale of surrogacy

Relationships predicting biodiversity value may be viewed as parts of a more general scale of surrogacy (Table 10.1). It is an alternative (not necessarily better or worse) view of the interrelationships among different aspects of biodiversity to that expressed by Noss (1990), in this instance from the particular perspective of seeking to measure one aspect of value. If we accept gene or character richness as a useful part of biodiversity value, then this can be measured relatively directly by phylogenetic or taxonomic diversity. These scores are likely to be approximated for large numbers of species by species richness. Higher taxa may also be useful, but lower taxonomic ranks are more likely to give greater precision, whereas higher ranks should be cheaper to survey (Williams & Gaston, 1994). Other approaches, measuring higher levels of biological organization or governing environmental factors, including classifications of vegetation, land and climate (Margules & Redhead, 1995; Faith & Walker, 1996*b*; Schmidt, 1996) may be regarded as surrogates that, although yet more remote from the level of genes or characters, are nevertheless expected to influence the distribution of this currency of diversity value and, again, are even cheaper to survey (Williams, 1996*b*). So, when designing a survey for estimating biodiversity value, this kind of scale may be useful for identifying a level of surrogate as an appropriate compromise between, on the one hand, the precision of a predictor and, on the other, the cost of data acquisition.

### AREA-SELECTION METHODS

Area-selection methods are sets of rules designed to achieve particular goals efficiently and with a transparency that aids accountability. Other properties may also be important, including the ability to identify flexibility for the planning process; speed to facilitate the exploration of alternative values, goals, data and flexible solutions; the ability to deal with incomplete data; and simplicity to aid communication. Accountability is important to the people giving conservationists their mandate so that they can see how their values are being acted upon and that limited resources are not being misused (Mittermeier *et al.*, 1994; Vane-Wright, 1996). This may become increasingly important as litigation obliges conservationists to defend area choices. Efficiency is important because the area of land available for conservation is usually limited as there is usually competition between conservation and incompatible land uses for managing particular areas (for definitions and measures of efficiency see Pressey & Nicholls, 1989*a*; Pressey, Humphries *et al.*, 1993; Castro Parga *et al.*, 1996). However, efficiency should always be considered in relation to the goal of ensuring viability and persistence in order to ensure that effective choices are made.

### Area-selection goals

The methods reviewed here can, in principle, be applied to measures of phylogenetic diversity, species, higher taxa, vegetation formations, or most of the other biodiversity surrogates identified in Table 10.1. The general form required of the data is of an areas by biodiversity–surrogates matrix. The general form of the problem is then one of seeking to maximize the representation of the chosen biodiversity surrogates (hereafter exemplified by species for simplicity) within the areas selected.

One kind of question that has often been asked is of the form 'which is the minimum set of areas within Madagascar required to represent all species of lemurs?', either to achieve at least one, or to achieve at least *n* representations within the area set. This expresses ideas of complete representation, usually in the first instance seeking representation of each species in at least one area. There are many pitfalls with this approach, not only concerning the problems of viability and threat that are discussed below, but also concerning the meaning of 'complete'. It is apparent that a single representation of a species will not represent all of the intraspecific variation. The problem becomes worse with yet more remote surrogates for biodiversity value, for example a single representation of every vegetation class from a classification will not always represent every species, let alone all intraspecific variation. Of course, the only solution to representing every difference is to include every area, although the premise of area-selection methods is that competition with incompatible land uses limits the area available for conservation. However, if we accept the fundamental value of cumulative richness in different genes or characters, then minimum-area sets for surrogates at least have the advantage that they are expected to improve in terms of this currency on an undirected selection for the same number of areas.

In practice, it may often prove more useful to pursue a goal of maximizing representation as a maximum coverage set of areas if not all kinds of organisms can be represented (Ackery & Vane-Wright, 1984; Faith & Walker, 1996b). This approach addresses frequently asked questions such as 'how can we choose 1% of the total area of Madagascar to represent the greatest number of lemur species?' Recently this problem has been stated formally (Church, Stoms & Davis, 1996; Camm et al., 1996), although the principle has long been recognized in approximate techniques for selecting ordered area sequences, for example in prioritizing areas by taxonomic diversity (e.g. Vane-Wright, Humphries & Williams, 1991).

### Combinatorial scoring

Area-selection is often expected to satisfy multiple criteria. Economists have addressed this problem by combining values in scoring systems. Conservationists have followed by summing scores for some of their different values (e.g. Ratcliffe, 1977, 1986; Margules & Usher, 1981; Pearsall, Durham & Eagar, 1986; van der Ploeg, 1986; Mittermeier, 1988; Myers, 1988, 1990; Prance, 1990, 1994; IBAMA, INPA & CI, 1991; Sisk et al., 1994).

Combinatorial scoring systems have been criticized because the scoring has been considered highly subjective (NCC, 1989; Turpie, 1995) and because explicitly or implicitly they weight some criteria more heavily than others (Margules, 1989). The problems cannot be avoided entirely by multiplying, adding exponents, or normalizing the component scores. A fundamental problem remains with multiple 'currency' measures of how to trade-off between unconvertible currencies, for which there is no objective solution.

Economists address subjectivity in combinatorial systems by making the process explicitly subjective: by asking people which weights they would give to the various factors. However, Margules (1986) showed that in two British studies, not only did weights given by panel members to different values vary between studies as expected, but they also varied among panel members within a study. This causes severe problems for accountability in tracing back precisely why each area was selected.

### Hotspots of diversity

Another approach has been to select hotspots of diversity. Hotspots is a term often associated with Myers' influential worldwide review (Myers,

1988, 1990) of regions that combine high richness, endemism and threat. Subsequently, others (Gibbons, Reid & Chapman, 1993; Prendergast, Quinn *et al.*, 1993; Prendergast, Wood *et al.*, 1993; Gaston & David, 1994; Lawton *et al.*, 1994; Williams, Gibbons *et al.*, 1996 have used the term in a narrower sense of high scores for species richness within continents or countries. In principle, it could be used, with appropriate qualification, for high-scoring areas on any value scale and on any spatial scale.

Choosing areas with the highest numbers of species as priorities for biodiversity conservation has been a popular method (Scott, Csuti *et al.*, 1987; Gibbons *et al.*, 1993; Prendergast, Quinn *et al.*, 1993; Prendergast, Wood *et al.*, 1993; Lawton *et al.*, 1994; Mittermeier *et al.*, 1994; WWF & IUCN, 1994; Turpie, 1995). For example, Prendergast, Quinn *et al.*, (1993) considered the consequences for species representation of selecting the top 5% of areas (10 km grid cells) within Britain by species richness as conservation areas. This method has the appeal of dealing with species-occurrence data with apparent quantitative rigour. It also has the advantage that knowledge of the identity of each species is not required, so it would be possible to use extrapolated richness scores (e.g. methods in Palmer, 1990; Prendergast, Wood *et al.*, 1993; Colwell & Coddington, 1994).

### Hotspots of rarity

Hotspots of rarity are essentially similar to hotspots of richness, but give greater weight to the more narrowly distributed species. For example, Terborgh & Winter (1983), working with South American birds, identified areas with high richness in just those species with range sizes of less than 50 000 km² as future protection priorities. Similar approaches using discontinuous (threshold) measures of rarity have been applied at a wide range of spatial scales (ICBP, 1992; Sætersdal, Line & Birks, 1993; Thirgood & Heath, 1994; WWF & IUCN, 1994). This approach has the advantage of requiring data for only the more restricted species. Furthermore, because the species are necessarily narrowly distributed, it is also likely to select for more highly complementary biotas and so lead to more complete representation of species.

Crowe & Siegfried (1993) criticized the adoption of any arbitrary range-size threshold because it will always miss important species with marginally larger ranges. From this point of view, a better technique would be to map a continuous function of range size, such as summing the inverse of species range sizes (e.g. Jefferson, 1984; Usher, 1986; Avery & Leslie,

1990; Howard, 1991; Williams, 1993*b*; Turpie, 1995; Williams, Gibbons *et al.*, 1996; Williams, Prance *et al.*, 1996). This escapes the criticism of threshold arbitrariness, although on the other hand there is no obvious 'natural' formula for the range-size weighting. The importance is that, at least with the continuous functions, all of the species in the data make some contribution to the scores.

### Complementary areas

Where identities of species or other biodiversity surrogates are known, many recent studies have chosen to use complementarity methods. These methods are used to seek areas that in combination have the highest representation of diversity. Complementarity was introduced into area selection by Kirkpatrick (1983), Ackery & Vane-Wright (1984), Margules & Nicholls (1987) and Margules, Nicholls & Pressey (1988), although the term was coined by Vane-Wright, Humphries & Williams (1991). It refers to the degree to which one or more sets of attributes contributes otherwise unrepresented attributes to one or more other sets of attributes (Vane-Wright, Humphries *et al.*, 1991; Colwell & Coddington, 1994). In the present context, the attributes are the valued characters, or surrogates such as species, and the sets are the biotas, which are usually defined by spatial volume, or (on land) by area. For example, if one area has a fauna consisting of a tiger, bear and lion, while another area has a fauna with a lion, zebra and giraffe, then the second area's fauna complements the first by the zebra and giraffe. As a concept, complementarity is independent of spatial scale, although actual numbers of complementary characters or species are not. 'Gap analysis' is sometimes used as a general term for the application of complementarity to area selection. However, the Gap Analysis Program in the USA (from which the term was derived) has not always used complementarity as it does now (Scott, Davis *et al.*, 1993; Kiester *et al.*, 1996), but in the past had focused on using the hotspots approach (Scott, Csuti *et al.*, 1987).

The use of complementarity usually requires knowledge of the identities of the surrogates in each area, although this is not essential if there is knowledge of some pattern that predicts their complementary value (Faith, 1994). This alternative is used by taxonomic and phylogenetic measures of diversity (e.g. Vane-Wright, Humphries *et al.*, 1991), and in multivariate approaches to higher surrogates such as species assemblages (Sætersdal & Birks, 1993; Belbin, 1995; Woinarski, Price & Faith, 1996), but is more clearly apparent in the use of techniques based on environmental surro-

**Table 10.2**

*Hotspots and complementary areas*

| Species | Areas | | | | |
|---|---|---|---|---|---|
| | 1 | 2 | 3 | 4 | 5 |
| a | · | ⊛ | · | ⊛ | · |
| b | · | ⊛ | · | ⊛ | · |
| c | ⊛ | ⊛ | · | ⊛ | · |
| d | ⊛ | ⊛ | · | · | · |
| e | ⊛ | · | ⊛ | · | · |
| f | ⊛ | · | ⊛ | · | ⊛ |
| g | ⊛ | · | ⊛ | · | ⊛ |
| h | · | · | ⊛ | · | ⊛ |

Example data matrix for records of eight species among five areas. The hotspot of richness is area 1, but this is not part of the minimum representative set, which is areas 2 + 3. After Underhill (1994).

gates (Faith & Walker 1996*a*, *b*). In contrast, complementarity is not necessarily indicative between groups of organisms (Williams, 1993*b*; Gaston *et al.*, 1995; Faith & Walker, 1996*a*). This is to be expected because the distribution of diversity in one group of organisms does not necessarily 'indicate' the distribution of diversity in others (Ryti, 1992; Prendergast, Quinn *et al.*, 1993; Williams & Gaston 1994; Gaston *et al.*, 1995; Gaston, 1996*a*; Fig. 10.2), particularly where the groups are associated with very different kinds of habitat because they are governed by very different factors. However, the complexity of some of the techniques using assemblage or environmental surrogates may present a challenge for accountability. Furthermore, use of environmental surrogacy may be based on assumptions of a uniform random distribution of species in niche space (or simple graded transformations thereof), and (more generally) of equilibrium distribution of organisms among patches of suitable habitat, which require checking for robustness.

The efficiency of solutions to area-selection problems obtained by using complementarity can be maximized. It is obvious from the simple species-by-areas data matrix in Table 10.2 that areas 2 + 3 complement one another perfectly to represent all species *a-h* between them. In this particular case the hotspot of species richness, area 1, is not needed for the minimum set of complementary representative areas (2 + 3).

Unfortunately, not all data sets are so straightforward. There is in fact no fast and general solution to the problem (an '*n-p* complete' problem: Church *et al.*, 1996; Pressey, Possingham & Margules, 1996). Exact sol-

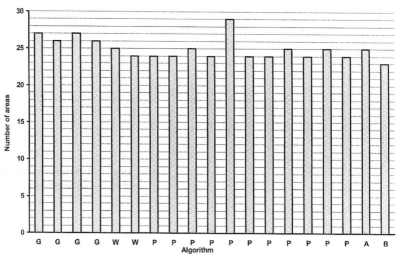

Fig. 10.4 Example of the minimum numbers of areas required for fully representative sets of Oregon vertebrates according to 19 different algorithms: (G) variations on greedy richness algorithms; (W) variations on weighted rarity algorithms; (P) variations on progressive rarity algorithms; (A) a simulated annealing algorithm; (B) branch-and-bound algorithm. After Csuti *et al.*, (1997).

utions can be achieved by exhaustive searches of all possible area sets, although these are too numerous to be practical for problems with all but very small numbers of areas. Techniques such as branch-and-bound algorithms (Fig. 10.4 column 'B') can give optimal solutions (Cocks & Baird 1989; Sætersdal *et al.*, 1993; Church *et al.*, 1996; Kiester *et al.*, 1996; Csuti *et al.*, 1997; Pressey, Possingham & Margules, 1996), but even they may take many hours or days to provide results when dealing with just a few hundred species and areas (Possingham *et al.*, 1993). This renders interactive assessment of priority areas out of the question (Williams, Gibbons *et al.*, 1996). The technique is also unsuitable for more complex selection goals (Pressey, Possingham & Margules, 1996).

For much faster solutions that may be only slightly less efficient, approximate, heuristic techniques are often employed and the popularity of complementarity has brought a tremendous proliferation of variations on these techniques. Csuti *et al.*, (1997) carried out one comparative study of many different complementarity-based area-selection algorithms (Fig. 10.4) applied to data for vertebrates as part of the Oregon Gap Analysis project (see Scott, Davis *et al.*, 1993). Their results illustrate some of the major features of the different groups of algorithms (iterated sets of rules).

**Table 10.3**
*Area selection by a heuristic rarity algorithm*

Near-minimum-area set
Selection rule summary by area sequence

| Choices | | Number | Selection rules |
|---|---|---|---|
| Step | Area | of ties | No.: Description |
| 1 | Kashmir | – | (irreplaceable taxon) |
| 2 | Afghanistan | – | (irreplaceable taxon) |
| 3 | Ecuador | 0 | 2: rarest + next rarest |
| 4 | Michoacan | 1 | 4: rarest + next rarest + next rarest + lowest cell |
| 5 | Qinghai | 3 | 4: rarest + (no next rarest) + lowest cell |
| 6 | N.E. India | 1 | 4: rarest + (no next rarest) + lowest cell |
| 7 | C. Bolivia | 0 | 1: rarest |
| 8 | N. California | 0 | 3: rarest + next rarest + next rarest |
| 9 | Uzbekistan | 2 | 4: rarest + (no next rarest) + lowest cell |
| 10 | Turkey | 1 | 4: rarest + next rarest + next rarest + lowest cell |
| 11 | Irkutsk | 0 | 2: rarest + next rarest |
| 12 | Big Horn | 11 | 4: rarest + (no next rarest) + lowest cell |

Example of the results of selecting a near-minimum-area set to represent all 43 species of bumble bees of the *sibiricus*-group among large equal-area grid cells (for details of the organisms and areas, see Vane-Wright, Humphries *et al.*, 1991). The table lists the areas in the order (step) in which they have been chosen, together with the rules used to choose them (Williams 1996a). Where a species occurs in only one grid cell, that cell is irreplaceable to meeting the selection goal (areas 1 and 2). Once all such species are accounted for, up to four rules may be applied (in this case) to make a subsequent choice at each step. The first rule is to select the area with the largest number of the rarest unrepresented species (e.g. for area 7). If there are tied areas for this rule, then the second rule is to choose among the ties in favour of the area with the largest number of the next-rarest unrepresented species (areas 3,11). If there are tied areas for this, then the third rule is to choose among them for the area with the largest number of the next-next-rarest unrepresented species (area 8). If ties persist or if there are no next- or next-next-rarest species, then a fourth arbitrary rule of choosing the cell with the lowest index number is used (areas 4,5,6,9,10,12; random choices might be used as one alternative, although then the results would be unrepeatable for test comparisons). The number of ties shown is the number persisting when the last rule at each step is applied.

Simple greedy richness algorithms (Fig. 10.4 column 'G'), whereby areas are chosen sequentially for their richest complements (Kirkpatrick, 1983; Thomas & Mallorie, 1985; Burley, 1988; Daniels *et al.*, 1991; Vane-Wright, Humphries *et al.*, 1991; Mickleburgh, Hutson & Racey, 1992; Rebelo & Siegfried, 1992; Sætersdal *et al.*, 1993; Kershaw, Williams & Mace, 1994; Kershaw, Mace & Williams, 1995; Rebelo, 1994; Vane-Wright, Smith

& Kitching, 1994; Vane-Wright & Peggie, 1994; Dobson et al., 1997), are fast but relatively inefficient in terms of numbers of areas required to represent all species. Depending on the range sizes of species and the degree to which they overlap in their distributions (Pressey, Possingham, Logan et al., in press), greedy algorithms usually require more areas for a particular representation goal (Underhill, 1994; Csuti et al., 1997).

The bulk of recent examples use rarity-based heuristic algorithms, designed to improve on greedy richness algorithms, to give fast (a few seconds on current PCs) though still approximate solutions to area-selection problems (near-minimum sets or near-maximum coverage). The idea is to select preferentially for areas with the more restricted species first. This is done either by using richness in a continuous measure of range-size rarity among species (e.g. Fig. 10.4 'W' rarity-weighted algorithms: Ackery & Vane-Wright, 1984; Rebelo & Siegfried, 1990, 1992; Kirkpatrick & Brown, 1991; Kershaw, Williams & Mace, 1994; Rebelo, 1994; Williams, 1994, 1996a; Turpie, 1995; Castro Parga et al., 1996; Kitching, 1996; Moreno Saiz et al., 1996; Williams, Gibbons et al., 1996; Williams, Prance et al., 1996; Csuti et al., 1997; Hacker et al., 1998; Fjeldså & Rahbek, this volume), or by choosing areas with the most restricted species first (a discontinuous measure of range-size rarity, Table 10.3), then areas with the next most restricted, and so on (e.g. Fig. 10.4 'P' progressive rarity algorithms: Margules, Nicholls & Pressey, 1988; Pressey & Nicholls, 1989b, 1991; Margules, Pressey & Nicholls, 1991; Bedward, Pressey & Keith 1992; Ryti 1992; Sætersdal et al., 1993; Margules, Cresswell & Nicholls, 1994; Margules, Nicholls & Usher, 1994; Pressey, Bedward & Keith, 1994; Freitag, Nicholls & van Jaarsveld, 1996; Williams, 1996a; Csuti et al., 1997). These rarity-based algorithms are very nearly as fast as greedy richness algorithms, but are often more efficient for near-minimum sets (Kershaw, Williams & Mace, 1994; Csuti et al., 1997). Differences in efficiency between the two formulations of rarity algorithms appear to be dependent on patterns within the data (unpublished data).

Heuristic algorithms can be supplemented with other procedures to improve their efficiency. These algorithms are often combined with checks to eliminate any early area choices that in retrospect are made redundant by later choices (e.g. Bedward et al., 1992; Williams, 1994, 1996a; Williams, Gibbons et al., 1996). This will ensure that the algorithms pass Underhill's (1994) simple test (Table 10.2) against the weaknesses of greedy richness algorithms by selecting only areas 2 + 3. However, they will still fail tests with more demanding data where optimal solutions require swapping

**Table 10.4**
*Area selections reordered by complementary richness*

Near-minimum-area set re-ordered by richness
(no within-set redundant areas detected)
Representation summary by area sequence

| Choices | | Species richness | | | |
|---|---|---|---|---|---|
| Step | Area | Absolute | Increment | Cumulative | % |
| 1 | Ecuador | 10 | 10 | 10 | 23.26 |
| 2 | Kashmir | 9 | 9 | 19 | 44.19 |
| 3 | Turkey | 7 | 6 | 25 | 58.14 |
| 4 | Michoacan | 4 | 4 | 29 | 67.44 |
| 5 | C. Bolivia | 8 | 3 | 32 | 74.42 |
| 6 | N. California | 4 | 3 | 35 | 81.40 |
| 7 | Irkutsk | 5 | 3 | 38 | 88.37 |
| 8 | Afghanistan | 5 | 1 | 39 | 90.70 |
| 9 | Qinghai | 8 | 1 | 40 | 93.02 |
| 10 | N.E. India | 5 | 1 | 41 | 95.35 |
| 11 | Uzbekistan | 4 | 1 | 42 | 97.67 |
| 12 | Big Horn | 4 | 1 | 43 | 100.00 |

Example of the results of re-ordering the near-minimum-area set shown in Table 3 that represents all 43 species of bumble bees of the *sibiricus*-group among large equal-area grid cells (for details see Vane-Wright, Humphries *et al.*, 1991). The areas are listed by complementary species richness: the order in which they contribute the largest number of previously unrepresented species (Williams 1996a). The complementary richness at each step or species increment is shown in the fourth column.

areas with others outside the initial set. One technique for attempting to address this is to swap selected areas for neighbouring areas and test for improved solutions. This is the basis of 'simulated annealing' algorithms (Fig. 10.4 'A') (e.g. Kirkpatrick, Gelatt & Vecchi, 1983; Csuti *et al.*, 1997).

Maximum-coverage problems can be addressed using heuristics in a similar way to minimum-set problems. Greedy richness has been most popular, and may be combined with redundancy tests (Williams, 1996a), although this becomes unreliable as the number of areas required approaches the size of the minimum set (see Csuti *et al.*, 1997: Fig. 1). The results may then be checked against an alternative technique, such as the simple expedient of re-ordering a heuristic near-minimum set of areas by their diversity complements (Table 10.4; Williams, 1994, 1996a; Williams, Prance *et al.*, 1996). This has been shown to provide a particularly good series of solutions to these maximum-coverage problems for more nearly complete sets (algorithm number 8 in Csuti *et al.*, 1997).

In reviewing these algorithms, it is important to appreciate that early greedy richness techniques were crude (Underhill, 1994), and consequently that there has been a move towards searching for true optimality. However, more recently the practical advantage of speed from heuristic techniques has come to be appreciated (just as in systematics, see Swofford, 1990), particularly as the cost to efficiency with rarity heuristics that incorporate redundancy checks is usually small (Pressey, Possingham & Margules, 1996).

### Comparison of area-selection methods

Pressey & Nicholls (1989a) have reported that scoring methods are consistently less efficient than complementarity-based algorithms in representing plant species or land classes in Australia.

Complementary areas can also be more efficient than hotspots of either richness or rarity. A joint study by Williams, Gibbons et al., (1996) of data for British breeding birds (Gibbons et al., 1993) followed Prendergast, Quinn et al.,'s (1993) goal of seeking to represent as many species as possible within 5% of the 10 km grid cells within Britain. Within this area limit, hotspots of richness and rarity did not even succeed in representing all of the species at least once, whereas complementary areas represented all of the species at least six times over (or included all representatives for the more narrowly distributed species) (Table 10.5). Inevitably, the hotspots of richness did give the highest total number of species-in-gridcell records.

Williams, Gibbons et al., (1996) also compared the frequencies of representations per species in the area sets from the three area-selection methods. Hotspots of richness included large numbers of repeat representations for the more widespread species, whereas many other more restricted species were represented only once. In comparison, rarity and complementary areas showed more even representation per species, although the complementary areas for a goal of six representations increased the numbers from single representations towards higher numbers for many of the rarer species.

## INTEGRATING VIABILITY AND THREAT

The study of British birds outlined above (Williams, Gibbons et al., 1996) highlighted the problem that while quantitative methods can be efficient in identifying sets of areas to represent diversity, ultimately they need to be

**Table 10.5.** *Comparison of area-selection methods*

| Representation achieved | Area-selection methods | | Complementary areas for | |
| --- | --- | --- | --- | --- |
| | Richness hotspots | Rarity hotspots | 1 representation | 6 representations |
| Percentage of occupied grid cells chosen (among 2827 cells) | 5.0 | 5.0 | 1.0 | 4.9 |
| Percentage of total species represented (among 218 species) | 89.0 | 97.7 | 100.0 | 100.0 |
| Percentage of total species-in-gridcell records represented (among 170 098 records) | 7.8 | 6.1 | 1.1 | 6.0 |

Efficiency of richness hotspots, rarity hotspots, and complementary areas in representing breeding birds among 10 × 10 km grid cells in Britain shown as percentage representation of species from the British totals. After Williams, Gibbons *et al.*, (1996).

successful in identifying viable areas and in dealing with threat in order to ensure the persistence of biodiversity (Witting & Loeschcke, 1993; Margules, Nicholls & Usher, 1994; Pressey, 1997). So how might this likelihood of persistence be improved? It is not possible to give an exhaustive review in this paper of how viability and threat have previously been integrated, but some of the more popular and promising approaches are discussed.

When adding criteria of viability and threat, the structure of area-selection methods might be reconsidered. Assuming that complementarity-based methods are to be used because of their potential for efficiency of species representation, we are again faced with the problem of dealing with multiple criteria. In order to avoid some of the problems of compromising accountability that are apparent with combinatorial scoring methods (see above), the additional viability and threat criteria might be applied in separate steps within a sequence or hierarchy of decisions. The idea is to retain accountability through making it possible to say exactly why each species or area is included or excluded at each step of the analysis (a less elegant and more laborious alternative with combined criteria would be to re-run the procedure with and without particular criteria in order to examine their effects).

A sequential structure based loosely on the 'steps' suggested by Bedward *et al.*, (1992) consists of prescription, preselection, selection, prioritization, postselection and reiteration, as detailed below. A treatment of viability and threat could then be integrated at *any* of these steps, although I shall concentrate on some of the possibilities at the preselection and postselection steps.

### Prescription

Prescription concerns deciding the values and goals of an area-selection exercise. Any area-selection procedure must begin with a clear idea of which value areas are to be chosen to represent. This is needed for a well-defined goal, so if the value to be conserved is in biodiversity, then decisions have to be made as to (i) which diversity-value surrogates to use; (ii) which areas to choose among (i.e. their location, grain size, and the extent of the survey area); and (iii) which representation target is to be achieved. Considering viability and threat, this representation target could vary among species depending on their differing vulnerabilities (e.g. Kirkpatrick & Brown, 1991).

### Preselection: modelling viability and threat

Preselection can be used to restrict which data (areas, species and records) from the raw data are to be included as candidates for selection during the main selection stage. This is done to tailor the data for pursuing the goals established at the prescription stage.

Triage (Myers, 1979; Vane-Wright, 1996) can be used as a form of preselection, which if required may be applied to exclude any areas and species that are beyond management, and also to exclude any areas and species that are considered never likely to require management. In this vein, the study of British birds (Williams, Gibbons *et al.*, 1996), included a supplementary analysis with some crude treatment of threat and viability. First, only Red Data book species were included, on the grounds that they are the most threatened and so are the highest priorities for conservation management. Second, to illustrate how complementarity can work to supplement existing conservation areas ('gap analysis'), the faunas of all grid cells with more than 50% area cover by Sites of Special Scientific Interest were excluded from the analysis (this is clearly an over-simplification of 'adequate' protection and was intended only for the purposes of illustrating the principle). And third, to enhance viability within any selected areas, only records with evidence of breeding were included, as a very crude measure of viability. This kind of preselection of data is often used, but crucially it does not guarantee that areas will not be selected that have very poor prognoses for some of the species.

One possibility is to use abundance data as a predictor of viability (e.g. Winston & Angermeier, 1995). As with any approach there are potential problems, in this case that high densities of individuals do not necessarily identify the most viable areas within populations (e.g. the distributions of density and of rates of increase may be different because of patterns of movement of individuals), at least when these areas become isolated. Use of abundance information is explored elsewhere in this volume (Nicholls, this volume).

Another possibility, to avoid the pitfall of including inviable candidates for area selection, is to exclude records for particular species from those areas where they have very poor viability prognoses, by using niche-based modelling of the local habitat suitability. This requires some means of using estimated probabilities of occurrence now to predict probabilities of occurrence in the future, as an estimate of local population viability. In principle, similar modelling techniques might also be extended to certain

# Pretreatment of data

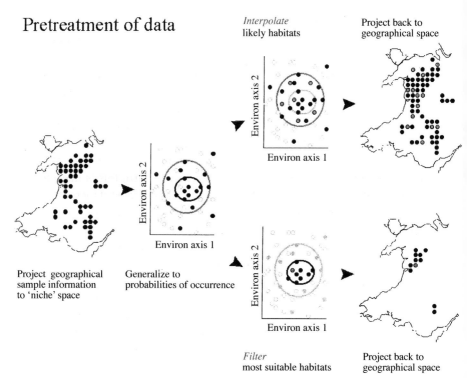

Fig. 10.5 Probability models have often been used for interpolating the expected distribution of moderately well-known and moderately widespread species. Spatial information is used to model niche space, which can then be used (upper row) by applying a threshold to predict the expected distribution among unsampled areas. Alternatively, probability models could also be used to seek 'viability centres' for each species (lower row). This might be achieved in part by increasing the threshold probability of occurrence for admitting records from the raw data so as to filter out all records from areas with lower habitat suitability.

kinds of threats, for example by modelling bulldozer 'habitat' (i.e. land that is reasonably flat and well drained: R. L. Pressey pers. comm.) as one form of area-based threat.

The use of probability models is familiar in the context of interpolating the expected distribution of moderately well-known and moderately widespread species (Fig. 10.5, upper row), where spatial information is used to model some aspects of 'niche space'. This is then used to predict the expected distribution among unsampled areas (e.g. Nicholls, 1989; Busby, 1991; Aspinall, 1992; Carpenter et al., 1993; Huntley et al., 1995; Margules

& Redhead, 1995). Interpolation is already well established as a routine part of Gap Analysis in the USA (Scott, Davis *et al.*, 1993; Butterfield, Csuti & Scott, 1994; Schmidt, 1996).

In contrast, probability models could be used to seek 'viability centres' for each species. This might be achieved in part by increasing the threshold probability of occurrence for admitting records from the raw data: in effect, to filter out and exclude as candidates for selection all records from areas with lower habitat suitability (Fig. 10.5, lower row). This procedure differs from excluding geographically marginal areas in that it goes more directly for ecologically central areas, within niche space. In turn, this is likely to relate more directly to population processes, such as net rates of increase. It is no doubt simplistic, particularly in regard to the need to consider interactions among species; the need to cater for large-scale foraging and migratory requirements (for birds, see, e.g. Lack, 1986; Pritchard *et al.*, 1992; Gibbons *et al.*, 1993); and the need for some geographically isolated areas to be excluded (see Thomas *et al*, this volume). Yet it may have advantages. First, in generalizing information from all data, consistency checks can identify ecologically outlying records that may require confirmation (Busby, 1991) and may not be reliable candidates for viable conservation. Second, it may be possible to identify apparently unoccupied yet highly suitable areas, which may have future significance for metapopulation dynamics (Doncaster, Micol & Jensen, 1996). Third, it may be possible to generate reasonably predictive models from distribution data and climatic data alone, without detailed autecological studies of each species, so that this procedure might be automated for dealing with larger numbers of species at relatively low cost.

### Selection

Selection is used to choose a set of areas for priority conservation management. Efficiency in representing biodiversity value per unit cost in area-selection methods comes from using complementarity-based algorithms applied at the main selection stage (see the discussion of complementary areas). This has often been seen as the primary purpose of this stage. Efficiency is required because the area of land available for conservation is usually limited and because there is often competition between conservation and incompatible land uses for managing particular areas.

None the less, efficiency of current representation is arguably not the primary criterion for conservationists concerned with persistence: rather it should be future representation, so that promoting viability and reducing threat is a vital component. In principle, these criteria could be added to supplement the sets of rules in heuristic algorithms, either by combining scores within one rule (e.g. choosing the area with the maximum score for weighted rarity + weighted viability + weighted threat), or by adding extra rules to a sequential list of rules to be iterated. When combining scores, the severe problems with subjectivity, accountability and efficiency that arise have been discussed above. On the other hand, the effect of adding extra rules depends on their position in the order in which the rules are applied. It may be that viability and threat are considered more important than current efficiency and so applied early in the order, which will have the consequence of appearing to compromise this measure of 'efficiency'. However, the conflict here might then prove to be illusory, because ultimately it is efficiency in the context of persistence that is important. Conflict arises when we are unable to measure properly the effect of these rules on future persistence (and thus their effect on efficiency). This is particularly apparent when we are obliged to implement 'rules of thumb' (e.g. selecting preferentially for contiguous areas) without being able to measure precisely their benefits for viability. For example, at least in certain circumstances, such as at large spatial scales or with very poorly dispersing species, rules such as selecting preferentially for contiguous areas might conceivably have very little advantage for promoting viability.

However, there are other means of allowing for viability and threat, even when they cannot be measured precisely. For example, preselection may be used (as discussed above) to limit area choices before the main selection step to just those local populations that are available for conservation and also most likely to remain viable. This might remove the need for some of the supplementary criteria at the main selection step. Preselection may appear to reduce current efficiency, but this extra 'cost' can be accounted for directly in terms of an increased probability for future persistence.

Supplementary criteria could still be included in the rules at the main selection step, such as selecting for areas with further increased viability scores (beyond the threshold for preselection) or preferentially selecting areas in proximity or contiguity. In order to avoid compromising accountability and efficiency (for a given probability of persistence), these supplementary criteria might be included as subordinate, tie-breaking rules at the end of the list of rules applied at each iteration of the algorithms.

With better knowledge of the organisms, it might be possible to avoid many of these complications by going even further down the road of using probability models in order to select directly for representation targets measured in terms of probabilities of persistence. For example, Margules & Nicholls (1987; or see accounts of this study in Margules, Pressey *et al.*, 1991; Margules, Cresswell *et al.*, 1994) have used a technique based on probabilities of occurrence that could equally be applied to probabilities of persistence.

### Prioritization

Prioritization within a priority-area set concerns which of the selected areas has the greatest urgency for conservation management to be applied. This is often unrelated to any ordering of areas produced by the main selection algorithms (Tables 10.3, 10.4), particularly when they are directed primarily towards efficiency of representation (Pressey, Possingham & Margules, 1996).

Pressey and colleagues (Pressey, Bedward *et al.*, 1994; Pressey, Johnson & Wilson, 1994; Pressey, 1997) have defined a measure of degrees of 'irreplaceability' from the frequency with which each area occurs among all of the different minimum-area representative sets. They view this as a measure of the conservation value of an area, summarizing the extent to which other options for reaching a representation goal exist among all other fully representative sets. Although this has the potential advantage of not being restricted to just one area set, it suffers from losing the links with knowledge of the particular goal-essential species (these depend on the context of a particular set, see below), which are important for accountability and biological management decisions.

A more direct approach to prioritizing a particular area set has been that if threat were predictable (e.g. Beissinger *et al.*, 1996), then this would be a popular criterion for re-ordering selected areas (Pressey, 1994; Pressey & Tully, 1994; Kershaw, Mace & Williams, 1995). Hence minimum-area sets or maximum-coverage sets can be re-ordered by measures of threat when this is known. Alternatively, if threat were unknown or could not be modelled, then the diversity complement could be used to ensure that the most diversity would be secured first against unpredictable threats (Table 10.4; Williams, Gibbons *et al.*, 1996; Williams, Prance *et al.*, 1996).

### Postselection: interactive exploration of flexibility

Postselection may be used to explore the consequences of modifying a selected area set to satisfy additional criteria. This is where the high speed of heuristic selection algorithms on even widely available computers has a particular advantage, because it permits truly inter-active exploration of area sets (Williams, Gibbons *et al.*, 1996; Pressey, Possingham & Margules, 1996).

One advantage of the complementarity method is that it enables precise identification of the goal-essential species that justify the inclusion of an area in an area set (Pressey, Humphries *et al.*, 1993). For minimum sets with a goal of a single representation for each species, the *goal-essential* species are those that occur in only one area within the area set (Rebelo, 1994). Some of these species may indeed occur in only one area within the extent of a particular survey, in which case their unique presence makes the area *irreplaceable* to achieving the representation goal. However, most species are usually more widespread, so that other areas where they occur provide *flexibility* for area selection (Pressey, Humphries *et al.*, 1993).

Using this information on goal-essential species, it is possible to map the selected areas as irreplaceable or as flexible, and to count the number of goal-essential taxa in each area (Fig. 10.6). Alternative area choices can then be applied inter-actively so that other criteria can be explored. If necessary, the new selections can be tested for their effect on efficiency by rerunning the area-selection algorithm and reprioritizing. This can be used to assess the sensitivity of particular area sets to the loss of particular areas (cf. 'irreplaceability', see above).

Furthermore, because the goal-essential species in each selected area are known and so too are their distributions, it is possible to plot maps of species richness in just these species (Fig. 10.6). In effect, these are maps of flexibility for the selected areas within a particular set. Any one of the other areas on these maps that has all of the same goal-essential species as the selected area under consideration (the black squares in Fig. 10.6) is therefore a perfectly flexible alternative, and could be swapped for it on the list of selected areas. Thus flexibility can be exploited to find a modified set of areas that is equally efficient and equally easily justified. Areas with fewer of the goal-essential species are only partially flexible, so that choosing them in place of the first area will be expected to reduce efficiency (occasionally when using heuristic algorithms this may not be the case, because it may be possible to find even smaller sets than the near-minimum approximations that heuristics provide).

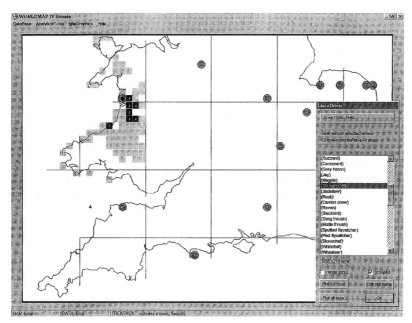

Fig. 10.6  Computer implementation of heuristic area-selection methods permits fast interactive exploration of flexibility in sets of representative areas, even with large datasets with many thousands of species. The complementary areas method can distinguish *irreplaceable* areas from *flexible* areas (using coloured circles that are not differentiated here) by identifying the *goal-essential* species that justify the choice of each selected area and registering how widespread they are. With the implementation of these methods in WORLDMAP software (Williams 1996*a*), clicking the mouse button with the cursor on a particular selected area (in this example, shown by the black spot on gridcell SH60 in North Wales) causes a map of richness in just these goal-essential species to be plotted, in effect providing a map of flexibility (e.g. for the selected area SH60: all black squares are perfectly flexible alternatives, whereas the light grey squares are only partly flexible because if substituted they would reduce efficiency). Double clicking the mouse button also opens a window (on the right), which lists the fauna of the particular selected area SH60 and highlights the goal-essential species (e.g. chough) and shows their range sizes within the dataset (e.g. 64 grid cells). For exploring alternative selections, the list of selected areas can then be called up, areas can be deleted or added as required, and the consequences for efficiency checked by re-running the complementarity algorithm. These methods can be applied to species or to most other biodiversity surrogates, and at any spatial scale or to areas of heterogeneous sizes.

### Reiteration

Finally, when changing values, goals or data, computer implementation of quantitative methods allows the entire procedure to be re-run as often as necessary, even with very large data sets for many thousands of species and areas.

## CONCLUSIONS

The area-selection methods preferred at present have three strengths. First, a scale of surrogacy based on a fundamental currency of gene/character richness can be used to judge appropriate compromises of precision and cost in choosing surrogates when designing surveys to measure more of biodiversity. Second, representation of species (or other biodiversity surrogates) among sets of areas can be optimized by the available quantitative algorithms that use complementarity. Third, the transparency of the area-selection process can be increased by replacing combinatorial scoring methods with sequential decision methods in order to aid public accountability.

These methods also have weaknesses, although they are mostly general to all attempts at area selection. For example, values and goals are not universal but idiosyncratic to particular people and situations. Data for representing biodiversity value can always be improved by reducing spatial, temporal and taxonomic bias in sampling. Information on viability and threat is potentially very expensive to collect even for single species, let alone for entire biota. Furthermore, there is no agreed procedure at present as to how viability and threat can best be integrated into quantitative area-selection methods, particularly without unduly compromising accountability and efficiency.

Doubtless these methods will continue to be improved, but the major challenges in the immediate future are how best to predict viability and threat from limited information and how best to integrate this information into area-selection methods.

## ACKNOWLEDGEMENTS

My thanks to Miguel Araujo, Dan Faith, Kevin Gaston, Chris Humphries, Melanie Kershaw, Helen de Klerk, Chris Margules, Nick Nicholls, Bob

Pressey and Dick Vane-Wright for discussion; to David Gibbons and the British Trust for Ornithology for collaborative work on British birds; to the Department of Entomology, the Natural History Museum, for providing facilities; and to the Institute for Advanced Study, Berlin, for funding this project.

## References

Ackery, P. R. & Vane-Wright, R. I. (1984). Milkweed butterflies, their cladistics and biology, being an account of the natural history of the Danainae, a subfamily of the Lepidoptera, Nymphalidae. *Publs Br. Mus. Nat Hist.* No. 893, 1–425.

Aspinall, R. (1992). An inductive modelling procedure based on Bayes' theorem for analysis of pattern in spatial data. *Int. J. Geogr. Inf. Syst.*, **6**, 105–21.

Austin, M. P. & Margules, C. R. (1986). Assessing representativeness. In *Wildlife conservation evaluation*: 45–67. (Ed. Usher, M. B.). Chapman & Hall, London.

Avery, M. & Leslie, R. (1990). *Birds and forestry*. Poyser, London.

Beccaloni, G. W. & Gaston, K. J. (1995). Predicting the species richness of Neotropical forest butterflies: Ithomiinae (Lepidoptera: Nymphalidae) as indicators. *Biol. Conserv.*, **71**, 77–86.

Bedward, M., Pressey, R. L. & Keith, D. A. (1992). A new approach for selecting fully representative reserve networks: addressing efficiency, reserve design and land suitability with an iterative analysis. *Biol. Conserv.*, **62**, 115–25.

Beissinger, S. R., Steadman, E. C., Wohlgenant, T., Blate, G. & Zack, S. (1996). Null models for assessing ecosystem conservation priorities: threatened birds as titers of threatened ecosystems in South America. *Conserv. Biol.*, **10**, 1343–52.

Belbin, L. (1995). A multivariate approach to the selection of biological reserves. *Biodiv. Conserv.*, **4**, 951–63.

Brewer, C. A. (1994). Color use guidelines for mapping and visualisation. In *Visualisation in Modern Cartography*: 123–147. (Eds MacEachren, A. M. & Fraser Taylor, D. R.). Pergamon Press, London.

Brooks, D.R., Mayden, R.L. & McLennan, D.A. (1992). Phylogeny and biodiversity: conserving our evolutionary legacy. *Trends Ecol. Evol.*, **7**, 55–9.

Burley, F. W. (1988). Monitoring biological diversity for setting priorities in conservation. In *Biodiversity*: 227–230. (Ed.Wilson, E.O.). National Academy Press, Washington DC.

Busby, J.R. (1991). BIOCLIM – a bioclimatic analysis and prediction system. In *Nature conservation: cost effective biological surveys and data analysis*: 64–68. (Eds Margules, C. R. & Austin, M. P.). Commonwealth Scientific and Industrial Research Organisation, Melbourne.

Butterfield, B. R., Csuti, B. & Scott, J. M. (1994). Modelling vertebrate distributions for GAP analysis. In *Mapping the diversity of nature*: 53–68. (Ed. Miller, R. I.). Chapman & Hall, London.

Camm, J. D., Polasky, S., Solow, A. & Csuti, B. (1996). A note on optimization models for reserve site selection. *Biol. Conserv.*, **78**, 353–55.

Carpenter, G., Gillison, A. N. & Winter, J. (1993). DOMAIN: a flexible modelling procedure for mapping potential distributions of plants and animals. *Biodiv. Conserv.*, 2, 667–80.

Castro Parga, I., Moreno Saiz, J. C., Humphries, C. J. & Williams, P. H. (1996). Strengthening the Natural and National Park system of Iberia to conserve vascular plants. *Bot. J. Linn. Soc.*, 121, 189–206.

Church, R. L., Stoms, D. M. & Davis, F. W. (1996). Reserve selection as a maximal covering location problem. *Biol. Conserv.*, 76, 105–12.

Cocks, K. D. & Baird, I. A. (1989). Using mathematical programming to address the multiple reserve selection problem: an example from the Eyre Peninsula, South Australia. *Biol. Conserv.*, 49, 113–30.

Colwell, R. K. & Coddington, J. A. (1994). Estimating terrestrial biodiversity through extrapolation. *Phil. Trans. R. Soc. Lond. B*, 345, 101–18.

Crowe, T. M. & Siegfried, W. R. (1993). Conserving Africa's biodiversity: stagnation versus innovation. *S. Afr. J. Sci.*, 89, 208–10.

Csuti, B., Polasky, S., Williams, P. H., Pressey, R. L., Camm, J. D., Kershaw, M., Kiester, A. R., Downs, B., Hamilton, R., Huso, M. & Sahr, K. (1997). A comparison of reserve selection algorithms using data on terrestrial vertebrates in Oregon. *Biol. Conserv.*, 80, 83–97.

Daniels, R. J. R., Hegde, M., Joshi, N. V. & Gadgil, M. (1991). Assigning conservation value: a case study from India. *Conserv. Biol.*, 5, 464–75.

Dobson, A. P., Rodriguez, J. P., Roberts, W. M. & Wilcove, D. S. (1997). Geographic distribution of endangered species in the United States. *Science*, 275, 550–3.

Doncaster, C. P., Micol, T. & Jensen, S. P. (1996). Determining minimum habitat requirements in theory and practice. *Oikos*, 75, 335–9.

Erwin, T. L. (1991). An evolutionary basis for conservation strategies. *Science*, 253, 750–2.

Faith, D. P. (1994). Phylogenetic pattern and the quantification of organismal biodiversity. *Phil. Trans. R. Soc. Lond. B*, 345, 45–58.

Faith, D. P. (1997). Biodiversity, biospecifics, and ecological services. *Trends Ecol. Evol.*, 12, 66.

Faith, D. P. & Walker, P. A. (1996a). How do indicator groups provide information about the relative biodiversity of different sets of areas?: on hotspots, complementarity and pattern-based approaches. *Biodiv. Letts.*, 3, 18–25.

Faith, D. P. & Walker, P. A. (1996b). Environmental diversity: on the best-possible use of surrogate data for assessing the relative biodiversity of sets of areas. *Biodiv. Conserv.*, 5, 399–415.

Freitag, S., Nicholls, A. O. & van Jaarsveld, A. S. (1996). Nature reserve selection in the Transvaal, South Africa: what data should we be using? *Biodiv. Conserv.*, 5, 685–98.

Gaston, K. J. (1996a). Spatial covariance in the species richness of higher taxa. In *Aspects of the genesis and maintenance of biological diversity*: 221–242. (Eds Hochberg, M. E., Clobert, J. & Barbault, R.). Oxford University Press, Oxford.

Gaston, K. J. (1996b). What is biodiversity? In *Biodiversity: a biology of numbers and difference*: 1–9. (Ed. Gaston, K. J.). Blackwell Science, Oxford.

Gaston, K. J. (1996c). Species richness: measure and measurement. In *Biodiversity: a biology of numbers and difference*: 77–113. (Ed. Gaston, K. J.). Blackwell Science, Oxford.

Gaston, K. J. & David, R. (1994). Hotspots across Europe. *Biodiv. Letts.*, **2**, 108–16.

Gaston, K. J. & Williams, P. H. (1993). Mapping the world's species – the higher taxon approach. *Biodiv. Letts.*, **1**, 2–8.

Gaston, K. J., Williams, P. H., Eggleton, P. & Humphries, C. J. (1995). Large scale patterns of biodiversity: spatial variation in family richness. *Proc. R. Soc. Lond. B*, **260**, 149–54.

Gibbons, D. W., Reid J. B., & Chapman, R. A. (1993). *The new atlas of breeding birds in Britain and Ireland: 1988–1991*. Poyser, London.

Groves, C. (1992). Beyond endangered species: Gap Analysis. *Idaho Wildl.*, **1992**, 26–7.

Hacker, J. E., Cowlishaw, G. & Williams, P. H. (1998). Patterns of African primate diversity and their evaluation for the selection of conservation areas. *Biol. Conserv.*, **84**, 251–62.

Howard, P. C. (1991). *Nature conservation in Uganda's tropical forest reserves*. World Conservation Union, Gland, Switzerland.

Humphries, C. J., Williams, P. H. & Vane-Wright, R. I. (1995). Measuring biodiversity value for conservation. *Annu. Rev. Ecol. Syst.*, **26**, 93–111.

Huntley, B., Berry, P. M., Cramer, W. & McDonald, A. P. (1995). Modelling present and potential future ranges of some European higher plants using climate response surfaces. *J. Biogeogr.*, **22**, 967–1001.

IBAMA, INPA & CI (1991). *Workshop 90 biological priorities for conservation in Amazonia* [map]. Conservation International, Washington DC.

ICBP (1992). *Putting biodiversity on the map: priority areas for global conservation*. International Council for Bird Preservation, Cambridge.

ISCBD (1994). *Convention on biological diversity. Text and annexes*. United Nations Environment Programme, Geneva.

Jefferson, R. G. (1984). Quarries and wildlife conservation in the Yorkshire Wolds, England. *Biol. Conserv.*, **29**, 363–80.

Kershaw, M., Mace, G. M. & Williams, P. H. (1995). Threatened status, rarity and diversity as alternative selection measures for protected areas: a test using Afrotropical antelopes. *Conserv. Biol.*, **9**, 324–34.

Kershaw, M., Williams, P. H. & Mace, G. M. (1994). Conservation of Afrotropical antelopes: consequences and efficiency of using different site selection methods and diversity criteria. *Biodiv. Conserv.*, **3**, 354–72.

Kiester, A. R., Scott, J. M., Csuti, B., Noss, R. F., Butterfield, B., Sahr, K. & White, D. (1996). Conservation prioritization using GAP data. *Conserv. Biol.*, **10**, 1332–42.

Kirkpatrick, J. B. (1983). An iterative method for establishing priorities for the selection of nature reserves: an example from Tasmania. *Biol. Conserv.*, **25**, 127–34.

Kirkpatrick, J. B. & Brown, M. J. (1991). Planning for species conservation. In *Nature conservation: cost effective biological surveys and data analysis*: 83–89. (Eds Margules, C. R. & Austin, M. P.). Commonwealth Scientific and Industrial Research Organisation, Melbourne.

Kirkpatrick, S., Gelatt, C. D. & Vecchi, M. P. (1983). Optimization by simulated annealing. *Science*, **220**, 671–80.

Kitching, I. J. (1996). Identifying complementary areas for conservation in Thailand: an example using owls, hawkmoths and tiger beetles. *Biodiv. Conserv.*, **5**, 841–58.

Kremen, C. (1992). Assessing the indicator properties of species assemblages for natural areas monitoring. *Ecol. Appl.*, **2**, 203–17.

Kremen, C., Colwell, R. K., Erwin, T. L., Murphy, D. D., Noss, R. F. & Sanjayan, M. A. (1993). Terrestrial arthropod assemblages: their use in conservation planning. *Conserv. Biol.*, **7**, 796–806.

Lack, P. (1986). *The atlas of wintering birds in Britain and Ireland*. Poyser, Calton.

Landres, P. B., Verner, J. & Thomas, J. W. (1988). Ecological uses of vertebrate indicator species: a critique. *Conserv. Biol.*, **2**, 316–28.

Lawton, J. H., Prendergast, J. R. & Eversham, B. C. (1994). The numbers and spatial distributions of species: analyses of British data. In *Systematics and conservation evaluation*: 177–195. (Eds Forey, P. L., Humphries, C. J. & Vane-Wright, R. I.). Oxford University Press, Oxford. (*Syst. Ass. spec. Vol.* **50**.)

Lee, M. S. Y. (1997). Documenting present and past biodiversity: conservation biology meets palaeontology. *Trends Ecol. Evol.*, **12**, 132–3.

Magurran, A. E. (1988). *Ecological diversity and its measurement*. Croom Helm, London.

Margules, C. R. (1981). *Assessment of wildlife conservation values*. D.Phil. thesis: University of York.

Margules, C. R. (1986). Conservation evaluation in practice. In *Wildlife conservation evaluation*: 297–314. (Ed. Usher, M. B.). Chapman & Hall, London.

Margules, C. R. (1989). Introduction to some Australian developments in conservation evaluation. *Biol. Conserv.*, **50**, 1–11.

Margules, C. R., Cresswell, I. D. & Nicholls, A. O. (1994). A scientific basis for establishing networks of protected areas. In *Systematics and conservation evaluation*: 327–350. (Eds Forey, P. L., Humphries, C. J. & Vane-Wright, R. I.). Oxford University Press, Oxford. (*Syst. Ass. spec. Vol.* **50**.)

Margules, C. R. & Nicholls, A. O. (1987). Assessing the conservation value of remnant habitat 'islands': Mallee patches on the western Eyre Peninsula, South Australia. In *Nature conservation: the role of remnants of native vegetation*: 89–102. (Eds Saunders, D. A., Arnold, G. W., Burbidge, A. A. & Hopkins, A. J. M.). Commonwealth Scientific and Industrial Research Organisation, Canberra.

Margules, C. R., Nicholls, A. O. & Pressey, R. L. (1988). Selecting networks of reserves to maximise biological diversity. *Biol. Conserv.*, **43**, 63–76.

Margules, C. R., Nicholls, A. O. & Usher, M. B. (1994). Apparent species turnover, probability of extinction and the selection of nature reserves: a case study of the Ingleborough limestone pavements. *Conserv. Biol.*, **8**, 398–409.

Margules, C. R., Pressey, R. L. & Nicholls, A. O. (1991). Selecting nature reserves. In *Nature conservation: cost effective biological surveys and data analysis*: 90–97. (Eds Margules, C. R. & Austin, M. P.). Commonwealth Scientific and Industrial Research Organisation, Melbourne.

Margules, C. R. & Redhead, T. D. (1995). *Guidelines for using the BioRap methodology and tools.* Commonwealth Scientific and Industrial Research Organisation, Dickson.

Margules, C. R. & Usher, M. B. (1981). Criteria used in assessing wildlife conservation potential: a review. *Biol. Conserv.*, **21**, 79–109.

Mickleburgh, S. P., Hutson, A. M. & Racey, P. A. (1992). *Old World fruit bats. An action plan for their conservation.* The World Conservation Union, Gland.

Mittermeier, R. A. (1988). Primate diversity and the tropical forest: case studies from Brazil and Madagascar and the importance of the megadiversity countries. In *Biodiversity*: 145–153. (Ed. Wilson, E. O.). National Academy Press, Washington D.C.

Mittermeier, R. A., Bowles, I. A., Cavalcanti, R. B., Olivieri, S. & da Fonseca, A. B. (1994). *A participatory approach to biodiversity conservation: the regional priority setting workshop.* Conservation International, Washington DC.

Moreno Saiz, J. C., Castro Parga, I., Humphries, C. J. & Williams, P. H. (1996). Strengthening the National and Natural Park system of Iberia to conserve pteridophytes. In *Pteridology in perspective*: 101–123. (Eds Camus, J. M., Gibby, M. & Johns, R. J.). Royal Botanic Gardens, Kew.

Myers, N. (1979). *The sinking Ark. A new look at the problem of disappearing species.* Pergamon, Oxford.

Myers, N. (1988). Threatened biotas: "hot spots" in tropical forests. *Environmentalist*, **8**, 187–208.

Myers, N. (1990). The biodiversity challenge: expanded hot-spots analysis. *Environmentalist*, **10**, 243–56.

NCC (1989). *Guidelines for selection of biological SSSIs.* Nature Conservancy Council, Peterborough.

Nicholls, A. O. (1989). How to make biological surveys go further with generalised linear models. *Biol. Conserv.*, **50**, 51–75.

Norton, B. G. (1994). On what we should save: the role of culture in determining conservation targets. In *Systematics and conservation evaluation*: 23–39. (Eds Forey, P. L., Humphries, C. J. & Vane-Wright, R. I.). Oxford University Press, Oxford. (*Syst. Ass. Spec. Vol.* **50**.)

Noss, R. F. (1990). Indicators for measuring biodiversity: a hierarchical approach. *Conserv. Biol.*, **4**, 355–64.

Otte, D. & Endler, J. A. (Eds) (1989). *Speciation and its consequences.* Sinauer Associates, Sunderland.

Palmer, M. W. (1990). The estimation of species richness by extrapolation. *Ecology*, **71**, 1195–8.

Pearsall, S. H., Durham, D. & Eagar, D. C. (1986). Evaluation methods in the United States. In *Wildlife conservation evaluation*: 111–133. (Ed. Usher, M. B.). Chapman & Hall, London.

Possingham, H., Day, J., Goldfinch, M. & Salzborn, F. (1993). The mathematics of designing a network of protected areas for conservation. In *Proceedings of the 12th Australian operations research conference*: 536–545. (Eds Sutton, D., Cousins, E. & Pearce, C.). Adelaide University, Adelaide.

Prance, G. T. (1990). Consensus for conservation. *Nature, Lond.*, **345**, 384.

Prance, G. T. (1994). The use of phytogeographic data for conservation planning.

In *Systematics and conservation evaluation*: 145–163. (Eds Forey, P. L., Humphries, C. J. & Vane-Wright, R. I.). Oxford University Press, Oxford. (*Syst. Ass. spec. Vol.* 50.)

Prendergast, J. R., Quinn, R. M., Lawton, J. H., Eversham, B. C. & Gibbons, D. W. (1993). Rare species, the incidence of diversity hotspots and conservation strategies. *Nature, Lond.*, 365, 335–7.

Prendergast, J. R., Wood, S. N., Lawton, J. H. & Eversham, B. C. (1993). Correcting for variation in recording effort in analyses of diversity hotspots. *Biodiv. Letts.*, 1, 39–53.

Pressey, R. L. (1994). *Ad hoc* reservations: forward or backward steps in developing representative reserve systems? *Conserv. Biol.*, 8, 662–8.

Pressey, R. L. (1997). Priority conservation areas: towards an operational definition for regional assessments. In *National parks and protected areas: selection, delimitation and management*: 337–357 (Eds Pigram, J. J. & Sundell, R. C.). University of New England, Centre for Water Policy Research, Armidale.

Pressey, R. L., Bedward, M. & Keith, D. A. (1994). New procedures for reserve selection in New South Wales: maximizing the chances of achieving a representative network. In *Systematics and conservation evaluation*: 351–373. (Eds Forey, P. L., Humphries, C. J. & Vane-Wright, R. I.). Oxford University Press, Oxford. (*Syst. Ass. Spec. Vol.* 50.)

Pressey, R. L., Humphries, C. J., Margules, C. R., Vane-Wright, R. I. & Williams, P. H. (1993). Beyond opportunism: key principles for systematic reserve selection. *Trends Ecol. Evol.*, 8, 124–8.

Pressey, R. L., Johnson, I. R. & Wilson, P. D. (1994). Shades of irreplaceability: towards a measure of the contribution of sites to a reservation goal. *Biodiv. Conserv.*, 3, 242–62.

Pressey, R. L. & Nicholls, A. O. (1989a). Efficiency in conservation evaluation: scoring versus iterative approaches. *Biol. Conserv.*, 50, 199–218.

Pressey, R. L. & Nicholls, A. O. (1989b). Application of a numerical algorithm to the selection of reserves in semi-arid New South Wales. *Biol. Conserv.*, 50, 263–78.

Pressey, R. L. & Nicholls, A. O. (1991). Reserve selection in the Western Division of New South Wales: development of a new procedure based on land system mapping. In *Nature conservation: cost effective biological surveys and data analysis*: 98–105. (Eds Margules, C. R. & Austin, M. P.). Commonwealth Scientific and Industrial Research Organisation, Melbourne.

Pressey, R. L., Possingham, H. P., Logan, V. S., Day, J. R. & Williams, P. H. (in press). Effects of data characteristics on the results of reserve selection algorithms. *J. Biogeog.*

Pressey, R. L., Possingham, H. P. & Margules, C. R. (1996). Optimality in reserve selection algorithms: when does it matter and how much? *Biol. Conserv.*, 76, 259–67.

Pressey, R. L. & Tully, S. L. (1994). The cost of *ad hoc* reservation: a case study in western New South Wales. *Aust. J. Ecol.*, 19, 375–84.

Pritchard, D. E., Housden, S. D., Mudge, G. P., Galbraith, C. A. & Pienkowski, M. W. (1992). *Important bird areas in the United Kingdom including the Channel Islands and the Isle of Man.* Royal Society for the Protection of Birds, Sandy.

Ratcliffe, D. A. (Ed.) (1977). *A nature conservation review* 1, 2. Cambridge University Press, Cambridge.

Ratcliffe, D. A. (1986). Selection of important areas for wildlife conservation in Great Britain: the Nature Conservancy Council's approach. In *Wildlife conservation evaluation*: 135–159. (Ed. Usher, M. B.). Chapman & Hall, London.

Rebelo, A. G. (1994). Using the Proteaceae to design a nature reserve network and determine conservation priorities for the Cape Floristic Region. In *Systematics and conservation evaluation*: 375–396. (Eds Forey, P. L., Humphries, C. J. & Vane-Wright, R. I.). Oxford University Press, Oxford. (*Syst. Ass. Spec. Vol.* 50.)

Rebelo, A. G. & Siegfried, W. R. (1990). Protection of fynbos vegetation: ideal and real-world options. *Biol. Conserv.*, 54, 15–31.

Rebelo, A. G. & Siegfried, W. R. (1992). Where should nature reserves be located in the Cape Floristic Region, South Africa? Models for the spatial configuration of a reserve network aimed at maximizing the protection of floral diversity. *Conserv. Biol.*, 6, 243–52.

Reid, W. V. (1994). Setting objectives for conservation evaluation. In *Systematics and conservation evaluation*: 1–13. (Eds Forey, P. L., Humphries, C. J. & Vane-Wright, R. I.). Oxford University Press, Oxford. (*Syst. Ass. Spec. Vol.* 50.)

Reid, W. V., McNeely, J. A., Tunstall, D. B., Bryant, D. A. & Winograd, M. (1993). *Biodiversity indicators for policy-makers.* World Resources Institute and The World Conservation Union, Washington DC.

Ryti, R. (1992). Effect of the focal taxon on the selection of nature reserves. *Ecol. Appl.*, 2, 404–10.

Sætersdal, M. & Birks, H. J. B. (1993). Assessing the representativeness of nature reserves using multivariate analysis: vascular plants and breeding birds in deciduous forests, western Norway. *Biol. Conserv.*, 65, 121–32.

Sætersdal, M., Line, J. M. & Birks, H. J. B. (1993). How to maximize biological diversity in nature reserve selection: vascular plants and breeding birds in deciduous woodlands, western Norway. *Biol. Conserv.*, 66, 131–8.

Schmidt, K. (1996). Rare habitats vie for protection. *Science*, 274, 916–18.

Scott, J. M., Csuti, B., Jacobi, J. D. & Estes, J. E. (1987). Species richness. A geographic approach to protecting future biological diversity. *BioScience*, 37, 782–8.

Scott, J. M., Davis, F., Csuti, B., Noss, R., Butterfield, B., Groves, C., Anderson, H., Caicco, S., D'Erchia, F., Edwards Jr, T. C., Ulliman, J. & Wright, R. G. (1993). Gap Analysis: a geographic approach to protection of biological diversity. *Wildl. Monogr.* No. 123, 1–41.

Sisk, T. D., Launer, A. E., Switky, K. R. & Ehrlich, P. R. (1994). Identifying extinction threats: global analyses of the distribution of biodiversity and the expansion of the human enterprise. *BioScience*, 44, 592–604.

Swofford, D. L. (1990). *PAUP: Phylogenetic analysis using parsimony version 3.0.* Illinois Natural History Survey, Champaign.

Terborgh, J. & Winter, B. (1983). A method for siting parks and reserves with special reference to Colombia and Ecuador. *Biol. Conserv.*, 27, 45–58.

Thirgood, S. J. & Heath, M. F. (1994). Global patterns of endemism and the conservation of biodiversity. In *Systematics and conservation evaluation*: 207–227. (Eds Forey, P. L., Humphries, C. J. & Vane-Wright, R. I.). Oxford

University Press, Oxford. (*Syst. Ass. Spec. Vol.* **50.**)

Thomas, C. D. & Mallorie, H. C. (1985). Rarity, species richness and conservation: butterflies of the Atlas Mountains in Morocco. *Biol. Conserv.*, **33**, 95–117.

Turpie, J.K. (1995). Prioritizing South African estuaries for conservation: a practical example using waterbirds. *Biol. Conserv.*, **74**, 175–85.

Underhill, L. G. (1994). Optimal and suboptimal reserve selection algorithms. *Biol. Conserv.*, **70**, 85–7.

Usher, M. B. (1986). Wildlife conservation evaluation: attributes, criteria and values. In *Wildlife conservation evaluation*: 3–44. (Ed. Usher, M. B.). Chapman & Hall, London.

van der Ploeg, S. W. F. (1986). Wildlife conservation evaluation in the Netherlands: a controversial issue in a small country. In *Wildlife conservation evaluation*: 161–180. (Ed. Usher, M. B.). Chapman & Hall, London.

Vane-Wright, R. I. (1994). Systematics and the conservation of biodiversity: global, national and local perspectives. In *Perspectives on insect conservation*: 197–211. (Eds Gaston, K. J., New, T. R. & Samways, M. J.). Intercept, Andover.

Vane-Wright, R. I. (1996). Identifying priorities for the conservation of biodiversity: systematic biological criteria within a socio-political framework. In *Biodiversity: a biology of numbers and difference*: 309–338. (Ed. Gaston, K. J.). Blackwell Science, Oxford.

Vane-Wright, R. I., Humphries, C. J. & Williams, P. H. (1991). What to protect? – Systematics and the agony of choice. *Biol. Conserv.*, **55**, 235–54.

Vane-Wright, R. I. & Peggie, D. (1994). The butterflies of northern and central Maluku: diversity, endemism, biogeography, and conservation priorities. *Trop. Biodiv.*, **2**, 212–30.

Vane-Wright, R. I., Smith, C. R. & Kitching, I. J. (1994). Systematic assessment of taxic diversity by summation. In *Systematics and conservation evaluation*: 309–326. (Eds Forey, P. L., Humphries, C. J. & Vane-Wright, R. I.). Oxford University Press, Oxford. (*Syst. Ass. spec. Vol.* **50.**)

Williams, P. H. (1993*a*). Salvaging more from the sinking Ark. *A. Rep. Sci. nat. Hist. Mus.*, Lond. **1992**, 30–1.

Williams, P. H. (1993*b*). Measuring more of biodiversity for choosing conservation areas, using taxonomic relatedness. In *International symposium on biodiversity and conservation*: 194–227. (Ed. Moon, T.-Y.). Korean Entomological Institute, Seoul.

Williams, P. H. (1994). *WORLDMAP priority areas for biodiversity. Using version 3.18*. Privately distributed, London, UK.

Williams, P. H. (1996*a*). *WORLDMAP 4 WINDOWS: Software and help document 4.1*. Privately distributed, London, UK.

Williams, P. H. (1996*b*). Measuring biodiversity value. *Wld Conserv.*, **1**, 12–14.

Williams, P. H. & Gaston, K. J. (1994). Measuring more of biodiversity: can higher-taxon richness predict wholesale species richness? *Biol. Conserv.*, **67**, 211–17.

Williams, P. H., Gaston, K. J. & Humphries, C. J. (1994). Do conservationists and molecular biologists value differences between organisms in the same way? *Biodiv. Letts.*, **2**, 67–78.

Williams, P. H., Gaston, K. J. & Humphries, C. J. (1997). Mapping biodiversity value world-wide: combining higher-taxon richness from different groups. *Proc. R. Soc. Lond.* B, **264**, 141–8.

Williams, P., Gaston, K., Humphries, C. & Vane-Wright, D. (1997). Biodiversity, biospecifics, and ecological services. *Trends Ecol. Evol.*, **12**, 66–7.

Williams, P., Gibbons, D., Margules, C., Rebelo, A., Humphries, C. & Pressey, R. (1996). A comparison of richness hotspots, rarity hotspots and complementary areas for conserving diversity using British birds. *Conserv. Biol.*, **10**, 155–74.

Williams, P. H. & Humphries, C. J. (1996). Comparing character diversity among biotas. In *Biodiversity: a biology of numbers and difference*: 54–76. (Ed. Gaston, K. J.). Blackwell Science, Oxford.

Williams, P. H., Prance, G. T., Humphries, C. J. & Edwards, K. S. (1996). Promise and problems in applying quantitative complementary areas for representing the diversity of some Neotropical plants (families Dichapetalaceae, Lecythidaceae, Caryocaraceae, Chrysobalanaceae and Proteaceae). *Biol. J. Linn. Soc.*, **58**, 125–7.

Winston, M. R. & Angermeier, P. L. (1995). Assessing conservation value using centres of population density. *Conserv. Biol.*, **9**, 1518–27.

Witting, L. & Loeschcke, V. (1993). Biodiversity conservation: reserve optimisation or loss minimisation? *Trends Ecol. Evol.*, **8**, 417.

Woinarski, J. C. Z., Price, O. & Faith, D. P. (1996). Application of a taxon priority system for conservation planning by selecting areas which are most distinct from environments already reserved. *Biol. Conserv.*, **76**, 147–59.

WWF & IUCN (1994). *Centres of plant diversity. Volume 1, Europe, Africa, South West Asia and The Middle East.* The World Conservation Union, Cambridge.

# 11

# Integrating population abundance, dynamics and distribution into broad-scale priority setting

A. O. NICHOLLS

## INTRODUCTION

Area-based selection (or priority-setting) methods are achieving recognition in the biological conservation literature (van Jaarsveld, 1995; Caughley & Gunn, 1996; Hunter, 1996), with research applications recorded for a number of continents or countries: Africa, (Kershaw, Williams & Mace, 1994), South Africa (Lombard 1995 and papers cited therein; Freitag, Nicholls & van Jaarsveld, 1996); America (Csuti et al., 1997; Kiester et al., 1996), Australia (Margules, Nicholls & Pressey, 1988; Pressey & Nicholls, 1989; Pressey, Bedward & Nicholls, 1990; Bedward, Pressey & Keith, 1992), Norway (Saetersdal, Line & Birks, 1993) and Thailand (Kitching, 1996). Two points emerge from this recognition. The first is that the methods are not without their critics. The criticisms range from inadequate, spotty distribution of selected sites (Bedward et al., 1992), to inefficient selection methods (Underhill, 1994), selection of populations at the margins of species' distributions (Branch et al., 1995) and doubts about the adequacy of the taxa used to act as surrogates for other taxa (Ryti, 1992). The second point, a major potential criticism, is that the methods fail to take account of biological processes (see Balmford, Mace & Ginsberg, this volume). In particular, viability of 'protected' populations is not addressed, and issues of landscape fragmentation, connectivity and the spatial distribution of species are not addressed. However, Nicholls and Margules (1993) addressed the consequences of modifying the selection method to find a solution that favours adjacent sites. The implications of temporal variability have also tended to be ignored, although Margules, Nicholls and Usher (1994) illustrate some potential consequences of such an omission.

Ecological and evolutionary processes are increasingly being subjected to mathematical and simulation modelling with predictions about the relationship between the processes and the real world becoming more common. The predictions being generated from such theoretical models vary greatly from very general qualitative statements through to explicit quantitative statements. One of the future challenges for area-based selection methods is to link these theoretical predictions with the area-based methods.

Given the range of ecological processes – an ecological process being one that acts on or is caused or influenced by an individual organism – that could legitimately be considered, it is impossible to illustrate in this chapter how all could be included in area-based selection methods. Evolutionary processes are those processes that maintain variety and cause selection. Both ecological processes and evolutionary processes need space and time to operate. Hence, if area-based selection methods can be devised to reflect spatial and temporal dynamics, it might be argued that ecological and evolutionary processes will be at least partially accommodated in solutions generated by such methods.

This contribution looks at some recent developments in the area-based selection methods that utilize quantitative data rather than presence/absence data. It then explores how abundance data displaying spatial and temporal dynamics or presence/absence data can be subjected to modified area-based selection methods so as to reflect the temporal or spatial dimensions explicitly. These are, in effect, additional constraints on the current area-based methods. The consequences of adding these features to the set of rules that drive the selection process are investigated. I conclude by returning from this exploration of how space and time might be incorporated into the selection methods to consider the fundamental prerequisites for area-based methods.

## ABUNDANCE AND DYNAMICS OF POPULATIONS

The majority of the reserve selection algorithms to date have worked with presence/absence data (Pressey & Tully, 1994). Clearly, this has limited appeal for managers when confronted with questions of minimum viable population size or probability of extinction of the attributes or features being managed. A partial solution to this is to move from presence/absence data to quantitative data and develop algorithms that will provide solutions to questions such as 'Which set of sites when taken together will represent some minimum proportion of each attribute?' or alternatively 'Which set of sites when taken together will represent all species by at least some minimum population size?'.

What might such data look like? Two examples can be cited to illustrate possible answers to this question and how such data might be used to answer the previous two questions. The first is the landscape units, or land systems (Christian & Stewart, 1953, 1968; Walker, 1991) used by Pressey and Tully (1994) in their comparison of the efficiency of different selection algorithms in western New South Wales. The second example is from the Kruger National Park and is based on annual censuses of 19 species, predominantly ungulates.

## Landscape units

Land systems are recurring patterns of landform, soil and vegetation defined subjectively from aerial photographs (Christian & Stewart, 1953, 1968; Mabbutt, 1968). The Western Division of New South Wales, an area of some 325 000 km², representing about one-third of the State, has been mapped into land systems (Walker, 1991). Pressey and Tully (1994) computed the area of each land system on each selection unit (for more details of the selection units see Pressey & Tully, 1994 but, in brief, selection units were areas of land roughly rectangular in shape and approximately equal in area to the local pastoral holdings). Each selection unit contains only a small number of land systems. To represent each land system a given number of times within a priority conservation network one could use one of the existing algorithms reviewed by Pressey, Humphries *et al.* (1993). Alternatively, to achieve some proportional representation the algorithm described by Pressey and Tully (1994) is appropriate. The objective of that algorithm is to represent each attribute, i.e. each land system, not by a minimum number of times but by some minimum proportion of the total area occupied by each land system. The basis for such an objective is to provide a greater realism to the representation of the attributes. What constitutes an appropriate proportion of each attribute is currently at the discretion of the user or land manager and current ecological theory does little to resolve what is adequate. Pressey and Tully illustrate the use of a minimum constant proportion to represent each attribute, but where it seemed appropriate a different minimum proportion for each landscape unit could be used. For example, landscape units that are rare could be represented by larger proportions than the more common landscape units.

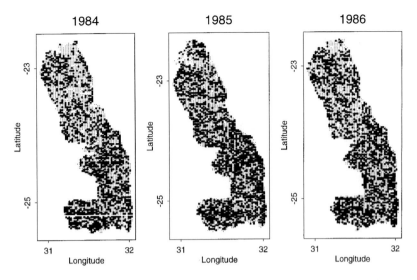

Fig. 11.1 The spatial distribution of *Tragelaphus strepsiceros* (kudu) across Kruger National Park in three years, 1984, 1985 and 1986, plotted (■) over the distribution of grid cells on which at least one of the 19 species were recorded (·).

## Population abundances

As part of the management of Kruger National Park, a number of species (predominantly mammalian herbivores) have been censused each year since 1977 (Joubert, 1983; Viljoen, 1989; Viljoen & Retief, 1994). A selection of those data (for years 1984, 1985 and 1986) were used to investigate how priority setting for conservation evaluation might be structured. The primary data for the priority-setting exercises are lists of attributes present on the selection units (Margules & Austin, 1994). For this illustration the selection units were grid cells and the attributes to be represented were species of large herbivores. Approximately 3500 one-fiftieth of a degree (approximately 5 km²) grid cells were assessed for the abundance of 19 species of large herbivores (see Fig. 11.1 for an example). The abundance and distribution of each species varies across the three years. For example, for a common species like *Tragelaphus strepsiceros* (kudu) the observed abundances varied from 8500 to over 11 000 and occupied from 1500 to around 1800 grid cells; in contrast, for *Hippotragus equinus* (roan antelope) the abundances varied from 340 to 450 occupying 75 to 100 grid cells. What this simple description of the dynamics does not reflect is the extent to which a grid cell in one year is occupied (or not occupied, as the case may be) by the same suite of species in subsequent years.

Two approaches to selecting a set of grid cells that represent the 19 species were used. The first used the Nicholls & Margules (1993) algorithm and utilized the presence of each species a given number of times as a basis for defining adequacy (Margules, Nicholls & Pressey, 1988). Even though the actual grid cells selected differ between years, this approach demonstrates that at a broad scale important areas within Kruger National Park, South Africa, do emerge particularly as the number of representations of each species increases (Fig. 11.2).

The second approach utilizes an independently developed algorithm that in terms of the first few rules is similar to that described by Pressey and Tully (1994). Additional rules were used to select individual sites from a set of sites that were otherwise of equal value (this avoided the use of a random selection rule: Pressey & Tully 1994). The object of the algorithm remains to select a small number of sites that, taken together, represent all attributes in terms of some user-defined minimum number of individuals or 'population size'. The impact of five different levels of minimum number of individuals, 25, 50, 100, 250 and 500, were investigated in terms of the number of grid cells selected. The spatial distribution of the selected grid cells for the five levels of representation for the one year are shown in Fig. 11.3. The number of sites necessary to achieve representation of each species a given number of times (10 to 50 separate occurrences) or by some minimum total population size (25, 50, 100, 250 and 500 individuals) for the years 1984, 1985 and 1986 is summarized in Table 11.1. As the number of representations per species necessary to achieve adequate representation increases from one to five, the number of grid cells increases from less than 0.5% of the grid cells to around 1% (Table 11.1). There is little difference in the number of grid cells selected across the three years. As expected, the number of grid cells necessary for representation increases as one increases the criterion for adequacy up to 50 grid cells per species, at which point around 10% of the grid cells are selected (Table 11.1). The comparable figures are from 1% to around 20% of the grid cells when representation is based on number of individuals and the criterion increases from 25 to 500 individuals. The percentage of the individual grid cells selected in each of the three solutions varies from zero to just over 4%, and the percentage of grid cells selected in any two solutions varies from 6% to 22% as the adequacy criterion changes from a minimum of 25 individuals to 500 individuals per species. This highlights, at the grid cell level, the subtle effects of

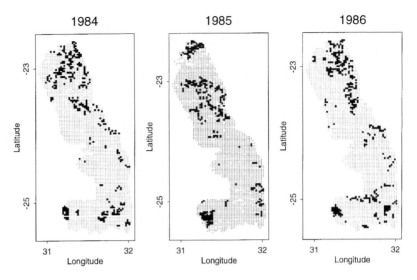

Fig. 11.2 The distribution of the selected grid cells (■) for the three years 1984, 1985 and 1986 based on the criterion of a minimum of 50 grid cells per species.

the spatial and temporal dynamics of the animal populations on the selection results.

### Temporal dynamics

Animal species comprise mobile organisms. Conservation measures must take this into account if conservation objectives are to be met into the future. The impact of temporal variability of species' distributions on reserve design has been documented for one example. Margules, Nicholls and Usher (1994) investigated the potential success that a reserve network based on presence/absence data might have achieved in the light of a subsequent survey of the sites some 11 years latter. They found that 36% of the species represented on the priority set in 1974 were not present on the same set of sites in 1985. To have maintained adequate representation of all species over the period 1974 to 1985 would have required a larger number of sites to have been selected in 1974.

For our example at Kruger National Park, how well does the 1984 priority set represent the 19 species in 1985 and 1986? If the 1984 criterion for

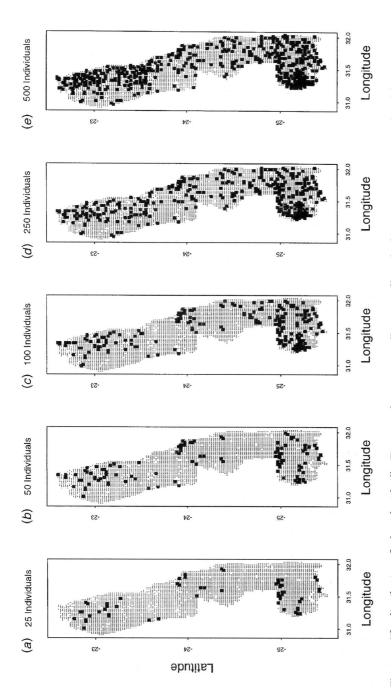

Fig. 11.3 The distribution of selected grid cells (■) required to represent all species of large herbivores in Kruger National Park by a minimum population size of 25 (a), 50 (b), 100 (c), 250 (d) and 500 (e) individuals per species, based on the census data from 1986.

**Table 11.1**

*Number of grid cells selected in three years to achieve different levels of representation of each of the selected 19 species of mammals in Kruger National Park, South Africa.*

(a) *The number of occurrences (based on presence/absence data)*

| Representation | 1984 | 1985 | 1986 |
|---|---|---|---|
| 1 cell/species | 5 | 5 | 4 |
| 2 cells/species | 12 | 14 | 11 |
| 3 cells/species | 18 | 16 | 20 |
| 4 cells/species | 26 | 24 | 28 |
| 5 cells/species | 32 | 31 | 37 |
| 10 cells/species | 70 | 66 | 76 |
| 20 cells/species | 140 | 132 | 171 |
| 30 cells/species | 220 | 201 | 236 |
| 40 cells/species | 285 | 272 | 293 |
| 50 cells/species | 341 | 346 | 353 |

(b) *A minimum population size (based on abundance data)*

| Representation | 1984 | 1985 | 1986 |
|---|---|---|---|
| 25 individuals/species | 38 | 44 | 59 |
| 50 individuals/species | 86 | 94 | 117 |
| 100 individuals/species | 195 | 204 | 230 |
| 250 individuals/species | 379 | 454 | 387 |
| 500 individuals/species | 602 | 667 | 564 |

adequate representation is retained in subsequent years, then the 1984 selected grid cells have about half of the species adequately represented in 1985 and again in 1986 (Table 11.2). This proportion rises marginally as the criterion for adequate representation is raised to 500 individuals. However, note that not all species could be represented at that level (i.e. for some species the total number of individuals observed is less than 500). If one takes the 1984 selected grid cells and then adds the grid cells necessary to achieve adequate representation in 1985 and then looks at the representation of the species in 1986 one finds a marginal improvement in the number of species adequately represented (Table 11.2).

The number of grid cells necessary to represent adequately all species in 1985 and 1986 starting from the 1984 selected grid cells approaches double the number selected in 1984 (Table 11.3). Table 11.3 also gives information on the number of grid cells selected in 1984 that were observed to contain individuals in the 1985 and 1986 censuses.

**Table 11.2**

*(a) Number of species of large herbivores in Kruger National Park considered to be adequately represented in 1984 (based on selection de novo) and the number adequately represented in 1985 and 1986 starting from the cells selected in 1984. The possible numbers of species that could be adequately represented in 1985 and 1986 are given for comparison*

| Representation | 1984 | 1985 | | 1986 | |
|---|---|---|---|---|---|
| 25 individuals/species | 18 | 8 | 18 | 8 | 19 |
| 50 individuals/species | 18 | 9 | 18 | 9 | 18 |
| 100 individuals/species | 14 | 9 | 18 | 9 | 17 |
| 250 individuals/species | 13 | 9 | 15 | 8 | 14 |
| 500 individuals/species | 12 | 9 | 12 | 8 | 12 |

*(b) Similar information for 1986 but starting from the combined set of cells selected from the 1984 data and added to using the 1985 data*

| Representation | 1986 | |
|---|---|---|
| 25 individuals/species | 12 | 19 |
| 50 individuals/species | 9 | 18 |
| 100 individuals/species | 10 | 17 |
| 250 individuals/species | 11 | 14 |
| 500 individuals/species | 10 | 12 |

## SPATIAL HETEROGENEITY WITHIN A SPECIES' RANGE

To date the explicit area-based selection methods have tended to ignore spatial considerations, although Faith and Walker (1993) utilized an ordination space to optimize representation, and Nicholls and Margules (1993) considered the implications of adding a rule to select preferentially adjacent or nearby sites.

In the absence of detailed knowledge of the spatial distribution of the biological attributes, Faith and Walker (1993) argued for setting priorities for areas based on the site distribution in an ordination space defined by either the biological attributes themselves (i.e. a species ordination), or surrogates of those biological attributes. Implicit in this approach is the assumption that the ecological continuum model (Austin, 1985) is appropriate to describe the distribution of species in the environmental space and that a selection of sites made from that space can maximize the representation of species if the distance from any point in the space to the selected sites is small (Faith & Walker, 1993; Faith, Walker *et al.*, 1996).

**Table 11.3**

*Number of grid cells selected in 1984, the number of grid cells observed to contain individuals in 1985 and 1986 (in parentheses) and the number of grid cells necessary to represent all species of large herbivores in Kruger National Park at the required level in 1985 and 1986 starting from the grid cells selected in 1984*

| Representation | 1984 | 1985 | | 1986 | |
|---|---|---|---|---|---|
| 25 individuals/species | 38 | (37) | 75 | (38) | 87 |
| 50 individuals/species | 86 | (82) | 158 | (84) | 182 |
| 100 individuals/species | 195 | (184) | 355 | (189) | 374 |
| 250 individuals/species | 379 | (363) | 719 | (360) | 655 |
| 500 individuals/species | 602 | (574) | 1045 | (561) | 932 |

The expected contribution of any additional area is proportional to the extent to which the addition reduces these distances. One of the potential applications of this technique, if a geographical ordination were applied, would be to select or nominate sites that would be spread across the region.

The abundance of a species is not uniform across its range (Brown, 1995; Lawton, 1996; Wiens, 1989). The reasons for this lack of uniformity are manifold and reflect the multiple factors influencing species' distribution and abundance. This, combined with the theoretical expectation that extinction risk may not be uniform across a species' range (Lomolino & Channell, 1995), leads one to ask 'should area-based priority setting methods take the spatial distribution of the biological attributes into account?' While the answer to this question is undoubtedly *yes*, the manner in which such information is incorporated is less clear. In particular, three approaches could be envisaged: a selection method that spreads the selected sites as uniformly as possible across the region of interest, a method that spreads the selected sites across the range of the individual species, or one that concentrates the selected sites in specific zones of the individual species' distributions, for example, within the centre or core of each species' range. For example, based on an analysis of the distribution of sites selected to represent tortoises and terrapins in southern Africa, Branch *et al.* (1995) have pointed out that the selected sites tend to be distributed towards the edge of individual species' distributions. They argue that the reserve-selection methods should nominate sites that are from, or towards, the centre of a species' distribution. Alternative viewpoints can be advanced, for example, see Lomolino and Channell (1995) for a discussion of the patterns of collapse of distributional ranges of endangered mammals.

The presence/absence distributions of 122 snake species in South Afri-

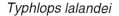

*Typhlops lalandei*                    *Typhlops schlegelii*

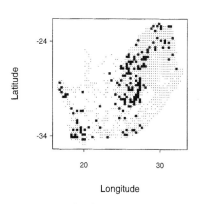
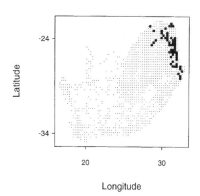

Fig. 11.4 The distribution of two South African snakes, *Typhlops lalandei* (Delalande's blind snake) and *T. schlegelii* (Schlegel's blind snake) (■) plotted over the distribution of grid cells in which any snake species was recorded (·) to illustrate two of the very divergent distribution patterns.

ca (Lombard, Nicholls & August, 1995) will be used here to illustrate the problem and possible solutions. Lombard *et al.* (1995) compiled a spatial database based on museum records and published maps. The selection units were one-quarter of a degree grid cells, approximately 625 km² (further details can be found in Lombard *et al.*, 1995). Examples of the variation in spatial distribution of two species of blind snakes are shown in Fig. 11.4. Figure 5 illustrates two of the Lombard *et al.*, (1995) solutions to the selection of grid cells to represent all species at least twice with and without an adjacency constraint (Nicholls & Margules, 1993). It is clear that the selected grid cells are distributed across the region (Fig. 11.5) but note that applying an adjacency constraint tends to reduce the geographic coverage for a given level of representation (compare Fig. 11.5(*b*) with 5(*a*)).

The question, 'How are the selected grid cells distributed with respect to the individual species' distributions within the region?' remains unanswered. Two ways of investigating that question are now explored. Dividing each species' range into four-quarters and tallying how many quarters are sampled for each species (by the selected grid cells) reveals that, although the majority of species are present in grid cells spread across three- or four-quarters at five representations per species, approximately one-quarter of the species are represented in the nominated network on only one- or two-quarters of their individual distributions within the region under study (Fig. 11.6(*a*)). Note that applying an adjacency constraint (Nicholls & Mar-

(a)

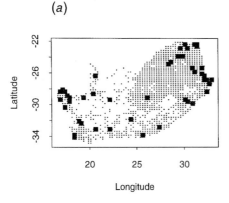

(b)

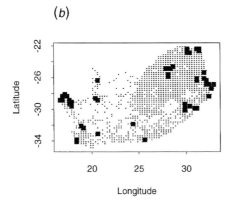

Fig. 11.5 The spatial distribution of selected grid cells for two solutions to represent all species of snakes in South Africa at least twice (■) plotted over the distribution of selection units for which there was recorded information (·). The first solution (a) is for the unconstrained algorithm and the second (b) is for the adjacency-constrained algorithm.

gules, 1993) reduces the proportion of species with representations spread across three- or four-quarters, albeit by a small amount (Fig. 11.6(b) compared with 6(a)).

The distribution of selected grid cells with respect to the core versus the periphery of the individual species' distribution was investigated by using the above adjacency-constrained algorithm (Nicholls & Margules, 1993). This was done by dividing the distribution of each species (within the area under study, not the full range for species that extend outside the study area) into nine sections arranged in three rows of three columns. The number of selected grid cells occupied by each species within the central section was expressed as a proportion of the total number of selected grid cells occupied by the species. The results demonstrate the high proportion of species for which the proportion of core grid cells was less than 10% (Fig. 11.7). Although the actual number of species in this category varied, the overall results for five, 10 and 15 grid cells per species and for unconstrained and adjacency-constrained solutions were very similar.

The algorithm was modified to select preferentially grid cells from the core of the species' distribution wherever possible. The criterion against which adequacy was judged was changed from a simple number of grid cells per species to number of core grid cells per species where possible, or all core grid cells plus as many peripheral grid cells as were required to meet a minimum number of grid cells per species. The change in the proportion of species with greater proportions of selected grid cells from the core of the species' distribution is apparent in Fig. 11.8. Approximately 20% fewer species have 10% or fewer of their selected grid cells in their core area compared to the unconstrained solution. However, the consequence of this core constraint on the number of grid cells selected is substantial (Fig. 11.9). There are increases of 1.5 to 1.8 times as many grid cells required, depending upon the number of grid cells considered necessary for adequate representation. The additional impact of applying an adjacency constraint is marginal in terms of the number of grid cells selected.

## DISCUSSION

There are three important issues that arise from these results: the relationship of the selection algorithms to ecological theory, the frequent lack of an explicit prediction from ecological theory and the cost, in terms of additional selection units, of adding the further constraints into the algorithms. A fourth issue then arises in the context of the questions 'Where to next?' and 'What is necessary for improved applications of area-based selection methods?'

To date the most important gap in current selection or priority-setting methods has been the lack of interface with ecological theory at either the population, community or landscape level. Selection algorithms have tended to concentrate on pragmatic features like the number of representations or the proportion of the abundance (however measured) required for representation (Margules, Nicholls & Pressey, 1988; Pressey & Tully,

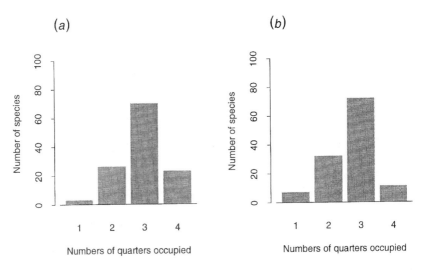

(a)    (b)

Fig. 11.6 The frequency of species of South African snakes present on one
to four quarters of their distribution for unconstrained (*a*) or adjacency
constrained (*b*) solutions based on five occurrences of each species of snake
in South Africa.

1994). The use of abundance data, for example population sizes of herbivores in Kruger National Park, not only provides another avenue to define
what might be considered as an adequate representation but, by combining
the results from analyses of long-term census data, also allows less arbitrary
criteria to be developed. Estimates of the probability of population extinction can be made by using stochastic diffusion models (Dennis, Munholland & Scott, 1991; Foley, 1994) or from more complex but process
orientated simulation models (Akcakaya & Ferson, 1992; Lacy, 1993; Possingham & Davies, 1995). Nicholls *et al.* (1996), using annual census data
from the period 1983 to 1992 for 12 herbivores, estimated the probability of
the populations declining one, two or three orders of magnitude in abundance. Of the 12 species investigated, the authors concluded that five appeared to be secure, four were vulnerable and three were at risk of declining
an order of magnitude within 100 years. All 12 species are included in the
database used here for priority setting. Also, in 1992 three of the species
had population sizes (from 68 to 571 individuals) substantially less than or
close to the 500 individuals used above as the maximum population size
considered the criterion for adequate representation. These three species
were all from the 'at risk' category (Nicholls *et al.*, 1996). Given the results
from the stochastic modelling, one would have to consider seriously sub-

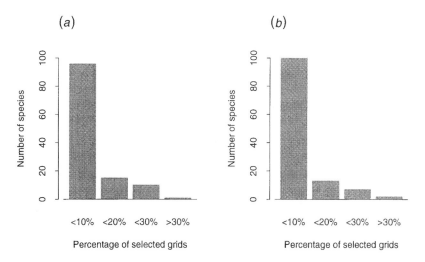

Fig. 11.7 The frequency of species of snakes of South Africa, grouped according to the number of selected grid cells drawn from their core distribution on which they occur expressed as a percentage of the total number of selected grid cells on which they occur. The frequencies are presented for results from (a) the unconstrained solution and (b) the adjacency-constrained solution for an adequacy criterion of 10 grid cells per species. For an explanation of core distribution, see the text.

stantially increasing the population size considered necessary for adequate representation. In passing, two points should be noted. It would be possible to set particular numbers of individuals for each species as the targets considered necessary for adequate representation, rather than the single general figure used here. Such a change would represent a very minor modification to the algorithm. The second point that needs to be made is that what is being illustrated here does not take into account the relationship between the number of individuals set as a criterion and their spatial distribution across the region. A reserve system based on the nominated grid cells would result in many very small groups of individuals that in the absence of interaction with other groups might not be viable, even though the total number of individuals might be above estimates of minimum viable populations. Solutions to this potential inadequacy could include the use of a much larger grid cell size or the use of a stronger adjacency rule from which to build up potential reserves from seed points (for an example of such an algorithm see Bull, Thackway & Cresswell, 1993; Margules & Redhead, 1995).

The use of discrete selection units, be they grid cells (Pressey & Tully,

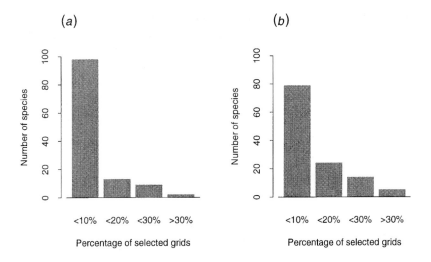

Fig. 11.8 The frequency of species of snakes South Africa, grouped according to the number of selected grid cells on which they occur. The frequencies are presented for results from (a) the unconstrained solution and (b) the core-constrained solution for an adequacy criterion of 15 grid cells per species. For an explanation of core distribution, see the text.

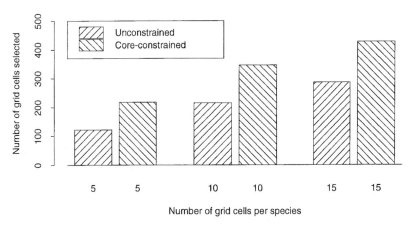

Fig. 11.9 The number of grid cells selected to achieve three levels of representation (5, 10 and 15 grid cells per species) for unconstrained and core-constrained solutions for snakes in South Africa.

1994; Lombard *et al.*, 1995; Freitag *et al.*, 1996) or irregularly shaped units (Margules, Nicholls & Pressy, 1988) offers the opportunity to apply meta-population theory (Gilpin & Hanski, 1991) to address the question, 'What is an adequate number of representations of each species?' Applying Levin's rule (Hanski, Moilanen & Gyllenberg, 1996) to estimate of the minimum amount of suitable habitat necessary for metapopulation persistence, one gets estimates of the number of patches ranging from around 1700 to near-ly 1800 across the three years for zebra. For impala, another widespread and common species, the figures are 1020 to 1160. Adding the constraint to Levin's rule that the minimum number of patches necessary for persist-ence is the proportion of unoccupied *suitable* patches (Nee, 1994) would reduce these estimates but leaves unanswered the questions of what is the definition of 'suitable' and how one estimates it for mobile species except from long-term studies. It has been argued that Levin's rule underesti-mates the number of patches necessary for persistence (Hanski *et al.*, 1996). Either way, the implication is that very many more patches may be necessary than have tended to be considered by the advocates of area-based methods or used here for illustrative purposes.

The other area of ecological theory investigated in this paper is that of the spatial heterogeneity of species' distributions and population dynamics within a species' range, or what Lawton (1996) refers to as the 'textures of abundance within ranges'. Here the theory is less well defined and perhaps would be better referred to as a scientific belief (Dan Botkin pers. comm.). I have demonstrated that it is possible to drive a selection algorithm towards a specific goal such as preferential selection of core sites. It would not be difficult to change such an algorithm from core selection to source-site selection, if that were considered a sound option. The source and sink con-cepts are well established as one explanation for the observed variation in density or abundance of individuals across a species' range (Pulliam, 1988; Lawton, 1996). As long as the selection units can be assigned to sources or sinks for each species it would be possible to drive a selection algorithm towards preferential selection of source areas for each species. The prefer-ential selection of core areas for South African snakes illustrated earlier suggests that the consequences of a sink-driven selection might be to in-crease further the number of grid cells selected. In passing it might be noted that the long-term cost of not making such a selection might be higher in terms of lost species.

There are quite important differences in the strength of the ecological theory utilized here. The contrast between population viability and metapopulation dynamics on the one hand and the ideas that emerge from consideration of the variable texture of abundance within species' ranges on the other is very marked. It is interesting that May (1991), in a discussion of the application of ecological theory to the planning of reintroductions of endangered species, points out that ecological theory does 'not necessarily mean mathematics and equations'. However, he chose to illustrate his point about the role of ecological theory by selecting three examples, each of which is capable of providing explicit quantitative predictions: minimum population sizes (genetic considerations), minimum population sizes (demographic considerations) and patch dynamics (May, 1991). Landscape ecology is an area that has provided many qualitative predictions with respect to conservation and landscape characteristics. In many instances these predictions may be easy to implement in an area-based selection algorithm (for example, select sites close together to aid potential dispersal, select sites connected by corridors). However, there is little guidance when the question is reframed in terms of how close sites must be to permit movement and what are the minimum dimensions of corridors to ensure movement of individuals.

The third issue that needs consideration is that of the consequent cost of adding additional constraints to the area-based selection methods. In the three examples presented here, tightening the criterion against which adequacy is judged or imposing spatial constraints on the solution increases the number of selection units required to meet the objective, sometimes quite dramatically (Margules, Nicholls & Pressey, 1988 and Fig. 11.9). However, the failure to recognize the importance of these additional constraints may lead to a greater long-term cost in terms of the loss of species.

Where to next? What is necessary for further application of area-based selection methods? Area-based selection methods are about making or setting priorities. Setting priorities is about making comparisons. Making comparisons is about judging one area against another in terms of a common set of attributes. Thus, data about the selection units are fundamental to the execution of area-based methods. The examples presented here reflect substantial investment in obtaining common data for all selection units. Regrettably, they are not typical of the world at large. There are examples of how point data can be used to infer spatial distribution of selected species (Nicholls, 1989; Osborne & Tigar, 1992; Buckland & Elston, 1993; Lindenmayer et al., 1995; Margules & Redhead, 1995). We have yet to take the next step and infer spatial and temporal dynamics from point data or from long-term census data.

In conclusion, I suggest that the future of area-based selection methods is not limited by our ingenuity to link our scientific beliefs or ecological or evolutionary theory to the methods. Rather, we will be limited into the foreseeable future by the lack of data to which such methods can be applied. It could also be argued that not only do the data not exist but there may be uncertainty as to what data are really necessary and how such data could be collected within time frames that will enable our theory to influence reserve design.

## ACKNOWLEDGEMENTS

I thank my South African colleagues for the opportunities to collaborate and for their permission for me to use their data, Mandy Lombard for access to the snake distribution data, and Petri Viljoen and Michael Knight for access to the Kruger National Park data; my Australian colleagues, Chris Margules, for keeping me focused and Peter Shaughnessy, for his critical comments on an earlier draft; and finally, the Zoological Society of London for their financial support and invitation that permitted me to attend the meeting.

### References

Akcakaya, H. R. & Ferson, S. (1992). *RAMAS/space: spatially structured population models for conservation biology, version 1.3.* Applied Biomathematics, New York.

Austin, M. P. (1985). Continuum concept, ordination methods, and niche theory. *A. Rev. Ecol. Syst.*, **16**, 39–61.

Bedward, M., Pressey, R. L. & Keith, D. A. (1992). A new approach for selecting fully representative reserve networks: addressing efficiency, reserve design and land suitability with an iterative analysis. *Biol. Conserv.*, **62**, 115–25.

Branch, W. R., Benn, G. A. & Lombard, A. T. (1995). The tortoises (Testudinidae) and terrapins (Pelomedusidae) of southern Africa: their diversity, distribution and conservation. *S. Afr. J. Zool.*, **30**, 91–102.

Brown, J. H. (1995). *Macroecology.* University of Chicago Press, Chicago.

Buckland, S. T. & Elston, D. A. (1993). Empirical models for the spatial distribution of wildlife. *J. appl. Ecol.*, **30**, 478–95.

Bull, A. L., Thackway, R. & Cresswell, I. D. (1993). *Assessing conservation of the major Murray–Darling Basin ecosystems.* Unpublished report, Environmental Resources Information Network (ERIN), Australian Nature Conservation Agency, Canberra.

Caughley, G. & Gunn, A. (1996). *Conservation biology in theory and practice.*

Blackwell Science, Cambridge, MA.

Christian, C. S. & Stewart, G. A. (1953). General report on survey of Katherine-Darwin Region, 1946. *Land Res. Ser. CSIRO Aust.*, **1**, 1–156.

Christian, C. S. & Stewart, G. A. (1968). Methodology of integrated surveys. *Nat. Resour. Res. (Paris)*, **6**, 233–80.

Csuti, B., Polasky, S., Williams, P. H., Pressey, R. L., Camm, J. D., Kershaw, M., Kiester, A. R., Downs, B., Hamilton, R., Huso, M. & Sahr, K. (1997). A comparison of reserve selection algorithms using data on terrestrial vertebrates in Oregon. *Biol. Conserv.*, **80**, 83–97.

Dennis, B., Munholland, P. L. & Scott, J. M. (1991). Estimation of growth and extinction parameters for endangered species. *Ecol. Monogr.*, **61**, 115–43.

Faith, D. P. & Walker, P. A. (1993). *DIVERSITY: a software package for sampling phylogenetic and environmental diversity. Reference and user's guide, v1.0.* CSIRO Division of Wildlife and Ecology, Canberra.

Faith, D. P., Walker P. A., Ive, J. R. & Belbin, L. (1996). Integrating conservation and forestry production: exploring trade-offs between biodiversity and production in regional land-use assessment. *Forest Ecol. Mgmt*, **85**, 251–60.

Foley, P. (1994). Predicting extinction times from environmental stochasticity and carrying capacity. *Conserv. Biol.*, **8**, 124–37.

Freitag, S, Nicholls, A. O. & van Jaarsveld, A. S. (1996). Nature reserve selection in the Transvaal, South Africa: what data should we be using? *Biodiv. Conserv.*, **5**, 685–98.

Gilpin, M. & Hanski, I. (Eds). (1991). *Metapopulation dynamics: empirical and theoretical investigations.* Academic Press, London.

Hanski, I., Moilanen, A. & Gyllenberg, M. (1996). Mininum viable metapopulation size. *Am. Nat.*, **147**, 527–41.

Hunter, M. L. (1996). *Fundamentals of conservation biology.* Blackwell Science, Cambridge, MA.

Joubert, S. C. J. (1983). A monitoring programme for an extensive national park. In *Management of large mammals in African conservation areas*: 201–212. (Ed. Owen-Smith, R. N.). Haum, Pretoria.

Kershaw, M., Williams, P. H. & Mace, G. M.(1994). Conservation of Afrotropical antelopes: consequences and efficiency of using different site selection methods and diversity criteria. *Biodiv. Conserv.*, **3**, 354–72.

Kiester, A. R., Scott, J. M., Csuti, B., Noss, R. F. Butterfield, B. Sahr, K. & White, D. (1996). Conservation prioritization using GAP data. *Conserv. Biol.*, **10**, 1332–42.

Kitching, I. J. (1996). Identifying complementary areas for conservation in Thailand: an example using owls, hawkmoths and tiger beetles. *Biodiv. Conserv.*, **5**, 841–58.

Lacy, R. C. (1993). VORTEX: a computer simulation model for population viability analysis. *Wildl. Res.*, **20**, 45–65.

Lawton, J.H. (1996). Population abundances, geographic ranges and conservation: 1994 Witherby Lecture. *Bird Study*, **43**, 3–19.

Lindenmayer, D. B., Ritman, K., Cunningham, R. B., Smith, J. D. B. & Horvath, D. (1995). A method for predicting the spatial distribution of arboreal marsupials. *Wildl. Res.*, **22**, 445–56.

Lombard, A. T. (1995). Introduction to an evaluation of the protection status of South Africa's vertebrates. *S. Afr. J. Zool.*, **30**, 63–70.

Lombard, A. T., Nicholls, A. O. & August, P. V. (1995). Where should nature reserves be located in South Africa? A snake's perspective. *Conserv. Biol.*, **9**, 363–72.

Lomolino, M. V. & Channell, R. (1995). Splendid isolation: patterns of geographic range collapse in endangered mammals. *J. Mammal.*, **76**, 335–47.

Mabbutt, J. A. (1968). Review of concepts of land classification. In *Land evaluation*: 11–28. (Ed. Stewart, G. A.). Macmillan, Melbourne.

Margules, C. R. & Austin, M. P. (1994). Biological models for monitoring species decline: the construction and use of data bases. *Phil. Trans. R. Soc. B*, **344**, 69–75.

Margules, C. R., Nicholls, A. O. & Pressey, R. L. (1988). Selecting networks of reserves to maximise biological diversity. *Biol. Conserv.*, **43**, 63–76.

Margules, C. R., Nicholls, A. O. & Usher, M. B. (1994). Apparent species turnover, probability of extinction and the selection of nature reserves: a case study of the Ingleborough Limestone pavements. *Conserv. Biol.*, **8**, 398–409.

Margules, C. R. & Redhead, T. D. (1995). *Guidelines for using the BioRap methodology and tools.* CSIRO, Dickson, ACT.

May, R. M. (1991). The role of ecological theory in planning re-introductions of endangered species. *Symp. zool. Soc. Lond.* No. 62, 145–163.

Nee, S. (1994). How populations persist. *Nature, Lond.*, **367**, 123–4.

Nicholls, A. O. (1989). How to make biological surveys go further with generalised linear models. *Biol. Conserv.*, **50**, 51–75.

Nicholls, A. O. & Margules, C. R. (1993). An upgraded reserve selection algorithm. *Biol. Conserv.*, **64**, 165–9.

Nicholls, A. O., Viljoen, P. C., Knight, M. H. & van Jaarsveld, A. S. (1996). Evaluating population persistence of censused and unmanaged herbivore populations from the Kruger National Park, South Africa. *Biol. Conserv.*, **76**, 57–67.

Osborne, P. E. & Tigar, B. J. (1992). Interpreting bird atlas data using logistic models: an example from Lesotho, Southern Africa. *J. appl. Ecol.*, **29**, 55–62.

Possingham, H. P. & Davies, I. (1995). ALEX: a model for the viability analysis of spatially structured populations. *Biol. Conserv.*, **73**, 143–50.

Pressey, R. L., Bedward, M. & Nicholls, A. O. (1990). Reserve selection in mallee lands. In *The Mallee Lands: a conservation perspective*: 167–178. (Eds Noble, J. C., Joss, P. J. & Jones, G. K.). CSIRO: Melbourne.

Pressey, R. L., Humphries, C. J., Margules, C. R., Vane-Wight, R. I. & Williams, P. H. (1993). Beyond opportunism: key principles for systematic reserve selection. *Trends Ecol. Evol.*, **8**, 124–8.

Pressey, R. L. & Nicholls, A. O. (1989). Application of a numerical algorithm to the selection of reserves in semi-arid New South Wales. *Biol. Conserv.*, **50**, 263–78.

Pressey, R. L. & Tully, S. L. (1994). The cost of ad hoc reservation: a case study in western New South Wales. *Aust. J. Ecol.*, **19**, 375–84.

Pulliam, H. R. (1988). Sources, sinks, and population regulation. *Am. Nat.*, **132**, 652–61.

Ryti, R. T. (1992). Effect of the focal taxon on the selection of nature reserves. *Ecol.*

*Appl.*, **2**, 404–10.

Saetersdal, M., Line, J. M. & Birks, H. J. B. (1993). How to maximize biological diversity in nature reserve selection: vascular plants and breeding birds in deciduous woodlands, western Norway. *Biol. Conserv.*, **66**, 131–8.

Underhill, L. G. (1994). Optimal and suboptimal reserve selection algorithms. *Biol. Conserv.*, **70**, 85–7.

van Jaarsveld, A. S. (1995). Where to with reserve selection and conservation planning in South Africa? *S. Afr. J. Zool.*, **30**, 164–8.

Viljoen, P. C. (1989). *Ecological aerial surveys in the Kruger National Park: objectives and methods*. National Parks Board, Skukuza, South Africa.

Viljoen, P. C. & Retief, P. F. (1994). The use of the Global Positioning System for real-time data collecting during ecological aerial surveys in the Kruger National Park, South Africa. *Koedoe*, **37**, 149–57.

Walker, P. J. (1991). Land systems of western New South Wales. *Tech. Rep. Soil Conserv. Serv. N.S.W.* No. 25: 1–65.

Wiens, J. A. (1989). *The ecology of bird communities* I. *Foundations and patterns*. Cambridge University Press, Cambridge.

# 12

# Global biodiversity priorities and expanded conservation policies

NORMAN MYERS

## INTRODUCTION

In face of a biodepletion crisis without precedent, there is a premium on determining priorities for conservation planning. Whatever the merits of our erstwhile approaches to the crisis, they have plainly been insufficient: the crisis has been growing ever-more critical, and the outlook must be doubtful indeed if the best we can do is a case of 'the same as before, only more so and hopefully better so'. Should we not recognize, then, that our approaches in the past have often been too scattered and hence too 'thin', and that they have sometimes been directed at less than the most productive targets? In other words, there has been insufficient attention to the key question of priorities – which is all the more vital at a time when our problems grow ever larger while our conservation resources are ever less capable of matching up to the challenge.

Fortunately there is now an increased focus on priorities. Ten years after the concept was first advanced in detail (Myers, 1983), the crucial planning tool of triage is now acknowledged as a fact of life – even if it means a fact of demise for certain species. Biodiversity is climbing up political agendas, as witness the Biodiversity Convention. Yet, our efforts increasingly fall short of what is needed. How can we better plan our conservation strategies, primarily by identifying and defining the topmost priorities? This chapter seeks to illuminate the prospect by considering a few options for conservation initiatives that offer most action leverage.

## HOTSPOTS REVISITED

One of the most productive priorities in conservation planning is to pin down 'hotspots' of biodiversity, these being areas where exceptional concentrations of endemic species face exceptional threat of habitat destruction. The strategy opens the way for 'silver bullet' responses on the part of conservation planners.

According to early analyses (Myers, 1988, 1990a), at least 20% of plant species are confined to 0.5% of Earth's land surface, and in 18 areas where habitat destruction is proceeding apace. Despite some misunderstandings about the nature and purpose of the hotspots strategy (for instance, it has always been limited to areas of the tropics and subtropics, hence application to areas such as Britain is irrelevant), it has already mobilized $165 million for conservation activities from the MacArthur Foundation and some $80 million from the Global Environment Facility, plus $100 million in the pipeline from the World Bank.

It has always been recognized that the original analyses were limited insofar as they were confined to higher plants. A recent updating through Conservation International in Washington DC (Myers et al., in prep.) reveals that 25 hotspots comprising less than 2% of Earth's land surface contain the sole remaining habitats of 34% of the four tetrapod groups of vertebrate species and 46% of higher plant species. Equally important, they harbour 60% of all species, including non-endemics, and at least 65% of Red Data Book species. The 25 areas are expected to lose most, if not virtually all, of their former habitats with the next two or three decades at most. For preliminary findings about these hotspots, see Table 12.1 (Myers et al., in prep.) More recent analyses can be found in Mittermeier et al. (in press).

Suppose that the average proportion of all species saved through the hotspots strategy were to be 25%. Suppose too that the mass extinction under way, if allowed to proceed largely unimpeded, were to eliminate 50% of all species. This means that a full half of the species extinction problem could be tackled through the hotspots strategy alone.


## THE FUTURE OF EVOLUTION

The mass extinction of species under way may not prove to be the most significant outcome of the biodiversity crisis. Of greater consequence could be the disruption and degradation of several basic processes of evolution. So far as we can discern from mass extinction episodes in the prehistoric past, the recovery period has been protracted, usually of the order of five million years (due primarily to speciation processes having to work with a

**Table 12.1**
*Biodiversity hotspots*

| Area/Region | Remaining habitat (km²) | Endemic plants | Endemic birds | Endemic mammals | Endemic reptiles and amphibians | Total endemic vertebrates |
|---|---|---|---|---|---|---|
| 1. Tropical Andes | 420 024 | 20 000 | 320 | 130 | 558 | 1008 |
| 2. Mesoamerican forests | 331 602 | 9000 | 185 | 50 | 400 | 635 |
| 3. Western Sundas | 442 979 | 8870 | 101 | 82 | 108 | 291 |
| 4. Madagascar | 52 034 | 8000 | 103 | 77 | 450 | 630 |
| 5. Mediterranean basin | 150 000 | 7600 | 2 | 2 | 11 | 15 |
| 6. Caribbean islands | 20 064 | 7000 | 157 | 42 | 148 | 347 |
| 7. Philippines | 19 328 | 6000 | 172 | 115 | 175 | 462 |
| 8. Brazil's Atlantic forest | 111 347 | 6000 | 199 | 73 | 260 | 532 |
| 9. Cape floristic province | 61 353 | 5850 | 4 | 22 | 66 | 92 |
| 10. Eastern Himalayas | 139 847 | 5000 | 25 | 1 | 7 | 33 |
| 11. Brazil's cerrado | 38 891 | 4200 | 29 | 19 | 63 | 111 |
| 12. South-western Australia | 24 640 | 4170 | 14 | 10 | 47 | 71 |
| 13. Darien-Choco and western Ecuador | 75 652 | 3760 | 84 | 17 | 304 | 405 |
| 14. Pacific islands | 17 297 | 3275 | 105 | 1 | 11 | 117 |
| 15. Wallacea | 153 936 | 3000 | 309 | 88 | 58 | 455 |
| 16. West African forests | 127 773 | 2960 | 40 | 34 | 97 | 171 |
| 17. Western Ghats/Sri Lanka | 37 873 | 2690 | 39 | 18 | 253 | 310 |
| 18. New Caledonia | 2880 | 2550 | 30 | 3 | 48 | 81 |
| 19. California floristic province | 69 601 | 2140 | 3 | 15 | 31 | 49 |
| 20. Northern Indochina | 132 882 | 2130 | 19 | 5 | 27 | 51 |
| 21. Khasi-Manipur | 120 758 | 2000 | 4 | 8 | 38 | 50 |
| 22. New Zealand | 92 480 | 1940 | 17 | 2 | 41 | 60 |
| 23. Central Chile | 54 370 | 1800 | 10 | 5 | 10 | 25 |
| 24. Succulent Karoo | 83 409 | 1750 | | | | |
| 25. Eastern Arc and coastal forests | | 1250 | | | | |
| Totals | 2 781 020 | 122 935 | 1971 | 819 | 3211 | 6001 |

*Source*: Myers *et al.* (unpublished data).

greatly reduced pool of species). But, because of certain unique features of the present mass extinction – notably the near elimination of biomes such as tropical forests, wetlands and coral reefs that have served as 'power-houses' of evolution in the past – the bounce-back phase this time could extend for far longer than five million years, conceivably as long as 25 million years.

Regrettably, this dimension of the biotic crisis receives virtually no attention from biologists. A computer check of *Evolution* and similar journals shows that hardly a single article in recent years makes even a passing reference to the notion that we could be at a crossroads stage in evolution's course. On the contrary, one could gain the impression that much biological research is proceeding as if in a world that features virtually no significant change – even though the perturbations of the next few decades will surely leave an impoverishing impact on evolution's course for several million years.

What could be some distinctive features of future evolution within the foreseeable future? We can reasonably surmise that there will be (i), in the short term, homogenization of biotas, a proliferation of opportunistic species, an outburst of speciation among certain taxa, and a pest-and-weed ecology; and (ii), in the long term, a decline of biodisparity, the elimination of many vertebrates, an end to speciation among large vertebrates, and severe limitations on origination, innovation and adaptive radiation.

These phenomena, impoverishing for the most part, would rank among the most prominent departures in the entire course of evolution. Yet, our knowledge and understanding of what may characterize future evolution remains largely a black hole of research. As a consequence, our conservation policies fail to reflect a profound problem of the biodiversity crisis, surely exceeding the better recognized problem of mass extinction of species.

The forces of natural selection can work only with the 'resource base' available (Mayr, 1982; Eldredge, 1991; Raup, 1991). If that base is drastically reduced, the result is a disruption of the creative capabilities of evolution, persisting far into the future. Following mass extinctions in the prehistoric past, the recovery period has lasted for at least five million years before there were as many species as before the extinction episode. To cite the graphic phrasing of Soulé & Wilcox (1980), 'Death is one thing; an end to birth is something else'.

But the evolutionary outcome this time around could prove yet more drastic (Myers, 1990b, 1996). The critical factor lies with the likely loss of key environments. Not only do we appear set to lose most if not virtually all tropical forests. There is progressive depletion of tropical coral reefs, wetlands, estuaries and other biotopes with exceptional abundance and diversity of species and with unusual complexity of ecological workings. These environments have served in the past as pre-eminent powerhouses of evolution in that they have thrown up more species than other environments. It has long been considered (Darlington, 1957; Mayr, 1982) that virtually every major group of vertebrates and many other large categories of animals originated in spacious zones with warm, equable climates, notably the Old World tropics, and especially their forests. It has likewise been supposed that the rate of evolutionary diversification – whether through proliferation of species or through emergence of major new adaptations – has been greatest in the tropics, especially in tropical forests (Stenseth, 1984; Stanley, 1991). In addition, tropical species, especially tropical forest species, appear to persist for only brief periods of geological time, which implies a high rate of evolution.

Furthermore, the species depletion of the current mass extinction will surely apply across most if not all major categories of species. This is almost axiomatic if extensive environments are eliminated wholesale. So the result will contrast sharply with the end of the Cretaceous, when not only placental mammals survived (leading to the adaptive radiation of mammals, eventually including man), but also birds, amphibians, and crocodiles and many other non-dinosaurian reptiles. In addition, the present extinction spasm looks likely to eliminate a sizeable share of terrestrial plant species, at least one-fifth within the next half century and a good many more within the following half century. During most mass-extinction episodes of the prehistoric past, by contrast, terrestrial plants have survived with relatively few losses (Knoll, 1984). They have thus supplied a resource base on which evolutionary processes could start to generate replacement animal species forthwith. If this biotic substrate is markedly depleted within the foreseeable future, the restorative capacities of evolution will be diminished all the more.

At the same time, a mega-extinction episode could trigger an outburst of speciation in some categories of species. A certain amount of 'creative disruption', in the form of, for example, habitat fragmentation, can readily lead to splitting-off of populations, followed by differentiation and termination of interbreeding, so that a population becomes distinctive enough to rank as a new race, then a subspecies, finally a species. Equally important, mass extinction leaves a multitude of niches vacant, allowing a few species to expand and then to diversify. Through these forms of creative disruption, we can discern incipient speciation in, for instance, the house sparrow and the coyote in the United States, both of which have developed several distinctive races, even subspecies, in short order.

But a marked acceleration of speciation through these processes will not remotely match the scale of extinctions envisaged. Whereas extinction can occur in just a few decades, and sometimes in a mere year or so (a ridge in a tropical forest with a pocket of endemic invertebrates can lose its forest habitats within a single season: Gentry, 1986), the time required to produce a new species is much longer. It takes decades for outstandingly capable contenders such as certain insects, centuries if not millennia for many other invertebrates, and hundreds of thousands or even millions of years for most mammals.

Among the reduced stock of species that survives the present extinction episode will surely be a disproportionate number of opportunistic species. These species rapidly exploit newly vacant niches (by making widespread use of food resources), are generally short-lived (with brief gaps between generations), feature high rates of population increase, and are adaptable to a wide range of environments. All of these traits enable them to exploit new environments and to make excellent use of 'boom periods' – precisely the attributes that enable opportunistic species to prosper in a human-disrupted world. Examples include the house sparrow, the European starling, the housefly, the rabbit, the rat, and other pest species, together with many 'weedy' plants. Not only are they harmful to humans' material needs, but they foster a homogenization of biotas by squeezing out less adaptable species. The house sparrow in North America is usurping the niches of bluebirds, wrens and swallows, while the herring gull in north-western Europe is adversely affecting the rarer terns.

While generalist species are profiting from the coming crash, specialist species, notably predators and parasites, will probably suffer disproportionately higher losses. This is because their lifestyles are generally more refined than the generalists', and their numbers are usually much smaller anyway. Since the specialists are often the creatures that keep down the populations of generalists, there may be little to hold the pests in check. Today, probably less than 5% of all insect species deserve to be called pests (Pimentel, 1991). But, if extinction patterns tend to favour clever species, the upshot could soon be a situation where these species increase until their natural enemies can no longer control them. In short, our descendants could shortly find themselves living in a world with a 'pest and weed' ecology.

These, then, are some of the issues for us to bear in mind as we begin to impose a fundamental shift on evolution's course. To date, however, we have given scarcely a moment's thought to this aspect of the biotic crisis. The impending upheaval in evolution's course could rank as one of the greatest biological revolutions of palaeontological time. In scale and significance, it could equal the development of aerobic respiration, the emergence of flowering plants, and the arrival of limbed animals. But, whereas these three departures of life's course rank as advances, the prospective depletion of many evolutionary capacities will rank as a profound setback.

In short, the future of evolution should be regarded as one of the most challenging problems that humankind has ever encountered. Yet, evolutionary biologists seem to give scant attention to this unique challenge – or indeed to the unprecedented opportunity for research into evolution in an incipient state of extreme turmoil. Surely, there is plenty of scope for innovative enquiry at a time when life's abundance and diversity on Earth seem poised for an exceptionally profound upheaval? With just a modicum of research, we could start to adapt and expand our conservation strategies so as to take account of basic evolutionary processes and how we are impoverishing them (Myers, 1996).

## FURTHER DEPARTURES IN CONSERVATION STRATEGIES

The principal approach to biodiversity conservation has hitherto comprised protected areas. While this approach has served us very well in many respects, it will be far less capable of doing so in the future. The present network of protected areas safeguards only a limited proportion of biodiversity at risk, and there is scant scope for bringing many more wildlands under protection within the foreseeable future because of rising human numbers and their proliferant demands on natural environments. Equally important, most protected areas are proving unable to preserve more than a modicum of their biodiversity in the long run.

More importantly, protected areas are increasingly subject to threats that even the best managed areas cannot resist (see chapters by Huntley, Mayer & Pimm, and Bond, this volume). These threats are not only well established in the form of, for instance, multitudes of landless and destitute peasants – a problem that seems set to grow for a good while to come (as many as one-third of developing-country parks and reserves are already being overtaken by agricultural encroachment). The new threats also stem from more distant and diffused problems, notably atmospheric pollution in the form of acid rain, ozone-layer depletion and global warming (Huntley, this volume). These various threats can be countered only by remedial measures that achieve much more than protection of specific, local wildland environments. The measures include efforts to slow, halt and even reverse problems such as desertification, deforestation, over-use of water supplies, acid rain and global warming. They also include population planning, relief of peasant poverty, and a host of other development activities. (For a detailed review of these multiple threats, see Myers, 1994.)

In short, we have reached a point where we can save biodiversity only by saving the biosphere. Hence we can best save biodiversity by doing many other things that we should be doing for many other cogent reasons. In turn, this implies that conservation planners should expand their policy approach to include action responses in lands far outside the main loci of biodiversity concentrations. Fortunately, then, there is much complementarity between our policy responses to the biodiversity problem and our responses to other problems of the biosphere.

This is not to deny that the protected-areas movement has a remarkable record. The total number of areas now totals over 25 000, and the aggregate expanse exceeds 5% of Earth's land surface (McNeely, Harrison & Dingwell, 1994). Many of these areas are in the tropical developing world, and especially in the biome that features greatest biotic richness and that experiences greatest depletion, the tropical forests. Especially heartening has been the recent upsurge in establishment of new areas, an additional five million square kilometres or so since 1970. For all this, the protected-areas movement deserves emphatic credit.

At the same time, it is increasingly clear that the present protected expanse is all too limited. For purposes of ecological comprehensiveness, it should be doubled at least. Moreover, many areas are too small to do their job adequately (see Mayer & Pimm, this volume). Many too are not sited in the best places; 2.2 million square kilometres are in the nearctic, twice as much as in the biotically richest zone on earth, the neotropics.

Worse, a good number of protected areas are not so well safeguarded as they might be, notably in developing countries – which, by and large, are co-extensive with the tropics. These areas are subject to poaching, logging, grazing and other forms of illegal resource exploitation; as many as 95% of all tropical parks and reserves are thought to suffer from some degree of poaching (Groombridge, 1992; McNeely, Miller et al., 1990). Many too are subject to extensive encroachment by small-scale cultivators (Brown & Pearce, 1994; Myers, 1995). Whatever the form of unwanted human incursion, the general result is a decline in the ecological integrity of protected areas, whereupon their conservation value is reduced. Worse, these derogations of protected status seem to be increasing, largely in response to pressures from multitudes of impoverished peasants – a familiar factor in developing countries (otherwise they would not be 'developing'). We have no good figures on how many protected areas are thus depleted, nor do we have a sound idea of how significant the damage is. But, the depletion appears to be widespread already, and it is becoming steadily more pervasive.

What of the future? Can we hope it will be a simple extension of the past, a case of 'the same as before, only more so and better so', i.e. a moderate success story for protected areas? Or should we anticipate that there will be some sharp divergences from the past, with non-linear changes of unusual sort? In particular, will there be a superscale increase in the pressures on protected areas, with a similarly superscale increase in their depletion? Or, could there also be a new approach, an imaginative and innovative approach that constructively addresses the rising tide of depletive pressures and, far from trying merely to build higher walls against the incoming tide, also seeks to divert the tide? Perhaps we should even go so far as to accept the creative speculation of McNeely, Miller et al. (1990) who propose there could eventually be no protected areas at all, on the grounds that either (i) they will have been over-run by land-hungry peasants of the developing world and by resource-hungry consumers of the developed world, or (ii) there will be no need for protected areas since humankind will have devised ways to manage all landscapes and ecosystems in a sufficiently rational way that the needs of wildlands and biodiversity will be catered for anyway.

## PERVERSE SUBSIDIES

The policy purview of conservation should now be expanded to include measures for resisting the tide of development pressures. A prime component of the tide is what can be called 'perverse' subsidies, these being subsidies that exert adverse impact of both environmental and economic sorts over the long run. The principal perverse subsidies are roughly estimated to be:

- agriculture, roughly 460 billion worldwide each year;
- fossil fuels and nuclear energy, $110 billion;
- road transportation, $639 billion;
- water, $220 billion;
- fisheries, $22 billion;
- forestry, $6 billion.

These estimates – preliminary and exploratory estimates, nothing more (and nothing less!) – make up a total of $1450 billion worldwide per year. Hence they exert a significant and sometimes distortive impact on the global economy of some $28 trillion. They are likewise deleterious to the environmental cause. Subsidies for agriculture can foster over-loading of croplands, leading to erosion and compaction of topsoil, pollution from synthetic fertilizers and pesticides, denitrification of soils, and release of greenhouse gases, among a suite of still further adverse effects. Subsidies for fossil fuels aggravate pollution effects such as acid rain, urban smog and global warming. Subsidies for water encourage misuse and overuse of water supplies that are increasingly scarce in many lands. Subsidies for fisheries foster over-harvesting, while subsidies for forestry encourage over-logging. Hence the environmental consequences can be pervasive and profound (Myers & Kent, 1998). In the case of biodiversity, these subsidies cause much degradation and destruction of wildlife habitat and species' life-support systems.

This is not to say that subsidies cannot serve many useful purposes. The key question is: which subsidies, of what sorts, of what scope and with what impacts, can be viewed as 'perverse', i.e. inimical to society's long-term interests? Clearly, this is a question of major import. Yet it has scarcely been identified as a salient issue of our times, let alone documented and analysed.

Equally clearly, we could do a great deal for the environmental cause in general and the biodiversity cause in particular by reducing or eventually phasing out these perverse subsidies. Moreover, these are monies going into unsustainable development. Consider the Rio Earth Summit's proposed annual budget for sustainable development, $600 billion – a sum that governments derided as quite unattainable in financially stringent times. I suspect that, in the biodiversity arena, there is no single initiative that could prove as lastingly productive as getting rid of perverse subsidies.

Similarly, it would behove conservationists to assess other aspects of the financial, fiscal and economic landscapes to see whether there are other macro-level measures with potential to support biodiversity in a manner far exceeding conventional measures such as establishing further protected areas. Consider, for example, that each day the amount of money despatched across international borders by the stock exchanges of the world tops $1.1 trillion (Korten, 1995). While many of the funds return next day, the sum offers huge scope to affect biodiversity. This is notably the case through investments as when, for instance, the stock of a timber corporation is suddenly boosted by an inflow of funds, enabling it to purchase another forest holding or concession in Amazonia, Borneo or Siberia. Funds of this scale can be exceptionally influential in land-use planning and other activities affecting biodiversity in all parts of the world.

There have been proposals (e.g. Overseas Development Institute, 1996) to exploit the daily $1 trillion by levying a tax of, e.g. 1% of 1% of turnover, yielding some $40 billion per year. These funds garnered from what is in effect a single worldwide stock exchange could be utilized for various international purposes, including safeguards for the planetary complement of species, or global commons such as the atmosphere and climate, and the oceans. There would be the additional economic benefit that it would help to damp down the more speculative and disruptive forms of currency trading.

## CONCLUSIONS

The over-arching point in the last section above is that there is far more leverage for conservationists – whether in policy, programme or project terms – in making a priority of addressing major economic forces than in the traditional strategy of establishing more protected areas. The biodiversity cause tends to be all too reactive. True, this approach has been moderately acceptable for decades. But to reiterate the vital point, defensive measures seek to protect biodiversity against something, and today that 'something' has grown unprecedently large – just as it is set to keep growing ever larger in light of the increasing numbers of humans with their increasing activities and demands. It is appropriate, then, for conservationists to see what better they can do about the 'something', and to become more proactive by getting to grips with the macro-economic forces that often drive the 'something'.

To be more specific: if we are to tackle that 'something', we need to establish what it consists of. It comprises much more than simply more people with more demands. It embraces all the leading factors (products, processes, etc.) of modern economies, notably investment and other financial flows, markets, trade, pricing systems, accounting procedures and discounting methods – plus the more prominent deficiencies of modern economies such as marketplace externalities and social inequities (for consideration of these further factors, see Pearce & Warford, 1993; Daly & Cobb, 1994; Cairncross, 1995).

Within the context of these potent forces, it is apparent that conservation policies are not primarily set by conservationists. Rather, and albeit by default, they are set by departments of economic planning, industry, agriculture, forestry, energy, trade, and human settlements, and also by bankers, investors and corporate leaders. When all these agencies have had their say, conservationists are left with little 'policy space' in which to pursue their purposes. It is in the interest of conservationists to understand the principal forces that shape the arenas within which they operate.

There would be, shall we say, a handsome payoff for conservationists in tackling these grand-scale forces. Equally, the conservation cause may prove a losing game in the long run unless we get to grips with what ultimately determines our scope for action. Priorities, anyone?

### References

Brown, K. & Pearce, D.W. (Eds) (1994). *The causes of tropical deforestation.* University College London Press, London.

Cairncross, F. (1995). *Green inc.* Earthscan Publications, London.

Daly, H. E. & Cobb, J. B. Jr. (1994). *For the common good: redirecting the economy toward community, the environment, and a sustainable future.* (Revised edn.). Beacon Press, Boston, MS.

Darlington, P. J. (1957). *Zoogeography: the geographical distribution of animals.* John Wiley, New York; Chapman & Hall, London.

Eldredge, N. (1991). *The miner's canary: unraveling the mysteries of evolution.* Prentice-Hall Press, New York.

Gentry, A. H. (1986). Endemism in tropical versus temperate plant communities. In *Conservation biology: the science of scarcity and diversity:* 153–181. (Ed. Soulé, M. E.). Sinauer Associates, Sunderland, MS.

Groombridge, B. (Ed.) (1992). *Global biodiversity: status of the Earth's living resources.* Chapman & Hall, London.

Knoll, A. H. (1984). Patterns of extinction in the fossil record of vascular plants. In *Extinctions:* 21–68. (Ed. Nitecki, M. H.). University of Chicago Press, Chicago.

Korten, D. C. (1995). *When corporations rule the world.* Earthscan Publications, London.

Mayr, E. (1982). *The growth of biological thought: diversity, evolution and inheritance.* Harvard University Press, Cambridge, MS.

McNeely, J. A., Harrison, J. & Dingwell, P. (1994). *Protecting nature: regional review of protected areas.* IUCN, Gland, Switzerland.

McNeely, J. A., Miller, K. R., Reid, W. V., Mittermeier, R. A. & Werner, T. B. (1990). Strategies for conserving biodiversity. *Environment,* **32**: 16–20, 36–40.

Mittermeier, R. A., Myers, N. & Mittermeier, C. (1998). *Biodiversity hotspots.* CEMEX publishers, Mexico City, Mexico (in press).

Myers, N. (1983). A priority-ranking strategy for threatened species? *Environmentalist,* **3**, 97–120.

Myers, N. (1988). Threatened biotas: 'hot spots' in tropical forests. *Environmentalist,* **8**, 187–208.

Myers, N. (1990a). The biodiversity challenge: expanded hot-spots analysis. *Environmentalist,* **10**, 243–56.

Myers, N. (1990b). Mass extinctions: what can the past tell us about the present and the future? *Global planet change,* **82**, 175–85.

Myers, N. (1994). Protected areas: protected from a greater 'what'? *Biodiv. Conserv.,* **3**, 411–18.

Myers, N. (1995). Tropical deforestation: population, poverty and biodiversity. In *The economics and ecology of biodiversity decline:* 111–122. (Ed. Swanson, T. M.). Cambridge University Press, Cambridge, UK.

Myers, N. (1996). The biodiversity crisis and the future of evolution. *Environmentalist,* **16**, 1–11.

Myers, N. & Kent, J. (1998). *Perverse subsidies: tax $$ undercutting our economies and environment alike.* international Institute for Sustainable Development, Winnipeg, Canada.

Overseas Development Institute (1996). *New sources of finance for development.* Overseas Development Institute, London.

Pearce, D. W. & Warford, J. J. (1993). *World without end: economics, environment and sustainable development.* Oxford University Press, Oxford.

Pimentel, D. (1991). Diversification of biological control strategies in agriculture. *Crop. Prot.,* **10**, 243–53.

Raup, D. M. (1991). *Extinction: bad genes or bad luck?* W.W. Norton, New York.

Soulé, M. E. & Wilcox, B. A. (1980). Conservation biology: its scope and its challenge. In *Conservation biology: an evolutionary–ecological perspective:* 1–8. (Eds Soulé, M. E. & Wilcox, B. A.). Sinauer Associates, Sunderland, MS.

Stanley, S. M. (1991). *The new evolutionary timetable.* Basic Books, New York.

Stenseth, N. C. (1984). The tropics: cradle or museum? *Oikos,* **43**, 417–20.

# Global conservation and UK government policy

(13)

ROBERT M. MAY AND KERRY TREGONNING

## INTRODUCTION

In discussing conservation and government policy, we must first consider the magnitude of the problem of conservation in a changing world. This involves extinction rates and numbers of species, and also the somewhat eccentric patterns of effort and attention we tend to devote to different groups. An outline of the principles that guide government policies in these areas, and actions that have arisen from these policies, follows. The chapter concludes with some ideas, based on a mixture of opinion and fact, about major things that we might do next. Much of what follows, in contrast to the global, overarching look of some of the earlier chapters, will describe small, discrete local actions in line with the maxim 'Think globally but act locally'.

## THE DIMENSIONS OF THE PROBLEM

The main business of recording the total number of species, and concern about its importance, only began quite recently. Linnaeus began the enterprise around 1758, recognizing about 9000 species. To date, we have recorded in the region of 1.7–1.8 million (May, 1988, 1990; Groombridge, 1992). We do not know exactly how many have been named. There is no central catalogue and there are difficulties associated with synonyms; the true count of named and distinct species may be nearer 1.4–1.5 million. The 1.7–1.8 million described species are distributed very differently among the various taxonomic groups. The most numerous by far are the insects at 57% of the total. The best known are mammals and birds. There are between 9000 and 10 000 species of bird, something over 4000 species of mammal and around 300 000 plant species. Not only are the insects most numerous, but among them the beetles account for about a quarter of all known species. Of the roughly 400 000 species of beetle named, about half are known from only one geographical location (N. E. Stork, pers. comm.). So, it is not surprising that there are problems with synonyms, that is the same thing being given different names in different places (Solow, Mound & Gaston, 1995; May & Nee, 1995). Lacking a centralized database, it is simply difficult to keep track.

If we do not know to within 10% how many species have been named and recorded, it is anybody's guess how many there may be in total. A variety of lines of argument of varying degrees of sophistication have been used to arrive at various figures. These are roughly summarized in Table 13.1. Several lines of empirical argument, backed up by a number of indirect theoretical estimates, suggest that the number of species currently on earth is in the range 3–10 million (Groombridge, 1992; May, 1988, 1990, 1994).

There are, however, revisionist estimates, based on one or other particular study, which extrapolate through a chain of arguments to hugely greater figures for the total. The most familiar is Erwin's (1982) estimate based on beetles in tropical canopies, but there are others based on British fungi (Hawksworth, 1991) and on seabed core samples from the North American continental shelf (Grassle & Maciolek, 1992), which indicate figures as high as 30–80 million for the total number of species. This is an order of magnitude higher than the more direct estimates of 3–10 million referred to above. Interesting though these higher numbers might be, and illustrative of the way they are connected with a fundamental understanding of the structure and function of ecological communities, we think they are, none the less, overestimates, for various technical reasons. For example, if Erwin were right, only about one in 30 species in his samples should be already known to science. However, in a recent article in the *New Scientist* he gives a figure of one in five already known, on the basis of direct 'keying-out' of some of his collections. If, indeed, the roughly one million known insects represent 20% of the total, then we arrive at a total number of insect species of five million (in contrast with Erwin's widely cited 30 million).

This illustrates a tendency among certain groups of individuals to think of the biggest number to which credence can be given, in the belief that this somehow produces political leverage. We think this is unhelpful. For one thing, the larger the number of species, then in some sense the lower the value of any individual one. For another thing, we might well hope the number of species on earth is not vast, because in that case we have a realistic chance of getting to know them, and to do something about con-

**Table 13.1**

*Total number of plant and animal species alive today, as estimated by various lines of argument*

| Basis for estimate | Roughly estimated total (millions) |
| --- | --- |
| *Empirically based* | |
| Extrapolation from past trends, group by group | 3–8 |
| Intuitive argument: for birds and mammals, roughly two tropical species for each temperate species; but much of recorded diversity is temperate invertebrates | 3–5 |
| Careful collection and keying-out of a group in a previously unstudied place, and assume the fraction of new species is typical | 3–5 |
| Compendium of opinions of experts in individual taxonomic groups | 5–10 |
| Look at one group in one place, and use various theoretical arguments to 'scale up', e.g. Erwin (1982) and beetles in tropical canopies; Grassle & Maciolek (1992) and benthic invertebrates off N.E. continental shelf of USA | 30 or more |
| *Theoretically based* | |
| Ratio of animal to plant species in different food webs, and use of relatively good knowledge of plant species to project animal species total | ~3 (ratio is of order 10, but highly variable and uncertain) |
| Patterns in numbers of terrestrial animal species in different size categories, and assume failure of roughly '$L^{-2}$ law' is caused by lack of recording (mainly tropical) species in 1–10 mm range | 3–10 |

For a more full discussion, see May *et al.*, 1995.

serving them. But, above all else, we should keep focused on getting the right answer, regardless of prejudices or desires to have the number small or large.

Given this order-of-magnitude uncertainty in our understanding of what the total number of species on earth is, it is all the more odd that we distribute our effort among taxonomic groups so unevenly. As discussed in more detail elsewhere (Gaston & May, 1992), and as summarized in their Table 1, taxonomic effort is partitioned roughly equally – in terms of numbers of people – amongst vertebrate animals, plants, and invertebrate animals. There are, however, something like 40 thousand (or at most 50 thousand) species of vertebrates, around 300 thousand species of plants, and at a conservative estimate three million or more species of insects.

**Table 13.2**

*Species in major taxa that have become extinct since 1600*

| Group | Number of species extinct since 1600 | | Approx. total of recorded species (in thousands) | Approx. % of group extinct (1996 figures) |
|---|---|---|---|---|
| | A as estimated by IUCN in early 1990s | B as assessed by IUCN in 1996 | | |
| **Animals** | | | | |
| Vertebrates | 229 | 296 | 47 | 0.6 |
| Birds | 116 | 104 | 9.5 | 1.1 |
| Mammals | 59 | 86 | 4.5 | 1.9 |
| Reptiles | 23 | 20 | 6 | 0.3 |
| Amphibians | 2 | 5 | 3 | 0.2 |
| Fish | 29 | 81 | 24 | 0.3 |
| Molluscs | 191 | 228 | 100 | 0.2 |
| Crustaceans | 4 | 9 | 40 | 0.02 |
| Insects | 61 | 72 | 1000 | 0.007! |
| Total (animals) | 485 | 605 | 1400 | 0.04 |
| **Plants** | | | | |
| Gymnosperms | 2 | – | 0.8 | 0.3 |
| Dicotyledons | 120 | – | 190 | 0.06 |
| Monocotyledons | 462 | – | 52 | 0.9 |
| Palms | 4 | – | 2.8 | 0.1 |
| Total (plants) | 584 | – | 240 | 0.2 |

Thus, on the basis of the taxonomic work force in relation to the job to be done (measured in numbers of species), the effort devoted to the average vertebrate species is roughly 10 times that for a plant species and 100 times that for the typical invertebrate species. This reflects accidents of intellectual fashion, rather than any considered appraisal. It would be difficult to argue, from the point of view of the functioning of food webs and ecosystems, that vertebrates are more important than invertebrates; certainly plants are more fundamental to the functioning of living systems than either.

So, we do not know the number of recorded species to within 10%, and we do not know the total number of extant species to within a factor 10. We know even less about future extinction rates.

Table 13.2 sets out numbers of recorded extinctions, for various groups, as certified by the IUCN Red Data Books. Table 13.2 shows the IUCN figures for the early 1990s (Smith *et al.*, 1993), and also the revised figures set out at the IUCN World Conservation Congress held in Montreal in the summer of 1996 (IUCN, 1996). It will be seen from Table 13.2 that a disproportionate fraction of recorded extinctions are for bird and mammal species. This, of course, reflects the attention these groups have received, rather than necessarily reflecting any inherently greater propensity for extinction. Every indication is that the most imperilled group of vertebrates is fish, and particularly freshwater fish, but on the other hand they have been less well studied. And the total of 61 recorded extinctions among insects underlines the problem: 43 of these insects are from Hawaii, and most of the rest are from islands studied by researchers (May, Lawton & Stork, 1995). Only nine are from continental areas (eight from the USA, one from Germany), and not a single one is from the tropics! Even for birds and mammals, where the combined rate of certified extinction has been about one species per year for the last century, this rate of certified extinction is almost surely an underestimate of the true figure. Thus Diamond's (1989) study of birds in the Solomon Islands noted 12 species which had not been seen for 50 years or so, and which are surely extinct; yet only one of these species appears in Table 13.2. A study of freshwater fish in Malaysia, thoroughly conducted over several years, found only 122 of the 266 species recorded in Victorian times, yet none of these apparently missing species is recorded as extinct in Table 13.2.

Because we are so uncertain about total numbers of species on earth, any estimate that convolves such uncertainties with the further imprecisions, greater in some groups than others, of Table 13.2 must lead to numbers which are virtually meaningless. There is, however, a more robust and analytic approach, which enables us to make reasonably precise statements (at least to within an order of magnitude) about recent changes in extinction rates (May et al., 1995). This approach begins by asking what is the average 'species lifetime', from origination to extinction, in the fossil record. This lifetime varies greatly, both among groups and within any one group. Broadly speaking, the average such lifetime of a species in the fossil record, at least over the last 600 million years, is in the range $10^6$ to $10^7$ years, although longer and shorter lifespans are seen. Now we turn to the past century. From Table 13.2, we have just noted that for the apparently well-studied birds and mammals, roughly one species has gone extinct each year, from a group embracing just over $10^4$ species. This statement can be inverted to say that, on the basis of events in the recent past, we would expect the average lifespan of a bird or mammal species to have shrunk to around $10^4$ years. Ten thousand years may seem like a long time, but in comparison with species lifetimes in the fossil record, it represents a speeding-up of extinction rates by a factor of something like 100 to 1000 above the background rate.

Looking toward the immediate future, three different approaches to estimating impending rates of extinction suggest species' life expectancies have shortened to around a few hundred years (May *et al.*, 1995). The most familiar of these approaches is based on species–area relations, coupled with assessments of current rates of habitat loss; this tends to give a projection of around 200–400 for expected species lifetimes over the coming centuries. The other two methods are based in different ways on the IUCN's catalogue of 'endangered' or 'vulnerable' species, as set out in Table 10.2, for better-known groups such as birds, mammals or palm trees (Smith *et al.*, 1993; Heywood *et al.*, 1994; Crosby *et al.*, 1994), or on even more detailed estimates for particular families of birds or mammals or reptiles (Mace, 1994). These two lines of estimates suggest lifetimes in the range of $10^2$ to $10^3$ years. Broadly speaking, if we take these three different lines of admittedly speculative estimates of future extinction rates to be suggesting species lifetimes of around a few hundred years, and contrast this with a fossil background species lifetime of around a few million years, we have extinction rates accelerating by a factor of $10^4$ (give or take one order of magnitude). This represents a sixth great wave of extinction, fully comparable with the Big Five mass extinctions of the geological past, but different in that it results from the activities of a single other species rather than from external environmental changes.

We conclude this globally orientated section by turning to focus on the UK.

The proportion of the world's species found in the UK varies widely from group to group. About half the world's species of protozoa and algae are found in the UK, and about one-sixth of the recorded fungi species. We have a lot of the world's known bryophytes (7%) and lichens (9%). On the other hand, we have relatively few flowering plants (0.5%), largely because they are still trying to re-establish themselves in the UK after the most recent ice age. About 2% of the global total of known insect species are represented in the UK, about 0.5% of freshwater fish species, and 0.1% of reptiles and amphibians. We do reasonably well with birds (2%), but less well with mammals (1.2%).

As can be seen from Table 13.3, about 1% of UK insect species have been recorded extinct in the UK this century (this does not mean they are globally extinct, only that they are no longer found within the UK); this local

**Table 13.3**

*Insect and other non-marine invertebrate species that have become extinct,*
*or are threatened with extinction, within Britain*

| | Extinct: formerly native to Britain, but not recorded since 1900 | Threatened: species listed as 'vulnerable' or 'endangered'[a] | Estimated number of species surveyed |
|---|---|---|---|
| Insects | | | |
| Coleoptera | 63 | 247 | 3900 |
| Diptera | 3 | 496 | 6000 |
| Lepidoptera | 16 | 49 | 2500 |
| (butterflies) | (3) | (5) | (56) |
| Hymenoptera | 18 | 49 | 580 |
| Trichoptera | 2 | 13 | 199 |
| Heteroptera | 6 | 20 | 540 |
| Orthoptera | – | 5 | 30 |
| Odonata | – | 6 | 41 |
| Total | 108 | 885 | 14 000 |
| Other invertebrates | | | |
| Mollusca | – | 17 | c. 202 |
| Arachnida | – 53 | 647 | |
| Crustacea | 1 | 3 | c. 70 |
| Myriapoda | – | – | c. 92 |
| Others[b] | – | 1 | c. 41 |
| Total | 1 | 74 | c. 1050 |

[a] For Lepidoptera, includes a few subspecies of macro-moths.
[b] Coelenterata, Nemertea, Bryozoa, and Annelida.

number for insects in the UK is (perhaps significantly, perhaps coinciden-
tally) very similar to the fraction of the world's better-known species of
birds and mammals recorded extinct this century (Hambler & Speight,
1996). The fraction of UK insects recorded as 'endangered' or 'vulnerable',
around 7%, is also similar to the global fraction of the world's birds in this
category (around 11%), although less than the global fraction of mammals
(around 25%). In the UK, a good deal of attention is concentrated on the
more attention-getting species which people would like to keep present in
the UK, even though they may be relatively common elsewhere. We think it
might be better to focus attention more on species which are on endangered or vulnerable lists, and which are endemic to the UK, or at least
where we have a large fraction of the world's total (see also Thomas *et al.*,
this volume). This view is gaining increasing currency, we think, among
conservation agencies in the UK (Avery *et al.*, 1995).

## UK GOVERNMENT POLICIES AND ACTIONS

The UK Government's broad approach to conservation and other environmental issues was clearly articulated in the 1993 White Paper *Our common inheritance* (HMSO, 1990: ch. 1 para. 14): 'The starting point for this Government is the ethical imperative of stewardship . . . we have a moral duty to look after our planet and hand it on in good order to future generations'. The first chapter of this White Paper also emphasizes that actions must be based upon facts, but that the precautionary principle must be the guide when we are faced with uncertainty.

Against the background of the principles spelled out in the White Paper on the Environment, a number of actions and initiatives can be identified. *Biodiversity: the UK action plan* (HMSO 1994) identifies a list of post-Rio commitments. Many other countries – although not all – have committed themselves to produce biodiversity action plans, but the UK is in the lead in its preparation of specific plans. Through the mechanism of a Biodiversity Steering Group, with representatives from Government departments, voluntary organizations, universities and Research Council institutes, and others, action plans have been produced for some 114 species categorized as being under some form of threat. There are concrete intentions to produce such plans for a further 286 species over the next 3 years. The Biodiversity Steering Group has produced a catalogue of 1252 species which have been recommended for statutory monitoring. In addition, 38 key habitats for conservation purposes have been identified. Costed action plans have already been published for 14 of these; plans for the remaining 24 key habitats will be developed over the next 3 years.

Underlying many aspects of the Biodiversity Action Plan is the problem of co-ordinating the large amount of information we already have about plants and animals in the UK. The flora and fauna of the UK is better known than that of any other country, largely as a result of the activities of a host of voluntary organizations, such as the RSPB, the Botanical Society, and many others. From an Australian perspective, one of us (RMM) would add that our relatively good knowledge also partly results from there being fewer plant and animal species in the UK than in most other countries! The task of bringing together, consolidating, and making available this wealth of information, which has been variously gathered over many years, is a tricky one. It involves both resources (because the databases are varied, extensive, and held by many different institutions) and delicate questions of reconciling ownership with wide availability. Much progress is being made

**Table 13.4**
*Darwin Initiative projects as of April 1997*

| Category | Country | Number of projects |
|---|---|---|
| 1. Overseas projects, directed at recording and/or understanding and/or preserving aspects of biological diversity | Africa | 35 |
| | East Asia and Pacific | 23 |
| | Central and South Asia | 11 |
| | Central and South America | 26 |
| | Eastern Europe | 11 |
| | Other | 6 |
| 2. Training programmes/courses, bringing researchers from developing countries to the UK for short periods | | 23 |
| 3. Miscellaneous/other | | 10 |
| Total | | 145 |

in solving these problems. Part of the preliminary planning for this enterprise comes fom the Systematics Forum, funded through the Office of Science and Technology. Ultimately, such a database could be a resource for schools and for certain kinds of local planning questions, as well as for research into questions of ecology and conservation biology.

Another post-Rio initiative in which the UK has, in our opinion, managed to do a lot of good with a relatively small amount of money is the Darwin Initiative. Its stated aim is to help those countries rich in biodiversity but poor in financial resources. The first projects were under way by the end of 1993, the year in which the Initiative was launched. The current funding of about £3 million per year is set to continue. While this is not a large amount of money, it is highly leveraged, and no other country has developed such a scheme. As of September 1996, 116 projects have been funded, with a good geographical spread (see Table 13.4). Of particular note is the project which has provided seed money to the Tropical Biology Association (TBA), and which aims at nothing less than establishing a European equivalent of the North American Organization of Tropical Studies, which has done so much to promote tropical studies in South America and Mesoamerica. The TBA brings together, in roughly equal numbers, African and European students on field courses in Africa during the summer. If it is a long-term success, it may create the same kind of 'invisible college' for the Old World as the OTS has in the Americas.

There are currently some 70 UK institutions involved with the Darwin Initiative. About 600 people from developing countries have received training either *in situ* or in the UK. To date, some 17 databases have been established, some 18 manuals and field guides published. All of this, and more, has taken place within a structure which brings together the UK and developing countries to create a knowledge base *in situ*, rather than co-opting postgraduate students from developing countries into the UK academic enterprise. The Darwin Initiative also funds some projects in Eastern Europe, and has a responsive-mode category to be open to novel ideas.

Another area in which the UK Government has been a leading player is the Commission on the International Trade in Endangered Species, CITES. The Appendices to CITES, within which species are listed to determine their status under the convention, are based on quantitative criteria for assessing extinction risk (Mace & Lande, 1991; IUCN Species Survival Commission, 1994). Translated into action, CITES scored a notable success in August 1996, shortly before the conference upon which this book is based, when UK officials confiscated some 124 rhinoceros horns reputedly worth around £3 million. The accumulation of many such small-scale successes is ultimately of considerable importance for the conservation of endangered species.

Not everyone realizes the extent to which the Ministry of Defence is an important factor in conservation in the UK. More generally, many of the places where wildlife flourish in the world are associated with military 'no go' zones: thus the Amur tiger (*Panthera tigris altaica*) persists in the zone between North and South Korea. Sydney Harbour, arguably the most beautiful harbour in the world, owes much of its unspoilt perimeter to the fact that large tracts of the foreshore are owned by the Australian Ministry of Defence. In the UK, MoD is a major player, with its estate comprising 240 000 ha or around 1% of the UK, in the form of 3200 separate sites, ranging from the 38 000 ha Salisbury Plain Training Area to individual small buildings and communication masts (MoD 1996). It has been described as the finest estate for wildlife in any single ownership in the UK. MoD operates a scheme to reward the best conservation project on MoD land. It is called the Sanctuary Award and is given annually. Recent examples of projects include: the use of artificial predator-free islands to act as nesting sites for common and little terns on the Shell Bank creek at Foulness Island; the use of coppicing in woodlands to increase the diversity of woodland flora and fauna which has contributed to dormouse population recovery; and the use of old ammunition boxes (450 of them) on Salisbury

Plain as nesting boxes for barn and tawny owls, which has contributed to their protection (MoD, 1996). It is clear that, although the primary use of MoD land is for training, there is a very positive attitude towards its potential for conservation.

## FOR THE FUTURE

We conclude with a list of issues which arguably deserve more attention.

More efforts should be directed toward marine communities and marine diversity. Here we need better understanding of the basic biology, as a foundation for addressing practical problems ranging from overfishing (especially with techniques which disturb benthic communities) to waste disposal of various kinds.

We welcome recent initiatives focused on the microbial diversity of soils. These include directed research initiatives by the Natural Environmental Research Council, and the reorganization and co-ordination of the UK culture collections (largely funded by the OST). Soil microbial diversity is a subject both of fundamental importance to understanding the functioning of ecological communities, and of practical importance in the light of likely climate changes.

As discussed above, there is also a clear need to do more to establish national databases of biological diversity. These should draw together the information we have, making it widely available for planning, for education, and for conservation purposes. The UK is taking a lead in international efforts to put together international databases, both within and outside the Systematics Forum.

More efforts should be devoted to problems associated with introduced organisms, such as Canada geese, muntjac deer, and many others. The Trondheim Conference in July 1996 (Schei, 1996) identified the spread of non-native species as the second most significant factor, after habitat loss, affecting biodiversity worldwide. In the UK, parts of the Wildlife and Countryside Act (subsection 14 and subsection 9) help to identify and give some defence against introduction of non-native species, but they provide no help against the spread of the species once they are introduced. By the same token, there are many important biological and policy issues associated with the release of genetically modified organisms (GMOs), although it can be argued that such issues tend to receive much more careful and deliberate attention than do introductions of non-native species.

Much conservation literature focusses on the problem of extinction

**Table 13.5**

*Recorded damage to Sites of Special Scientific Interest (SSSI) in England, Scotland, and Wales, 1990–1995*

| Category of damage | 1990/91 | 1991/92 | 1992/93 | 1993/94 | 1994/95 |
|---|---|---|---|---|---|
| Short-term<br>'Could recover, in less than 15 years, with favourable management' | 212 | 196 | 126 | 111 | 76 |
| Long-term<br>'lasting reduction of SSSI, or more than 15 years to recover' | 31 | 47 | 46 | 39 | 48 |
| Partial loss<br>'result in denotification of part of SSSI' | 10 | 6 | 7 | 11 | 14 |
| Total loss | 0 | 1 | 0 | 0 | 0 |
| Overall totals | 253 | 250 | 179 | 161 | 154 |

Total number of SSSIs is around 5500.

rates of species in the Third World, where something like 1% of tropical forest is lost each year. It is salutary to compare this with conservation problems in the UK. In the UK, we have something like 6000 sites of special scientific interest (SSSI); hindsight might suggest that a smaller number of more consolidated sites would have been better. Be this as it may, we keep increasingly good statistics about damage done to these sites. These are summarized in Table 13.5. The statistics cover 'short-term damage' (reversible in 15 years or less under favourable management), 'long-term damage' (having a lasting effect or taking more than 15 years to recover under favourable management), 'partial loss' (resulting in denotification of part of the SSSI), and 'total loss' (of which there has only been one example in recent years). Happily, these rates of damage to SSSIs have been steadily decreasing over the past 5 years, even though our monitoring and data-keeping has been improving. There is, however, no room for complacency. Much of the damage suffered by SSSIs is indeed minor, but it is experienced by around 2% of all sites in recent years. If we consider only long-term damage or partial loss, the incidence is around 1% per year. Arrestingly, this is roughly the same as the rate at which tropical deforestation is occurring. In other words, conservation problems are not confined to the tropics, but rather the underlying problems are general and widespread.

The UK Dependent Territories raise questions which, in one sense, relate to global conservation, but in another sense are UK responsibilities.

**Table 13.6**

*Number of endemic species in UK Dependent Territories (from HMSO 1994: 133)*

| Place | Vascular plants | Terrestrial invertebrates | Reptiles and amphibians | Birds[a] |
|---|---|---|---|---|
| **Caribbean** | | | | |
| Anguilla | 1 | – | – | – |
| British Virgin Is. | NK[b] | 1 | 5 | – |
| Cayman Is. | 24 | 38 + | 19 | – (16) |
| Montserrat | 2 | 6 + | 5 | 1 |
| Turks and Caicos Is. | 9 | 2 + | 8 | – |
| **Atlantic** | | | | |
| Ascension | 10 | 13 | – | 1 |
| Bermuda | 14 | 1 | – | 1 |
| Falkland Is. | 12 | 70% of all insects | – | 1(16) |
| St. Helena | 46 | *ca.* 300 | – | 1 |
| South Georgia | 1 | 30% of all insects | – | 2 |
| South Sandwich Is. | – | NK | – | – |
| Tristan da Cunha | 40 | 60 + | – | 5(4) |
| **Pacific** | | | | |
| Pitcairn Is. | 19 | 170 + | 1? | 4 |
| Hong Kong | 20 | 20 + | 3 | – |
| **Local** | | | | |
| Gibraltar | 5 | 3 | – | – |
| Guernsey | – | – | – | – |
| Jersey | – | – | – | – |
| Isle of Man | – | – | – | – |

[a] Subspecies in brackets; [b] NK = not known.

The UK still has obligations to a large number of Dependent Territories in the Caribbean, the Atlantic, the Pacific, and elsewhere. In sum, these far-flung territories have much more in the way of endemic and unique biological richness than the UK has. Table 13.6 makes this abundantly clear. But, in the aftermath of the Rio Conference, the biodiversity action plans for most of the Dependent Territories are not nearly as advanced as those of the UK. The Foreign and Commonwealth Office is well aware of this, and is taking action to remedy the situation. The difficulties, however, should not be underestimated.

## CONCLUSION

We began with a comparatively analytic estimate of current and likely future rates of extinction. This estimate, which avoids the uncertainties of how many species there may be on earth, points unambiguously to a contemporary acceleration of extinction rates, by a factor of around 10 000 faster than the average rate seen over the sweep of the fossil record. We are clearly standing on the breaking tip of a sixth great wave of mass extinctions in the history of life on earth.

Against the immensity of that backdrop, our chapter has described relatively modest measures that can be, and are being, taken to ameliorate the consequences. The principles that underpin UK Government policies, and the actions that are being taken, point in the right direction. In proportion to resources, measured by population size or by GDP, few other developed countries are doing as much as the UK. Clearly, however, it is possible to wish that more could be done.

## ACKNOWLEDGEMENTS

We are indebted to John Plowman and Sarah Collins of the Department of the Environment, Transport and the Regions, Colonel James Baker of the Ministry of Defence, and Dr Andrew E. Brown of the Joint Nature Conservation Committee for their help in providing material for this chapter.

### References

Avery, M., Wingfield Gibbons, D., Porter, R., Tew, T., Tucker, G. & Williams, G. (1995). Revising the British Red Data List for birds: the biological basis of U.K. conservation priorities. *Ibis*, **137**, (Suppl.), S232–9.

Crosby, M. J., Stattersfield, A. J., Collar, N. J. & Bibby, C. J. (1994). Predicting avian extinction rates. *Biodiv. Letts.*, **2**, 182–5.

Diamond, J. M. (1989). The present, past and future of human-caused extinctions. *Phil. Trans. R. Soc. B*, **325**, 469–77.

Erwin, T. L. (1982). Tropical forests: their richness in Coleoptera and other arthropod species. *Coleopts Bull.*, **36**, 74–5.

Gaston, K. J. & May, R. M. (1992). The taxonomy of taxonomists. *Nature, Lond.*, **356**, 281–2.

Grassle, J. F. & Maciolek, N. J. (1992). Deep-sea species richness: regional and local diversity estimates from quantitative bottom samples. *Am. Nat.*, **139**, 313–41.

Groombridge, B. (Ed.) (1992). *Global biodiversity: status of the earth's living resources*. Chapman & Hall, London.

Hambler, C. & Speight, M. R. (1996). Extinction rates in British nonmarine invertebrates since 1990. *Conserv. Biol.*, **10**, 892–6.

Hawksworth, D. L. (1991). The fungal dimension of biodiversity: magnitude, significance, and conservation. *Mycol. Res.*, **95**, 441–56.

Heywood, V. H., Mace, G. M., May, R. M. & Stuart, S. N. (1994). Uncertainties in extinction rates. *Nature, Lond.*, **368**, 105.

HMSO (1990). *This common inheritance: Britain's environmental strategy*. HMSO, London.

HMSO (1994). *Biodiversity: the UK action plan*. HMSO, London.

IUCN (1996). *1996 IUCN red list of threatened animals*. IUCN, Gland; Conservation International, Washington DC.

IUCN Species Survival Commission (1994). *IUCN red list categories*. IUCN, Gland.

Mace, G. M. (1994). An investigation into methods for categorizing the conservation status of species. In *Large scale ecology and conservation biology*: 295–312. (Eds Edwards, P. J., May, R. M. & Webb, N. R.). Blackwell, Oxford.

Mace, G. M. & Lande, R. (1991). Assessing extinction threats: toward a reevaluation of IUCN threatened species categories. *Conserv. Biol.*, **5**, 148–57.

May, R. M. (1988). How many species are there on earth? *Science*, **241**, 1441–9.

May, R. M. (1990). How many species? *Phil. Trans. R. Soc.* B, **330**, 293–304.

May, R. M. (1994). Conceptual aspects of the quantification of the extent of biological diversity. *Phil. Trans. R. Soc.* B, **345**, 13–20.

May, R. M., Lawton, J. H. & Stork, N. E. (1995). Assessing extinction rates. In *Extinction rates*: 1–24. (Eds Lawton, J. H. & May, R. M.). Oxford University Press, Oxford.

May, R. M. & Nee, S. (1995). The species alias problem. *Nature, Lond.*, **378**, 447–8.

MoD (1996). *Conservation on the defence estate*. Ministry of Defence Conservation Office, London.

Schei, P. J. (Ed.) (1996). *Chairman's report on Norway/UN conference on alien species*. Trondheim, Norway.

Smith, F. D. M., May, R. M., Pellew, R., Johnson, T. H. & Walter, K. R. (1993). How much do we know about the current extinction rate? *Trends Ecol. Evol.* **8**, 375–8.

Solow, A. R., Mound, L. A. & Gaston, K. J. (1995). Estimating the rate of synonymy. *Syst. Biol.*, **44**, 93–6.

# *Index*

Page references in *italics* refer to figures, tables or their captions.

abundance data 233, 252–60, 264–5
acid rain 32
adaptations
  to disturbances 25
  disturbance-dependent plant species
    13–14, 87–102
adjacency constraints 263, 264
agriculture, subsidies for 282
algorithms
  branch-and-bound 226
  for conservation area selection 2, 3, *226*,
    227–30, 252–3, 264
  heuristic *227*, 228–9, 236, 238
  priority-setting 22, 252–3, 264
Allee effect 37–8
Amazonia
  bird conservation 139–57
  bird diversity 170
  reserves
    Amazonia National Park 66
    protection 23–4
  *see also* Neotropics
Andes
  conserving biodiversity 22–3, 141–57
  *see also* Neotropics
Andrew, Hurricane 60, 61
antbirds 153–4
antelope, roan 255
ants, litter-inhabiting 186
archipelagos
  extinction rates 34
  species–area relationship 54
area effects 174–5
area-selection, for conservation 2, 3, 21,
    211–40, 261
  methods 220–30, *231*, 251–69
aspen 101

Australia
  forests and woodlands 90, 91
  land systems of New South Wales 253
autecology 69

Baikal Region National Park 66
bats, diversity along elevational gradients
    177–8
bees, bumble, conservation area selection
    227
beetles
  dung, as indicator species 22, 182,
    187–201
  fossil 9–10
  number of species 288
  tiger, species richness 187, 201
Bergmann's rule 12
Big Cypress National Preserve 56–66
biodiversity
  assessed using indicator taxa 181–209,
    217–18
  avian diversity with elevation in the
    Neotropics 168–75
  conservation of 2, 79–80
    area-selection methods for 2, 3,
      211–40
    and biodiversity value 211, 212, 213–20
    and gene or character richness 215–20
    and higher taxon richness 218–20
    scale of surrogacy *219*, *220*, 240
    in South America 22–3, 139–57
    and species richness 217–18
    and WORLDMAP computer program
      140
  global priorities 273–84
  surrogates 217–20
Biodiversity Action Plan 294

Biodiversity Steering Group 294
*Biodiversity: the UK action plan* (1994) 294
biogeography 69–70
birds
  and ecotone habitats 20–1
  endemism *see* endemism, avian
  extinction(s) 291
    risk of 30, 176
  metapopulations in tropical forests 15, 17
    and elevation 161–79
    Neotropics 139–57, 161–79
    and speciation 20, 21, 152–3
  number of species 287
  with small geographical ranges 54
Biscayne National Park 56–7, *58*
Bolivia, Parque Nacional Noel Kempff
      Mercado, dung beetle surveys
      187–201
Brazil
  conserving biodiversity 22–3
  Serra dos Orgãos National Park 177
breeding, selective 39–40
butterflies
  distribution patterns 107, 108–15
  Edith's checkerspot, and climate change
      *10*, 11
  and habitat isolation 124–32
    on islands 133
  as indicator species 184, 186, 187
  marsh fritillary, conservation 15, *16*
  metapopulations 117–24
  milkweed, metric tree *216*
  population dynamics and the niche
      model 115–17, 132

Cameroon, forest–savanna ecotone habitat
      *20–1*
Cape Sable seaside-sparrow 7, 53–67
carbon dioxide, and the climate 9, 79
Caribbean, coral reef faunal collapse 7–8
catastrophes, environmental 32–3
Central America
  parks and protected areas 55
  *see also* Neotropics
character richness 215–*16*, 217
charcoal 90
Chile, matorral shrubs 99
cichlids, species diversity and pollution
      18–*19*, 39
CITES 183–4, 296
climate
  and butterfly distribution 108–9
  and butterfly population dynamics
      115–17
  change 8–9
    and choice of area for conservation 24

dynamic response of species to 9–13,
      69–80
  modelling responses to 74–5
  and risks of extinction 76–9
  *see also* global warming
clonal species, of plants 95
combinatorial scoring systems, for area
      selection 222
complementarity methods, for area
      selection 224–30, *231*, 235, 240
computer methods, for conservation area
      selection 239, 240
Conquista 156
conservation areas *see* area-selection;
      reserves
coral reefs
  faunal collapse 7–8
  recruitment of species to 17–*18*
corridors, between habitats 11, 35
Costa Rica, migration of the resplendent
      quetzal 17
cowbirds 38
critical patch size 38

damming, of rivers 13, *14*
Darwin Initiative *295*, 296
databases, on-line 203
DDT 32
'declining population paradigm' 2, 94
deforestation 176
degraded landscapes 132–3
demographic potential 35
demographic stochasticity 37
deterministic population models 45
*Diadema*, and Caribbean reef communities
      8
discounting, economic 30–1
disease resistance 44
dispersal
  butterfly 124–32
  local population 34–7
distribution, geographical *see* range of
      species, geographical
disturbance-dependent plant species 13–14,
      87–102
disturbances, anthropogenic 1, 25, 29–32,
      279–81
  and disturbance-dependent species
      13–14, 87–102
  and neotropical montane bird species
      176
diversity
  hotspots of 222–3, 230, *231*
  *see also* biodiversity
dogs, hybridization 39
*Drosophila*, inbreeding depression 40

dynamic processes, and conservation 2, 3
dynamic responses, to external challenges
    5, 9–14, 69–80

Earth Summit, Rio 282
ecologcal theory 267–8
ecological processes, and conservation area
    selection 251–2
ecological threats to extinction 32–8, 45
economic discounting 30–1
Ecuador, protected areas 54–5
edge effects 38
emigration see migration
endemism, avian 147, 149, 150, 152, 155,
    156–7, 161
    and extinction/threat 167–8, 175, 178
    and human populations 140, 151, 152, 155
    and montane elevation 161–79
environment
    changing phenotypes 11–13, 72
    fluctuations and catastrophes 32–4
    see also climate, change
epidemics 33
'establishment effect' 36
eutrophication, and species diversity of
    cichlids 18–19
Everglades National Park 23
    and the Cape Sable seaside-sparrow 7,
    53–67
evolution, future of 274–9
'evolutionary potential', species with 214
extinction 29, 300
    counter-extinction strategies 79–80
    future episode of 274–5, 277–9, 292
    insect 133
    in isolated populations 124–5, 133
    mass 274–6, 292, 300
    mean time to 32–3, 34, 35, 45
    numbers of recorded 290–1
    and the palaeoecological record 73–4,
    77–8, 79
    probabilities of 5–7, 25, 54, 265
    recovery period from 274–6
    risks 76–9
        across a species' range 260–1
        anthropogenic 1–2, 6, 29–32, 45,
        76–9
        and CITES lists 296
        ecological 32–8, 45
        genetic factors 38–45, 46
        modelling 78–9
        see also climate, change
    thresholds 36
    'vortices' 45

Fagaceae 218

families, surrogates for gene or character
    richness 218
fire
    and the Cape Sable seaside-sparrow 63
    fire-adapted species 13–14, 88–9
fish
    extinctions 291
    overexploitation on coral reefs 7–8
    restocking 39
fisheries
    overexploitation 30
    subsidies for 282
fitness, and inbreeding depression 40–1
floods 13, 14
flycatchers, New World, South American
    distribution 141, 144
forestry, subsidies for 282
forests
    forest–savanna ecotone habitat 20–1
    Pleistocene extinction 74
    tropical
        anthropogenic extinctions 1
        clearing 38
        elevational gradients in bird diversity
        161–79
        generation of new species in 20, 21,
        152–3
        importance of habitat patches to birds
        15, 176–7
    see also trees
fossil fuels, subsidies for 282
fragmented habitats see habitat(s), patches
Franklin–Soulé number 43–4
fynbos vegetation 89, 91, 92, 99

Gap Analyses 142, 148, 150, 151, 154–7, 224
    Oregon Gap Analysis project 226–7
genera, surrogates for gene or character
    richness 218
genetics
    and conservation 5, 18–21
    gene richness 215–16
        surrogates for 217–20
    genetic effects in small populations
    38–45
    genetically modified organisms 297
    loss of genetic variation 41–4
    random genetic drift 42, 44
Ginko biloba (maidenhair tree) 100
global conservation 287–92, 300
Global Environmental Facility 274
global warming 9, 22, 43, 45
    and choice of area for conservation 24
    and risks of extinction 76–9
GMOs (genetically modified organisms)
    297

goats, degradation attributed to 92
grasshoppers, in different habitats 116
grasslands 90
grazing *see* herbivory
greenbuls, little, speciation 20–1
greenhouse gases, emissions 9, 22

habitat(s)
  corridors between 11, 35
  degraded 132–3
    and indicator taxa response 185–6
  and edge effects 38
  heterogenous 116–17
  loss
    on continents versus islands 6, 7
    and indicator taxa response 185–6
    and threat to montane avifauna 176
  patches
    butterfly response to 121–2
    and climate change 11
    and conservation 15–17, 24, 25–6, 131,
      132
    critical patch size 38
    importance of the matrix between 15,
      25–6, 124, 176–7
    leading to extinctions 107, 124
    migration between 17, 121–3, 124–32,
      176–7
    occupancy 35–6, *118*, 119–*21*
    recruitment on coral reefs 17–*18*
    *see also* metapopulations
    selection by birds 168
    *see also* range of species, geographical;
      reserves/parks
  harvesting strategies 31
    selective 39
Hawaii, introduced plant species 31
herbivory, and disturbance processes 13,
    92, 93
hominids, evolution 91
hotspots
  of diversity 222–3, 230, 231, 273–4, 275
  of rarity 223–4, 230, 231
humans
  conservation aiding local human
    populations 25
  demands for resources 24, 139
  governmental subsidies 22, 281–3
  habitat destruction and birds 176
  human-dominated habitats beyond
    reserves 25–6
  populations and avian endemism 140,
    151, *152*, 155
  *see also* disturbances, anthropogenic
hurricanes 60, 61, 64
hybridization, interspecific 38–9

ibis, white 65
immigration *see* migration
inbreeding, depression in fitness 40–1
Inca Empire 156
indicator taxa, for biodiversity assessment
  22, 181–209, 217–18
individualism, of species 72–3
insects
  extinctions 291
  as indicators of biodiversity 181–2
    *see also* beetles, dung
  as pests 278
  proportion of all species 287
introduced species
  on continents versus islands 6–7
  danger to endemic species 31
  for restocking 38–9
  in the UK 297
islands
  and extinction 34, 64, 133
  species–area relationship 54
IUCN 290–1
  and threat 5, 6, 97

jackals, Simien 39

Kenya, animals outside reserves 25
kite, snail 58–9
Kruger National Park, herbivore
  abundances 254–60, 264–7
kudu *254*, 255

Lakeside Daisy 38
land development, and extinction 29, 30, 45

land systems 253
landscape ecology 268
landscape units 253
landscapes, degraded 132–3
latitude, and species richness 174
Levin's rule 267
lime
  small-leaved 75–6
  sprouting 100
Linnaeus 287

MacArthur Foundation 274
maidenhair tree 100
mammals
  evolution of herbivorous 91
  in North American reserves/parks 64–5
  number of species 287
  threatened 6–7
matorral shrubs 99
metapopulations
  avian *see* birds

metapopulations (*cont.*)
  butterfly 117–24
  and conservation 15–17, 24, 131
  emigrations and immigrations 121–3,
    124–32, 176–7
    *see also* migration
  extinctions and colonizations 15, 34–7,
    42, 107, 118–19
  extinctions 107
  persistence 267
    *see also* habitat(s), patches
metric tree *216*
MIGRATE model 75
migration
  between habitat patches 17, 121–3,
    124–32
    for montane tropical birds 176–7,
      178–9
  models of 75–6, 125–32
military land 23, 296–7
Minstry of Defence 23, 296–7
models
  ecological 69, 251–2
  evolutionary 251–2
  migration 75–6, 125–32
  probability distribution *234–5*
  risks of extinction 78–9
  of spatial responses to environmental
    change 74–6
montane habitats 154
  avian diversity and endemism with
    elevation 161–79
  butterfly distribution 114
morphology, changes in 11–13, 72
mutations *43*, 44–5

Neotropics
  dung beetles as indicator species 187–201
  elevational gradients in bird diversity
    161–79
    *see also* South America
New South Wales, land systems 253
Ngorongoro Conservation Area 66
niche theory/model, and butterfly
    distribution 107, 108, 109, 115–18,
    132
North America
  parks and protected areas 55, 66
    *see also* Everglades National Park
North Yukon National Park 66

oaks, North American 'climax' 87
*Our common inheritance* (1993) 294
ovenbirds and woodcreepers, South
    American distribution 141, 143–4,
    149–51

overexploitation, resource, by humans 30–1
owls
  barred 39
  northern spotted 36, 39

palaeoecology
  and Amazonian bird species 152–3
  and environmental changes 9–10, 11–12,
    13, 71–4
  and extinction 73–4, 77–8, 79
panther, Florida 41
parks *see* reserves/parks
Parque Nacional Noel Kempff Mercado
    (PNNKM), dung beetle surveys
    187–201
parrots, South American distribution 141,
    143, 149–51
patches, habitat *see* habitat(s), patches
persistence
  butterfly 117
  plant 94–101, 102
persistence niche 94–5, 97, *98*, *99*
Peru, Manu National Park 147
'perverse subsidies' 22, 281–3
pesticides 32
pests 278
phenotypes, environment causing changes
    in 11–13, 45, 72
Pinaceae 218
plants
  disturbance-dependent species 13–14,
    87–102
  dynamic responses to external
    challenges 69–80
  longevity 95
  number of species 287
  persistence 94–101, 102
  species distribution 274
  sprouting 95, *96–7*, 99–101
PNNKM (Parque Nacional Noel Kempff
    Mercado), dung beetle surveys
    187–201
poaching 280
pollution
  extinction risk from 32
  subsidies encouraging 282
  water, and species diversity of cichlids
    18–19
population dynamics 15–18, 252–60
  butterfly 115–17
populations
  abundances *254–8*
  'bottlenecks' 42
  environmental fluctuations and
    catastrophes 32–4
  minimum effective size 12–13, 43–4

small 45
  and ecological effects 37–8
  and genetic effects 38–45, 46
  source and sink 15, 268
  for tropical montane birds 177, 178
  *see also* metapopulations
prairies, remnant 13–14
precipitation, change in future 79
priorities
  area-based 21–2, 212, 237, 251–69
  global biodiversity 273–84
process-related concerns 3, 4–21
  incorporated into priority-setting
    procedures 21–2, 251–69
  recommendations for 21–6
protected areas 279–81
  *see also* reserves/parks

questions, asked/answered by
  conservationists 3–4
quetzal, resplendant, migration between
  habitats 17

rain, acid 32
range of species, geographical
  butterfly distribution patterns 107,
    108–15
  and choice of area for conservation 24,
    223–4
  and climate 70–2, 74–6
  of extinction-threatened birds 54
  marginal and core 15–17, 108, 109,
    114–15, 117
  shift in 9–11
  spatial heterogenity within 260–4, 267–8
  *see also* habitat(s)
Rapaport's rule 171–4
rarity hotspots 223–4, 230, 231
rats, introduced 31
recruitment 101–2
  *see also* metapopulations
Red Data Books 163, 290
regeneration 76
  of 'climax' oaks 87
  and plant persistence 95–7
'rescue effect' 36
reserves/parks 53–6, 261
  external threats to 66
  as islands 64–6
  size
    and environmental catastrophes 3–4
    and extinctions 64–5
    small and isolated 25
    usefulness of large reserves 23–4,
      33–4, 64–5
  *see also* area-selection, for conservation;

Everglades National Park; habitat(s);
  protected areas
restocking 39
Rio Earth Summit 282
risk factors, and mean time to extiction 33,
  *34, 35*
rivers, damming 13, *14*
rodents, diversity along elevational
  gradients 178

salmon, restocking 39
savanna 90, 91
  forest–savanna ecotone habitat *20–1*
  trees sprouting 96
scaling laws, for mean time to extinction
  33, *34, 35*, 45
scoring systems, combinatorial, for area
  selection 222
sea-urchins, and Caribbean reef
  communities 8
seaside-sparrow
  Cape Sable 7, 53–67
  dusky 59
Serengeti National Park 66
Serra dos Orgãos National Park 177
sites, for conservation *see* area-selection, for
  conservation
Sites of Special Scientific Interest (SSSI)
  *298*
'small population paradigm' 2, 93–4, 101
snakes, South African, distribution *261–4,
  265,* 268
social interactions, and population sizes
  37–8
South Africa
  fynbos vegetation 89, 91, 92, 99
  Kruger National Park, herbivore
    abundances *254–60, 264–7*
  plants threatened with extinction 93
South America
  conservation processes 139–57
  parks and protected areas 55
  *see also* Neotropics
sparrows
  grassland 61
  *see also* seaside-sparrow
spatial responses
  to climate change 71–2
  modelling 74–6
species
  average lifetime 291–2
  goal-essential 238, *239*
  individualism with respect to climate
    change 72–3
  introduced *see* introduced species
  opportunistic 278

species (*cont.*)
richness 217–18, 223
*see also* biodiversity
speciation 19–21
birds in South America 152–3
during any future mass extinction
event 277–8
in ecotone habitats 20–1
in ecoclimatically stable areas 20, 21
species–area relationship 25, 54
total number of 287–9
'species dynamo areas' 214
sprouting, by plants 95, 96–7, 99–101
SSSI (Sites of Special Scientific Interest)
298
stochastic population models 32–3, 45
stork, wood 58–9, 65–6
subsidies, governmental 22, 281–3
Systematics Forum 295, 297

taxonomic groups, and conservation
289–91
terrapins, distribution in southern Africa
261
threats 5–9
and conservation area selection 230–40
to protected areas 279–80
*see also* disturbances, anthropogenic
tortoises, distribution in southern Africa
261
transition zones *see* ecotones
trees
climate preferences of European trees
218

extinction in the Quaternary 74, 77
stem diameter and population status 97,
*98*
Tropical Biology Association (TBA) 295–6

United Kingdom
conservation policy 292–300
Dependent Territories 298–9
distribution of the marsh fritillary *16*
and global warming 24
proportion of the world's species in 292
species extinct 292–3
United States
national parks 53–4
*see also* Everglades National Park
United States Agency for International
Development (USAID) 181, 185

vertebrates, number of species 289
viabile areas, for conservation area
selection 230–40

water, subsidies for 282
Wildlife and Countrside Act 297
woodcreepers and ovenbirds, South
American distribution 141, 143–4,
149–51
woodrat, bushy-tailed, size and
environmental temperature *12*
World Bank 181, 185, 274
World Wide Web 203
WORLDMAP software 140, 141, *239*
wrens, South American distribution 141,
*144, 147, 149–51*